THE MARCH OF THE WOMEN

A REVISIONIST ANALYSIS OF THE CAMPAIGN
FOR WOMEN'S SUFFRAGE
1866–1914

MARTIN PUGH

OXFORD
UNIVERSITY PRESS

This book has been printed digitally and produced in a standard specification in order to ensure its continuing availability

OXFORD

UNIVERSITY PRESS

Great Clarendon Street, Oxford OX2 6DP

Oxford University Press is a department of the University of Oxford.
It furthers the University's objective of excellence in research, scholarship,
and education by publishing worldwide in

Oxford New York

Auckland Cape Town Dar es Salaam Hong Kong Karachi
Kuala Lumpur Madrid Melbourne Mexico City Nairobi
New Delhi Shanghai Taipei Toronto
With offices in
Argentina Austria Brazil Chile Czech Republic France Greece
Guatemala Hungary Italy Japan South Korea Poland Portugal
Singapore Switzerland Thailand Turkey Ukraine Vietnam

Oxford is a registered trade mark of Oxford University Press
in the UK and in certain other countries

Published in the United States
by Oxford University Press Inc., New York

Oxford is a registered trade mark of Oxford University Press
in the UK and in certain other countries

Published in the United States
by Oxford University Press Inc., New York

© Martin Pugh 2000

The moral rights of the author have been asserted

Database right Oxford University Press (maker)

Reprinted 2004

ISBN 0-19-925022-7

for Hannah

ACKNOWLEDGEMENTS

I would like to express my gratitude to a number of scholars who have commented on drafts or advised on specific issues arising from the preparation of this book including Diane Atkinson, Catriona Burness, David Doughan, Claire Eustance, Brian Harrison, Janet Howarth, Angela John, Jon Lawrence, Leah Leneman, Bill Purdue, and Chris Wrigley. Specific references in the footnotes also record my debt to the authors of several theses and manuscripts: Claire Eustance, 'Daring to be Free: The Evolution of Women's Political Identities in the Women's Freedom League, 1907–1930', Ph.D. thesis (York University, 1993); Julie Gottlieb, 'Women and Fascism in Inter-War Britain', Ph.D. thesis (Cambridge University, 1998); David Neville, 'The Women's Suffrage Movement in the North East of England, 1900–1914', M.Phil. thesis (University of Northumbria, 1991); Joan Elizabeth Parker, 'Lydia Becker: Her Work for Women', Ph.D. thesis (Manchester University, 1990); Kirsten Seltorp, 'The Women's Suffrage Movement in Bristol, 1868–1906', unpublished MS in the Fawcett Library.

My research in the primary sources over many years has been greatly assisted by the archivists and librarians in the following institutions: The Fawcett Library, the Public Record Office, the Museum of London, the British Library, the British Library Newspaper Library (Colindale), the India Office Library, the Marx Memorial Library, the British Library of Political and Economic Science, the House of Lords Record Office, Newcastle-upon-Tyne Literary and Philosophical Society Library, Gateshead Public Library, Newcastle Central Library, the Robinson Library, Manchester Central Library, the John Rylands University Library, Oldham Local Studies Library, the National Library of Scotland, the Mitchell Library, Bristol University Library, Edinburgh University Library, and Cumbria County Record Office.

Finally, I gratefully acknowledge the financial support given to me by the British Academy's Small Grants in the Humanities in 1996 and 1997.

M.D.P.

June 1999
Slaley

CONTENTS

LIST OF TABLES

LIST OF ABBREVIATIONS

AFL	Actresses' Franchise League
CUWFA	Conservative and Unionist Women's Franchise Association
EFF	Election Fighting Fund
ELF	East London Federation
ICW	International Council of Women
ILP	Independent Labour Party
NEC	National Executive Committee
NLF	National Liberal Federation
NLOWS	National League for Opposing Women's Suffrage
NMF	Northern Men's Federation
NSWS	National Society for Women's Suffrage
NUWSS	National Union of Women's Suffrage Societies
WCG	Women's Co-operative Guild
WFL	Women's Freedom League
WLF	Women's Liberal Federation
WLGS	Women's Local Government Society
WSPU	Women's Social and Political Union

The March of the Women

Composed and Dedicated to the Women's Social and Political Union by
Ethel Smyth, Mus. Doc.

(1)

Shout, shout—up with your song,
  Cry with the wind, for the dawn is breaking;
March, march, swing you along,
  Wide blows our banner, and hope is waking.
Song with its story, dreams with their glory,
  Lo! they call, and glad is their word!
Hark, hark, hear how it swells,
  Thunder of freedom, the voice of the Lord!

(2)

Long, long—we in the past
  Cowered in dread from the light of heaven,
Strong, strong—stand we at last,
  Fearless in faith and with sight new given.
Strength with its beauty, Life with its duty
  (Hear the call, oh hear and obey!)
These, these—beckon us on!
  Open your eyes to the blaze of day.

(3)

Hail, hail—ye who have dared
  First in the battle to strive and sorrow!
Scorned, spurned—nought have ye cared,
  Raising your eyes to a wider morrow.
Ways that are weary, days that are dreary,
  Toil and pain in faith ye have borne;
Hail, hail—victors ye stand,
  Wearing the wreath that the brave have worn.

(4)

Life, strife—these two are one.
  Naught can ye win but by faith and daring.
On, on—that ye have done
  But for the work of to-day preparing.
Firm in reliance, laugh a defiance—
  (Laugh in hope, for sure is the end).
March, march—many as one,
  Shoulder to shoulder and friend to friend.

Introduction

NOT since 1967 when Constance Rover's *Women's Suffrage and Party Politics in Britain* was published has there been an attempt to assess the entire campaign to secure the parliamentary vote for women. Since 1967 a great deal of primary material has become available and a number of studies of specific aspects of the movement have helped to change our perspective on the cause. However, in view of the importance of the subject and the popular interest it still engenders, it cannot be said that a great deal has been published. Several aspects of the topic remain neglected, and the treatment of it seems unbalanced in many ways. Some authors continue to approach it by attacking the straw men of the past—that is the accounts written by George Dangerfield in *The Strange Death of Liberal England* as long ago as 1935, and by Roger Fulford in *Votes for Women* as long ago as 1957, neither of which were, in fact, based on primary source material. It is easy to criticize such works, but this is to avoid the real issues involved in an analysis of the campaign.

Received impressions about the centrality of the Pankhursts took a dent when Andrew Rosen's *Rise Up Women! The Militant Campaign of the Women's Social and Political Union, 1903–1914* (1974) appeared. Indeed, much subsequent work has in effect modified the original interpretation bequeathed by the Pankhurst family. The marginalization from which the non-militant suffragists had suffered began to be revised first by Lesley Parker Hume's *The National Union of Women's Suffrage Societies, 1897–1914* (1982) and then by Sandra Stanley Holton's *Feminism and Democracy: Women's Suffrage and Reform Politics in Britain, 1900–1918* (1986). We now have a far clearer picture of the ideas of the non-militants as a result of the valuable revisionist biography by D. W. Rubinstein, *A Different World for Women: The Life of Millicent Garrett Fawcett* (1991); the non-militants have also been brought into focus by June Hannam, *Isabella Ford* (1989); Jill Liddington, *The Life and Times of a Respectable Rebel: Selina Cooper* (1984); Barbara Caine, *Victorian Feminists* (1992), which includes the important but neglected Frances Power Cobbe; and Brian Harrison, *Prudent Revolutionaries* (1987). As a result of Olive Banks's *Becoming a Feminist: The Social Origins of First Wave Feminism* (1986), it is now possible to generalize about the kinds of political and social factors that lay behind the movement. Patricia Hollis in *Ladies Elect: Women in English Local Government* (1987) remedied a major gap in our explanation for the development of the late Victorian movement, though Hollis herself doubted that local government materially advanced the suffragist cause. Susan Kingsley Kent argued for a reinterpretation of the movement as a radical attempt to overthrow conventional gender relations in her *Sex and Suffrage in Britain 1860–1914* (1987), a thesis difficult to square with Banks's empirical study. A much-needed attempt to explain the male role in the movement appeared in 1997 in Angela V. John and Claire Eustance (eds.), *The Men's Share: Masculinities, Male Support and Women's Suffrage in Britain 1890–1920*. For the first time the Anti-Suffragist movement was treated seriously by Brian Harrison in *Separate Spheres: The Opposition to Women's Suffrage in Britain* (1978); this is now complemented by biographical studies of leading Antis: John Sutherland, *Mrs Humphry Ward* (1990); Jane Lewis, *Women and Social Action* (1991), which discusses Violet Markham; and Helen Jones (ed.), *Duty and Citizenship: The Correspondence and Papers of Violet Markham* (1994). Despite the general change of emphasis, the analysis of the suffragettes has continued. A pioneering essay by Brian Harrison on 'The Act of Militancy: Violence and the Suffragettes' in his *Peaceable Kingdom* (1982) was the first attempt to explain sympathetically what led certain women to adopt militancy; but it has been surprisingly neglected by other writers in the field. Although we are still lacking scholarly studies of suffragism at local level some valuable work has been published notably by Leah Leneman, *A Guid Cause: The Women's Suffrage Movement in Scotland* (1991), and by Jill Liddington and Jill Norris on Lancashire in *One Hand Tied Behind Us: The Rise of The Women's Suffrage Movement* (1978); there is also an essay on Welsh suffragism by Kay Cook and Neil Evans in Angela V. John (ed.), *Our Mothers' Land: Chapters in Welsh Women's History 1830–1939* (1991), and a more general survey in Leah Leneman's chapter in Maroula Joannu and June Purvis (eds.), *The Women's Suffrage Movement: New Feminist Perspectives* (1998). Surprisingly, there is still no good, scholarly biography of either Emmeline or Christabel Pankhurst, though Sylvia has attracted attention in Patricia Romero, *E. Sylvia Pankhurst* (1987) and Barbara Winslow, *Sylvia Pankhurst* (1996). Other militants have recently been studied by Angela V. John in *Elizabeth Robins: Staging a Life 1862–1952* (1995) which, like the local studies, demonstrates how individuals shifted between militancy and non-militancy; Lis Whitelaw, *The Life and Rebellious Times of Cicely Hamilton* (1990); and Andro Linklater, *An Unhusbanded Life: Charlotte Despard, Suffragette, Socialist and Sinn Feiner* (1980).

Although the present volume follows a broadly chronological pattern, it is not designed as another narrative account of the campaigns of suffragists and suffragettes; it is instead organized in ten essays which focus on specific questions of interpretation or aspects of the topic. Chapter 1 begins the examination of suffragist tactics and methods by emphasizing the initial difficulties involved in pushing the issue to the fore even within the context of the women's movement itself. By implication it suggests, contrary to received opinion, that the early emphasis on a parliamentary approach was both rational and successful; but the chapter also highlights some of the inherent weaknesses in the movement—its loose federal structure, the lack of inspirational leadership, the avoidance of party political commitments, the narrow nature of suffragist demands, especially the reluctance to incorporate married women, and the broader issue of adult suffrage. Chapter 2 analyses the *debate* over women's enfranchisement—a key theme but surprisingly neglected, perhaps because scholars traditionally accepted the Pankhursts' claim that no progress had been made before the 1900s. The chapter aims to remedy the deficiency by demonstrating how the debate fluctuated over time as suffragists varied their case in order to take advantage of changing conditions; it also identifies those areas of debate in which Anti-Suffragist views became discredited or redundant. This leads to the conclusion that by the turn of the century the suffragists had largely won the debate; little of any significance was added during the Edwardian period. Following on from this Chapter 3 challenges the traditional view that the suffragist cause entered a decline or at least stagnated between the 1880s and 1900. It suggests, on the contrary, that the 1890s proved to be the decade of breakthrough for the suffragists as demonstrated by the shift of parliamentary support in their favour, a trend not hitherto recognized. Chapters 4, 5, 6, and 7 develop and substantiate this broad theme by examining aspects of the change in more detail. The implication is that the traditional chronology of the suffrage movement in Britain no longer fits the facts. The achievements of the Victorian suffragists have been underrated. Since their success *preceded* the militant phase it obviously has major implications for the significance attributable to it; when the WSPU was founded in 1903 it was in some ways a *symptom* of the improving fortunes of suffragism rather than simply a cause. Chapter 4 complements this thesis by putting the domestic movement in the context of *international* suffragism. In particular it seeks to demonstrate how the enfranchisement of women in New Zealand and Australia, and to a lesser extent the United States, advanced the cause in Britain by discrediting some of the alarmism of the Antis and lending credibility to the suffragist case. The political dimensions to the problem are discussed in Chapters 5 and 6 which emphasize, on the one hand, the fluctuations in Liberal support for the cause and, on the other, the significant rise in sympathy amongst Conservatives from the 1880s. It is argued that traditional accounts fail to take account of this latter aspect.

Indeed, while some more recent writers claim that the movement has been seen as too conservative, the argument here is that, on the contrary, we have underestimated the conservatism and the Conservatism in women's suffrage, and thereby lost an important part of the explanation for the eventual success of the cause. Chapter 7 approaches suffragism through the perspective of its opponents. It shows among other things the fitful nature of organized Anti-Suffragism and emphasizes that its chief efforts came too late in the day to offer any effective check to the long-term social and political trends which worked in the suffragists' favour. It also underlines the fundamental flaws in Anti-Suffragism, notably its attempt to combine male Antis with female Antis who were often *feminists*. In Chapter 8 the book moves on to an analysis and evaluation of militancy which is designed to show it as a far more varied and in some ways subtle movement than is usually thought. Militancy is revealed as involving a wide spectrum of participation including purely nominal and temporary involvement by many women. Emphasis is placed on the extent to which suffragettes and suffragists crossed the supposedly clear line between militancy and non-militancy, which suggests that the divisions over tactics assumed far less significance at local level than they did in London and among the leadership ranks. Some fresh light is also thrown on the character of the WSPU by juxtaposing the radicalism of its methods and its reputation with the reality of its members' position within the economic and social establishment, and by highlighting the inconsistency involved in attacking private property while simultaneously exploiting private wealth to sustain the campaign. The chapter concludes by explaining, partly with neglected PRO material, that the WSPU had decisively failed and had entered a decline by 1914. In Chapter 9 an attempt is made to assess one of the central claims made by the Pankhursts to the effect that they had mobilized the force of public opinion against the government of the day. *Inter alia* this involves for the first time an analysis of the Edwardian by-election record which the WSPU flourished as proof of its success. Finally, Chapter 10 completes the re-evaluation of suffragism by examining the extent to which the non-militant campaign expanded into a mass movement, the significance of the alliance between the Labour Party and the National Union of Women's Suffrage Societies and the latter's attempt to develop a working-class base during the last two and a half years before the outbreak of war. It is here, rather than in the better-known suffragette campaigns, that the central explanation for the eventual success of the women's movement lies.

Part I

The Issues

1

The Tactical Dilemmas

'IN the years that I have passed in Government offices,' Florence Nightingale told John Stuart Mill in 1867, 'I have never felt the want of a vote.'[1] Nightingale's comments, from the standpoint of a pro-suffragist it should be remembered, underline the fundamental, but easily overlooked, tactical issue that faced the early suffragist campaign: how much significance attached to the parliamentary vote in relation to all the other goals and grievances of the Victorian feminist movement? Though the question was never formally resolved, over time the vote gradually assumed greater priority until it became the central object.

Initially the franchise represented no more than one amongst a range of goals tackled by the single-issue pressure groups which had emerged between the late-1850s and mid-1860s, largely inspired by the so-called 'Ladies of Langham Place' in London. The leaders of this early women's movement—Barbara Leigh Smith (later Bodichon), Bessie Rayner Parkes, Jessie Boucherett, Frances Power Cobbe, Emily Davies, Maria Rye, Adelaide Proctor, Elizabeth Garrett, and Elizabeth Blackwell—followed a pattern well-established in middle-class, mid-Victorian Radical circles. They founded the Society for Promoting Women's Employment in 1859, tried to extend higher education for women, promoted female emigration to the colonies, and demanded entry into the medical profession; they established the Married Women's Property Committee and the Ladies National Association for the Repeal of the Contagious Diseases Acts.[2] Only in the aftermath of John Stuart Mill's election at Westminster in May 1865 did the parliamentary vote emerge as a significant goal. Barbara Leigh Smith, who had

---

[1] Florence Nightingale to J. S. Mill, 11 Aug. 1867, Nightingale Papers, British Library, Add. MS 39927, fo. 62.

[2] See Candida Ann Lacey, *Barbara Leigh Smith Bodichon and the Ladies of Langham Place* (Routledge, 1987); Sheila Herstein, *A Mid-Victorian Feminist* (Yale University Press, 1985); Olive Banks, *Becoming A Feminist* (Brighton: Harvester, 1986); Ray Strachey, *The Cause* (G. Bell & Sons, 1928).

campaigned for Mill but wondered whether she was doing him more harm than good, joined with Davies, Boucherett, and Garrett, to form a committee in Kensington; they collected signatures for the women's suffrage petition which Mill subsequently presented to the House of Commons in 1866.

The Status of the Vote

However, for some time the significance of the franchise amongst this congeries of ad hoc pressure groups remained unclear. The very range of issues inevitably spread the efforts of the small stage army of activists thinly, thereby limiting their impact. On the other hand, the wider the variety of issues the more women were likely to become involved. Some preferred to focus on one cause, for example, Emily Davies on higher education and Josephine Butler on the repeal of the Contagious Diseases (CD) Acts. But the analysis of 'first wave' feminists by Olive Banks has shown that the activists were likely to be involved in anything up to five campaigns. Significantly she found that 89 per cent of her sample participated in the suffrage movement, a much higher level than that for any other cause.[3] Moreover, participation was distinctly lower amongst the older women, which underlines how, over time, the vote became increasingly central to the women's movement.

What determined how much emphasis was given to the different feminist causes? In the first place, success and failure frequently dictated changes in the level of activity. For example, the passage of the divorce law reform in 1857 had the effect of depriving the campaign for married women's property of its momentum for several years at least. Conversely, when the Ladies National Association achieved the final repeal of the CD legislation in 1886, its activists diverted their efforts into related campaigns dealing with moral conduct. Tactical considerations were also important. Barbara Leigh Smith made shrewd judgements about which goals were attainable and thus worth concentrating on; she calculated, for example, that the issue of married women's property could be resolved without unduly antagonizing male opinion, whereas female enfranchisement seemed to her an ambitious aim unlikely to be achieved except in the long term. As Nightingale put it: 'it will be years before you obtain the suffrage for women. And in the meantime there are evils which press much more hardly on women.'[4] Despite this, feminists such as Lydia Becker and Millicent Fawcett concentrated their efforts largely on the vote, and took a strict line on the association between this

---

[3] Banks, *Becoming*, 50–2.   [4] Nightingale to Mill, 11 Aug. 1867.

campaign and other causes. Though they sympathized strongly with Butler's attack on the CD Acts, they avoided public involvement with it because it seemed certain to detract from the respectability of their campaign. Indeed, the London suffragists refused to be represented in parliament by Jacob Bright because of his links with Butler.[5] The preoccupation with respectability featured prominently in the case of Elizabeth Wolstenholme (later Mrs Wolstenholme Elmy) who was known to be living with a man, Ben Elmy, to whom she was not married; Becker, Fawcett, and others insisted that she could not be secretary of the Married Women's Property Committee without damaging the cause.[6] Nor was this untypical. Banks found that only 13 per cent of first wave feminists became involved with Butler's campaign, and only 19 per cent with the issue of birth control. Whether this sprang from disapproval or from tactical considerations, it underlines the perceived need to present the case for the vote in the best possible light.

In addition to tactical calculations the feminists' handling of the franchise also reflected the impact of a series of political contingencies. For example, the sudden death of the prime minister, Lord Palmerston, in 1865, which led to the introduction of a parliamentary reform bill in 1866 by Lord John Russell and W. E. Gladstone, suddenly elevated the whole question of reform and carried women's suffrage with it. Also, many women who had originally seen the vote largely as a symbol of female inequality came in time to regard it as a greater priority, partly because it appeared to be the key to further changes. By 1873 Josephine Butler recognized the greater urgency of the vote: 'We cannot always depend on the self-sacrificing efforts of noble men . . . to right our wrongs, and now that the labourers are going to be enfranchised, our case becomes the worse.' During the 1890s leading members of the Women's Liberal Federation reached the conclusion that they were wasting their time in passing annual resolutions and would be better advised to accelerate the whole process by focusing on the women's vote.[7] The post-1905 strategy of the Women's Social and Political Union represented a logical extension of this thinking; the Pankhursts argued not just that the vote should be the priority but that the government should be compelled to suspend all other business until the demand had been satisfied.

Above all, the significance attributed to the vote was heightened by the example set by other contemporary Radical movements. Throughout their

---

[5] Strachey, *The Cause*, 267–9; Barbara Caine, 'John Stuart Mill and the English Women's Movement', *Historical Studies*, 18 (1978), 59–62.

[6] Barbara Caine, *Victorian Feminists* (Oxford: Oxford University Press, 1992).

[7] Ibid. 182, quoting J. Butler to Mrs C. M. Wilson, 12 Nov. 1873, Butler Papers; Women's Liberal Federation, *Annual Report*, 1899, 17.

campaign the suffragists reacted to the activities of the Irish Nationalists both in and out of parliament. From the general election of 1874 onwards the Home Rulers enjoyed direct representation in the Commons, and after the extension of the county franchise in 1885 they commanded at least eighty seats, a position which enabled them to obstruct legislation and occasionally to hold the balance of power. In Ireland they sustained a violent agitation, while in the English constituencies they mobilized the Irish vote and periodically withheld it from their Liberal allies in order to extract pledges on Home Rule from vulnerable candidates. All this made an indelible impression on the Pankhursts who attributed the defeat of Dr Richard Pankhurst at a Manchester by-election in 1883 to the obstructionism of Irish Catholics.[8]

The emergence of the Labour Movement also had a galvanizing effect. By enfranchising substantial numbers of workingmen the 1867 reform act raised the expectations of trade unions, especially those, such as coal miners, whose members now dominated some constituencies; as a result, from 1874 onwards several of their leaders sat as 'Lib-Lab' members, thereby creating direct working-class representation for the first time. Subsequently their activities provided not merely an example for feminists but a provocation, for the union representatives energetically promoted protective legislation designed to exclude women from employment, ostensibly on the grounds that it endangered their health or morals, but in reality because they wished to reduce competition between the sexes which, in their view, lowered wage levels. Thus, although women achieved some of their goals during the 1870s and 1880s, despite their exclusion from the electorate, the changing character of parliamentary representation appeared to put them at a greater disadvantage, and thus gave greater urgency to female enfranchisement. By the 1890s further advance for women appeared to be blocked or at least likely to be very slow until parliament became more representative.[9] Gradually the vote ceased to be merely symbolic and became the key to wider change.

Organization and Leadership

By comparison with the Edwardian suffragettes the Victorian suffragists have made little impact on popular perceptions; even academics have invariably minimized their role. This is symptomatic of their somewhat obscure organizational structure and the character of their leadership. The London

---

[8] E. Sylvia Pankhurst, *The Suffragette Movement* (Virago, 1977), 63.
[9] Ignota, 'Women's Suffrage', *Westminster Review*, 148 (Oct. 1897), 365.

National Society for Women's Suffrage emerged in 1867 under Clementina Taylor, Barbara Leigh Smith, and Emily Davies. Shortly after, societies appeared in Manchester, led by Lydia Becker, and in Edinburgh, founded by Flora Stevenson and Priscilla, a sister of Jacob Bright, which affiliated to the National Society.[10] Similar groups emerged in Bristol under Annie Priestman and Lady Anna Gore, and at Birmingham under Mr and Mrs Osler, so that by the early 1870s clusters of suffragists in the regional capitals had created a loose federal organization which persisted throughout the life of the campaign.[11] While the London suffragists coordinated the parliamentary strategy it was largely left to the regions to take initiatives to promote the cause as they thought appropriate. Consequently, tension developed between provincial activists, who were more attuned to campaigning, and London which, to its critics, appeared cautious and reluctant to seek popular support. After 1900 this pattern offered an easy target for Mrs Pankhurst who, along with her husband, had in fact participated in the suffragist society in Manchester. However, the Pankhurst critique overlooked the fact that volunteer activists could not easily be dictated to; attempts to do so invariably resulted in breakaway factions as the Pankhursts discovered after 1903. This was all the more true since the early suffragists, men and women alike, tended to be classic liberal individualists, insistent on consulting their consciences on every issue.

As a result the central organization never exercised effective control over the movement. It was in any case handicapped by its limited financial resources, at least until the Edwardian period. During the 1870s, for example, central income amounted to around £1,000 to £1,300 per annum, but dwindled to only £300 to £400 during the 1880s. The resources of the constitutional movement remained largely concentrated at the local level. The Manchester Society, for example, attained an annual income of over £2,000 by 1872 and maintained it at around that level until 1885 when it declined.

The combination of opinionated members and a weak centre inevitably made the history of Victorian suffragism a history of splits. As early as 1872 the London Society refused to join the Central Committee of the National Society for Women's Suffrage because some of its members were associated with the campaign to repeal the CD Acts, though it retracted in 1877. A major split occurred in 1888 when a majority, which called itself the Central National Committee for Women's Suffrage, agreed to allow the affiliation of

---

[10] Leah Leneman, *A Guid Cause* (Aberdeen: Aberdeen University Press, 1991) discusses the development of the movement in Scotland.

[11] See Kirsten Seltorp, 'The Women's Suffrage Movement in Bristol, 1868–1906', unpublished MS, Fawcett Library.

women's party political organizations; the minority objected so strongly that it withdrew to form the Central Committee of the National Society. It is symptomatic of the introspection of the dispute that the successor bodies adopted such confusing and unmemorable titles! In 1889 another splinter group emerged in the form of the Women's Franchise League which wanted to include married women in suffrage legislation rather than restrict it to single and widowed women. The Women's Emancipation Union, formed in 1892, also aimed at a more democratic appeal. However, by 1897 most of these groups had been reunited in the National Union of Women's Suffrage Societies under the Presidency of Millicent Fawcett.[12]

In spite of this record it would be a mistake to exaggerate the significance of internal divisions within suffragism. At the grass roots the disagreements over legislation were not of great practical importance. Virtually all suffragists agreed about the use of constitutional methods in this period, and in London their campaign operated efficiently enough. In her capacity as Parliamentary Agent Lydia Becker coordinated the efforts of politicians and local societies, and she took the initiative in forming a parliamentary committee of suffragist MPs in June 1887. Though Mill believed that men ought to be excluded from the suffragist organization, his view did not prevail. Nonetheless, men's role was kept under control; at a demonstration in Edinburgh in 1884 the press complained that men had been confined to the gallery and 'made to pay half-a-crown for the privilege of hearing themselves abused!'[13] In effect women occupied all the officers' positions in the organization but maintained an element of male representation. In 1889, for example, the National Society's executive included three MPs (Leonard Courtney, Captain Edwards-Heathcote, and T. W. Russell), while the much larger general committee included twenty-eight politicians.

The other unifying element in the movement lay in two journals, the *Englishwoman's Review*, founded by Barbara Leigh Smith in 1866, and the *Women's Suffrage Journal* which Lydia Becker started in 1870. The former adopted a cautious and conservative approach, while the latter came closer to being a campaigning journal in that it reported extensively on local activities. Both suffered from precarious finances. Leigh Smith sustained the *Englishwoman's Review* from her own private income and with help from Jessie Boucherett who reportedly sold her diamonds for the cause.[14] So dependent on Becker

[12] See Lesley P. Hume, *The National Union of Women's Suffrage Societies, 1897–1914* (New York: Garland Publishing, 1982).

[13] Leneman, *Guid Cause*, 27.

[14] Theodora Bostick, 'The Press and the Launching of the Women's Suffrage Movement, 1866–67', *Victorian Periodicals Review*, 13/4 (1980).

was the WSJ that on her death in 1890 it promptly folded. Not until the Edwardian period were these early papers effectively superseded by the more successful journals—*Votes for Women* (1907) and *The Common Cause* (1909).

The impact of Victorian suffragism was also hindered by the fact that, although it attracted some very able women, it lacked a single charismatic leader. Indeed, for much of the pre-1900 period there was no real leader at all, but a collection of leading figures. Although Mill gave vital inspiration and intellectual weight to the cause, he never became important as an active participant in the campaign outside Westminster.[15] At best he remained aloof, apparently believing that the vote could be won comparatively easily without requiring an elaborate campaign. After 1867 he performed little further service to suffragism, and his death in 1873 was thus of no great significance for the cause. Unfortunately, Mill suffered from the academic's inability to recognize his own organizational deficiencies, and his stepdaughter, Helen Taylor, who proved to be an intransigent and divisive element, exploited his authority in her attempts to dominate the London Society in its early years. Helen variously objected to the inclusion of men, to the exclusion of married women from suffrage legislation, and to any links with Josephine Butler's campaign; she even jibbed at the title—which at one stage was the London Society for *Woman* Suffrage—on the grounds that she could never join an organization that was ungrammatical![16] As a result Helen and her father quit the London Society in order to work with the Manchester suffragists; but they found Becker and Bright no more to their liking. Fortunately, Taylor soon diverted herself to other activities, but in effect several years had been absorbed with attempts to keep the two Mills happy which vitiated any concerted leadership in London.

Up to 1890 the most influential single individual in the movement was probably Lydia Becker, an indefatigable, intellectually tough but slightly academic advocate of the vote. Her thorough grasp of parliamentary procedure, mastery of detail, and persistence in dealing with politicians made Becker formidable. But like her successor, Millicent Fawcett, she was not flamboyant. Fawcett also enjoyed close familiarity with Westminster, not least because her husband, Henry, had sat in Liberal cabinets under Gladstone. Calm, measured, and very well-informed, Fawcett's forte was the systematic rebuttal of ill-supported Anti-Suffragist arguments. However, she lacked the

---

[15] See Caine, 'Mill and the Women's Movement'.

[16] Ibid. 20; A. P. W. Robson, 'The Founding of the National Society for Women's Suffrage, 1866–67', *Canadian Historical Journal*, 8 (Mar. 1973).

inspirational qualities of a real leader. According to one account, when asked to sign a petition which described the vote as passionately desired by women, she demurred: '*must* I be passionate?'[17] An ideal leader actually existed in Josephine Butler who possessed the essential ability to articulate the women's case in moral terms. Indeed, Butler brought the kind of inspirational qualities later associated with the Pankhursts as well as their shrewd sense of the visual impact that could be made, for example, by women's prayer meetings. 'Never was there such an exhibition of silent power as Mrs Butler gave,' wrote Florence Fenwick Miller, 'her presence, her beautiful saintly face, her magnetic inspiring power, were felt throughout.'[18] Butler was also a better Liberal than either Becker or Fawcett, and as such she was more likely to have mobilized the party support which the others alienated. However, she concentrated on the Ladies National Association up to the 1880s, and remained marginal to the suffragist campaign, an unrealized asset.

The Parliamentary Strategy

Following the example of Victorian single-issue pressure groups, the suffragists focused their efforts around parliament; they compiled detailed records of their supporters in the House of Commons and cultivated members willing to introduce bills, present petitions, and arrange deputations to ministers. With the benefit of hindsight it was easy for the Pankhursts to disparage this approach; indeed, historians have often implicitly endorsed their critical view. Yet the virtues of the parliamentary strategy—in the early stages at least—were compelling. Parliament proved to be invaluable for getting over the immediate problem: how to launch the campaign. For many Victorians a political cause was simply not to be taken seriously unless it had been debated in parliament. In fact the suffragists capitalized brilliantly on the parliamentary situation so as to promote what was, after all, a very novel issue, into the forefront of debate. The death of Palmerston led to the introduction of a Liberal reform bill in 1866 whose defeat stimulated popular demonstrations organized by the Reform League over a period of several months. This suited the women because it kept the whole question of franchise reform topical and gave them time to organize. By persuading John Stuart Mill to present a petition to the Commons in June 1866 they contrived to

---

[17] See Joan E. Parker, 'Lydia Becker: Her Work for Women', Ph.D. thesis (Manchester University, 1990); H. M. Swanwick, *I Have Been Young* (Gollancz, 1935), 185.
[18] Quoted in Caine, *Victorian Feminists*, 173.

provoke a debate in the press. Emily Davies drew up a list of some five hundred newspapers to whom articles and copies of the petition were sent.[19] The lectures delivered by Barbara Leigh Smith to the congress of the Association for the Promotion of Social Science at Manchester in October 1866 also gained publicity partly because of the status of the host organization. Newspapers such as the *Pall Mall Gazette* agreed to print summaries of the suffragist petition and the names of leading signatories; others simply criticized women's suffrage editorially which was almost as useful at this stage; the worst response was that of *The Times*, a consistent antagonist over many years, which decided to ignore the question altogether. Much depended on the accident of editorial or proprietorial preference; for example, the *Fortnightly Review* suddenly became interested in 1867 when John Morley took over as editor.

Yet despite these efforts it was not easy for a handful of middle-class suffragists to force the issue into the limelight. Fortunately, the resignation of the Liberal Government and its replacement by a vulnerable minority Tory administration under Lord Derby and Benjamin Disraeli in the summer of 1866 created a fine opening for them. Not until February 1867 had the new government decided to introduce a reform bill of its own. For the suffragists the advantage lay in the fact that, as a minority administration, the Tories could not hope to remain in office for long unless they could maintain the divisions among the Liberals; consequently Disraeli was obliged to accept a series of amendments proposed by Liberal backbenchers which had the effect of turning the bill into a far more radical measure than intended. In this situation, with the bill changing from day to day on the floor of the House, Mill's amendment to include a franchise for women was a far less quixotic effort than it would otherwise have been. Though novel, it was scarcely more so than the amendments designed to incorporate large numbers of workingmen in which Disraeli's backbenchers, contrary to all expectations, acquiesced.

In the event Disraeli decided, despite his personal sympathy for female enfranchisement, that Mill's amendment would be a bridge too far; and it was defeated by 196 votes to 73, which was rightly regarded as more than satisfactory by his supporters. The choice of Mill had been shrewd. Though not a major politician—he had first been elected in 1865—he was an intellectual heavyweight who gave credibility to the new cause. It emerged subsequently that a number of Liberals had agreed to support the proposal more out of personal regard for Mill than because of any enthusiasm for female suffrage; and

---

[19] Bostick, 'The Press and the Women's Suffrage Movement', 125–7.

although suffragists complained bitterly for many years that MPs treated the issue frivolously, the fact remains that at a stroke votes for women had become a serious question. The initial debate in parliament gave the campaigners a base on which to build and a focus for wider efforts. Though Mill lost his seat in 1868, they found a suitable alternative champion in Jacob Bright the brother of John Bright, famous for his success over the repeal of the Corn Laws. As a result debates on women's suffrage took place in the Commons almost every year for the next decade and a half: 1870 (twice), 1871, 1872, 1873, 1875, 1876, 1877, 1878, 1879, 1883, and 1884 (twice). At a time when the national and provincial press used parliamentary material to fill its columns, this was an excellent expedient for keeping the issue in the public eye. The debates created a focus for local petitions and the formation of new societies, and helped to obscure the fact that the campaign was being run on the basis of minimal resources.

In retrospect this emphasis on parliament came to be seen as misplaced partly because it necessarily involved relying on cooperative backbench members whose legislation stood little or no chance of passing into law. In fact, this was much less true in the nineteenth century than it was to be in the twentieth; but even so, the odds were not encouraging. In 1870, for example, only 26 out of 84 private members' bills succeeded, and in 1872 only 17 out of 109. As a result of the expansion of government business the only propitious time in the year for backbenchers was around February before the cabinet's programme was ready. Yet if backbench legislation offered a dubious option, what alternative was there? To wait for government reform bills, which appeared at very irregular and infrequent intervals, would have been bad for morale. In any case, in the early stages of the campaign it was not remotely likely that any government would have legislated for women's suffrage. But by repeatedly initiating debates on backbench bills the suffragists managed to build up their support in parliament and in the country which, in the long run, offered the best means of encouraging governments to take up the issue.

However, the parliamentary strategy certainly entailed certain drawbacks. It inevitably put the suffragists in the hands of a small number of politicians who were willing to devote the time and accept the risks involved in promoting feminist legislation.[20] For example, in 1874 the new spokesman, William Forsyth, took it into his head to modify the bill by explicitly excluding married women, a course which Lydia Becker violently opposed because she knew it would upset some MPs previously pledged to the bill. The dispute

[20] Sir G. O. Trevelyan told Lydia Becker (6 Mar. 1879, Manchester Central Library, Becker Correspondence, M50/1/2) not to expect more than his vote as he could not take on too many causes at once.

was a distraction, it meant the loss of a debate in 1874, and in the end Forsyth largely got his way.

There are also some grounds for thinking that the suffragists allowed their campaign to be dictated more than was wise by the exigencies of the parliamentary situation. To become immersed in the endless complications of parliamentary tactics and the management of MPs was to risk neglecting the mobilization of support in the country. Some suffragists certainly entertained a very narrow view of the campaign. When Mill addressed a meeting in Edinburgh in January 1871 it was the *only* occasion on which he ever spoke on women's suffrage outside London.[21] He made no secret of his distaste for what he called the 'common vulgar motives and tactics' of the Manchester suffragists, and he refused to believe that public opinion was really ready for female enfranchisement. Emily Davies, who shared his doubts about the value of popular demonstrations, wished to avoid following the example set by the Reform League's agitation.[22] She once accepted a donation to the Kensington Women's Suffrage Society on the understanding that the members would abstain from campaigning for the vote for a year! However, such caution was hardly typical. Most of the leading suffragists overcame their understandable hesitation about public propaganda. Becker, Fawcett, and others traversed the country addressing meetings; the chief limitation was physical—Fawcett eventually restricted herself to four speeches a week.

In time Becker and Fawcett accumulated a fund of parliamentary expertise. But playing the parliamentary game sometimes led them astray. During the early 1880s Becker attempted to take advantage of the Liberals' readiness to introduce a bill to enfranchise agricultural labourers. She argued that it was pointless to expect Tory suffragists to support a women's bill for fear that this would make it awkward for them to oppose the Liberal measure.[23] As a result no women's bill was introduced for several years, a gap which has often been interpreted as a loss of momentum for the cause but which actually reflected over-sophisticated tactics. Becker argued that once the Liberal bill had appeared the Conservatives should be encouraged to amend it by means of a women's clause; but this misfired because it offended the radicals and played into Gladstone's hands (see Chapter 6). Throughout the campaign the cause suffered from attempts to find a formula that would satisfy the interests of all parties, and one suspects that the suffragists would have done better to avoid clever parliamentary manoeuvres and concentrate on

[21] Leneman, *Guid Cause*, 19.

[22] Sandra Stanley Holton, *Suffrage Days* (Routledge, 1996), 23, 37; Strachey, *The Cause*, 110–11.

[23] Lydia Becker to Mrs Ashworth Hallett, 2 Apr. 1880, in Helen Blackburn, *Women's Suffrage: A Record of the Women's Suffrage Movement in the British Isles* (Williams and Norgate, 1902), 149.

propagating their case. Of course, the validity of the parliamentary strategy changed over time. By the 1890s some suffragists had become restive about the traditional emphasis on Westminster. Valentine Munro-Ferguson complained that 'the result of patience so far has been that a less and less serious view is being taken of our cause. We are too cautious about offending either party in parliament.'[24] Such sentiments heralded the Pankhursts' initiatives in 1903.

But from the start it had been recognized that the parliamentary spokesmen for women's suffrage would carry more clout if they were seen to represent more than just a minority of disaffected women. In the early years the chief remedy for this was the presentation of petitions, a method traditionally employed by reformers in Britain. To some extent the petition was symbolic; in 1866 Mill had enthusiastically declared 'Ah, this I can brandish with effect', after receiving a petition containing only 1,499 signatures.[25] Subsequently petitions expanded to reach a peak in 1872–5 before falling off sharply, though during the 1890s the figures returned to the earlier high levels. Petitions were a useful form of local activity and could be used to embarrass MPs who claimed that the women in their constituencies showed no interest in the vote.[26]

TABLE 1.1. Women's suffrage petitions (number of signatures) presented to the House of Commons

1869	61,475	1872	355,806	1875	370,166
1870	134,561	1873	329,206	1877	266,263
1871	186,890	1874	430,343	1878	173,521
				1879	35,000

However, it remains doubtful whether these petitions tell us much about popular opinion. Since the suffragists employed canvassers, the figures are strictly an indication of the resources devoted to petitioning by the organizers as much as a sign of fluctuations in public support for the cause. Even Helen Blackburn admitted that petitions quickly lost impact because they were too easy to organize and were not regarded as a spontaneous expression of feeling.[27] In any case the Anti-Suffragists could easily spoil the effect by raising counter-petitions of their own. That petitions were deemed

[24] Valentine Munro-Ferguson to Millicent Fawcett, 12 Feb. 1896, Fawcett Library, Fawcett Letters, 89/1/20.
[25] Blackburn, *Women's Suffrage*, 55.
[26] See *Women's Suffrage Journal*, 2 Mar. 1874 (referring to K. Hodgson, Bristol and E. A. Leatham, Huddersfield), 49.
[27] Blackburn, *Women's Suffrage*, 198.

necessary at all was a tribute to the memory of the huge Chartist petitions, for however discredited they may have become, they almost dictated that a reform movement should demonstrate its seriousness in a similar fashion. But after the initial impact familiarity soon meant that they were simply laid on the table in the Commons and then rapidly swept away.

Militancy?

The Victorian suffragists are generally considered to have differed fundamentally from the Edwardian suffragettes because they adhered strictly to constitutional methods. This, however, oversimplifies considerably. Definitions of militancy naturally fluctuate over time. Between 1866 and 1869 when a small group of middle- and upper-middle-class ladies—Barbara Leigh Smith, Mrs Clementina Taylor, Lydia Becker, Millicent Fawcett, and Lady Amberley—first began to advocate female enfranchisement on public platforms, the tactic was described disparagingly as 'mixed speaking', since men were also present, and was widely thought to be rather shocking. One MP complained that two wives of members (Fawcett and Taylor) had disgraced themselves in this way, but he declined to add to their shame by naming them! Lady Amberley, of whom Queen Victoria memorably declared that she 'ought to get a good whipping', noted: 'people expressed surprise to me afterwards to see that a woman could lecture and still look like a lady!'[28] Naturally the sheer novelty of these occasions attracted large audiences; and by the 1880s ladies routinely addressed large meetings for the Girls Friendly Society, the Primrose League, the Mothers' Union, and the Women's Co-operative Guild. But in the late 1860s, one should remember, the suffragists who mounted public platforms were the *militants*.

It was not until 1905 when the WSPU's adoption of militant tactics posed a challenge to the existing societies that they felt obliged to clarify their position by claiming to be strictly law-abiding and non-violent. It comes as a surprise to find Lydia Becker writing in 1868: 'it *needs* deeds of bloodshed or violence before the British Government can be roused to do justice'.[29] Conversely Richard and Emmeline Pankhurst sat on the executive of the Manchester Society during the 1880s when constitutional methods were the norm. In view of the continuity of personnel between the two phases of

[28] Strachey, *The Cause*, 118, 121; Sir Theodore Martin, *Queen Victoria as I Knew Her* (Blackwood, 1908), 69.

[29] Lydia Becker to Esther Becker, 28 Apr. 1868, Manchester Central Library, Becker's Letter Books, M50/1/3.

suffragism it is hardly surprising to find that at least two of the tactics associated with Edwardian militancy were copied from the earlier period. For example, reports in the *Women's Suffrage Journal* suggest that as early as the 1870s women began refusing to pay taxes as a protest against their disfranchisement.[30] They quoted historical precedents in their support: Hampden's refusal of Ship Money, the late eighteenth-century American colonists, and the more recent resistance by Nonconformists to Church rates. In 1907 Margaret Ashton apparently persuaded the members of the Manchester Society that non-payment was justified in principle, though despite the widespread support, no attempt was made to coordinate this form of protest.[31]

A more troublesome form of militancy, at least for the politicians, involved intervention at by-elections usually designed to split the vote of Liberal candidates. As early as 1873 Lillias Ashworth promoted a pro-suffrage Liberal against an anti-suffrage Liberal at Bath, though this seems to have been an exceptional case.[32] In this period the technique was more associated with the Ladies National Association under Josephine Butler who used it controversially at by-elections in Colchester and Pontefract in 1870 and 1872. However, as a result of the lack of organizational strength and the non-party strategy of the suffragists, by-election interventions were infrequent before 1906 when the Pankhursts began to target Liberal candidates. They calculated that more was to be gained by working with the politicians than against them. Despite this, many members of the Women's Liberal Federation favoured applying women's suffrage as a test question for Liberal candidates before undertaking work on their behalf in the 1890s; they were, thus, halfway to Edwardian militancy.

There is also some suggestion that the tactics of Victorian suffragists varied regionally. The caution and gradualism characteristic of the London leaders has been contrasted with the more populist instincts of the Manchester suffragists for example.[33] The latter attempted to bypass the laborious legislative route by launching a legal challenge for the vote. Most of the early suffragists chose to regard women's exclusion from the electorate as an anomaly or legal disability that had arisen almost accidentally; and they hoped to exploit the legal and historical precedents which proved that women had previously been registered as parliamentary voters, especially as this was a form of argument to which politicians were susceptible. In 1867 a

[30] *Women's Suffrage Journal*, 1 Aug. 1872, 115; 2 June 1873, 103; 1 Dec. 1873, 175; 1 Aug. 1874, 115; 2 Nov. 1874, 151.

[31] *Annual Report*, Manchester Society for Women's Suffrage, 1907.

[32] *Women's Suffrage Journal*, 1 Nov. 1873, 158.

[33] This view is suggested in Parker, 'Lydia Becker'.

Manchester woman, Lilly Maxwell, who found herself on the register, cast her vote for Jacob Bright in a by-election, and she was far from being the first woman to do so. The case for allowing female ratepayers to enjoy the vote was threefold. In earlier times people in possession of this qualification had voted without distinction of sex; an Act introduced in 1850 by Lord Romilly provided that in all legislation the use of the masculine gender included females unless otherwise stated; and the reform act of 1867 had adopted the term 'man', not 'male persons' as in the 1832 reform act, and thus by implication included women.

Regardless of the validity of this claim, it proved an attractive initiative not just in Manchester but for suffragists in Scotland and other northern towns because it offered a means of demonstrating that women really did want the vote. In Manchester over 90 per cent of female ratepayers, a total of 5,346, agreed to make a claim to be registered before the revising barristers.[34] On being rejected they appealed to the Court of Common Pleas where the case was put by Sir John Coleridge and Richard Pankhurst (the case of Chorlton versus Lings) on 7 November 1868. London-based suffragists such as Mill regarded this tactic, along with the lobbying of MPs and deputations to the prime minister, as 'exceedingly mischievous'.[35] However, the difference between London and the industrial regions seems largely a matter of degree. In any case Becker, the leading Manchester suffragist, spent much of her time operating in London and dealing with the politicians; like Fawcett, she had an unshakeable confidence in the ultimate power of rational argument to secure the women's goal.

The Non-Party Strategy

Despite its original reliance on Liberal members, the campaign was from the outset firmly based on non-party lines. This had fundamental implications for the movement right up to 1914. In the beginning this approach seemed sensible in view of the need to maximize recruitment. In any case neither party had an agreed policy on women's enfranchisement, and the Conservative women were so strongly entrenched within the original suffrage committees that a firm commitment to the Liberals would simply have provoked another split in the small organization. A non-party strategy also seemed consistent with the concentration on backbench bills; the societies needed a

---

[34] *First Annual Report*, Manchester Society for Women's Suffrage, 1868, 7; for Edinburgh, see the Edinburgh Branch of the NSWS, *Report*, 17 Jan. 1870 (National Library of Scotland, 194.5/23).

[35] Parker, 'Lydia Becker', 140.

measure that could be handed on from Liberal to Tory members. This line of thinking was to culminate in the Conciliation Committee which promoted a bill backed by members of all four parties during 1910–12.

Nonetheless, the tactic suffered from major flaws. It was inevitably complicated by the fact that the organization included, on the one hand, dedicated Radicals such as Eva McLaren and Priscilla Bright who came from partisan Liberal families, and, on the other, staunch Conservatives such as Frances Power Cobbe and Emily Davies. From time to time the suffragist bill developed a bias, due to the member currently promoting it, which could be interpreted as favouring one party.[36] Yet for decades the suffragists proceeded as though party differences were merely a minor complication which should not stand in the way of the principle. Their naivety was dramatically underlined in 1911–12 when the huge majority won by the Conciliation Bill collapsed partly because Liberal members, who feared it would give an advantage to their opponents, dropped it when they saw the chance of a more democratic measure.

Many of the Victorian and Edwardian suffragists were not so much non-party as *anti*-party. Despite their close personal connections with parliament, they acquired a contempt for the whole business of party politics which years of prevarication and patronizing treatment from politicians merely exacerbated. Annie Kenney's heartfelt plea to A. J. Balfour summed up the feeling: 'there seems to be such hypocracy [*sic*],' she wrote, 'such insincerety [*sic*], such lying and a lot of humbug.'[37] Even the more sophisticated suffragists like Becker and Fawcett allowed their hostility to party to get the better of their judgement on occasion. When they found themselves in a minority in 1888 over the affiliation of the women's party associations to the National Society they simply walked out, and Becker contemplated quitting the movement altogether.[38] Though Fawcett has usually been regarded as the embodiment of the unemotional, non-party suffragist, the only modern biography of her portrays her as a rather rigid partisan especially after 1888 when she became a Liberal Unionist. During the 1890s Fawcett expressed the case for the women's vote in highly Conservative language and was scarcely credible as the spokesman for a movement claiming to be neutral between the main parties.[39]

---

[36] For example, in 1874 William Forsyth, a Conservative, proposed to insert a statutory disqualification for married women into the bill which antagonised many radicals. He found a compromise of sorts by substituting the words 'no woman under coverture' for 'no married woman', but the opportunity for a debate was thrown away as a result of the dispute.

[37] A. Kenney to A. J. Balfour, 18 Dec. 1909, British Library, Balfour Papers, Add. MS 49793, fo. 117.

[38] Strachey, *The Cause*, 281–2.

[39] D. Rubinstein, *A Different World for Women* (Brighton: Harvester, 1991), 119, 139.

Apart from the difficulties in adhering to a non-party strategy, there are grounds for regarding the whole approach as rather anachronistic.[40] The Victorian feminists drew much of their inspiration from the great moral crusades such as the campaign to repeal the Corn Laws which had triumphed over vested interests earlier in the century. However, the expansion of the electorate in 1867 had altered the balance between pressure groups and political parties to the disadvantage of the former. The parties felt obliged to develop a larger membership and more sophisticated and disciplined organizations to cope with the extra voters and the greater frequency of contested elections. Consequently, though the parties resented interference by pressure groups as much as ever, they coped better because they themselves reflected public opinion more closely and could mobilize enough support to withstand marginal losses of votes at by-elections. In short party loyalty was a phenomenon against which single-issue pressure groups often pitted themselves in vain. To some extent the suffragists were misled about the efficacy of interventions at elections by the pressure exerted by the Irish Nationalists on the Liberal Party. A disciplined body of voters such as the urban Irish could be switched from one party to another with some ease; but even with their advantages the Nationalists under John Redmond eventually accepted that only through cooperation with the Liberals were they ever likely to gain Home Rule.

In some ways the Pankhursts showed themselves realistic in the lessons they drew from this earlier experience. They accepted that party dominance had become a fact of life at Westminster, and concluded that the indefinite cultivation of an all-party majority for backbench suffrage bills was futile. They therefore demanded nothing less than government legislation. The flaw was that in holding Liberal governments responsible in this way they consistently antagonized their best allies and lost credibility on the left. They also continued to have an exaggerated faith in by-elections as a means of pressurising governments.

On the other hand, it is obvious why the suffragists felt so reluctant to modify their tactics so as to offer a form of enfranchisement acceptable to the Liberal Party. Until 1894 Gladstone remained an obstacle; and in any case, when the Liberals were in office they seemed increasingly unable to get their legislation past the House of Lords. Yet by the Edwardian period even they recognized belatedly the failure of their traditional approach when, the National Union of Women's Suffrage Societies, out of sheer exasperation, agreed an electoral pact with the Labour Party.

[40] Brian Harrison, 'Women's Suffrage at Westminster 1866–1928', in M. Bentley and J. Stevenson (eds.), *High and Low Politics in Modern Britain* (Oxford: Oxford University Press, 1983), 92–8.

The Question of Married Women

During the entire period from the 1860s to 1914 most of the women's suffrage bills debated in parliament involved enfranchising women on the same terms as men, a proposal which sounded radical but, in practice, affected single women and widows who were heads of households; in the 1870s this would probably have involved 300,000 to 400,000 women, and about one million by the 1900s. Why did the suffragists restrict their proposal in this way? In the first place it reflected the original assumption of the mid-Victorian feminists that single women *needed* political influence most urgently because of the obstacles they faced in trying to support themselves. Secondly, it appeared to Becker, Fawcett, and others that single women had an unanswerable case, politically, in that, as ratepaying householders they met the conventional notion of citizenship. Thirdly, being modest in scope and simple in law, the proposal seemed to be feasible. 'We should limit ourselves strictly to the disabilities of *sex* and leave the marriage question alone,' insisted Becker in 1874, 'the common law disabilities of married women effectively preclude them from the exercise of the franchise.' She concluded that the issue should be left to some later date.[41] In this the suffragists made a crucial tactical judgement—or misjudgement. They calculated that the inclusion of wives would antagonize men both because it would create a female majority amongst the electorate and because it could be seen as threatening the stability of marriage itself.

Yet from the outset some suffragists regarded this reasoning as flawed and even indefensible. As Emily Davies observed, the exclusion of married women was 'dishonest as misrepresenting our real opinions . . . When the wedge is inserted, you can go for more.'[42] However, others seemed unconvinced that it was even desirable. Fawcett, for example, claimed that if wives were enfranchised 'changes will be introduced into home life which have not been adequately considered'. Nor could she accept the need for wives' enfranchisement, for, 'the effect, in ninety-nine cases out of a hundred, would be to give two votes to the husband. Wives are bound by law to obey their husbands . . . it seems inexpedient to allow political independence (which would only be nominal) to precede actual independence.'[43] This remarkably frank statement underlines the conventional and even illiberal elements within

[41] Lydia Becker to Mr Eastwick, 4 Mar. 1874.
[42] Emily Davies to Helen Taylor, 6 Aug. 1866, British Library of Political and Economic Science, Mill–Taylor Papers, XIII, quoted in Robson, 'Founding', 11.
[43] Millicent Fawcett, 'Female Suffrage: A Reply', *The Nineteenth Century*, 209 (July 1889).

Fawcett's thinking. The logic led her to argue that as most women were likely to marry eventually, and in time become widows, their status would change from being voters to non-voters: 'In this way the direct representation of some women would become the indirect representation of all women.' This was by no means an eccentric idea, for many *men* passed in and out of the electoral registers as their circumstances changed; but Fawcett was, in effect, adopting the Anti-Suffragist view about virtual representation.

Indeed, that tactic played straight into the hands of opponents who simply derided the emphasis placed upon single women. 'Is it any proof,' demanded Edward Leatham, MP, 'because a woman happens to have failed, from one cause or another, in the role of her own sex, that she can adequately discharge the more difficult and less congenial part of man?' Another member, P. B. Smollett, cuttingly observed: 'Under this Bill, elderly virgins, widows, a large class of the demi-monde and kept women ... would be admitted to the franchise, while the married women of England—mothers who formed the mainstay of the nation—were rigidly excluded.'[44]

Moreover, the exclusion of married women introduced a long-running division into the suffrage movement, for many Radical Liberals, both men and women, wished to promote a more democratic measure. As early as 1870 Sir Charles Dilke and Jacob Bright withdrew from the London Society when a proviso excluding wives was added to the suffrage bill.[45] Subsequently bills designed to include women under coverture were introduced by Richard Haldane (1889, 1890, 1892), by Dr Clarke (1893, 1894, 1895), by Dilke (1894, 1906), by Walter McLaren (1895), by Henry York Stanger (1908), by Geoffrey Howard (1909), by Sir Charles McLaren (1910), and by W. H. Dickinson (1907, 1909, 1911, 1913). Every one of these was a Liberal. The suffragist leaders were very slow to take the point they were making—that many of the most loyal supporters of the cause believed in the desirability for a democratic and representative first instalment of women's suffrage. The same case was urged by Ursula Bright, Clementina Taylor, Mrs Wolstenholme Elmy, Emmeline Pankhurst, Josephine Butler, and others who formed the Franchise League in 1889. Though this splinter group enjoyed only a small membership, they believed, with some reason, that they were working with the grain of politics. As a result of the Married Women's Property Acts a number of wives who were ratepayers in their own right were included on local registers. In 1893 Walter McLaren and James Stansfeld successfully pressed the Liberal Government to include wives as voters in their Local Government

[44] *Hansard, House of Commons Debates,* 3rd Series, CCXXIII, 7 Apr. 1875, c. 449.
[45] Notes for Autobiography, Dilke Papers, BL, Add. MS 43931, fos. 58–9.

Bill if they paid rates on separate property, that is, they could not be registered for the same property as their husbands.[46] Eventually corroboration for
the views of the Radical members came during the First World War when the
Speaker's Conference recommended the vote for women qualified as local
government electors *and* for those who were married to local government
electors. Nothing, however, deflected the suffragist leaders from their conviction that it would be easier to enact a simple bill for single women.

Adult Suffrage and the Working Class

The controversy over married women was symptomatic of the wider
dilemma facing Victorian Suffragists: whether to attempt to advance the
cause via a broader movement for complete adult suffrage. During the 1860s
and 1870s the case for caution appeared compelling. Even the third reform
act of 1885 left Britain with an electorate of only 5.7 million—about six adult
men in every ten. The advance towards democracy continued to proceed by
a series of steps at irregular intervals; surely the same logic would apply in the
case of women? Tactics thus required the suffragists, in Becker's words, to
present 'what is theoretically a great change as practically a very small measure'.[47] In effect, they proposed to introduce about one million women into
what, by the Edwardian period, was a male electorate of 7.9 million—modest
enough to be reassuring. By contrast, adult suffrage still appeared dangerous
because it implied a working-class majority. As Professor Harrison has
emphasized, much of the Anti-Suffragists' hostility reflected not simply or
even primarily their view of women, but their wider fears about the drift
towards complete democracy.[48]

Yet while the aim of reassuring the politicians seemed shrewd enough in
theory, it was fatally vitiated by the narrowness of the proposal. Most Victorian politicians found unmarried women more threatening than reassuring.
And since they insisted on seeing the modest women's suffrage bills in the
context of adult suffrage, the cautious strategy became rather futile. Suffragists refused to face the paradox at the heart of their cause: that they were striv-
ing to achieve a democratic reform while denying a democratic rationale,

---

[46] *Hansard, HC Deb.*, 4th Series, XVII, 16 Nov. 1893, c. 111–13; 21 Nov. 1897, c. 1388; Scottish
Women's Liberal Federation, executive minutes (Edinburgh University Library), 5 Dec. 1893, and
Memorial to G. O. Trevelyan, 1 Jan. 1984.

[47] *Women's Suffrage Journal*, 2 May 1870, 18.

[48] Brian Harrison, *Separate Spheres: The Opposition to Women's Suffrage in Britain* (Croom Helm,
1978), 33.

and in the process, depriving themselves of the potential of a popular movement. It must be significant that at the end of the day parliament actually granted the vote, not to one million women, but to 8.4 million, far from the cautious first step that most suffragists had anticipated. Contrary to expectations the politicians found it easier to be radical than to be conservative; this, after all, was exactly how they had behaved in 1866–7 in rejecting a modest measure in favour of a far more sweeping one. Even in 1884–5, when a further extension of the electorate took place, the suffragists continued to draw the wrong lessons. Understandably angered at women's exclusion from the bill, they failed to see that as more and more men became enfranchised it was increasingly anomalous that educated, intelligent, tax-paying and politically aware women remained excluded. Yet both constitutional and militant suffragists refused to accept that each move towards adult suffrage was in the line of progress and thus helpful to women; they insisted that the next reform must be a purely women's measure. But in effect this meant that they failed to make common cause with the millions of men who still remained excluded, and kept the working class of both sexes at arm's length for many years.

Some historians, offended by the assumption that Victorian feminism was essentially a middle-class movement, have insisted that working-class support has simply been overlooked. This, however, depends very much on which region of the country one examines, and also on the chronological period. Victorian suffragists typically relied on the well-worn technique of drawing-room meetings which were intimidating for working-class wives and, moreover, held at inconvenient times of day. Working women certainly attended public meetings in Scotland and Lancashire for example, though in the early years this was essentially a by-product of the campaign not an attempt to enrol such women in the suffrage organization.[49] Most of our evidence for the deliberate mobilization of working women comes from the Lancashire textile districts where Esther Roper and Eva Gore-Booth attracted enthusiastic audiences to open air meetings; female members of the Weavers Union endorsed female enfranchisement at branch meetings in Bolton, Clitheroe, Colne, Nelson, Hyde, and Haslingden for example.[50] However, this activity was a feature of the 1890s and early 1900s rather than the earlier period. Similarly, the Women's Co-operative Guild, though founded in 1883, did not take up the vote for women until the 1890s, to some extent under the influence of middle-class leaders.

[49] Leneman, *Guid Cause*, 18, 24.
[50] Jill Liddington and Jill Norris, *One Hand Tied Behind Us* (Virago, 1978); Lewis Gifford, *Eva Gore-Booth and Esther Roper* (Pandora, 1988); *Annual Report*, Manchester Society for Women's Suffrage, 1903.

If suffragism proved slow to mobilize the working class, the fault was not to be laid entirely at the door of the suffragists. There is abundant evidence that until the Edwardian period male trade unionists in Lancashire, Yorkshire, and the North-East resented the attendance of their wives at political meetings of any kind.[51] Isabella Ford, who devoted herself to persuading the Labour Movement in Leeds and the West Riding that the interests of women were inextricably linked with those of workingmen, found the experience dispiriting; and she never managed to emulate the relative success with female workers in neighbouring Lancashire.[52] Not that the obstacles were solely male. Most of the leading women in the pre-1914 Labour Movement—Margaret Bondfield, Mary MacArthur, Margaret MacDonald, Marion Phillips, Katherine Bruce Glasier—campaigned for adult suffrage rather than for a separate women's bill. Bondfield explained that she was 'never able to approach the question from the standpoint of women's rights'.[53]

Although none of this proves that suffragist tactics were wrong, it does underline the point that by focusing on a limited measure of women's suffrage they handicapped themselves by making it more difficult to realize their potential support; it is at least arguable that their cautious approach contributed to the length of time taken to win the vote. No doubt this was far from obvious in the early years of the campaign. However, by the 1880s experience with cautious measures in parliament should have inspired some reassessment of strategy, as it clearly did amongst some Liberal MPs. By the 1890s an alternative route to enfranchisement had been pioneered in New Zealand where full male suffrage greatly simplified the introduction of votes for all women; it also showed the value of close cooperation with Liberals or with a Liberal–Labour alliance. In Britain this would have involved certain risks, for it was at this time that more Conservatives were taking up the cause, and suffragists naturally felt reluctant to alienate them. Above all, the leading feminists justified their tactics on the grounds that no great demand for the enfranchisement of all *men* had yet materialized in Britain, as was conceded even by sympathetic Labour politicians such as Philip Snowden.[54] When pressure groups such as the Adult Suffrage Society and the People's Suffrage Federation, led by Margaret Bondfield and Arthur Henderson, respectively,

---

[51] See Mrs Sim reporting on Gateshead, Women's Labour League, Labour Party Archives WLL/1/93; Jill Liddington, *The Life and Times of a Respectable Radical: Selina Cooper* (Virago, 1984); Martin Pugh, 'Labour and Women's Suffrage', in K. D. Brown (ed.), *The First Labour Party* (Croom Helm, 1985).

[52] See June Hannam, *Isabella Ford* (Oxford: Blackwell, 1989), 34, 47, 80–1, 89–90.

[53] M. Bondfield, *A Life's Work* (Hutchinson, 1948), 82.

[54] *The Common Cause*, 3 June 1909, 102.

emerged they seem to have been small, lacking resources and distinctly marginal to the struggle for the vote.[55] In any case these initiatives came so late in the day that the women's suffragists believed that their own claim should take priority. Yet their own rank and file were unconvinced; in 1909 one member derided Fawcett's rejection of adult suffrage as 'laughable', arguing that a 'bold appeal for the enfranchisement of the great mass of the working women, the class who most need the protection of the vote' was the best way to impress the government.[56] The political logic of the Edwardian period—dominated by a Liberal–Labour alliance based on working-class votes—pointed inexorably towards adult suffrage.

Suffragism and the 'Sex War'

This evidence about the caution of Victorian suffragists' demands and about their desire to work within the existing political system has contributed to a view of the movement which may not fully reflect its character. In recent years some feminist scholars, looking back from the perspective of the modern women's movement, have criticized this tradition for presenting British suffragism as unduly conservative and as too narrowly political. In 1987, for example, Susan Kingsley Kent suggested a broad reinterpretation of the movement: 'In fighting for enfranchisement, the suffragists sought no less than the total transformation of the lives of women.' Scholars, she argued, would be wrong to dismiss the 'sex war' as an aberration or a sidelight, for it was in fact 'the crux of the suffrage campaign'.[57] From this perspective the campaign to repeal the Contagious Diseases Acts, for example, can be seen as directly advancing the cause of suffragism, and later initiatives such as Christabel Pankhurst's 1913 attack on marriage and venereal disease appears as part of a continuing theme rather than as an isolated example. Thus, the reluctance of contemporary suffragists to express their radical views in public whether on politics or morality, must be regarded as wholly tactical in motive not as reflecting their real ideology and aims.

This view is valid to the extent that the moral tradition within feminism was a long-standing one stretching back to evangelical influences earlier in the century; and throughout the period one finds abundant evidence of

---

[55] See the Adult Suffrage Society's statement of accounts, 24 Jan. 1908 which shows £49 income for 1907, Roland Muirhead Papers (National Library of Scotland, Box 153/10).

[56] See Lillian Harris, *The Common Cause*, 27 May 1909, 97.

[57] Susan Kingsley Kent, *Sex and Suffragism in Britain, 1860–1914* (Princeton: Princeton University Press, 1987), 3, 5.

feminist criticism of the double standard in moral and sexual standards practised by men. However, the approach adopted by Kent suffers from several
major flaws, both empirical and interpretational.

Selective quotation from feminists' views on marriage, morality, and masculinity does not offer convincing proof and needs to be put into context. The
thesis takes no account of the systematic analysis of 'first wave' feminists
undertaken by Olive Banks. Among other things this quantifies the participation by Victorian feminists in a whole range of causes and pressure groups. It
reveals that whereas 89 per cent of first wave feminists participated in suffragism, only 13 per cent took part in the campaign against the CD Acts.
Moreover, although 85 per cent of women involved in Josephine Butler's
work also backed votes for women, only 13 per cent of active suffragists participated in her campaign.[58] These findings somewhat undermine the claim
that moral issues were a central force behind the movement to win the vote.

Banks's analysis also throws light on the wider relationship between first
wave feminists and the male sex. Although active feminists were less likely to
be married than women as a whole, a clear majority did in fact marry. Moreover, active feminism appears to have been associated with a happy marriage
rather than reflecting a reaction against a failed one.[59] Husband and wife
partnerships in which both members supported women's causes were not
uncommon—George and Josephine Butler, Henry and Millicent Fawcett,
Richard and Emmeline Pankhurst, and Fred and Emmeline Pethick-
Lawrence are prominent examples. Positive relations with men extended
beyond husbands. Banks found that feminism was not a reaction against an
autocratic or prejudiced father but was likely to be associated with positive
encouragement by a father for his daughter's ambitions as in the cases of
Elizabeth Garrett Anderson, Josephine Butler, Barbara Leigh Smith, and
Margaret Llewelyn Davies. Brothers also proved to be sympathetic influences for such feminists as Harriet Martineau, Anne Jemima Clough, Emily
Davies, and Constance Lytton. Broadly Banks concluded that far from
rejecting contemporary attitudes, the first wave feminists 'lived within the
sexual conventions of their time'.[60]

Feminists' criticism of masculine sexual behaviour and of legal discrimination against married women must be seen in this context. Millicent Fawcett,
for example, relentlessly exposed male immorality; she also opposed the
spread of birth control material because it simply exacerbated existing male
irresponsibility: 'if we don't level up we shall have to level down'.[61] It seems

---

[58] Banks, *Becoming*, 51, 64.   [59] Ibid. 34–5.   [60] Ibid. 37.
[61] M. G. Fawcett to A. J. Balfour (copy), 26 Mar. 1894, Fawcett Letters 90A, in Rubinstein,
Different World, 86–8.

likely that after her husband's death she became more radical, or perhaps readier to express her views in this respect as is suggested by her support for W. T. Stead's campaign to stop the traffick in children and to raise the age of consent. Yet Fawcett fully accepted the institution of marriage as a desirable goal for women; she simply felt that women ought not to be coerced into marriage if they were not suited to it and that the alternatives ought to be open to them. She agreed with Lydia Becker who wrote: 'the notion that the husband ought to have the headship or authority over his wife is the root of all social evils. It is a doctrine demoralizing alike to men and women.'[62] But none of this made her hostile to marriage as such. The reform of certain unfortunate aspects of marriage would lead to a more general experience of the companionate marriage that she and Henry Fawcett had enjoyed. Suffragists of her generation undoubtedly expected women's enfranchisement to have wider ramifications in helping women to become more equal partners and more able to support themselves financially. Barabara Leigh Smith, for example, took a positive view of marriage and employment for women; to encourage a girl to obtain the means of supporting herself was not, in her view, to divert her from domesticity, but to enable her to become a better wife: 'women must have work if they are to form equal unions. Work will enable women to free themselves from petty characteristics, and therefore ennoble marriage.'[63] In effect the feminism of these women combined a belief in greater equality with an emphasis on sexual difference. Josephine Butler also wished to maintain women's femininity and disapproved of what she called the 'masculine-aiming woman' who sought to eradicate the differences between the sexes.[64] Similarly, Fawcett's repeated references to the special experiences, skills, and qualities engendered by women's domesticity was surely more than merely a tactical justification for their enfranchisement. To suggest that the demand for the vote implied a fundamental challenge to the separate spheres ideology on the part of these women seems to be a misunderstanding of their views; indeed, they endorsed a good deal of the conventional idea of gender roles. That this was more than a passing feature of the movement is evident from the evolution of feminism during the 1920s and 1930s when leaders such as Eleanor Rathbone attempted to adjust its objectives so as to reflect even more closely the domestic needs of the average woman.

The other complication in the 'sex war' thesis, and a formidable one in the context of an analysis of the fortunes of the suffrage campaign, is interpretational. Kent's depiction of Victorian suffragism closely echoed the criticisms

---

[62] Becker in Theodore Stanton (ed.), *The Woman Question in Europe* (Sampson Low, 1884), 42.

[63] Barbara Leigh Smith, 'Women and Work', 1857.

[64] Quoted in Caine, *Victorian Feminists*, 95.

levelled against it by contemporary *Anti-Suffragists* who were naturally keen to prove that it harboured subversive intentions behind its reassuring exterior. Goldwin Smith alleged that the vote was part of 'an attempt to change the general relations between the sexes' and to encourage women 'to think that rearing children is a poor object for (their) aspirations'.[65] Yet if this had been the case the chances of parliament agreeing to female enfranchisement would have remained slight. Thus, to interpret the movement as driven by a radical attack on gender roles is merely to dig oneself deeper into an analytical hole, from which no means of extrication are offered. How, in short is one to explain why growing numbers of politicians backed the vote for women, and why over eight million were eventually enfranchised? Politicians obviously did not understand the movement as a threat to existing society and politics. On the contrary, they concluded that though votes for women represented a risk, it was one that could reasonably be taken without jeopardizing marriage and the family.

There is a tradition deriving from contemporary opinion amongst both constitutional and militant suffragists that female enfranchisement was a good cause effectively propagated but frustrated by trickery and weakness on the part of dishonourable politicians. This examination of suffragist tactics and strategy suggests that this is an inadequate explanation for the protracted struggle to win the vote. Despite the skill and determination of its advocates, the cause suffered from some serious operational flaws. In particular, the insistence on excluding married women and on following a non-party strategy showed a lack of realism; and in general the attempt to pass off female enfranchisement as though it meant a marginal modification rather than a major innovation was essentially disingenuous. Suffragist leaders were slow to learn from experience and failed to resolve the dilemmas of the early years, which is why the politicians eventually cut through the problems by imposing a solution of their own in 1917.

[65] Goldwin Smith, 'Conservatism and Female Suffrage', *The National Review*, 10 (Feb. 1888), 747.

2

The Debate

'WE should have been a better country today if we had stuck to men voters.'[1] This comment by the late A. J. P. Taylor, written as late as 1958, forty years after women first obtained the parliamentary vote, reflected a view of the female mentality which had survived apparently unchanged from an earlier era. It reminds us that on an issue of this kind the argument can never be said to have been completely settled. Fundamental prejudices about the role and the qualities of men and women are very slow to change; and for the Victorian suffragists, therefore, victory consisted not so much in altering basic convictions about gender, as in modifying perceptions about the implications of enfranchisement. Men in particular had to be convinced that extending the vote would not wholly subvert existing politics and society in Britain.

Yet the *debate* over women's suffrage—as opposed to the campaigns waged by suffragists and suffragettes—has been surprisingly neglected by scholars.[2] This may reflect an assumption that the arguments became highly repetitive and thus unimportant, or that the issue became stuck in rhetorical trench warfare. This is true—but only up to a point. One of the objects of this chapter is to examine the interplay between the two sides in the debate, bearing in mind that, as in most arguments, the protagonists sometimes preferred to ignore what their opponents said. It is especially important to analyse the debate over time, for to present it as a static dialogue of the deaf is to oversimplify enormously. It would be misleading, for example, to assume that the

---

[1] *Woman's Mirror*, 31 Oct. 1958, 11. He declared, *inter alia*, that good voters had to have common sense in public affairs: 'Men argue. Women feel'. In fairness one should allow for the possibility that Mr Taylor did not believe what he wrote; then as now, impecunious historians sometimes felt obliged to earn an honest penny by expressing extravagantly reactionary views in the right-wing press.

[2] Apart from the outstanding analysis in Brian Harrison, *Separate Spheres: The Opposition to Women's Suffrage in Britain* (Croom Helm, 1978), there is also a short account in Constance Rover, *Women's Suffrage and Party Politics in Britain 1866–1914* (Routledge, 1967).

case against enfranchisement was overwhelmingly strong at the start. In 1867 Mill professed quiet satisfaction over the poor quality of the arguments used against his proposal. At this stage the Antis had simply not thought much about the issue; they were largely going on their instincts. Their case probably became most formidable during the 1870s and 1880s but was increasingly undermined by political and social changes during the later 1880s and the 1890s, a view which is inconsistent with the usual assumption that suffragism entered a decline in that period. A chronological perspective helps to reveal how the suffragist case varied as new ideas gained prominence; and, on the other hand, it highlights those aspects of Anti-Suffragism which became obsolete or lost credibility. The debate was also complicated because neither side presented a monolithic case, though naturally there was a large area of common ground. Liberals and Conservatives, for example, expressed the case for the vote differently; and the Antis suffered from fundamental divisions because some of their leading figures held feminist views (see Chapter 7).

Equal Rights Versus Expediency

For the mid-Victorian advocates of votes for women the basis of the claim lay in the belief that in any community individuals possessed rights and that these rights attached to individuals regardless of their social relations. Since women comprised over half of the population, as Lydia Becker observed, it could hardly be desirable for them to remain uninterested in or uninvolved in a political order which obviously affected them. The law, after all, did not require citizens to be clever or literate in order to enjoy formal political influence, but simply to possess some stake in the country or to contribute to it, usually in the form of property or taxation; on this basis how, asked the suffragists, could one justify withholding political rights from women?[3] Seen from this perspective the women's vote did not really interfere with existing principles of representation, but 'would rather make our Constitution more consistent with itself' as Barbara Leigh Smith put it.[4] Even the Edwardian Tory Leader, A. J. Balfour, accepted that after the enfranchisement of the

---

[3] Lydia Becker, 'Female Suffrage', *Contemporary Review*, 4 (Mar. 1867), 308; 'The Women Ratepayers' Right to Vote', *Westminster Review*, 122 (1884), 377.

[4] Barbara Leigh Smith, speech to the National Association for the promotion of Social Science, Oct. 1866.

artisans and labourers it had become 'ludicrous to attempt a distinction of principle between the adults of one sex and the adults of another'.[5]

On the whole, however, the debate was not conducted in terms of principle or abstract ideas about rights; indeed Millicent Fawcett denied that the claim was based on inalienable rights for women, and Beatrice Webb explained that her own original opposition to the vote was based 'principally on my disbelief in the validity of any abstract rights'.[6] Partly for tactical reasons and partly from their own inclinations, the suffragists adopted a pragmatic or expedient approach, resting their case on experience and on the implications of reform. They thus engaged the Antis on their own ground. Professor A. V. Dicey, one of the most vigorous protagonists, argued that the vote was not a right for the individual but a function for the citizen to use for the public good; liberal claims to rights, he suggested, had gone out with Burke and Bentham.[7] Even Mill in *The Subjection of Women* had attacked the legal subordination of one sex to the other not only in terms of its inherent injustice but also for the utilitarian reason that it had damaging consequences for society. When he articulated the case in the House of Commons he shifted the emphasis even further away from individual rights: 'My whole argument is one of expediency,' he declared, 'to lay a ground for refusing the suffrage to any one, it is necessary to allege either personal unfitness or public danger.'[8] In fact Mill and the other early suffragists were adopting the fashionable argument of the 1860s, to the effect that a workingman who contributed to national taxation was responsible enough to exercise the parliamentary vote. When Frances Power Cobbe flourished a list of nine reasons for enfranchising women in 1869 she gave priority to the claim of women who possessed property and paid their rates.[9]

Amongst Gladstonian Liberals the no-taxation-without-representation argument seemed hard to resist in the 1860s. Later, however, Liberals such as James Bryce who had initially accepted the logic of the women's claim, retracted on the basis that since virtually everyone paid taxes of some sort, even if only on their drink and tobacco, the claim was not a valid one. In a way the suffragists' original argument had succeeded rather too well; for it appealed to Conservatives so strongly as to arouse doubts in the minds of Radicals. Right-wing politicians undoubtedly felt the force of the claim that

---

[5] A. J. Balfour to Christabel Pankhurst, 23 Oct. 1907, Balfour Papers, BL, Add. MS 49793.

[6] Fawcett in Stanton (ed.), *Woman Question*, 5; Webb in *The Times*, 5 Nov. 1906, 8.

[7] A. V. Dicey, *Letters to a Friend on Votes for Women* (John Murray, 1909), 7, 14.

[8] *Hansard, HC Deb.*, 3rd Series, CLXXXVI, 20 May 1867, c. 818.

[9] See Millicent Fawcett, 'The Electoral Disabilities of Women', *Fortnightly Review*, 7 (1870), 622; Frances Power Cobbe, 'Why Women Demand the Vote', 1869.

all property ought to be represented regardless of the sex of its owner, and the more the vote was extended to unpropertied sections of society the more urgent it seemed to find fresh forms of representation for private property. Consequently, in time this line of argument was heard less frequently on Liberal lips and became more typical of Tory suffragists.

A Necessity or an Indulgence?

During the 1870s two-thirds of adult men occupied the same position as women in being excluded from the electoral registers; this enabled opponents of reform to argue that women had no major grievance, being subject to 'virtual representation' in common with many men, and, moreover, enjoyed an advantage as a result of their *indirect* influence over men which more than compensated for a lack of formal recognition. This soon became a central element of the Anti-Suffragist case: 'The fundamental error of all this reasoning is that women constitute a class apart . . . for all practical purposes women are already represented by their husbands, sons and brothers.'[10]

Significantly this was endorsed by women such as Mrs Humphry Ward, the famous novelist, who commented in 1889: 'during the past half-century all the principal injustices of the law towards women have been amended by means of the existing machinery . . . and with regard to those that remain we see no signs of any unwillingness on the part of Parliament to deal with them'.[11] Even in the 1890s politicians such as James Bryce and H. H. Asquith continued to urge this view. Others pointed out that the bills put forward for women would in any case give a vote to maiden ladies with property who did not particularly need it, but not to the poor women for whom a stronger case might be made. Though not entirely accurate, this did expose the narrowness of the proposals; opponents clearly found it easy to discredit the women's cause by presenting it as essentially a *symbol* of inequality for well-to-do women rather than as a substantial grievance. The language used by Barbara Leigh Smith, for example, gave some substance to the claim: 'citizenship is an honour', she said, 'those who . . . are debarred from full participation in the rights and duties of a citizen lose more or less of social consideration and

[10] E. A. Leatham, *Hansard, HC Deb.*, 3rd Series, CCXXIII, 7 Apr. 1875, c. 415–16. Another way of putting this was to say that female enfranchisement would mean two votes for male relations. Fawcett rebutted this ('Electoral Disabilities of Women', 623), but also contradicted herself by rejecting a vote for married women on the grounds that it would give two votes to husbands.

[11] 'An Appeal Against Women's Suffrage', *The Nineteenth Century*, 209 (June 1889).

esteem'.[12] Hence Lady Salisbury, already generously endowed with social esteem, derided the whole claim: 'What earthly good will it do to any woman to have a vote?' According to one MP, 'Women should be satisfied with the great power they now possess indirectly, which is far greater than anything they can hope to attain directly.'[13]

Yet the suffragists felt confident about debating these points. Lydia Becker challenged her opponents to explain exactly by what means women exercised their influence on men before they voted. Mill condemned the very idea on the grounds that indirect influence, if it existed at all, was irresponsible and undesirable. He probably had in mind the role of ambitious hostesses whose role during the mid-Victorian period was far from simply social. In 1852 Millicent, Duchess of Sutherland, used her Stafford House connections to lead an anti-slavery campaign which attracted criticism on the grounds that she was going beyond a woman's place and even demeaning female moral authority. Significantly, Gladstone had been on the receiving end of the Duchess's pressure.[14]

As to whether women's interests were already dealt with, Barbara Leigh Smith adopted a very tentative line, suggesting only that any class was likely to be neglected if left unrepresented. Others observed that the same had been said about workingmen before 1867. Jacob Bright exploded the notion of virtual representation: 'I have seen Members of this House sit here till daylight to defeat the Married Women's Property Bill . . . and I have seen the same Hon. Members competing in this House in their desire to protect the funds of trade unionists and to protect trade unions themselves. This is the effect of the franchise.'[15] Mill and Fawcett itemized the grievances that lay unresolved by parliament: the lack of property rights for married women, the denial of guardianship rights over children, exclusion from educational endowments, and subjection to domestic violence which went unpunished by the courts.[16] In so far as women were naturally weaker or disadvantaged, they argued, they stood all the more in need of the protection of the law and of parliament.[17]

---

[12] Barbara Leigh Smith, speech, Oct. 1866.

[13] Lady Frances Balfour, *Ne Obliviscaris: Dinna Forget* (Hodder and Stoughton, 1930), i. 148; Edward Bouverie, *Hansard, HC Deb.*, 3rd Series, CCI, 12 May 1870, c. 613.

[14] See Lydia Becker, 'Female Suffrage', *Contemporary Review*, 4 (Mar. 1867), 310; *Hansard, HC Deb.*, 3rd Series, CLXXXVII, 20 May 1867, c. 824–5; K. D. Reynolds, *Aristocratic Women and Political Society in Victorian Britain* (Oxford: Oxford University Press, 1998), 125–6.

[15] *Hansard, HC Deb.*, 3rd Series, CCI, 4 May 1870, c. 199–200.

[16] See Fawcett, 'Electoral Disabilities of Women', 623; *Hansard, HC Deb.*, 3rd Series, CLXXXVII, 20 May 1867, c. 824–5.

[17] Frances Power Cobbe, 'Why Women Demand the Vote', 1869; *Hansard, HC Deb.*, 3rd Series, CCI, 12 May 1870, c. 622.

Despite the fact that several major female grievances had been tackled during the 1870s and 1880s, leading opponents of the suffrage including Gladstone himself readily conceded that the reformers had a valid point; they simply argued that it was not a major one. A. V. Dicey, for example, agreed that women had been unfairly treated over employment and married women's property, but felt that as women were not a class it was rare for their interests to conflict with those of men as a class.[18] Violet Markham admitted that she would have been a suffragist if she had been convinced that gaining the vote would have had the effect of raising women's wages, which suggests that issues of this sort ought to have been given higher priority by the suffragists before the Edwardian period.[19] A. J. Balfour betrayed an interesting confusion on this point in that he accepted that the position on women's employment was 'productive of injustice', but also felt there was no real difference between the views of men and women, and that if their interests did diverge, 'I should regard this as a strong, and even overwhelming, argument *against* women's suffrage.'[20]

One concludes from all this that having begun on apparently strong ground in arguing that the vote was largely symbolic, the Antis were gradually put on the defensive. In fact, during the Edwardian period they began to offer innovations designed to correct any injustice done to female interests by parliament. One suggested appointing a third chamber of parliament, comprising women elected by women, which the other houses might consult; another floated the notion of a cabinet minister for women, supported by an advisory council, as an alternative to the vote.[21] These were symptoms of a losing cause.

On the other hand, for many years the Antis believed that their case was strongly corroborated by the absence of any general demand for the vote on the part of women themselves; some, they claimed, positively opposed enfranchisement, and most remained indifferent. Millicent Fawcett recognized this as one of the more formidable objections in terms of practical politics, however irrelevant it may have been in terms of principle.[22] Mr Osborne Morgan spoke for many MPs when he declared that he 'could not consent to make a revolution for the sake of a handful of fanatics', while Gladstone insisted 'there has never within my knowledge been a case in which the

[18] Dicey, *Letters*, 21–2.   [19] *Manchester Guardian*, 20 Oct. 1910.

[20] A. J. Balfour to Christabel Pankhurst, 23 Oct. 1907, to Annie Kenney, 3 Jan. 1910, Balfour Papers, BL, Add. MS 49793.

[21] Caroline E. Stephen, 'Women and Politics', *The Nineteenth Century*, 61 (1907), 231; S. M. Mitra, 'Voice for Women—Without Votes', *The Nineteenth Century*, 74 (1913), 996–7.

[22] Fawcett, 'Electoral Disabilities of Women', 628.

franchise has been extended to a large body of persons generally indifferent about receiving it'.[23] A succession of women reiterated the point.[24] Even Fred Pethick-Lawrence, who loyally supported the cause, clearly felt the force of the argument. He explained that he had not originally bothered much about votes for women because he saw little evidence that women themselves cared strongly; his own wife's interest, he thought, was 'mainly academic ... I failed to see what the average sheltered woman of the middle classes had to complain about'.[25]

Suffragists attempted to rebut the charge of indifference in four ways. First, they observed since voting was not compulsory, the apathetic need not exercise their rights; it was sufficient that *some* women wanted to. Second, they invoked the classic liberal rationale, expressed by Mill, that if women were uninterested then it merely proved how far their minds and consciences had stagnated; once granted, the vote would stimulate their intellect and broaden their interests.[26] Third, they endeavoured to discredit the Antis by questioning whether they themselves represented opinion beyond that of the upper ten thousand who were too comfortable and secure to have any understanding of the needs of ordinary women. Interestingly, Gladstone, in the context of general opposition to the suffrage, accepted this criticism as valid.[27] Fourth, suffragists argued that although women were 'not prepared to break any railings, material or metaphorical', in Cobbe's words, they cared enough to sign petitions demanding the vote.[28] This, however, was a double-edged weapon in that their opponents claimed that all those who had *not* signed must be against enfranchisement; and MPs often justified their own opposition or even withdrawal of support on the grounds of absence of visible pressure from their constituents.

Female apathy proved a very persistent obstacle. One finds women such as Louise Creighton and Mrs Ward citing the failure of women to take up the opportunities available to them in local government as proof that it would be unwise to burden them with even more public duties.[29] As late as 1909 Balfour, though sympathetic, continued to believe that 'a very large electorate, of which only a small proportion use their privileges, is not a very satisfactory

---

[23] *Hansard, HC Deb.*, 3rd Series, CCXI, 1 May 1872, c. 56; and 4th Series, III, 11 Apr. 1892, c. 257.
[24] Ward, 'Appeal Against Women's Suffrage'; Mrs Theo Chapman, 'Women's Suffrage', *The Nineteenth Century*, 107 (1886), 561–2; Mildred Ransom, *Daily Mail*, 30 Oct. 1906.
[25] F. W. Pethick-Lawrence, *Fate Has Been Kind* (Hutchinson, 1942), 68–9.
[26] *Hansard, HC Deb.*, 3rd Series, CLXXXVII, 20 May 1867, c. 823–4.
[27] *Hansard, HC Deb.*, 3rd Series, CCVI, 3 May 1871, c. 92.
[28] Cobbe, 'Why Women Demand the Vote', 1869.
[29] Louise Creighton, 'The Appeal Against Female Suffrage: A Rejoinder', *The Nineteenth Century*, 209 (1889), 350.

instrument of government'. To which Christabel Pankhurst reposted: 'If only you would say what you would regard as proof that a demand exists!'[30] By this time, however, the argument about what the majority of women wanted was becoming irrelevant simply because a majority of members of parliament had become converts to the cause. This is why one finds Lord Curzon, among others, arguing that as women's suffrage had not been an issue at any general election, the House of Commons had no mandate to pass a bill on the subject.[31] Similar claims had been made, however, in 1866–7, for the artisans' vote had not figured prominently in the election of 1865; in any case, Curzon's use of the notion of the mandate seemed a transparently partisan ploy, associated with the Tory peers whose pretensions had been rudely rejected at two elections in 1910. It was a sign of growing desperation among the Antis that at this stage some of them considered advocating a referendum on female enfranchisement (see Chapter 7).

The Qualities of Women

Inevitably much of the argument focused around the common belief that men and women were characterized by different moral and intellectual qualities with which they had been endowed by God or by Nature in order to perform their separate functions in society. Interestingly, the two sides found a measure of agreement on this point; it was rather the political implications of gender difference which divided them. Though male Antis invariably regarded women's intellect as inferior, they avoided saying so directly. As one member put it:

> It was not a question whether the male or the female intellect were the superior one. He simply said they were different... There were in the world women of a man-like mind—a Mrs Somerville or a Miss Martineau... but he reasoned from the generality and not from marked exceptions. Reason predominated in the man, emotion and sympathy in the woman.[32]

Right up to 1914 this theme remained central to the opposition's case. Gladys Pott, one of the leading Anti-Suffragist organizers, claimed that women focused on detail but were apt to lose sight of broader issues; according to one pamphleteer, 'the difference is fundamental owing to physiological reasons

---

[30] A. J. Balfour to Mrs Templeton, 20 Oct. 1909; Christabel Pankhurst to A. J. Balfour, 28 Oct. 1907, Balfour Papers, BL, Add. MS 49793.
[31] Speech at Glasgow, 1 Nov. 1912, Curzon Papers, BL, F112/38.
[32] Beresford Hope, *Hansard, HC Deb.*, 3rd Series, CCVI, 3 May 1871, c. 100–1.

which no training can obliterate. Women are more easily swayed by sentiment, less open to reason, less logical, keener in intuition, more sensitive than men.'[33] These assumptions were supported by medical opinion about the implications of the female reproductive function which was believed to be the fundamental formative factor affecting a woman's behaviour and intellect. However, Anti-Suffragists usually avoided explicit discussions of this kind because of the indelicacy of the whole subject. Exceptionally William Cremer chose to deploy the argument in the Commons in 1904: 'Women unfortunately suffered from infirmities from which men were altogether exempt ... there were physiological considerations which ... made it very difficult for women frequently to exercise their mental faculties and their judgement as clearly as they did at other periods of their lives.'[34] Cremer's remarks can be interpreted as an indication that by 1904 the Antis had been forced back onto their ultimate line of defence now that other arguments had lost their force; the hostile reaction aroused by Sir Almroth Wright when he used similar arguments in 1912 suggests that they were becoming counter-productive (see Chapter 7).

Perhaps because scientific opinion appeared to be against them, the suffragists on the whole avoided the physiological argument, and simply denied that they claimed intellectual equality between the sexes; the aim, for them, was to develop whatever natural capacity men and women had to start with. Barbara Leigh Smith conceded the critics' case up to a point but tried to minimize it: 'granted that women are ignorant of politics, as are many male ten pound householders'.[35] Liberal suffragists pointed out that though artisans and agricultural labourers had been regarded as intellectually deficient before their enfranchisement, they had subsequently proved themselves quite capable. In contrast the Unionist suffragist, Lord Selborne, reflected his party's thinking: 'we know perfectly well that there are very many thousands of men who are not fit'.[36] This simply invited the counter-argument that it could hardly be wise to add even more ignorant electors; moreover, as Violet Markham put it, men's ignorance could be corrected, whereas women's deficiencies were constitutional![37]

[33] *Anti-Suffrage Review*, Nov. 1911, 228; 'Why Women Should Not Vote', Women's National Anti-Suffrage League, 1909; Chapman, 'Women's Suffrage'.

[34] *Hansard, HC Deb.*, 3rd Series, CXIII, 16 Mar. 1904, c. 1356.

[35] Barbara Leigh Smith, speech, Oct. 1866; Millicent Fawcett, 'Women's Suffrage: A Reply', *The Nineteenth Century*, 107 (1886), 742.

[36] *Hansard, HC Deb.*, 3rd Series, CCLXXIX, 12 June 1884, c. 200; Lord Selborne, *Conservative and Unionist Women's Franchise Review*, Apr. 1911, 104; Frances Power Cobbe ('Why Women Desire the Franchise', 1869) noted that the enfranchisement of uneducated men in 1867 had silenced one argument against women.

[37] *Manchester Guardian*, 20 Oct. 1910.

Suffragists were on stronger ground in attacking the flaws in their opponents' reasoning. Fawcett pointed out that there was no means of proving
whether women were intellectually inferior; and the point seemed irrelevant
for no one ever attempted to establish whether one group of men was less able
than another with a view to withholding the franchise from the inferior. In
any case, no one could reasonably claim that *all* women were inadequate or
inferior to all men. This seems to have forced several Antis to modify their
views about the separate spheres, including Gladstone and Lady Tullibardine (later the Duchess of Atholl) who conceded: 'there are many women in
this country who could intelligently exercise a vote'.[38] From the outset suffragists had flourished lists of outstanding women including Harriet Martineau, Florence Nightingale, Miss Burdett Coutts, Mary Carpenter, Louisa
Twining, Emily Davies, Dorothea Beale, and Josephine Butler, on the
assumption that few would regard them as unworthy of a vote. But as they
were obviously untypical women, Fawcett preferred to emphasize the practical, realistic nature of the work undertaken by female philanthropists and
social reformers rather than their special qualities. From this it was a short
step to making the link between the practical work of women and the kind of
legislation discussed by parliament; were men really more competent than
women in making judgements about licensing, housing, poor law reform, or
old age pensions?[39]

By far the favourite variation on the *ad hominem* argument was the royal
one. The petition of 1866 had reminded politicians that 'women in these
islands have always been held capable of sovereignty'. Judging by the regu-
larity with which suffragists dragged Queen Victoria into their propaganda
they evidently felt that the example she set discredited their opponents' case.
'Our gracious Queen fulfils the very arduous duties of her calling and man-
ages also to be the mother of many children,' wrote Barbara Leigh Smith as
early as 1857. Fawcett frequently pointed out that the Queen's duties 'do not
prevent her from being every inch a woman'.[40] From the suffragists' perspective the value of the Queen lay precisely in the fact that she was not an
unusual woman in terms of intellect, though this was not easy to express tactfully; one anonymous but shrewd writer described her as 'essentially a
commonplace woman'.[41]

[38] Fawcett, 'Electoral Disabilities of Women', 625–6; Lady Tullibardine, speech, 1 Nov. 1912,
Curzon Papers, BL, F112/38.
[39] Fawcett, 'The Women's Suffrage Bill', *Fortnightly Review*, 46 (1889), 561–2; F. H. Barrow, 'The
Political Responsibility of Women', *Westminster Review*, 170 (1908), 252.
[40] Barbara Leigh Smith, 'Women and Work', 1857; Millicent Fawcett, 'Women's Suffrage: A
Reply', *The National Review*, 11 (1888), 52; and 'Electoral Disabilities of Women', 630.
[41] Ignota, 'Women's Suffrage', 372.

The Antis countered with constitutional arguments, pointing out that Queen Victoria was no absolute monarch and did nothing except on the advice of her ministers, which was true, but only up to a point for she undoubtedly exercised influence with the politicians.[42] One wonders whether the Antis saw in her partisanship and excitability some corroboration for their own misgivings about women dabbling in national politics, especially where war and foreign diplomacy were involved. Unfortunately for the suffragists their claims were complicated by the Queen's rooted hostility to female enfranchisement, which eventually became public knowledge in 1908 when Sir Theodore Martin published his volume of reminiscences. However, during the 1890s when pride in Queen Victoria's long reign reached a peak, the balance of this particular argument seems to have favoured the suffragists. So much so that in 1897 Sir Wilfred Lawson and others suggested that it would be appropriate to mark her diamond jubilee by enacting a women's suffrage bill.[43] The parliamentary majority achieved in that year suggests that the cause may well have derived some benefit from the sentiment generated by the national celebrations.

If the protagonists disagreed over women's intellectual qualities, they reached near-unanimity over the proposition that women enjoyed a more highly developed *moral* sense than men. But was their moral contribution so vital that it could not be jeopardized by forcing them into politics? Or, as suffragists claimed, did women have a duty to place their moral assets at the disposal of the nation? 'I regard women as superior to men', commented Violet Markham, 'and therefore I don't like to see them trying to become men's equals.' Mrs Humphry Ward argued that to drag women into political controversy would be to turn them into partisans and thereby undermine the nation's reserves of moral force.[44] Mill, on the other hand, questioned whether those who had responsibility for the moral education of the future voters could themselves be unfit to form opinions, and whether parliament ought not to be prepared to learn from the experience of women whose daily task was to manage small sums of money judiciously. Jacob Bright summed up the female attributes: 'Women are less criminal than men; they are more temperate than men … less vicious in their habits than men; they are more thrifty, more provident; they give more to the family and take less to themselves.' These were precisely the qualities which would raise the standard of British

---

[42] Goldwin Smith, 'Female Suffrage', *Macmillan's Magazine*, 30 (1874), 148; Sir Frederick Banbury, *Hansard, HC Deb.*, 5th Series, 94, 19 June 1917, c. 1645.

[43] *Hansard, HC Deb.*, 4th Series, XLV, 3 Feb. 1897, c. 1214; Ignota, 'Women's Suffrage', 372.

[44] *Manchester Guardian*, 29 Oct. 1910; Ward, 'Appeal Against Women's Suffrage'.

politics.[45] In fact, by the 1890s this had become a central element of the suffragist case, largely displacing earlier arguments about individual rights and about the representation of taxpayers. Fawcett in particular developed a cogent appeal based on the motherhood of women. She went half-way to accepting the separate spheres position by welcoming the fact that most women expected a life of marriage, motherhood, and domesticity, and acknowledging that their different experience of life made women unlike men. However, her point was that the difference, 'instead of being a reason against their enfranchisement, seems to me the strongest possible reason in favour of it; we want the domestic side of things to count for more in politics…than they do at present'.[46] The discharge of her routine domestic duties, so the argument ran, endowed women with relevant skills in terms of financial management, knowledge about health, hygiene, and education, and cultivated in them a fuller sense of injustice and self-sacrifice. By the turn of the century concern about the role and the skills of motherhood had become fashionable among politicians of all kinds, and increasingly the needs of the wife and mother were regarded as vital to the national interest; to this extent women's claims for formal recognition by the state became helpfully merged with questions of national politics. This view gained credibility among Liberals and Socialists through the expansion of elective local government, in which women participated, and the growth of state social reform from the early 1900s; but it also commended itself to Conservatives and imperialists, fearful that Britain's external role could not be maintained without giving greater priority to the social conditions and issues that dominated women's lives.[47] Suffragism, in short, was working with the grain of politics.

The Political Consequences

For the opponents of votes for women the simplest and most effective tactic consisted in exploiting fears of the unknown. They pointed out with some justification that what the suffragists presented as a modest proposal to amend the franchise actually involved a fundamental change with long-term implications which they seemed reluctant to acknowledge. Conceding the vote would settle nothing; for a vote surely implied the right of a woman to

---

[45] *Hansard, HC Deb.*, 3rd Series, CLXXXVII, 20 May 1867, c. 820; speech on 'The Electoral Disabilities of Women' (National Library of Scotland, Women's Suffrage collection, 19945.5/23).

[46] Millicent Fawcett, 'Home and Politics', not dated.

[47] See Anna Davin, 'Imperialism and Motherhood', *History Workshop Journal*, 5 (1978).

become an MP, to hold cabinet posts, to sit on juries, and so forth.[48] To these challenges the feminists offered no convincing answers. They invariably claimed simply that the right to vote and the right to be elected were separate things; and they never advocated the idea of female MPs.[49] This was a little disingenuous because in local government they tried to capitalize on the precedent set by the school board system which had made the voter eligible to stand for election. Fawcett came close to admitting to feminist ambitions when she wrote that it would simply be left to the constituencies to choose their candidates as they already did with men; Lady Galloway frankly met the Antis' challenge when she argued that women's role on the school boards proved that they helped to expedite business, but she was virtually alone in this.[50] Of course, the Antis contradicted themselves by arguing, on the one hand, that women would try to enter parliament and, on the other, that they showed themselves reluctant to take their opportunities in local government. Even considered purely as a franchise measure, the women's vote was a more radical proposal than it seemed; Goldwin Smith graphically described the bill as 'the crowbar by which the next barrier will be speedily forced'. Both Tory and Liberal critics alleged that the first instalment, however small, must inevitably lead to universal adult suffrage and thus to both a working-class and a female majority.[51] To open this pandora's box would expose British society to unending disasters. Some critics felt that something deep within their temperament made women susceptible to arbitrary government and undermined their love of liberty; as a result they posed a danger to free institutions especially in countries such as France where their influence might lead to the restoration of the Bourbons and to religious crusades against Protestantism.[52] Assumptions about female susceptibility to priestly influence loomed large in Liberal suspicions of women's enfranchisement which appeared likely to hand an advantage to the Conservatives.[53] Once again, however, the Antis showed themselves inconsistent in their anxiety to

---

[48] Smith, 'Female Suffrage', 139; W. E. Gladstone to Samuel Smith, 11 Apr. 1892; Mrs Theo Chapman, 'Women's Suffrage Again!', *The Nineteenth Century*, 32 (1897), 171; Dicey, *Letters*, 62; 'Women's Suffrage and After', WNASL, No. 2, 1909.

[49] Becker, 'Female Suffrage', 314–15; Fawcett, 'Electoral Disabilities of Women', 628; and 'Women's Suffrage: A Reply', 57; W. Lyon Blease, *The Emancipation of Women* (Constable, 1910), 216–17.

[50] Countess of Galloway, 'Women and Politics', *The Nineteenth Century*, 107 (1886), 899.

[51] Smith, 'Female Suffrage', 139; *Hansard, HC Deb.*, 3rd Series: Edward Bouverie (Liberal), CCXI, 1 May 1872, c. 26; Earl Percy (Conservative), CCXV, 30 Apr. 1873, c. 1250; Beresford Hope (Conservative), CCXXIII, 7 Apr. 1875, c. 467; Sir Henry James (Liberal), CCCXXIII, 7 Apr. 1875, c. 480.

[52] Smith, 'Female Suffrage', 145.

[53] For example, Osborne Morgan, *Hansard, HC Deb.*, 3rd Series, CCXI, 1 May 1872, c. 55–6.

discredit suffragism; they claimed that the women's vote would strengthen both clericalism and Socialism.[54] Fawcett characteristically pointed out that opposition to women on the grounds that they might vote Conservative was an objection to representative government itself, and even implied that Conservatives ought to be disenfranchised.[55] Yet this cut little ice with the machine politicians for whom party advantage loomed larger than logic or democratic principle. The only effective counter lay in emphasizing women's natural enthusiasm for promoting peace, sobriety, education, and free trade.

However, this in turn implied that women would alter the character of parliamentary business by focusing it more on the social and philanthropic issues which some politicians felt were already promoted by sectional interests at the expense of the nation as a whole. Beresford Hope, a veteran Anti, warned:

> you will find yourselves drifting on a sea of impulsive philanthropy and sentimentalism, where you are now at anchor on the principles of political economy . . . we should have more wars for an idea, or hasty alliances with scheming neighbours, more class cries, permissive legislation, domestic perplexities and sentimental grievances. Our legislation would develop hysterical and spasmodic features, partaking more of the French and American system.[56]

Such a catalogue of predictions could not be damped down except by reference to the actual role of women in local government and to the effects of their enfranchisement in other countries. This explains why, from 1870 onwards, virtually every member who introduced a suffrage bill argued that the municipal franchise had set a precedent for the parliamentary vote. The principle that women were entitled to representation where their interests were involved had already been conceded. Further, since local elections occurred every year, the idea that voting at a parliamentary election every seven years would be a burden for women now looked absurd. Suffragists argued that women had used their local franchise with advantage and demonstrated that the fears about their participation were groundless. The more parliament chose to legislate on matters such as pauperism and education the more anomalous the exclusion of women appeared to be.[57] In effect the steady extension of the female role in local government helped to shift the whole debate further away from unprovable, abstract arguments towards

---

[54]   Samuel Smith, *Hansard, HC Deb.*, 4th Series, III, 27 Apr. 1892, c. 1481.

[55]   Fawcett, 'Electoral Disabilities of Women', 630.

[56]   *Hansard, HC Deb.*, 3rd Series, CCI, 3 May 1887, c. 229.

[57]   *Hansard, HC Deb.*, 3rd Series, CCI, 4 May 1870, c. 195, 206, 221; 4th Series, III, 27 Apr. 1892, c. 1454.

largely empirical considerations. Several MPs drew upon the municipal experience to justify their support for or even conversion to women's enfranchisement.[58] Even Gladstone admitted that the municipal franchise had created 'a presumptive case for advocating some change in the law', and some members now saw the parliamentary vote as the logical next step (see also Chapter 3).[59]

This naturally put the Anti-Suffragists onto the defensive. Mrs Humphry Ward instinctively assumed that the burden of local politics would consume all a woman's energies, and right up to 1914 she continued to argue that either lack of energy or lack of ambition inhibited women from capitalizing on their existing opportunities. More thoughtfully, Samuel Smith pointed out that the municipal franchise had been granted almost accidentally, and certainly not with the intention of helping women to win the parliamentary vote; moreover, local authorities were essentially administrative rather than law-making bodies, so that a clear distinction of type could be made regardless of the fact that they were involved with some of the same topics as parliament.[60] Above all, the Antis tried to distinguish between the essentially domestic functions of local authorities and the external and imperial responsibilities of parliament which, they claimed, remained beyond women's proper sphere and understanding. By granting the municipal vote, so the argument ran, parliament had once again satisfied women's legitimate demands; the only further extension might be some machinery to enable local authorities to express their views on legislation affecting, say, health or factory conditions, for the benefit of the Home Office or the Local Government Board.[61]

Despite this counter-attack, it is clear the Antis were forced to give ground as a result of local government developments, and the effect was compounded by female participation in party political organizations and in parliamentary elections especially from the 1880s onwards. Suffragists enjoyed mocking politicians for their inconsistencies over this form of activity, suggesting, for example, that if politics was a damaging distraction from a woman's role it might be necessary to suppress the Primrose League in the national interest! 'I have never observed that the opponents of woman suffrage declined to allow women to canvass at elections', remarked

---

[58] Lord John Manners, *Hansard, HC Deb.,* 3rd Series, CCVI, 2 May 1871, c. 95; Joseph Henley, *Hansard, HC Deb.,* 3rd Series, CCXV, 30 Apr. 1873, c. 1254.

[59] *Hansard, HC Deb.,* 3rd Series, CCXI, 3 May 1871, c. 92.

[60] *Hansard, HC Deb.,* 4th Series, III, 27 Apr. 1892, c. 1472.

[61] Chapman, 'Women's Suffrage', 564; Heber Hart, 'Is Woman Suffrage Inevitable?', WNASL, No. 5.

Lord Robert Cecil in 1908.[62] More subtly, Millicent Fawcett invited the politicians to consider whether, since many women now enjoyed an active political role, it would not be wise to give some scope to the more typical domestic woman who would participate *only* by exercising a vote and not by electioneering.[63] In this way she forced the Antis towards accepting the logic of their own belief in the importance of the ordinary woman.

Marriage and Femininity

Faced with a dangerous accumulation of empirically-based arguments which largely favoured their opponents, the Antis found themselves going back to basics. From the perspective of the late twentieth century some of their language appears apocalyptic, but it reflected contemporary concern about changes in British society during the 1880s and 1890s. As perceived threats to the British Empire grew, so the alarmist predictions about the debilitating effects of sex equality and the confusion of roles consequent upon it, gained credibility. Women's suffrage, declared one MP, 'contained the germ of a great social revolution'; as Gladstone put it, 'the stake is enormous'; Goldwin Smith wrote: 'The very foundations of Society are touched when Parliament tampers with the relations of the sexes.' As late as 1907 Marie Corelli argued: 'with women alone rests the Home, which is the foundation of Empire; when they desert this, their God-appointed centre, the core of the national being, then things are tottering to a fall'.[64] In the face of such charges suffragists desperately played down any revolutionary ambitions: 'we admire and wish to cherish what is womanly in women' in Fawcett's words.[65] But would participation in the unruly world of politics not detract from the femininity of the average woman? At the start of the campaign this was widely believed to be only too likely in view of the disorder, drunkenness, and violence which frequently attended parliamentary elections; personal voting by ladies was, in Gladstone's words, 'an objection of great force'. Speaking in 1866 even Barbara Leigh Smith accepted that women should avoid a disorderly poll, and Lydia Becker conceded that voting would be difficult in some places. Consequently Becker and Gladstone envisaged

[62] Lyon Blease, *Emancipation*, 210; Lord Robert Cecil, Address, CUWFA, 1908.

[63] Millicent Fawcett, 'Women's Suffrage: A Reply', *Fortnightly Review*, 46 (1889), 124.

[64] Edward Bouverie, *Hansard, HC Deb.*, 3rd Series, CCXV, 30 Apr. 1873, c. 1218; W. E. Gladstone to Samuel Smith, 11 Apr. 1892; Smith, 'Female Suffrage', 139; Marie Corelli, 'Woman or Suffragette', 1907.

[65] Fawcett, 'Women's Suffrage: A Reply', 52.

allowing women to cast their votes without actually attending polling stations, an idea which had to wait for the crisis of the First World War before being implemented. Meanwhile Becker suggested that female involvement would exert 'the same humanising and softening influence over the rougher elements as is confessedly the case in social life', while Fawcett urged that whenever women spoke at public meetings they had a calming effect and encouraged men to behave better. Later, suffragists drew upon evidence from the United States to suggest that a female electorate really did have a morally improving impact on the men.[66]

However, the proximate solution to the problem of electoral disorder lay in the secret ballot as Gladstone freely admitted in 1871. After the enactment of this reform in 1872 the suffragists lost no time in claiming that the objection to female participation had been removed: 'now the voting is as solemn as a funeral and as quiet as a Quaker's meeting', declared William Forsyth, with, one feels, a little exaggeration.[67] The ballot by no means put an end to electoral bribery, and in view of the undoubted pressures to which small borough electors were habitually subject, politicians continued to wax eloquent about the need to save 'helpless female lodgers, seamstresses and such' from energetic canvassing techniques. Suffragists simply covered all this in ridicule; to talk about diminishing the purity and delicacy of women at elections was to overlook the far greater and more exacting daily pressures withstood by women who struggled to earn a living. Fawcett shrewdly questioned whether femininity, if ordained by Nature, could really be as fragile and vulnerable as the Antis claimed. Similar fears had, after all, been expressed about the damaging effects upon women of exposure to higher education: 'It was thought that if a woman knew Greek she would not love her children, and that if she learned mathematics she would forsake her infant for a quadratic equation.'[68]

But the Antis persisted in demanding to know whether women had appreciated the full consequences of equality with men; would they wish to sacrifice the courtesy and indulgence with which they were invariably treated? Fawcett briskly dismissed all this as no more than a matter of minor social courtesies which could scarcely be weighed against the value of full citizenship; interestingly the aristocratic Lady Selborne took an equally disparaging

[66] *Hansard, HC Deb.*, 3rd Series, CCXI, 3 May 1871, c. 90–1; Barbara Leigh Smith, speech, Oct. 1866; Becker, 'Female Suffrage', 312; Fawcett, 'Women's Suffrage: A Reply', 57; J. O. P. Bland, 'Woman Suffrage in the United States', *The Nineteenth Century*, 74 (1913), 1337–9.

[67] *Hansard, HC Deb.*, 3rd Series, CCXV, 30 Apr. 1873, c. 1196, CCXXIII, 7 Apr. 1875, c. 425; Fawcett, 'Electoral Disabilities of Women', 630.

[68] William Woodall, *Hansard, HC Deb.*, 4th Series, III, 27 Apr. 1892, c. 1491; Millicent Fawcett, 'Home and Politics', not dated.

view, suggesting that male chivalry was worth little to women especially when compared with 'the solid advantage which the vote would give'.[69] On balance the suffragists probably had the better of this argument; the prominence of ladylike women in the suffragist campaign and their participation in public life at home and abroad made their opponents' fears look unrealistic. To some extent suffragette militancy after 1905 revived these earlier misgivings about the loss of femininity, but by then it was too late to have a decisive impact.

On the other hand, the suffragists could not easily refute the claim that in the long run political equality might have the effect of raising women's aspirations and thereby undermining their commitment to the ideal of marriage and domesticity. Indeed, their emphasis on votes for single women who had no family obligations and had the opportunity to make a contribution to public life played to this weakness.[70] The vote almost appeared as a reward for remaining unmarried, something which politicians had not the slightest inclination to encourage. One MP declared that it was laughable to seek the opinions of 'that portion of the other sex which for some cause had failed to be womanly (laughter)'. According to Mrs Ward the passage of an 'equal terms' bill meant that 'large numbers of women leading immoral lives will be enfranchised, while married women, who, as a rule, have passed through more of the practical experiences of life than the unmarried, will be excluded'. A. V. Dicey simply declared that wives were 'best qualified to exercise the franchise without disadvantage to the nation'.[71] As usual the Antis tried to have it both ways; they objected to the exclusion of married women as being the more deserving section, but also to their inclusion on the grounds that this would introduce political dissension into the relations between husband and wife, so that 'the domestic peace of many households in the country would be destroyed'.[72]

Although the Antis' concentration on the implications of enfranchisement for the institution of marriage was tactical, they undoubtedly spoke to the concerns of late Victorian Britain. During the 1880s and 1890s a prolonged debate took place on the question: 'Is marriage a failure?'. The decrease in the rate of marriage among women in their twenties was easily ascribed to the progress already made towards female emancipation, and it seemed

---

[69] Fawcett, 'Electoral Disabilities of Women', 630; Lady Selborne, *Conservative and Unionist Women's Franchise Review*, Apr.–June 1912, 193.

[70] Barbara Leigh Smith, speech, Oct. 1866; Fawcett, 'Electoral Disabilities of Women', 627, and 'Women's Suffrage', 747.

[71] E. A. Leatham, *Hansard, HC Deb.*, 3rd Series, CCXXIII, 1 Nov. 1875, c. 436; Ward, 'Appeal Against Women's Suffrage'; Dicey, *Letters*, 58.

[72] Henry Labouchere, *Hansard, HC Deb.*, 4th Series, CXXXI, 16 Mar. 1904, c. 1342.

plausible that political emancipation might accelerate the trend.[73] Even worse, the census showed that from the late 1870s onwards the British birth rate had begun to fall. In an era increasingly dominated by the mass armies of continental Europe and the threats of foreign invasion, politicians inevitably speculated about the implications for national strength of a population that was diminishing relative to that of our major competitors. As late as 1916 Earl Grey argued for strengthening the link between family life and citizenship by bestowing an additional vote for each man and woman who had produced four children, on the grounds that such people had 'had an additional experience of life, and their vote is therefore of more value. Further, they have rendered a service to the state without which the state could not continue to exist.'[74]

That this created some disarray amongst the suffragists is evident from the variety of their responses. Some, such as William Forsyth, strongly opposed enfranchising married women, but others, like Leonard Courtney, MP, supported the idea but admitted it might create political disputes within marriage. On the other hand, it seemed unreasonable to give a vote to a single woman only to take it away from her when she married.[75] Lydia Becker, J. S. Mill, and Barbara Leigh Smith, while not pressing for votes for wives, tackled the issue obliquely by challenging the suggestion that voting would constitute a major distraction from women's existing functions; women, they said, would combine voting with their normal occupations just as men did.[76] Few protagonists tackled the issue directly. W. Lyon Blease, for example, frankly accepted that as the feminist movement developed it would gradually alter the institution of marriage, but not necessarily weaken it; he contended that it would become more of a partnership as women felt increasingly reluctant to sacrifice their independence.[77] This echoed some of Mill's remarks in the 1867 debate when he claimed 'there has taken place around us a silent domestic revolution; women and men are, for the first time in history, really each other's companions'. In this he was surely anticipating developments, influenced perhaps by his own domestic relationship, and one doubts that his view on this point carried much conviction at the time.

---

[73] Adele Crepaz, *The Emancipation of Women* (Swan Sonnenschein, 1893), 51; Smith, 'Female Suffrage', 142.

[74] 'A Memorandum on Franchise Reform', Earl Grey Papers, Durham CRO, 236/3, quoted in Martin Pugh, *Electoral Reform in War and Peace, 1906–1918* (Routledge, 1978), 44.

[75] *Hansard, HC Deb.*, 3rd Series, CCXL, 19 June 1878, c. 1870; and CLXXXIX, 12 June 1884, c. 124, 130.

[76] Becker, 'Female Suffrage', 313; J. S. Mill, *Hansard, HC Deb.*, 3rd Series, CLXXXVI, 20 May 1867; Barbara Leigh Smith, speech, Oct. 1866.

[77] Lyon Blease, *Emancipation*, 206.

Millicent Fawcett, almost alone, dealt briskly and confidently with the argument over marriage.[78] As she observed, it was not the vote itself but political partisanship that caused dissension; yet women could scarcely be prevented from holding political opinions, let alone religious beliefs which were far more divisive than politics. In any case, if marriage was in difficulties, she argued, one would hardly restore the stability of the institution by banning women from politics. Not everyone was fitted for marriage, and to coerce reluctant women into becoming wives would be in no one's interest. Finally, Fawcett challenged the Antis to say frankly whether they wanted English husbands to be despots in their own homes and to exclude wives from all political knowledge and opinions—a state of affairs not so far from that actually prevailing in the households of senior figures such as Joseph Chamberlain and W. E. Gladstone. Up to a point her counter-attack was effective, but largely as a debating exercise; in view of the widespread concern about marriage, the birth rate, and national security the suffragists would probably have been better advised to have challenged their opponents to back up their fine words about married women by enfranchising them.

Race, Progress, and Empire

The shortage of contemporary evidence about female participation in politics, at least until the 1890s, encouraged both sides in the debate to ransack history for support and inspiration. On the one hand, the Antis flourished a gruesome catalogue of disasters apparently attributable to women's influence, beginning with the decline of the Roman Empire! They suggested that the Victorian suffragists were attempting to ape the role of men just as their predecessors had done in imperial Rome when, lacking other excitements, they had tried to become gladiators. However, female responsibility for the fate of Rome was vigorously disputed on the grounds that it was female license, not liberty, which had produced the moral decline; by contrast the modern women's movement dedicated itself to morality and motherhood.[79] Another favourite disaster was the French Revolution during which, it was alleged, women's excitability and lack of self-control had led to the worst excesses of the Reign of Terror. Professor Goldwin Smith unearthed a phalanx of female rulers including Margaret of Anjou, Henrietta Maria,

---

[78] Fawcett, 'Electoral Disabilities of Women', 623–4, and 'The Future of Englishwomen', *The Nineteenth Century*, 4 (1878), 351–2; J. E. Cairnes, 'Woman Suffrage: A Reply', *Macmillan's Magazine*, 30 (1874), 385–6.
[79] Smith, 'Female Suffrage', 143; Lyon Blease, *Emancipation*, 206–7.

Catherine II of Russia, Maria Theresa, and Madam de Pompadour, who, through their aggressive temperament, had provoked international war and civil strife. Even Queen Elizabeth I's reputation for patriotic statesmanship, which had begun to wither under the scholarship of J. A. Froude, was traduced to undermine the women's claim; for according to Goldwin Smith, Elizabeth had been exposed as a victim of the usual female flaws, in particular her 'partiality for handsome scoundrels like Leicester'.[80]

However, as in the best academic disputes, the two sides carefully selected their evidence to suit their prejudices. Suffragists largely followed the practice of nineteenth-century Radicals in looking back to the rough-and-ready democracy of Anglo-Saxon England in which women had participated in assemblies under the Saxon kings and sat in council with the Saxon Witas; this golden age had been disrupted by the Norman Conquest which swept away women's rights. This offered a satisfying way of associating the Antis with alien influences and presenting female emancipation as part of the true English tradition.[81]

Historical perspectives loomed large not simply because the past offered a convenient source of supporting material, but also because, as members of the mid-Victorian generation, the participants could not help being strongly influenced by notions of progress; indeed, by the 1880s both sides were stimulated by the fashionable concern about the capacity of the British race to maintain its hitherto pre-eminent position in the civilization of the world. Consequently they found common ground in the belief that the position occupied by women constituted a test of any society's culture. They differed in that the Antis believed that the trend towards the assimilation of the sexes would lead to racial decadence, as already manifested in the falling birth rate, whereas the suffragists argued that the greater emancipation of women accelerated the progress of the nation.[82] Indeed, from the start assumptions about racial superiority seem to have been a central element in suffragism. Frances Power Cobbe, for example, drew comparisons between English women and their Italian counterparts who suffered, she felt, from a lack of education, the absence of constructive charitable work, and from the influence of the Catholic Church in suppressing political debate.[83] Throughout

---

[80] Smith, 'Female Suffrage', 147–9; and 'Conservatism and Female Suffrage', *The National Review*, 10 (1888), 744.

[81] Smith, 'Female Suffrage', 143, and 'Conservatism and Female Suffrage', 744.

[82] Lydia Becker, 'The Rights and Wrongs of Women in Local Government', 24 Jan. 1879; Mrs Wolstenholme Elmy, 'Justice between the Sexes', *Westminster Review*, 169 (1908), 36–8; Gladys Jones, 'Suffragists Again', *Westminster Review*, 169 (1908), 292.

[83] Crepaz, *Emancipation*, 6; Frances Power Cobbe, 'Women in Italy', *Macmillan's Magazine*, 6 (1862), 363.

the period up to 1914 the suffragists effectively capitalized on conventional racial-religious prejudices. They implied that adherence to the separate spheres was tantamount to keeping women as life-long prisoners: 'that is the Oriental theory', declared Lord Robert Cecil, 'to my mind such a theory is grotesque in England'.[84] Suffragists repeatedly urged that Islamic societies were failing to progress precisely because of their reluctance to free their women from seclusion, ignorance, and subjection. Was Turkey a really masculine nation, Fawcett demanded to know? As for Egypt, even Lord Cromer, one of the leading Edwardian Antis, had admitted that until its women had been educated the country could never benefit from European civilization.[85] The conclusion appeared inescapable that continued female emancipation offered not a recipe for decadence but the best means of maintaining the fitness and competitiveness of the British race.

Conversely their opponents believed it to be almost self-evident that women would constitute a liability if they participated in male affairs such as wars and international diplomacy: 'imagine the foreign policy of England determined by women', suggested Goldwin Smith, 'while that of other countries is determined by men; and this in the age of Bismarck'.[86] Right up to the Edwardian period female Antis such as Mrs Ward and Gladys Pott continued to emphasize the dangers of involving women in imperial and foreign issues, arguing that the risks were even greater than in the 1860s in view of the increase in the size and complexity of the Empire.[87] In particular they argued that masculine rule was almost a condition of Britain's retention of India, for she would otherwise forfeit the respect of the native population. Lord Curzon, among other imperial statesmen, threw his authority as a former viceroy behind this view.[88]

It would, however, be a mistake to assume that the Antis enjoyed all the advantages even in the debate over empire. Other Indian experts observed that there was actually no evidence that British authority would be weakened by female suffrage; Indians had been accustomed to female rulers among their own princely families, and had reacted favourably to Queen Victoria as

---

[84] Barbara Leigh Smith, 'Women and Work', 1857; Lord Robert Cecil, Address, CUWFA, 1908, 10.

[85] Millicent Fawcett, 'The Women's Suffrage Bill', *Fortnightly Review*, 46 (1889), 557; Barrow, 'Political Responsibility of Women', 248.

[86] Smith, 'Female Suffrage', 140.

[87] See report of speech by Pott, *Anti-Suffrage Review*, Oct. 1911, 212–13; Mrs Humphry Ward, speech, 1908, WNASL, No. 3; John Sutherland, *Mrs Humphry Ward* (Oxford: Oxford University Press, 1990), 302.

[88] Heber Hart, *Woman Suffrage: A National Danger* (P. S. King, 1912), 36; Lord Curzon, speech, 1 Nov. 1912, Curzon Papers, BL, F112/38.

Empress since 1876. In any case, since Britain governed India autocratically, alterations in her domestic political system were of fairly marginal significance.[89] More typically, the suffragists attempted to dismiss imperial arguments as irrelevant, for by the 1890s the business of parliament largely revolved around matters that fell unambiguously within women's sphere.[90] By the turn of the century they felt increasingly confident about challenging the Antis' imperial arguments. This was to some extent a reflection of the evidence accumulating from Australia and New Zealand which not only suggested that enfranchisement held few risks, but that it even promoted the unity of the Empire. This claim was vigorously propagated by visitors from New Zealand and by the Conservative and Unionist Women's Franchise Association which emphasized the patriotism of colonial women as manifested in their support for military training and for sending troops to help Britain during the South African War.[91] To this end they distributed lantern slides on such themes as 'Women's Work in the Empire' and 'Lands Where Women Have the Vote'. Suffragists also claimed that during the war with the Boers British women had shown themselves no less patriotic and imperially-minded than men.[92] The Antis were forced to concede that there had been no ill-effects in Australia, but contended that this offered no guide to the impact of the vote on European women. These exchanges put the external aspect of the suffrage debate into perspective. Though it proved to be a persistent and prominent element in the Anti-Suffragist case, this was not so much because it went unchallenged as because, by the Edwardian period, other lines of argument once deployed by them had lost force or credibility.

Physical Force

For the Antis the imperial arguments were closely connected with the belief in the physical inferiority of women which they regarded as another irrefutable aspect of their case. Physical force actually comprised several distinct arguments. Basically the Antis believed that the modern state depended for its existence on naval and military power, diplomacy and finance to which women could make no significant contribution. As early as

---

[89] Lyon Blease, *Emancipation*, 221–2.
[90] Leonard Courtney, *Hansard, HC Deb.*, 4th Series, III, 27 Feb. 1892, c. 1575.
[91] *Hansard, HC Deb.*, 4th Series, XLV, 3 Feb. 1896, c. 1176; CXXXI, 16 Mar. 1904, c. 1334, 1359; Anna Stout, 'Under the Flag', *Conservative and Unionist Women's Franchise Review*, Feb. 1910, 16; 'The Imperial Aspect of Women's Suffrage', CUWFR, 16; Apr. 1911, 106.
[92] Barrow, 'Political Responsibility of Women', 249–50.

1889 Mrs Humphry Ward had pronounced: 'the emancipating process has now reached the limits fixed by the physical constitution of women'.[93] Suffragists offered no challenge to the idea that women lacked the physical strength of men because it complemented their emphasis on the *moral* superiority of women. But they attacked the implications drawn from this. 'Any man in the country', argued Goldwin Smith, 'can in the last resort, be called upon to defend the country, if necessary with his life. That fact gives him a claim of some sort to have a voice in the conduct of its affairs which women do not possess.'[94] However, his assumption proved, on examination, more dubious than originally supposed. For in contrast to the continental system of compulsory military training, the British took great pride in their traditional reliance on voluntary recruitment into the armed forces; indeed, the link between gender and citizenship was particularly weak in that most soldiers had no vote, whereas most male voters knew that they would never be called upon to fight for their country.[95] Moreover, as the suffragists were quick to point out, the state demanded services and qualities other than the purely physical which women could and did supply. 'What is the Voter's part in War?' ran suffragist propaganda, 'He is called upon to PAY THE BILL. Are Women physically incapable of this? Apparently NOT.' Even the Tory Leader, A. J. Balfour, endorsed this view, somewhat to the discomfort and irritation of the Antis.[96]

However, they employed a more subtle variation on the physical force theme by arguing that a female electorate would render the parliamentary system unstable by undermining respect for the law. The rationale behind this lay in the belief that the law rested ultimately upon force, which was necessarily a male monopoly; consequently men might refuse to obey laws enacted on the basis of a female majority of voters. As early as 1874 Goldwin Smith floated this thesis in the context of legislation enacted by or for the negro majorities in the Southern states of America which could be sustained only by the force commanded by the North.[97] Though little discussed, this idea burst into life again in the Edwardian period when A. V. Dicey argued that the sovereignty of parliament would be put in danger by legislation passed in the face of male opposition. 'In such a case', he wrote, 'the ominous

[93] Mrs Humphry Ward, speech, WNASL, No. 3, 1908.
[94] 'Why Women Should Not Vote', WNASL, No. 12, not dated.
[95] Jacob Bright, speech at Edinburgh, 17 Jan. 1870 (National Library of Scotland, Women's Suffrage Collection, 1945.5/23).
[96] 'Anti-Suffrage Arguments', NUWSS pamphlet, Nov. 1912; *Hansard, HC Deb.*, 4th Series, III, 27 Apr. 1892, c. 1510; Cairnes, 'Woman Suffrage: A Reply', 382–3; Fawcett, 'Women's Suffrage: A Reply', 49–51.
[97] Hart, *Woman Suffrage*, 19–24; Smith, 'Female Suffrage', 145–6.

result would ensue that...the body possessed of predominant strength would be strongly opposed to the law.'[98] This appears at first sight somewhat far-fetched, and both Smith and Dicey admitted that since the interests of men and women largely coincided, it would be rare for such a clash to arise. The most likely areas of disagreement were thought to be suppression of the liquor trade, regulation of sexual vice, and entry into war. However, after the turn of the century the scenario sketched by Dicey took on more substance when some Nonconformists adopted passive resistance to the 1902 Education Act. But above all it was the return of Irish Home Rule to the top of the agenda after 1911 that exposed the fragility of parliamentary authority in the face of determined physical opposition.

Nonetheless, the Anti-Suffragist arguments here remained highly speculative, and there was still no evidence that opinion amongst women on questions like Home Rule did in fact differ from that among men. In the last resort, as Lyon Blease observed, people obeyed the law because they had participated in making it, and the moral force of public opinion stood behind the police in the exercise of force when it proved necessary.[99] It may be significant that this particular variation on the physical force argument was used by academics and constitutional authorities rather than by practising politicians, for it remained difficult to take seriously except perhaps in the context of Ireland. In any case, by expressing the point in the form of a specific example they inevitably muddied the constitutional principle by introducing a party political element. Antis who favoured the physical force argument tended to be those who adopted a highly pessimistic view of British society largely because they were on the losing side in the various controversies of the Edwardian period; they concluded rather too easily that society had reached a state of collapse because their own opinions had been rejected in several successive general elections. In the last resort the Antis hesitated to make too much use of the Irish example because they could not risk alienating their Liberal allies within the government.

Conclusions

The first point to be made about the protracted debate over women's enfranchisement is that it was far from merely a static exchange. Both men and women moved in each direction. It is often overlooked, for example, that several of the Liberal academic-politicians such as Goldwin Smith, James Bryce,

---

[98] Dicey, *Letters*, 68–9.   [99] Lyon Blease, *Emancipation*, 225–6, 228–9.

Thorold Rodgers, and A. V. Dicey, soon deserted the suffragist cause either because they were influenced by women's own opposition to the vote or because they came to regard it as detrimental to Liberal electoral interests. This meant abandoning the intellectual rationale originally derived from Mill. Goldwin Smith attempted to discredit Mill by suggesting that his judgement had deserted him on this question due to 'his hallucinations . . . as to the unparalleled genius of his wife'![100] Converts in the opposite direction usually cited women's success in local government (Joseph Henley, MP), their role in party political organizations (John Morley), and the disappearance of the distinction between parliamentary politics and local government (Beatrice Webb). Essentially the suffragists showed more flexibility in adapting their case; they soon dispensed with abstract arguments about individual rights, which offered little prospect of advance, in order to exploit the changes in women's role in society and the shift in the national political agenda towards the domestic questions in which women were acknowledged to have an interest and a contribution to make. In particular the suffragist case gained ground through the introduction of the secret ballot, the steady extension of elective local government, the acceptance of female work at elections, and the example offered by several British colonies which granted the vote during the 1890s (see Chapter 4). Consequently, by the turn of the century substantial parts of the Anti-Suffragist case had become irrelevant or lost force. Receiving a deputation of suffragists in 1906 the new prime minister, Sir Henry Campbell-Bannerman, frankly accepted that the case for the vote had been established.[101] Even some Antis conceded this up to a point: 'theoretically the advocates of the cause have proved their case . . . so far as logic and justice are concerned there is nothing to be said against [the women's vote] . . . It is only when we come to practical results . . . [that] the objections are advanced.'[102] In 1911 when Gladys Pott was challenged to say whether the Antis would advise women to use their votes if they were given them, she replied that it would be a woman's duty to vote in spite of her inadequacies, which seemed to imply that it would be less than a disaster.[103] In effect the opponents of enfranchisement had been forced back onto a fairly narrow range of traditional arguments by this time; they continued to stress the defects of the female intellect and temperament, the danger of infringing the separate spheres, and the inappropriateness of their involvement in foreign policy, defence, and empire. As late as June 1917, when parliament was putting the women's amendment into the Representation of the People Bill,

[100] Smith, 'Female Suffrage', 140, and 'Conservatism and Female Suffrage', 744–5.
[101] Deputation, 19 May 1906, 12.   [102] Mildred Ransom, *Daily Mail*, 30 Oct. 1906.
[103] *Anti-Suffrage Review*, Oct. 1911, 212–13.

Sir Frederick Banbury, firmly taking his stand in the last ditch, insisted that women were 'likely to be affected by gusts and waves of sentiment' just as Anti-Suffragists had done in the 1870s.[104]

After 1900 no fresh arguments were introduced into the debate. At the most, suffragette militancy helped revive earlier claims about the female temperament, which encouraged the Antis; also the popular preoccupation with invasion scares, the German naval building programme, and the mass continental armies added a certain topicality to the physical force argument. But by this time, as we shall see, members of parliament had substantially been converted to the cause. The *principle* of women's enfranchisement had largely been won by the turn of the century; it remained to resolve the complicated question of the precise terms on which women were to receive the vote.

[104] *Hansard, HC Deb.*, 5th Series, 94, 19 June 1917, c. 1645.

Part II

Winning the Advantage

3

Decline or Revival?
Women's Suffrage in the 1890s

F OR the man or woman in the street the campaign for women's enfranchisement is still to be equated with the Pankhurst family and the
Edwardian suffragette escapades. Although excavations in the archives by
historians have unearthed a much longer history for organized feminism, the
assumption remains widespread, even amongst scholars, that until the emergence of the suffragettes little significant progress had been made towards
winning the vote.[1] In the words of an Edwardian militant, Teresa Billington-
Greig, the Victorian suffragists 'assumed that argument, right and reason
would finally triumph'; Sylvia Pankhurst described them disparagingly as 'so
staid, so willing to wait, so incorrigibly leisurely'.[2]

Many suffragists undoubtedly left themselves wide open to criticism.
Take Millicent Fawcett's observations in 1886:

women's suffrage will not come ... as an isolated phenomenon, it will come as a necessary corollary of the other changes which have been gradually and steadily modifying, this century, the social history of our country. It will be a political change, not
of a very great or extensive character in itself, based upon social, educational and
economic changes which have already taken place.[3]

Today what strikes the historian is how perceptive Fawcett was when she
wrote this. But for contemporary campaigners, especially the youthful ones,

[1] Lesley P. Hume, *The National Union of Women's Suffrage Societies, 1897–1914* (New York: Garland Publishing, 1982), 3, suggests that after 1884 the suffragists lost enthusiasm and the cause
'ceased to attract attention or adherents'; Andrew Rosen, *Rise Up Women!* (Routledge, 1978), 12, says
that the period between 1884 and 1897 'marked the nadir of the women's suffrage movement'.

[2] T. Billington-Greig, 'The Militant Policy of the Women's Suffragists', 12 Nov. 1906, Fawcett
Library, Billington-Greig Papers Box 404, file 3; E. Sylvia Pankhurst, *The Suffragette Movement*
(Virago, 1977 edition), 92, 484.

[3] Millicent Fawcett, 'Women's Suffrage: A Reply', *The Nineteenth Century*, 107 (1886), 746.

her approach appeared excessively measured and even complacent, suggesting a culpable lack of urgency and passion for the cause. For the Edwardian
suffragettes, the Victorian suffragists had been too patient in the face of prevarication and betrayal by politicians; consequently constitutional methods
had been 'outgrown by circumstances. They are condemned by results. Neither enthusiasm nor growth resulted from them.'[4]

Yet however superficially persuasive, this view is essentially *propagandist*; it
gave the Pankhursts their justification for the adoption of militancy after
1905 and helped them to recruit members for the Women's Social and Political Union. Of course, effective propaganda invariably contains elements of
truth; but the historian is obliged to examine such claims sceptically. This
does not imply that they should award credit for women's enfranchisement to
either militants or to non-militants; to some extent the two campaigns surely
complemented each other's efforts. But the received view is so unbalanced
that a reassessment of the early campaigns now seems necessary. This
involves some reconsideration of the broad chronology of suffragism. It has
been tempting to distinguish four phases of the movement: the first from the
launch in the 1860s to the early 1880s, the second from the mid-1880s to the
early 1900s when it supposedly stagnated or even declined, the third, a
revival associated with the suffragettes from 1905 to 1914, and finally the
wartime period when both campaigns were largely abandoned before the
women's vote had been won.[5]

The Loss of Momentum

But did suffragism fall into a decline during the last fifteen years of the century as is so often claimed? The negative view seems easier to appreciate
simply because divisions and failures tend to leave copious documentation in
their wake, whereas the progress of a cause often manifests itself in more subtle
and indirect ways. At first sight the evidence for decline and demoralization within late Victorian suffragism seems impressive. After two decades of
continuous activity the issue had inevitably lost its novelty value; when start-
ing from scratch the suffragists had found it comparatively easy to win fresh
recruits each year and create a sense of momentum. But by the 1880s politicians had grown familiar with the arguments, and the battle lines had

---

[4] Billington-Greig, 'The Militant Policy', BGP Box 404, file 3.
[5] Martin Pugh, *Women and the Women's Movement in Britain 1914–1959* (Macmillan, 1992),
7–9, 36.

become more firmly fixed. In the absence of fresh tactics and ideas the cause began to suffer from dwindling funds and personnel, and from a lower parliamentary profile.

However, this thesis is valid only in part. It is, for example, true that suffragist petitions which had run at 300,000–400,000 signatures in the mid-1870s, fell to 178,000 by 1878, and to even lower levels by the early 1880s. But these figures were essentially symptomatic of the effort put in; unless a suffrage bill was before parliament it was not deemed to be worth the trouble. The pattern was easily reversed in 1892 when 248,000 signatures were obtained in support of a bill of which the suffragists entertained high hopes.

Another indicator may be found in the financial resources of the movement. Brian Harrison has examined the funds of several feminist organizations from the late 1860s onwards and found that after the initial spurt they stabilized during the 1870s, then diminished sharply after setbacks in parliament in 1884–5, and did not revive until around 1900.[6] However, the significance of these fluctuations is not always clear. Some pressure groups such as the Ladies National Association naturally became less active once it had achieved its object by 1886. Many suffragists, as we shall see, diverted their efforts into local government or into the new party political organizations for women during the 1880s, which reflected not a loss of momentum for the cause but a variation of tactics. It is also difficult to know how great the funds of the non-militants actually were because their resources remained largely dispersed in the regions.

None of these qualifications can explain away the evidence for internal division amongst the suffragist leadership during the 1880s which was symptomatic of uncertainty about tactics. The longer they were frustrated by the leading politicians the more difficult it became to maintain an even-handed approach towards the parties. Although some suffragists saw the development of party organizations for women as a new opportunity, this also created friction leading to a formal split in December 1888. The majority in the National Society for Women's Suffrage (NSWS) took the view that the women's party organizations should be allowed to affiliate; it eventually reformed itself as the Central National Society for Women's Suffrage. The complication lay in the fact that while Women's Liberal Federation Associations were free to join and were often keen to do so, the habitations of the Conservatives' Primrose League were not; moreover, since the women Liberals greatly outnumbered the suffragist societies, they could easily have

[6] Brian Harrison, 'Women's Suffrage at Westminster, 1866–1928', in M. Bentley and J. Stevenson (eds.), *High and Low Politics in Modern Britain* (Oxford: Clarendon Press, 1983), 87–8.

swamped the movement and effectively destroyed its claim to non-party status. Such a prospect seemed especially unwelcome to pro-Conservative suffragists like Cobbe and to those such as Fawcett and Becker who had become increasingly anti-Liberal as a result of Gladstone's obstructionism. In the event some 68 Women's Liberal Associations affiliated to the majority group while Becker and the minority withdrew to form the Central Committee of the NSWS. The movement thus remained formally divided for eight years. However, the consequences seem much less significant at the grass roots than at the centre. Nowhere in the provinces were two rival organizations in competition, and some suffragists clearly maintained membership of both factions.[7]

On the other hand, the wear and tear generated by these disputes diverted effort from the cause itself. Becker nearly retired, and in 1890 she died. The immediate effect of her death was that the *Women's Suffrage Journal* ceased publication and was not replaced until *The Common Cause* appeared in 1908. Beyond that, however, Becker's loss was probably not as great a setback as is sometimes imagined. Though an indefatigable worker, Becker had by this time become a divisive figure. She inspired those already converted to votes for women, but made a less favourable impact on the wider world. One pro-suffragist, the young David Lloyd George, went to hear her speak at Porthmadog in 1879 but was unimpressed: 'she was rather sarcastic' he noted.[8] In the event, Becker was replaced by Millicent Fawcett, a very skilled speaker, a prolific writer, and equally at home in the world of parliamentary politics.

The Impact of Gladstone and Home Rule

To some extent the problems associated with funds, affiliations, and leadership were symptomatic of the dilemma facing the cause by the mid-1880s; firmly committed to the parliamentary route, suffragists found their path increasingly blocked at Westminster. In this perspective the introduction of the third parliamentary reform bill by Gladstone's government in March 1884 appears to have been a crucial missed opportunity. This measure extended the franchises for householders and lodgers, which had been introduced in 1867, to men in the county constituencies. Relying on its established methods, the NSWS organized a Liberal member, William Woodall, to

---

[7] Rosamund Billington, 'Women, Politics and Local Liberalism: From Female Suffrage to Votes for Women', *Journal of Regional and Local Studies*, 5 (1985), 5–6.

[8] Herbert Du Parcq, *The Life of David Lloyd George* (Caxton, 1912), i. 33.

introduce an amendment to the bill, and seventy-nine Liberals memorial-
ized Gladstone in his support. But in the debate on Woodall's amendment the
prime minister intervened to announce that if it were carried, the bill would
be abandoned. This was largely bluff. Gladstone had been manoeuvred into
the reform bill by his own radical Liberals who believed he had squandered
the victory won in 1880 by ignoring their legislative programme during the
previous four years; consequently Gladstone could not ditch the franchise
bill, which was a major concession to radical pressure, without provoking further controversy and undermining his own leadership. But his claim—that
the women's amendment would merely encourage the House of Lords to
reject the whole measure—did seem plausible. Ultimately the Liberal members, confidently anticipating an electoral advantage from the agricultural
labourers' vote, did not think the gain worth risking for the unknown quantity of a female electorate; they therefore cooperated with Gladstone in voting heavily against Woodall's proposal. Not surprisingly the NSWS angrily
denounced the prime minister's action as 'an infringement of a free parliament and an aggression on the rights of the people'.[9] Though Gladstone's
opposition to votes for women was hardly new, exclusion from the 1885
reform act seemed in retrospect to be a major setback not least because there
was to be no more government legislation on the subject until 1912.

But was the pessimism exaggerated? Up to 1885 women's suffrage did not
enjoy a majority in the House of Commons, and so, regardless of Gladstone's
attitude, it was unlikely to be successful; in any case the peers, with whom
even Gladstone was obliged to compromise in order to pass a bill, were
almost certain to reject the women's vote. Thus, it cannot really be claimed
that a good opportunity had been lost at this stage. On the other hand, the
implications of the episode loomed large subsequently in suffragists' imagination. The number of electors had been increased from around three million
to six-and-a-half million by the 1890s, with the result that most sections of
male society, including even the poorest, now found it possible to get onto the
parliamentary register even if only periodically. As a result politicians
regarded the general question of reform as less urgent, which could be interpreted as disadvantageous for women.[10] Yet there was another side to the
coin. The glaring contrast between the large number of poor and ill-
educated men now eligible to vote, and female ratepayers, property-owners,
and university graduates who could not, helped to strengthen the feeling,
especially among Conservatives, that the continued exclusion of *all* women
had become indefensible.

[9] *Annual Report*, 1884, Manchester National Society for Women's Suffrage.
[10] Ignota, 'Women's Suffrage', *Westminster Review*, 148 (Oct. 1897).

The fact that women's suffrage legislation was introduced far less frequently after 1885 than it had been during the 1870s might be interpreted as
an indication of the hopelessness of the situation in parliament or as a sign of
demoralization amongst the activists. But this would be erroneous. The
decline in backbenchers' bills was largely a by-product of the growing control over the parliamentary timetable exercised by governments. In this
period only six to eight private members' bills could obtain a sufficient
opportunity for debate each year, and even they remained vulnerable to
intervention by the government; for the next four years after 1886, for example, the day originally designated for women's suffrage was appropriated
for government business. There was also an element of luck involved; in 1895,
for example, when nineteen members balloted with a view to introducing a
women's bill, the highest place obtained was sixteenth, and so no debate took
place at all.[11] In short, late Victorian backbenchers enjoyed far fewer effective opportunities to legislate than they had at the beginning of the suffrage
campaign.

No sooner was the third reform bill and the subsequent general election of
1885 out of the way than British politics became convulsed by a major crisis
over the first Irish Home Rule Bill of 1886 which left Gladstone's party split
and helped to keep the Liberals out of office for most of the next twenty years.
At first sight Home Rule appears yet another blow for the women's cause; but
the ramifications were complex and by no means uniformly unhelpful. By
excluding the Liberals from office the split effectively weakened Gladstone's
influence over the party which began to yield dividends for the suffragists
during the 1890s. Conversely, Home Rule strengthened the Conservatives,
hitherto the more hostile towards the women's vote. Yet during the late
1880s and 1890s a significant change occurred as Conservatives began to per-
ceive the attractions of female participation in politics (see Chapter 5); the
propaganda undertaken by Anglo-Irish ladies designed to highlight the 'outrages' committed by the Nationalists was regarded as a valuable contribution
to the Conservatives' success at the election of 1886. According to the NSWS
that election actually returned *more* pro-suffrage members—343 out of
670—and they claimed a rising total of 354 in 1887 and 365 by 1889.[12]

Yet there are grounds for thinking that the Home Rule controversy did
more than merely modify the fortunes of the political parties. It has long been
believed that the prospects of radical causes generally were closely linked to
broader fluctuations in the political climate; thus suffragism had enjoyed its

---

[11] *Annual Report*, 1895, Manchester NSWS.
[12] *Annual Report*, 1886, Manchester NSWS.

initial expansion when Liberalism was buoyant, and was to benefit in a similar way during the Edwardian period; conversely it dwindled during the last fourteen years of the century when Conservatism became dominant.[13] To some extent constitutional reform was displaced in public debate by the Union with Ireland, by perceived threats to the Empire, by weaknesses in national defence, the loss of export markets and by dramatic revelations about poverty and urban degeneration. In this way the agenda of politics changed during the 1890s in such a way as to focus debate on precisely the kinds of issues which, according to the opponents of women's suffrage, were simply beyond the comprehension of women.

While there is some validity in this, it would be a mistake to overlook the positive implications of the new agenda for women. Even imperial crises sometimes pushed women into prominence. For example, during the South African War female critics of Lord Kitchener's policy of concentration camps played a distinctive part in the debate; this encouraged the government to appoint the more patriotic Millicent Fawcett to go to South Africa to help the investigation into conditions in the concentration camps. In one sense this represented a diversion from the suffrage campaign. But it effectively involved women more closely in national and imperial issues. This is why the suffragists made a point of celebrating Queen Victoria's Diamond Jubilee in 1897 with a view to exploiting her popularity and success in combining the roles of mother and monarch. In any case, between the late 1890s and the early 1900s the political debate shifted again. It has been suggested that issues such as tariff reform, education, licensing, and trade union disputes in the early 1900s simply crowded women's suffrage out of public attention.[14] But this is to miss the underlying significance of such questions. The popular interest in food prices, the birth rate, children's health and poverty generally around the turn of the century effectively helped to turn the agenda into a domestic one in which women's involvement was taken for granted. Throughout the 1890s the Women's Co-operative Guild (WCG) among other pressure groups had been capitalizing upon the fashionable idea that behind the Empire stood hard-pressed mothers, ill-fed children, and poorly-educated workers. The WCG gained the ear of politicians because they accepted that it represented ordinary housewives unlike most of the feminist organizations. Yet although the WCG had not originally interested itself in votes for women, by 1894 it had adopted the cause and subsequently backed the efforts of the suffragists especially in connection with the 1897 bill.

[13] Harrison, 'Women's Suffrage at Westminster', 91.
[14] Hume, *The National Union*, 21.

Trojan Horses

Despite the prominence of great questions such as Home Rule during the late Victorian era, beneath the surface of politics structural changes were also taking place which ultimately proved advantageous for women. In fact the progress made by suffragism in this period took the form of *indirect* gains rather than frontal assaults on Anti-Suffragism. To some extent the reduction in the activities and resources of the official suffragist organizations reflected a deliberate diversion into alternative means of achieving the objectives of the movement. One obvious example of this was the Women's Local Government Society (WLGS) whose leaders, Eva McLaren, Annie Leigh Browne, and Louisa Twining, aimed at promoting the election of women to local authorities.[15] The WLGS proved especially attractive to women Liberals anxious to find fresh ways of advancing the case for the parliamentary vote. Much the most blatant Trojan Horses however, were the new party political organizations for women. During the 1880s many Liberal suffragists concluded that they had achieved about as much as they could as a non-party pressure group; why not try to undermine the parliamentary Anti-Suffragists from *within* the party political organizations? Developments at local level before the eventual establishment of the Women's Liberal Federation in 1887 suggest this was indeed a central motive. As early as 1881 Liberal women in Bristol set up their own association under Anna Maria Priestman in order to 'prepare women for the further duties and responsibilities which will in no long time fall to their share'.[16] The ladies shrewdly argued that the more women were seen to be active in the Liberal cause the sooner suspicions about women's natural Conservatism would be discredited. At Hyde in Lancashire where a suffrage society had been formed in 1882, the majority of its members promptly joined the local Women's Liberal Association when it was set up in 1888; the new branch defined its aim as the extension of the political role of women.[17] On a larger scale the constitution adopted by the Scottish Women's Liberal Federation included among its objects: 'to secure just and equal legislation and representation for women, especially with reference to the Parliamentary Franchise and the removal of

---

[15] Founded under a different name in 1888, it became the WLGS in 1893.

[16] Quoted in Kirsten Seltorp, 'The Women's Suffrage Movement in Bristol 1868–1906', Fawcett Library, unpublished MS, 80.

[17] Joan E. Parker, 'Lydia Becker: Her Work for Women', Ph.D. thesis (Manchester University, 1990), 134–5.

all legal disabilities on account of sex'.[18] While the Federation assisted the Liberal Party at general elections, in between times it effectively functioned as a feminist pressure group with one foot in the party and the other in the women's movement. To a considerable extent the members were simply using the new party organization as a vehicle to advance the cause of women's suffrage, partly by giving women a political training and partly by obtaining greater leverage with the politicians. The very fact that the women Liberal activists remained predominantly loyal to their party served to promote this objective by making it very difficult for the parliamentary leaders to repudiate them despite their feminist orientation.

By comparison with the Women's Liberal Federation (WLF) the Primrose League was unassertive and never attempted to pressurize the party into adopting a women's suffrage policy. Nonetheless, its long-term significance proved to be similar to and arguably even greater than that of the WLF (see Chapter 5). Millicent Fawcett, who for all her dislike of party organizations, was fully alive to the potential of these bodies, took care to extract from both Liberals and Conservatives written confirmation of the electoral work performed by their female auxiliaries.[19] At successive general elections in 1892, 1895, and 1900 the parties' reliance upon female activists for canvassing, transporting voters, checking on removals, and even writing election addresses for husbands who were absent during the campaign, grew steadily.[20] Grateful candidates began to acknowledge their debt: 'I do believe that my election was won by ladies,' declared Sir John Rolleston on his victory as a Tory in radical Leicester.[21] John Morley, a prominent Gladstonian who had opposed votes for women in the 1880s, admitted that in view of women's electoral work 'it is absurd . . . to pretend either that women are incapable of political interest and capacity, or that the power of voting on their own account must be injurious to their womanhood'.[22] The suffragists were not blind to the fact that the volunteers were to some extent being taken advantage of by the politicians, and that expressions of gratitude did not guarantee support for the women's vote; but they felt confident that the regular cooperation with the men would count even if unconsciously 'on the

[18] See Scottish Women's Liberal Federation, executive minutes 5 May 1891, 21 Apr. 1892, 5 Dec. 1893, 2 Jan. 1894, 29 Mar. 1895, 15 Jan. 1895, Edinburgh University Library.

[19] Emlyn Boyes to Millicent Fawcett, 26 Sept. 1892, Manchester Central Library, Fawcett Papers M50/2/26/29; George Lane Fox to Millicent Fawcett, 27 Sept. 1892, M50/2/26/30.

[20] Lady Joan Dickson-Poynder (NW Wiltshire) and Mrs D. Bagot (Kendal) wrote their husbands' addresses in 1900.

[21] Quoted in D. Rubinstein, *Before the Suffragettes* (Brighton: Harvester, 1986), 155; for similar examples, see *The Gentlewoman*, 10 Nov. 1900, 619.

[22] 'The Rt. Hon. John Morley on Women's Suffrage', NUWSS pamphlet, 1905.

minds of both the candidates themselves and of the public. The old asseveration that women have nothing to do with politics has had its complete quietus.'[23]

Women and Local Government

In the same period women were also penetrating the political system in a distinctly Fabian fashion at the municipal level. In this respect they were the indirect beneficiaries of the prolonged expansion of elective local government during the last thirty years of the nineteenth century. But it is also fair to say that several suffragist leaders perceived the advantage to be gained by exploiting the local franchise as, in effect, the thin end of the wedge. The process began in June 1869 when Sir Charles Dilke and Jacob Bright put down amendments to the Municipal Franchise Bill designed to include female ratepayers in the municipal electorate.[24] They argued that this simply restored to women a right of which they had been deprived by the 1835 Municipal Corporations Act.[25] When the Home Secretary, H. A. Bruce, accepted Bright's proposal on the grounds that it involved 'no novelty', the reform was incorporated in the bill with virtually no controversy even in the House of Lords; the Earl of Lichfield for example observed that as women paid rates they had 'the same interest in an economical administration of municipal funds and in the efficient management of municipal affairs as any other inhabitants'.[26] At that stage politicians assumed that the business handled by local authorities—the poor, health, education, and so on—represented no more than a natural extension of the duties and responsibilities of women as wives and mothers. 'Poor Law work', pronounced the *Westminster Review*, 'is especially fitted for women; for it is only domestic economy on a larger scale.'[27] By thus encouraging women's municipal work they expected to *consolidate* rather than to undermine conventional gender roles; in effect the traditional distinction between the functions of national and local government gave institutional expression to the separate spheres of men and women.

---

[23] *Report*, Bristol and West of England Society for Women's Suffrage, 1899–1900, 7.

[24] Dilke Papers, BL, Add. MSS 43909, fo. 116, and 43932, fos. 33–5.

[25] Women could qualify for older local bodies, but were excluded by the 1835 Act which thus appeared an anomaly; moreover, existing female ratepayers lost their rights if they lived in a town which was subsequently elevated to the status of a municipal borough; see M. Ostrogorski, *The Rights of Women* (Swan Sonnenschein, 1893), 97.

[26] *Hansard, House of Lords Debates*, 3rd Series, CXCVII, 13 July 1869, c. 1417.

[27] 'The Work of Women as Poor Law Guardians', *Westminster Review*, 123 (1885).

Like the contemporary politicians, historians have usually regarded this development as of marginal significance. The parliamentary vote for women, as Patricia Hollis put it, 'owed little or nothing to women's local government work'.[28] However, this assumption deserves to be questioned. Seen in a long-term perspective local government was one of those small keys that help to unlock large doors. Certainly the Victorian suffragists showed themselves fully alive to the potential advantages of this as a route to obtaining the vote. In 1868 Dilke had told the London Society for Women's Suffrage that the municipal franchise was 'only the first step towards adult suffrage'.[29]

In 1870 Emily Davies, Elizabeth Garrett Anderson, and Lydia Becker promptly sought election to the new school boards, not because they were particularly interested in elementary education, but because they believed that their participation would have beneficial long-term effects for the status of women.[30] It was with a view to accelerating this process that the Women's Local Government Society was founded. In a pamphlet of 1879 Becker argued that participation by women in local government represented the continuation of an English tradition stretching back to Anglo-Saxon times, and claimed that 'political freedom begins for women as it did for men, with freedom in local government'.[31] Her purpose at that stage was almost certainly to persuade more women to come forward for fear that their opponents would cite their reluctance to seek election as proof that women lacked interest in public affairs. Several formidable obstacles, quite apart from inexperience, impeded them; for example, up to 1894 poor law guardians were required to possess a property qualification which could be as much as a forty pound rating.

In spite of the slow start Becker and the WLGS were surely correct about the underlying significance of the municipal role. For one thing the comparatively minor innovation made in 1869 proved to be merely the start of a major extension of elective local government in Britain over the next thirty years. In 1870 Jacob Bright went out of his way to remind the House of Commons that the ratio of female to male voters—1:6 in Manchester, 1:7 in Bristol, and 1:8 in Newcastle for instance—was perfectly safe.[32] By the late 1890s female voters numbered 729,000 in England and Wales or 13.7 per cent of the municipal electorate—large enough to be taken seriously but not so large as to be a threat. Female ratepayers were already eligible as voters and

[28] Patricia Hollis, *Ladies Elect: Women in English Local Government 1865–1914* (Oxford: Clarendon Press, 1987), 463.

[29] Dilke Papers, BL, Add. MS 43931, fos. 33–5.   [30] Hollis, *Ladies Elect*, 39.

[31] Lydia Becker, 'The Rights and Duties of Women in Local Government', 24 Jan. 1879.

[32] *Hansard, HC Deb.*, 3rd Series, CCI, 4 May 1870, c. 195.

guardians of poor law boards.[33] In 1870 W. E. Forster's Act allowed them both to vote for and be elected to the new school boards. The 1888 legislation setting up County Councils gave women votes. Finally, when Gladstone's last government created elective parish councils, and urban and rural district councils in 1894 it took it for granted that women should vote and serve as councillors. As a result of intervention by the Liberal backbenchers, Walter McLaren and James Stansfeld, the 1894 reform included *married* women electors, though they could not qualify on the basis of the same property as their husbands. Interestingly, though the Home Secretary initially resisted this proposal, the vote went against the government which then capitulated; the episode was an indication of the growing feeling in Liberal circles that enfranchisement ought to apply to wives, though most suffragist leaders remained slow to appreciate the point.

TABLE 3.1. Female members of Local Authorities (England and Wales), 1870–1920

	School Boards	Poor Law Boards	RDCs	UDCs	Town & County Councils, including London
1870	3				
1875	17	1			
1880	71	8			
1885	78	37			
1890	*c.*100	80			(2)[a]
1895	128	893[b]	140	2	
1900	*c.*270	1,147	170	2	
1905	594[c]	1,157	112	4	
1910	641	1,310	147	4	22
1914–15	679	1,546	200	15	48
1919–20	*c.*680	2,039	263	67	320

[a] Two were elected in 1889 but forced to resign by a legal ruling.
[b] Poor law figures include RDC members from 1895.
[c] From 1903 women were co-opted onto county education committees not elected.

Source: Patricia Hollis, *Ladies Elect* (1987), 486.

As Table 3.1 shows, the 1890s proved to be the decade of major expansion for female representation. The lifting of the property qualification for guardians in 1894 had an immediate impact as is shown by the return of nearly nine hundred female guardians in 1895. By 1909 the total had reached 1,141 amongst 24,613 guardians in all.[34] School Boards also appear to have

---

[33] Since 1834 women had been eligible to vote, but their right to be elected as Guardians remained untested until 1875 when Martha Merrington was returned at South Kensington.

[34] *Anti-Suffrage Review*, Mar. 1909, 2.

been a relatively attractive form of participation for women. This probably owed something to the unusual system of election: the cumulative vote. Thomas Hare advised the women electors that 'any earnest and intelligent minority' could maximize its impact using this system by concentrating its votes rather than distributing them over several candidates.[35] The extraordinary successes scored by Elizabeth Garrett Anderson, whose poll of 47,000 was nearly four times that of the second candidate, and Emily Davies and Annie Besant who topped the poll in Greenwich and Tower Hamlets, respectively, suggest that his advice was adopted. In addition Anderson, who became married while she sat on the school board, established that wives would not be disqualified under the 1870 Act, contrary to previous assumptions.[36]

Inevitably some women experienced resistance from the party political organizations.[37] Some of them responded to this by standing as Independents which split the party vote and forced some local politicians to realize that it made more sense to co-opt women onto the ticket so as to maximize its appeal especially at school board elections.[38] Thus, despite the friction generated in some areas, women began to emerge as assets to their parties. Three women had even been chosen as mayors by the Edwardian period: Sarah Lees at Oldham, Frances Dove at High Wycombe, and Elizabeth Garret Anderson at Aldeborough.[39] The relatively modest increase in the number of women elected during the Edwardian period is not to be interpreted as a lack of interest amongst women, but more as a sign that efforts were now being focused on the final push to win the parliamentary vote. Also many of the Liberal and Labour women candidates were vulnerable to the swing back towards the Conservatives after 1906. The Anti-Suffragists claimed that female candidates suffered from a popular reaction against the suffragettes, but this is difficult to verify.

However, the significance of local government experience lay less in the numbers involved than in its effects on male and female perceptions. Women had to demonstrate their ability to withstand the pressures of a competition for votes; at this time it was usual for school board candidates to take to the platform in order to make their case, not simply to canvass.[40] Electoral experience increased their self-confidence and often had a politicizing effect

---

[35] *Women's Suffrage Journal*, 1 Oct. 1870, 79.
[36] *Women's Suffrage Journal*, 1 Apr. 1871, 37.
[37] Liddington, *Respectable Rebel*, 109–12; G. Mitchell (ed.), *The Hard Way Up* (Faber and Faber, 1968), 122–4.
[38] Hollis, *Ladies Elect*, 137–40, 156–8.
[39] See Lees Papers, Oldham Local Studies Library, D LEES/152.
[40] Hollis, *Ladies Elect*, 35.

especially on women who approached local government from a background in philanthropic work such as workhouse visiting. Charlotte Despard and Emmeline Pankhurst, for example, were influenced partly by their earlier work on local authorities to take up the campaign for the parliamentary vote. Once elected the women became responsible for policy-making including the raising of local rates. They also enjoyed certain advantages over their male colleagues. As guardians, for instance, women were able to inspect closely the conditions in which the inmates of workhouses lived because as women they could enter where men feared to tread; they also had more leisure time to devote to the work than most of the men. Moreover, women who came from a higher social class often exercised a natural authority especially where moral issues were involved. Although many women chose to conform to male expectations by rationalizing their role in terms of philanthropy, others played a more radical and political part by helping to pioneer innovations which had important implications for national government. Annie Besant in London, Margaret Macmillan in Bradford, and Flora Stevenson in Edinburgh promoted such policies as free school meals, the abolition of fees, and the payment of trade union rates.[41] The cumulative effect of all this was to undermine the claims once confidently made by opponents of female enfranchisement about the flaws of intellect and temperament suffered by women.

Above all, it has not been sufficiently appreciated that the implications of participation in local government changed over *time*. For although the Victorians regarded social welfare as the proper preserve of local authorities, by the 1890s pressure had grown for national government to assume a much larger measure of responsibility. As a result, the post-1906 Liberal governments intervened over free school meals, school medical services, old age pensions, health and unemployment insurance, labour exchanges, and minimum wages. In the process they went a long way to turning national politics into local politics and, as a crucial if unintended by-product, they materially diminished the distinction between the male and female spheres.

Yet the consequences for the women's cause went still further. Anti-Suffragists found themselves thrown onto the defensive and eventually fell out amongst themselves as they tried to reconcile their position with the empirical facts of women's local government work (see Chapter 7). James Bryce and H. H. Asquith, who had originally accepted the concessions to women, tried vainly to draw the line in 1888 when Salisbury's government legislated on county councils. They argued that county councils were more parliamentary

---

[41] Hollis, *Ladies Elect*, 112–16.

in style than the other local authorities, by which they meant that they were more party-orientated.[42] The new bodies certainly represented a step towards national government partly because they commanded far greater resources and also because of the issues with which they became involved; on the London County Council for instance the Progressives took up interventionist policies such as minimum wages and municipal house-building.

Although the 1888 legislation followed precedent in enfranchising female ratepayers, it failed to grant women the right to be elected; in fact it seems to have been assumed by this time that the right to vote now carried the right to serve. Consequently, two Liberals, Jane Cobden and Lady Margaret Sandhurst, were duly elected to the new London County Council, while Emma Cons was appointed an Alderman. However, when the defeated Conservative candidates went to court to challenge Cobden's and Sandhurst's right to sit, the judges ruled women ineligible. As a result numerous attempts were made in both Houses to correct what now seemed an anomaly by Walter McLaren (1889), Lord Meath (1890 and 1895), James Stuart (1891), Lord Aberdeen (1901), and Lord Beauchamp (1904). Two further reforms kept the issue alive. In 1899 the London Government Act, which created twenty-eight Metropolitan Boroughs, allowed women to vote but not to be elected; the explanation appears to be that by this stage the municipal franchise was increasingly regarded as a stalking horse for the parliamentary vote.[43] Then in 1902 came Balfour's Education Act which, by abolishing the school boards, struck a blow at female representation, though not intentionally. Yet Balfour's reform also gave striking recognition to women's role by requiring all county councils to include at least one woman on their education committees. As a result female representation rose from 270 on the old boards to over six hundred on the new committees. The same principle was incorporated into the Unemployed Workmen's Act of 1905 which stipulated that women should be included in all local distress committees.

These measures underline how far opinion had shifted since 1869. Then the women's vote had been seen simply as an extension of their domestic role, but by the early 1900s the contribution made by women meant that they had become a necessary element. It was in this spirit that in 1907 the new Liberal government introduced a bill to allow women to be elected to county councils. Though a marginal concession in itself, the significance of the measure may be gauged from the fact that both its supporters and its critics considered it from the perspective of the *parliamentary* franchise. In the Commons

[42] Ibid. 41.   [43] Rubinstein, *Before the Suffragettes*, 177.

Viscount Helmsley condemned it as 'the first step in the downward path to female suffrage'.[44] In the upper house Lord Halsbury commented: 'Why, there is hardly any subject which Parliament can deal with which a County Council cannot'; and Lord Lansdowne, who praised women's work in local government, declared that the arguments used for the bill 'would go very far indeed towards justifying not only a change with regard to the Parliamentary franchise, but even the admission of women to legislative powers'.[45] Such remarks underline the extent to which thirty years of gradual penetration of local authorities had effectively blurred the distinction between the two spheres of administration, thereby altering assumptions and diminishing the novelty in the idea of a parliamentary vote for women.

The Parliamentary Breakthrough

One of the flaws in the pessimistic view of the suffragism during the late Victorian period is that it tends to neglect some of the most relevant criteria by which the progress of the cause may be measured, notably the fluctuations in the level of support for the women's vote amongst MPs. This no doubt reflects an assumption that the voting did not matter because MPs were luke-warm, unreliable, or even downright deceitful in their expressions of support for the cause. No doubt many were. As Willoughby Dickinson put it: 'if you asked me to name a dozen members who would have gone through fire and water for the cause of women's suffrage I could not do it ... as a rule they are not the sort of persons who go through fire and water for any political cause'.[46] But this is to miss the point. Ultimately suffragists had to convert these polit-icians whatever their personal weaknesses; and three hundred faint-hearted supporters was a distinct advance on fifty. A reassessment of the progress of suffragism at the parliamentary level is therefore overdue.

During the period between the 1867 Reform Act and the mid-1880s women's suffrage bills and amendments were consistently rejected in the Commons with two exceptions, neither of which is of any significance; majorities were gained in 1870 because the Anti-Suffragists failed to turn out, and in November 1884 when a total of only forty-one members voted. The largest vote in favour of female enfranchisement was 157, recorded in 1873. This may be contrasted with the list of supporters compiled by the

[44] *Hansard, HC Deb.*, 4th Series, 180, 12 Aug. 1907, c. 930.
[45] *Hansard, HL Deb.*, 4th Series, 175, 12 June 1907, c. 1351–2.
[46] Speech, 23 Mar. 1918, W. H. Dickinson Papers, Greater London Record Office.

NSWS in 1889 which claimed 364 out of 670 members.[47] However, these estimates were evidently over-optimistic since only 153 of the 364 had actually voted for a women's suffrage bill; others admittedly had spoken in favour, signed memorials, or written letters.

Yet it was at this stage that a qualitative improvement occurred in support for suffragism. This initially took the form of a shift amongst the Conservatives. Encouraged by several speeches made by Lord Salisbury, the NSWS decided to capitalize on the prime minister's prestige by persuading the National Union of Conservatives and Unionist Associations to debate a women's suffrage resolution at its annual conference in Birmingham in November 1891, and to invite Millicent Fawcett to address the gathering.[48] When this was carried by a large majority at the conference, the Tory MP and Primrose Leaguer, Sir Algernon Borthwick, agreed to introduce a bill; this was then taken over by another Conservative, Sir Albert Rollit who had secured the earliest place in the ballot.[49] The resulting debate in April 1892 was taken unusually seriously by both sides. The Anti-Suffragists hastily organized a whip signed by twenty prominent figures including Sir William Harcourt, H. H. Asquith and A. J. Mundella from the Liberals, and Sir Michael Hicks Beach, Henry Chaplin, and Lord Randolph Churchill among the Tories; meanwhile they circulated a letter from Gladstone opposing the bill written to a Liberal backbencher, Samuel Smith. A. J. Balfour and George Wyndham spoke for Rollit's bill while Asquith and Bryce spoke against. In the event it was defeated, but by only twenty-three votes (175 to 152 or 202 to 179 including pairs). Immediately the NSWS presented a 4,000 signature Address of Thanks to Rollit to mark what they regarded as a breakthrough;[50] it certainly began to look as though Gladstone's influence had diminished. Moreover, the Conservatives had backed the bill by 78 votes to 64.

After the general election of July 1892 the Liberal suffragist Walter McLaren summoned a meeting of all the parliamentary friends of the cause on the first day of the new parliament. However, although many members agreed to ballot on behalf of women's suffrage, none was successful for several years.[51]

[47] List of Parliamentary Friends of Women's Suffrage, Apr. 1889, National Library of Scotland, Women's Suffrage Collection, 1889/18/10.

[48] *Report*, NSWS, executive, 31 May 1892, National Library of Scotland, Women's Suffrage Collection, 1892/18/2.

[49] Ibid.

[50] Address of Thanks, 1892, NSWS, National Library of Scotland, Women's Suffrage pamphlets, 4/119/9.

[51] *Report*, NSWS, 11 July 1893, National Library of Scotland, Women's Suffrage Collection, 1893/18/11.

A heavy Liberal defeat at the 1895 election made no overall difference to the movement now that suffragism was so obviously gaining ground among the Conservatives. In May 1896 another Primrose Leaguer, F. Faithfull Begg, prepared to introduce the bill again; however, the day was appropriated by the government. By this time the suffragists were keen to test their strength as they felt increasingly confident about the members' views.[52] Eventually Faithfull Begg's bill came up for debate in February 1897. He achieved a comfortable majority of 71 (230 votes to 159); the Liberals, the Conservatives, and the Irish members recorded more votes in favour than against, only the Liberal Unionists remaining hostile on balance.

This 1897 division undoubtedly represented the real breakthrough for women's suffrage; for it reflected a gradual accumulation of support during the decade which had not been obvious largely because for several years the House had had few opportunities to vote on the issue. Far from being an isolated victory, the 1897 vote set a *pattern*; subsequent bills in 1904, 1909, 1910, and 1911 continued to record pro-suffrage majorities which were enhanced as successive general elections swept fresh generations into parliament regardless of fluctuations in party fortunes. After the 1900 election the suffragists calculated that the members elected for the first time favoured women's suffrage by a 7–1 margin.[53] The Liberal landslide of 1906 brought in 200 Liberals who had never sat before in addition to the 29 Labour members, most of whom were also newcomers. As a result the suffragists won divisions in the Commons by margins of 273–94 in 1908, by 301–192 in 1910, and by 257–91 in 1911.

No doubt certain qualifications must be made about these parliamentary votes. Few MPs regarded women's suffrage as a priority or as a cause for which they would take major risks or to which they were prepared to devote much time. Some remained susceptible to the influence of their party leaders, though more so on the Liberal than on the Conservative side; the Irish members considered suffrage legislation as worth sacrificing if it threatened to impede or endanger the Home Rule Bill. Many members undertook to support the bills under pressure from female activists in their constituencies rather than from enthusiasm, but were liable to be antagonized by aggressive tactics as their reactions to suffragette militancy demonstrated. Above all, in these divisions members were recording their vote for the general principle of female enfranchisement on bills which no one

---

[52] Appendix, *Report*, NSWS executive, 2 July 1896, National Library of Scotland, Women's Suffrage Collection 1896/23/8.

[53] *Annual Report*, Manchester NSWS, 1900; for a similar view of the outcome of the 1895 election, see Blackburn, *Women's Suffrage*, 210.

expected to become law. Inevitably matters grew more complicated when they were obliged to move from the broad principle to considering the precise terms for enfranchising women, for this forced the issue of party interest to the fore and, in the process, exposed the heterogeneity of the suffragist majority.

Nevertheless, when all these qualifications are accepted, the point remains that since Mill's pioneering amendment had been rejected by just 73 votes to 196 in 1867, the campaign of the constitutional suffragists had gained enormously in support and credibility. By the turn of the century a suffragist majority had been created where it mattered most, and this *before* militant tactics had made their appearance. In view of this it would clearly be a misrepresentation to define the 1890s as on balance a period of failure for the cause, and to that extent the criticisms made by the Pankhursts and their followers in the early 1900s were without foundation. The problem still facing the Edwardian suffragists was not primarily one of propaganda and conversion, but the more intractable question of how to translate parliamentary sympathy into support for a detailed measure of female suffrage.

Reunification

One by-product of the parliamentary successes of the 1890s was an improvement in the morale of the suffragists which encouraged them to put aside their differences and stimulated a wider campaign in the country. The election of 1895 saw a cooperative effort by the NSWS, the Central Committee and the Manchester Society to petition every candidate in the country to support votes for women.[54] This activity helped promote the reunification of the movement. In January 1896, following a suggestion by Fawcett, the three groups, along with the societies based in Edinburgh and Bristol, established a joint committee to organize the campaign in parliament.[55] From this it was a short step to a conference representing all the main suffrage societies held at Birmingham in October. This conference defined the territorial boundaries within which each local society was to campaign. It also reconstituted the central organization as a federal body, the National Union of Women's Suffrage Societies (NUWSS), under the Presidency of Millicent Fawcett, with an executive committee and an annual conference. Though affiliated to the NUWSS, the societies enjoyed effective autonomy in their

---

[54] *Report*, Manchester NSWS, executive, 1895.
[55] *Annual Report*, Central Committee NSWS, 1897, 5–6.

areas.[56] The National Union laid several controversies to rest by deciding to be neutral towards the political parties and by confining its aims to winning the parliamentary vote 'on the same terms as it is, or may be, granted to men'.

1897 brought not only a formal reunification, but also a shift of emphasis towards active campaigning in the country. The local societies aimed to place an organizing secretary in every constituency who would prepare a list of supporters with a view to creating new societies and putting pressure on local MPs. This work developed furthest in the Manchester-based North of England Society where Eva Gore-Booth and Esther Roper tried to build a mass movement by involving working-class women in the campaign and thus shed the image of suffragism as a fad for well-to-do ladies.[57] Their efforts multiplied the number of societies in Cheshire, Lancashire, and Yorkshire and produced a petition with 66,000 signatures in 1901.

This expansion had several indirect consequences for the movement. First, the activity in the north-west helped to stir the National Union into adopting a bolder election strategy in the Edwardian period. By October 1903 when the breakdown of Balfour's government created general expectations about an early election, the National Union had decided to try to ensure the adoption of pro-suffrage candidates as well as to seek new pledges from existing ones.[58] It is in this extra activity that the origins of the Women's Social and Political Union are to be found, for it was through her collaboration and friendship with Eva Gore-Booth and Esther Roper in Lancashire that Christabel Pankhurst discovered her own interest in votes for women.[59] In this sense the suffragette movement itself was a *symptom* of the revival of suffragism around the turn of the century rather than simply or primarily a cause of that revival. Far from repudiating traditional methods of propaganda, the Pankhursts continued to practise them at least until 1906. The change of emphasis in the movement also helped to raise the parliamentary profile of the cause. The House of Commons debated the issue four times between 1904 and 1906 on proposals put forward by the Liberals, Walter McLaren, Sir Charles Dilke, and Bamford Slack, and the Labour member, Keir Hardie. Although the election of 1906 was fought largely on such questions as free trade, some 415 candidates gave promises of support for women's enfranchisement, and the rapidly rising expectations generated by the

[56] Hume, *The National Union*, 5–7; Billington, 'Women, Politics and Local Liberalism', 8–10.

[57] Liddington and Norris, *One Hand Tied Behind Us*, 143–9; *Annual Reports*, NSWS, 1901, 1902, 1903.

[58] Hume, *The National Union*, 22–3.   [59] Pankhurst, *Suffragette Movement*, 164–8.

Liberal landslide gave further momentum to the cause. The readiness of the new prime minister, Sir Henry Campbell-Bannerman, to receive a deputation of suffragists in May 1906 appeared to reflect the higher priority now attaching to votes for women; he frankly accepted that they had now established their case and effectively won the argument of principle.

4

The Impact of International Developments on Women's Suffrage

'I think Australia is doomed.' Professor Goldwin Smith delivered himself of this dismal prophecy to the *New York Post* in July 1904.[1] He based his verdict on three alarming trends in the Antipodes: the decrease in the birth rate, low immigration, and the fact that a million Australian women had voted in the recent elections there. Though few of the participants in the suffrage debate adopted such apocalyptic language, the professor's remarks serve to remind historians that contemporaries were fully alive to the implications of female enfranchisement abroad for the campaign at home. The general neglect of the international dimension in analyses of suffragism in Britain is, therefore, a significant and surprising one. When confronted with suffragist successes abroad, Anti-Suffragists instinctively adopted an attitude of supercilious dismissal. In 1892 Samuel Smith described Wyoming, which had enfranchised women in 1869, as 'this newly formed state on the outskirts of civilisation'. 'Generally speaking', observed C. W. Radcliffe Cooke, MP, referring to the colonies, 'the children follow the example of the parents, not the parents the example of the children.'[2]

Yet the pro-suffragists shared similar cultural and political assumptions. This explains why the Victorian reformers were so surprised to discover that the breakthrough in women's political rights had been achieved not, as they had expected, in the sophisticated, metropolitan areas, but in sparsely-populated frontier societies ostensibly far removed from advanced political and social thought. Even Mill had believed that Australia would follow Britain in enfranchising women, largely because she had fewer *unmarried* women than the home country and was consequently less susceptible to

---

[1] Arnold Haultain, *Goldwin Smith: His Life and Opinions* (T. Werner Laurie, 1913), 167.
[2] *Hansard, HC Deb.*, 4th Series, III, 27 Apr. 1892, c. 1479; XLV, 3 Feb. 1897, c. 1186.

female pressure for equal access to employment and other rights.[3] Of course, this was an assumption typical of the 1860s; by the 1890s it had become apparent that all over the world colonial states were setting the pace. Mill's attitude highlights again one of the crucial misjudgements of the British suffragists, namely their inability to recognize that marriage was a helpful factor in winning the vote for women rather than a drawback.

Influences from Abroad

The absence of the international dimension from accounts of British suffragism suggests that scholars have followed some of these contemporary assumptions. Although comparative studies of feminism have often been undertaken, especially in Britain, France, and the United States, there has been little attempt to employ this perspective in order to *explain* the course of events in Britain; moreover, it is now clear that the societies usually selected in comparative studies are not necessarily the most relevant ones.[4] Yet international experience was relevant in several ways. For example, in view of the bias in the British campaign towards empirical rather than abstract methods of argument, foreign practice could tip the balance of the debate. Fear of the unknown inevitably posed a major handicap for the women's movement which their opponents exploited to considerable effect, especially during periods of perceived national decline, by making all manner of dire predictions about the consequences of female enfranchisement. Though the Antis largely failed to substantiate their claims, as long as little solid evidence existed the suffragists had no convincing means of refuting their charges. It was thus of no small importance *which* Western societies became the first to experiment with women voters. On the one hand, practical experience with a female electorate might deflate the prophets of doom; on the other hand, it could as easily discredit the reformers as naïve idealists.

Although most of the suffragist leaders were almost quintessentially English, by the 1890s they had increasingly interested themselves in the

---

[3] J. S. Mill to Catherine Spence, quoted in Marion Sawyer and Marion Simms, *A Woman's Place* (Weidenfeld and Nicolson, 1984), 2.

[4] Two very useful exceptions which do discuss the interaction between the campaign abroad and the domestic movement are: Raewyn Dalziel, 'Presenting the Enfranchisement of New Zealand Women Abroad', in C. Daley and M. Nolan (eds.), *Suffrage and Beyond* (Pluto Press, 1994); and Barbara Caine, 'Vida Goldstein and the English Militant Campaign', *Women's History Review*, 2/3 (1993). For general accounts, see Richard Evans, *The Feminists* (Croom Helm, 1977); and Martin Pugh, 'The Rise of European Feminism', in Pugh (ed.), *A Companion to Modern European History 1871–1945* (Blackwell, 1997).

progress of the cause abroad. Improvements in communications throughout the second half of the nineteenth century greatly accelerated the exchange of ideas and personnel across national boundaries. Feminist writing, for example, was widely translated and disseminated throughout Europe and North America, particularly Mill's *The Subjection of Women* (1869), August Bebel's *Women in the Past, Present and Future* (1878), and Ellen Key's *The Strength of Woman Misused* (1896). The theatre also proved to be a valuable vehicle for transmitting feminist ideas to a wider audience. The first British performance of *A Doll's House* by the Norwegian playwright, Henrik Ibsen, in 1889 fuelled the debate over marriage which dominated the 1890s. Ibsen's portrayal of the dilemmas and injustices faced by married women helped not only to arouse the feminism in the actress Elizabeth Robins, but also to convert the young David Lloyd George to women's suffrage, where speeches had left him unmoved.[5]

External developments also impinged upon the cause in the sense that they helped to maintain the morale of small groups of beleaguered suffragists scattered across the country. In one of the earliest editions of *The Women's Suffrage Journal* Lydia Becker reported on women's suffrage speeches delivered as far away as Nelson in New Zealand, and this habit was maintained by all the journals up to 1914.[6] Moreover, by cultivating links with fellow campaigners the suffragists created an illusion of greater strength. While the press might ignore purely local women's meetings, they invariably treated any international gathering more respectfully, even when the majority of the delegates actually came from the host country. Not surprisingly, then, an International Association of Women was launched as early as 1868, though it lasted only until 1871. A more enduring organization, the International Council of Women (ICW), appeared in 1888 through the initiative of the leading American suffragists, Elizabeth Cady Stanton and Susan B. Anthony. Lady Aberdeen served as President of the ICW which had attracted representation from most European countries by 1900. Those who found the ICW too cautious established the Women's Suffrage Alliance at Berlin in 1904, a group to which suffragists from twenty-one states had affiliated by 1911. These organizations achieved their greatest influence during the First World War and in the 1920s when they helped to promote women's contribution to the anti-war movement throughout the Western world. Contacts with foreign countries also offered some tangible advantages

---

[5] Angela V. John, *Elizabeth Robins: Staging a Life* (Routledge, 1995), 62; A. J. P. Taylor (ed.), *Lloyd George: A Diary by Frances Stevenson* (Hutchinson, 1971), 43.
[6] *Women's Suffrage Journal*, 2 May 1870, 24.

to the Edwardian suffragists from time to time. Mrs Pankhurst, for example, made several timely visits to the United States which provided a welcome refuge from the British authorities and a fruitful source of funds, while Christabel Pankhurst found Paris a congenial bolt-hole from which to direct suffragette operations while recuperating from the effects of forcible feeding.

Above all, the significance of international suffragism lay in the intangible but profound impact it made on perceptions about the women's vote in Britain. The chronology of female enfranchisement before 1914 must be kept in mind here, for although successes occurred as early as the 1860s, it was during the 1890s and early 1900s that external changes impinged most strongly on the domestic debate. Back in 1869 the Rocky Mountain territory of Wyoming had enfranchised its female population, followed by Utah in 1870. Neither aroused much attention at the time, but when these territories entered the Union as states in 1890 and 1896, respectively, the original decision had to be reaffirmed in the face of federal opposition; fortunately no significant misgivings had developed in the interim. The cause continued to gain momentum from the referenda conducted among the men of Colorado in 1893 and Idaho in 1896 which led to further extensions of the vote. Altogether eleven states of the USA had granted the franchise to women by 1914.[7] Though geographically extensive, these areas could be represented as marginal politically, and their decisions as equivalent to municipal enfranchisement in Britain. The same could hardly be said, however, of the more comprehensive innovations in New Zealand, where all adult women gained the vote in 1893, and in Australia where the federal vote was granted in 1902; there the process had begun in South Australia in 1894, followed by Western Australia (1896), New South Wales (1902), Tasmania (1903), Queensland (1904), and finally Victoria (1908).[8] In Europe the pioneers were Finland in 1906 and Norway in 1913.[9] In the British context the nearest approach to enfranchisement had come in 1881 when the Isle of Man extended the vote to women in elections to the House of Keys.[10]

---

[7] The others were Washington, Oregon, California, Arizona, Kansas, Nevada, and Montana.

[8] See the analysis in Patricia Grimshaw, *Women's Suffrage in New Zealand* (Auckland: Auckland University Press, 1972); and Audrey Oldfield, *Woman Suffrage in Australia* (Cambridge: Cambridge University Press, 1992).

[9] Ida Blom, 'The Struggle for Women's suffrage in Norway, 1885–1913', *Scandinavian Journal of History*, 5 (1980); Riitta Jallinnoja, 'The Women's Liberation Movement in Finland, 1880–1910', *Scandinavian Journal of History*, 5 (1980); Evans, *The Feminists*, 69–90.

[10] Ostrogorski, *Rights of Women*, 51–2; Millicent Fawcett, in Stanton (ed.), *Woman Question*, 27–8.

The American Example

In view of the variety of societies which generated feminist movements in the late nineteenth century, one hesitates to generalize about the implications for British suffragism; advances in some states proved to be more advantageous than others; some attracted considerable attention while others were neglected. North American experience appears to have been a distinctly mixed blessing in the British context. During the mid-Victorian period Radical workingmen had often found a source of inspiration in American democracy, and from this perspective the vote for women could be regarded as a natural part of the rough-and-ready egalitarianism of a frontier society. The British and American women's movements used similar language, employed the same tactics at least until 1905, and shared a common emphasis on moral causes such as temperance and anti-slavery.[11]

However, during the two decades after 1867 American political practice came to be seen as more of a liability or a warning in Britain. Conventional parliamentary politicians characterized it as a system sunk in corruption and its electoral practice as almost calculated to devalue the personnel of politics; thus conservatives in both parties could plausibly argue that Britain should hesitate before making any ill-considered dash towards democracy.[12] This coloured the thinking of those Liberals who reacted against the innovations associated with Joseph Chamberlain—the local 'caucus' and the National Liberal Federation of 1877—which appeared to be little more than Brummagem imitations of the political machines typical of North American cities. Consequently opponents of female suffrage found it tempting to try to discredit the cause by depicting the feminist movement of the United States as another symptom of a political system emasculated by the influence of ignorant and gullible voters. Certainly Goldwin Smith, who had been among the original supporters of Mill's suffrage amendment, professed to have been alienated by evidence of the role of women in public life on his visits to the United States, and thus became a convinced Anti-Suffragist.[13] Though his critics accused him of allowing pure prejudice to defeat his intellect, this hardly erased the damage done by his defection. However, the professor's colourful language probably went some way to undermining his credibility. 'In one backwoods state', he wrote contemptuously, 'the vote has been given

---

[11] Olive Banks, *Faces of Feminism* (Oxford: Blackwell, 1981); Jane Rendall, *The Origins of Modern Feminism* (Oxford: Blackwell, 1985); Christine Bolt, *Feminist Ferment* (UCL Press, 1995).

[12] Haultain, *Goldwin Smith*, 117–18.

[13] J. E. Cairnes, 'Woman Suffrage: A Reply', *Macmillan's Magazine*, 30 (1874), 382–3.

to women probably for much the same reason which leads the denizens of an Australian mining camp to dance round a petticoat on a pole.'[14] But his wider analysis of the feminist movement as an aberrant feature of Western societies surely carried more weight because it coincided with existing worries at home. He argued that in the United States certain impediments to marriage had left many women 'without an object in life', and in this situation 'there is a passion to emulate the male sex' which led women to seek careers for themselves.[15] Already, so the critics claimed, America was leading the way towards the virtual abolition of marriage and the destruction of family life.[16] In view of the evidence that young women in Britain were postponing the age of marriage, this naturally fuelled the fears about the implications of female enfranchisement for the family and population levels.

As so often, however, the Antis' tendency to exaggeration deprived their case of some of its credibility. Goldwin Smith contrived to lay the blame for the American civil war on women; and he argued that they wanted to inflict capital punishment for sexual offences and impose stringent controls over the consumption of alcohol. Such examples were widely employed to illustrate the dangers of allowing the law to be determined by a majority that lacked physical force.[17] Inconsistent as usual, the Antis managed both to blame women for the civil war and accuse them of inhibiting the USA from declaring war; as late as 1917 Sir Frederick Banbury claimed that all the states with women voters had supported Woodrow Wilson in the presidential elections because of his opposition to entry into the First World War, rather overlooking the fact that his opponent took an identical view.[18]

At the very least the American evidence appears to have stimulated the Anti-Suffragists and corroborated their claims about the potential damage arising out of votes for women. Fortunately for the suffragists, however, its impact proved to be limited in several ways. In the first place, as a succession of states followed Wyoming and Utah right up to 1914, it became increasingly difficult to demonstrate convincingly that enfranchisement had major drawbacks. On the contrary, suffragists made great play with claims about the morally improving effects of female voters in the lawless communities of the West. In 1878 they published an account of a typical election in Wyoming before female enfranchisement which made English practice look decidedly tame: 'there was a perfect Pandemonium. The saloons were all open, whisky was dealt out freely by the candidates to all who would vote for them. The

---

[14] Goldwin Smith, 'Conservatism and Female Suffrage', *The National Review*, 10 (1888), 743.
[15] Goldwin Smith, 'Female Suffrage', 142–3.   [16] Ibid. 149.
[17] Ibid. 146, 149.   [18] Ibid. 146.

streets were filled with men partially intoxicated, all armed with knives and pistols . . . the bullets were flying at random, and many were severely wounded.'[19] But at the next election, according to this account, 'perfect order prevailed, and has prevailed ever since. Not a single case has occurred of a lady being insulted or treated with disrespect at elections.' It soon became a staple item of British suffragist propaganda to claim that female voters had helped to cleanse the politics of the western states, and that women had discriminated in favour of respectable candidates, even if that meant ignoring the party ticket. Though this was necessarily difficult to prove, by dint of repetition the suffragists gave the claims some credibility. California's decision to enfranchise 600,000 women in 1911 was cited as evidence that Americans had been impressed by the improving effects of women in the other states.[20] Suffragists also produced the Speaker of the Wyoming House of Assembly, a former opponent of female suffrage, who graciously acknowledged his error: 'it has worked well and been productive of much good to the Territory, and no evil that I am aware of'.[21] This seems typical of the tactics adopted by the suffragists who largely contented themselves with a negative line of argument: no one in the United States had identified any undesirable consequences.

A further mitigating factor lay in the timing; for although the women's movement in America was more advanced in some ways than that in Britain, it failed to obtain the national vote until 1919 by which time Britain had already taken the plunge. This proved to be advantageous for the cause in Britain because it prevented the Antis from making dire predictions based on the impact of women on the legislature. In particular, the introduction of Prohibition in the 1920s, which was widely attributed to the influence of female voters, would have been a gift to Anti-Suffragist propaganda. Even though the temperance cause had dwindled considerably in Britain by this time, its potential for damage may be glimpsed in the political career of Nancy Astor, the first woman to sit in the Commons. As an American and an unapologetic critic of the sale of alcoholic drink, Astor became vulnerable to charges of wishing to foist prohibition on Britain. This led the brewers to run an independent candidate against her at Plymouth in the 1922 election.[22] As a result her majority fell, and she was a little lucky that the issue no longer had the resonance it enjoyed in its Victorian heyday.

---

[19] *Women's Suffrage Journal*, 1 Jan. 1878, 4.
[20] Millicent Fawcett, 'The Women's Suffrage Bill', *Fortnightly Review*, 46 (1889), 564; J. O. P. Bland, 'Woman Suffrage in the United States', *The Nineteenth Century*, 74 (1913), 1339.
[21] Fawcett, 'The Women's Suffrage Bill', 565.
[22] Martin Pugh, *Women and the Women's Movement in Britain, 1914–1959* (Macmillan, 1992), 174.

Yet to argue that the suffragists contained the potential damage arising out of developments in the United States is not to claim any significant advantage from them. This negative conclusion was implicitly acknowledged by the British suffragists who showed a preference for focusing attention on other societies which they saw either as more relevant or as more helpful to their case. In this connection one notices the way in which Millicent Fawcett introduced the Isle of Man into the discussion in the 1880s, which was symptomatic of the conservative drift of the suffragist rationale at that time. She emphasized that the Isle of Man represented a more significant example of female enfranchisement than Wyoming partly because it enjoyed a larger population of 54,000, compared to only 9,000, and also because its legislature was independent of Westminster, whereas Wyoming was merely a territory, and, subsequently, a state of the Union.[23] Moreover, the Isle of Man appeared to be an indisputably traditional, conservative society whose assembly, the House of Keys, enjoyed an even longer history than that of the Westminster parliament. That such a body had felt able to risk enfranchising women illustrated perfectly the suffragists' claim that a female electorate posed no threat to the status quo.

The Australasian Experience

Although the Australasian states, like those of North America, made a virtue of their youth, egalitarianism, and innovative spirit, they nonetheless served the suffragists' purpose rather better in that they resembled British society more closely. By the early 1900s 95 per cent of Australia's population was of pure British origin as Sir John Cockburn pointed out, and its experiment with a female electorate therefore seemed likely to offer a realistic guide to the effect on Britain.[24] The fact that several prominent figures practised as politicians in both Britain and New Zealand and used similar party labels, further underlined the common political culture. Consequently New Zealand and Australia figured much more prominently than North America in suffrage propaganda, and by the turn of the century they occupied a central position in the debate, not least because many eminent and articulate Australasians of both sexes visited Britain to spread the message. 'Scarcely anything does more good to women's suffrage in England', wrote Mary Priestman, 'than seeing

---

[23] Fawcett, in Stanton (ed.), *Woman Question*, 27–8.
[24] Sir John Cockburn, 'Women's Suffrage in New Zealand and Australia', NUWSS, 1905.

those who speak from personal experience.'[25] This was all the more true as
those who visited Britain in the 1890s and 1900s were heavily biased in favour
of votes for women. In fact only two notable Antis spoke with any authority
about New Zealand, one being John Cathcart Wason, the MP for Orkney and
Shetland, who attempted to minimize the significance of New Zealand politics, and Lady Glasgow, whose husband had been Governor in 1893, and who
later became President of the Glasgow Branch of the National Anti-Suffrage
League. Her claim that New Zealand elections were very disorderly after
women won the vote was squashed by eyewitness accounts by Maud Pember
Reeves and Lady Anna Stout who pointed out that Lady Glasgow's position
excluded her from venturing among the crowds of voters to see for herself.[26]

Amongst the female visitors the majority appear to have been non-
militants including Kate Shepherd, Anna Stout, Ellen Ballance, Edith Searle
Grossman, and Maud Pember Reeves, all of whom circulated their views in
NUWSS pamphlets during the Edwardian period.[27] Particularly influential
was Kate Shepherd, the leader of the campaign in New Zealand, who spent
1894–5, 1903, and 1908 in Britain when she addressed rallies for women's suffrage and temperance. Even in the hostile newspapers Shepherd attracted
flattering comment as 'a good representative of Colonial woman at her best,
strong physically and mentally'.[28] Anna Stout, the wife of the New Zealand
Chief Justice, visited Britain from 1909 to 1912, and, like Shepherd, helped to
disabuse the political Establishment of its prejudice. Even *The Times* printed
a pro-suffrage article by her, and her campaign was taken so seriously that in
Manchester the branch of the Anti-Suffrage League found it necessary to
employ a New Zealander to counter her propaganda.[29] Several of the visitors,
including Dora Montefiore, Mrs Nellie Martell, and Vida Goldstein associated themselves with militancy. In an eight-month tour in 1911 Goldstein
addressed rallies for the WSPU, but one has the impression that she had difficulty concealing her pride in the superiority of Australian women and her
shock over the discrimination suffered by women in Europe. Goldstein also
began to realize how far women still had to go, even in Australia, before
achieving real emancipation; it seems, therefore, that her visit made more
impact on her own thinking than on the British campaign for the vote.[30]

[25] Mary Priestman to Kate Shepherd, 2 Feb. 1895, Shepherd Papers, quoted in Dalziel, 'Presenting the Enfranchisement', 53.
[26] *The Times*, 26 Jan. 1912, and 1 Feb. 1912.
[27] See 'Women's Suffrage in New Zealand and Australia', NUWSS, 1905.
[28] *The Times*, 19 Nov. 1909.
[29] Lucy T. Lewis to Miss Moir, 22 Dec. 1911, Manchester Central Library, Manchester League
for Opposing Women's Suffrage, M131/3.
[30] *The Times*, 1 May 1911; *Votes for Women*, 5 May 1911; Caine, 'Vida Goldstein', 369–72.

Distinguished male visitors included the former New Zealand premiers Sir George Grey (1894) and Richard Seddon (1897 and 1902), the Chief Justice Sir Robert Stout, and Sir Edmund Barton, the premier of South Australia. Seddon and Barton, who had originally opposed votes for women, now testified to the unqualified good that had resulted.[31] In November 1910, following violent clashes between police and suffragettes attempting to march to the House of Commons, both houses of the Australian parliament dispatched resolutions to Asquith urging him to learn from their experience: 'though disaster was freely predicted, the reform has brought nothing but good'.[32] William Pember Reeves, whose books, *The Long White Cloud* (1898) and *State Experiments in Australia and New Zealand* (1902), were widely quoted in suffragist literature, exercised an indirect influence on the debate. Pember Reeves placed the enfranchisement of women in a wider context of innovation, thereby making it appear more natural and less alarming. He and his wife, Maud, moved freely in Fabian-Liberal circles, where they propagated a picture of New Zealand as a laboratory for social reform in which old age pensions and votes for women were simply part of the broad Liberal achievement, a useful correction to the conservative bias which had crept into the campaign in Britain. Both Fawcett and Shepherd took issue with Pember Reeves because he minimized the role of the suffrage campaign in New Zealand, making the end result appear an almost effortless triumph. But though misleading, his account was by no means unhelpful in the British context in that he contrived to present the women's vote as something that could be accommodated quite naturally by a liberal society rather than as a change that involved major upheavals.

Australasian experience also impinged upon the argument in Britain by throwing extra light on the much-debated claim that women themselves lacked any strong desire for the vote. After the passage of the Bill in New Zealand in 1893 only six weeks remained in which to register women for a general election. In the event 78 per cent were enrolled, thus creating a female electorate of 109,461, of whom no fewer than 90,290 actually voted. Although the turnout diminished slightly in subsequent elections, doubtless as the novelty wore off, it remained high in absolute terms and very similar to that among male electors; also the proportion of spoilt ballot papers was only slightly higher than usual.[33] By the early 1900s any claim that New Zealand women did not want the vote had been decisively exploded. On the other

[31] *Annual Report*, Edinburgh NSWS, 1903, 9–10.
[32] Quoted in Oldfield, *Woman Suffrage*, 236.
[33] W. Pember Reeves, *State Experiments in Australia and New Zealand* (Grant Richards, 1902), 122.

hand, in Australia the turnout proved to be consistently lower than that for men especially in the federal elections, though the level clearly reflected general fluctuations in political interest state by state, and the lower profile of federal elections.

TABLE 4.1. Turnout in New Zealand General Elections (percentage)

	1893	1896	1899	1902	1905	1908	1911
Men	69	76	79	78	84	81	84
Women	85	76	75	74	82	78	84

Sources: Bishop George Frodsham, 'The Women's Parliamentary Franchise in Practice', *The Nineteenth Century*, 74 (Nov. 1913); and W. Pember Reeves, *State Experiments in Australia and New Zealand* (1902).

TABLE 4.2. Turnout in Australian Elections (percentage)

	1910 South Australia	1911 Western Australia	1907 New South Wales	1912 Queensland	1911 Victoria	1909 Tasmania
State Elections						
Men	77	74	72	70	68	60
Women	64	75	61	70	59	43
	1903 House of Representatives	1903 Senate	1906 House of Representatives	1906 Senate	1910 House of Representatives	1910 Senate
Federal Elections						
Men	56	53	57	56	68	67
Women	43	39	44	44	57	56

Source: Bishop George Frodsham, 'The Women's Parliamentary Franchise in Practice', *The Nineteenth Century*, 74 (Nov. 1913).

Suffragists also argued that practical experience would corroborate their view about the beneficial effects of female participation on the conduct of elections. Grey and Shepherd upheld this claim, while Reeves wrote: 'women are not afraid to go to the voting booths . . . there are no signs of disorder at the polls'.[34] Some observers even compared the experience of voting with going shopping! In New South Wales the 1903 elections were described as 'the most orderly that have ever been held in the state'.[35] On the other hand, Seddon denied that women had had any purifying effect, and others pointed out that as elections in New Zealand were already fairly orderly there was little room for

[34] Dalziel, 'Presenting the Enfranchisement', 51–2; Pember Reeves, *State Experiments*, 136.
[35] Dalziel, 'Presenting the Enfranchisement', 51–2.

improvement![36] If any change occurred it was probably the result of restrictions introduced specifically in order to facilitate female voting; the authorities closed the public houses and declared a public holiday on polling day, while the parties abstained from canvassing or interfering with voters at that stage.

More significant were the ramifications of the new electorate for parliament, the political parties, and legislation. New Zealand practice corroborated the suffragists' pleas that the women's vote did not automatically imply the right to sit in parliament, which was not in fact granted until 1919. In Australia where women did enjoy the right of election, no woman stood in the 1903 federal elections, and none managed to get elected until 1943! In the state of South Australia, which allowed women to stand in 1894, no woman won a seat until 1959. This extraordinarily negative record at least helped to deprive the Antis of any convincing evidence with which to frighten nervous British parliamentarians about the threat to their male club. By comparison women proved to be far quicker about establishing a footing in the two European countries which granted the vote before 1914. In Finland, for example, nineteen women, representing 9 per cent of the places, were returned in 1906.[37] Part of the explanation for their relative success lay in the use of proportional representation by means of multi-member constituencies which placed the parties under pressure to maximize their appeal by including female candidates in each seat. However, the European elections seem to have attracted little attention in the British press.

The impact on the party system also appears to have been minimal. Both hostile and sympathetic observers of New Zealand politics had expected the women's vote to strengthen prohibition and to threaten the system of secular education, in the process damaging the Liberal Party which was then in office.[38] However, such prognostications were rapidly discredited when in the first elections the government won 54 out of the 74 constituencies; indeed, as the Liberals retained power for nineteen years it appeared that the new franchise had fostered continuity rather than change. 'The innate Conservatism of women is, I am convinced, a myth', concluded Enid Grossman in 1908, reflecting on a record which cannot but have been reassuring for British Liberals.[39] Inevitably the other side of this coin was disappointment among Conservatives as Lord Onslow pointed out: 'I think it

---

[36] Norwood Young, 'The Truth about Female Suffrage in New Zealand', *Westminster Review*, 142 (1894), 672.

[37] *Daily Express*, 24 May 1907, reported that the nineteen women deputies were 'not particularly beautiful, the majority being determined-looking and angular'.

[38] R. H. Bakewell, 'New Zealand under Female Franchise', *The Nineteenth Century*, 35 (1894), 272; Pember Reeves, *State Experiments*, 111–12.

[39] Enid Grossman, 'The Woman Movement in New Zealand', *Westminster Review*, 170 (1908), 50.

has had a considerable effect in checking the ardour of our friends now in Opposition here for following in the footsteps of New Zealand.'[40]

As far as the legislative record was concerned the suffragists had to tread a fine line between claiming too much for the women's vote and thereby frightening male politicians, and claiming too little and thereby confirming the misgivings of the Radicals. Kate Shepherd suggested rather tentatively that women had helped to strengthen pressure for social and moral reform, while other suffragists pointed to a catalogue of innovatory and improving legislation including the 1895 Liquor Act, which introduced partial prohibition, equal divorce, the raising of the age of consent, and changes in women's working conditions.[41] Both Seddon and Reeves conceded that New Zealand had achieved very advanced labour laws, partly through female influence, but contended that this benefited men just as much.

Yet this optimistic view was inconsistent with Anna Stout's conclusion that 'experience has proved that the women's vote does not cause any revolution', and Maud Pember Reeves's claim that no legislation had been introduced specifically as a result of female pressure.[42] The key issues were drink and education. New Zealand already enjoyed a system of compulsory, free, and secular education, but, despite earlier predictions, the women declined to support the clergy in attacking it. Similarly, in 1894 when an opportunity arose to vote by district to reduce the number of licensed houses, the new voters failed to swing the result against the drink interest.[43] Claims and counter-claims continued to be made, with the Antis variously suggesting that women had put an end to drinking and that their enfranchisement had resulted in increased expenditure on alcohol! According to Anna Stout, writing in 1911, spending on drink had fallen since women won the vote and consumption of beer stood at nine gallons per head compared with 29.5 gallons in Britain.[44] However, it was difficult for either side to demonstrate convincingly that what had happened since 1893 could be attributed to female influence; it seemed more credible that they had reinforced existing tendencies because, as Pember Reeves put it, 'families as a rule vote together'. Some commentators concluded that women were having a stabilizing effect in the sense that they voted with married men against the single men or 'floating population'.[45] By 1914 a very similar perspective was being adopted by

---

[40] Lord Onslow to Sir John Hall, 27 Jan. 1894, quoted in Grimshaw, *Women's Suffrage*, 104.
[41] Grossman, 'The Woman Movement in New Zealand', 49.
[42] *The Times*, 19 Nov. 1909; *The Queen*, 26 Sept. 1908.
[43] Young, 'The Truth about Female Suffrage', 670–1.
[44] *Manchester Guardian*, 16 Jan. 1911, 4.
[45] W. Pember Reeves, *The Long White Cloud* (G. Allen and Unwin, 1898), 379; Edward Reeves, 'Why New Zealand Women Get the Franchise', *Westminster Review*, 143 (1895), 35–6.

British Conservatives such as Lord Selborne who also hoped that the female element would consolidate the family influence in politics.

Such an interpretation had obvious implications for the wider questions about the impact of enfranchisement on gender roles: had it provoked antagonism between men and women, disrupted marriage or undermined femininity? Seddon was an ideal figure to refute these charges, for although sympathetic towards the women's vote after 1893, he was no radical in gender relations; originally he had warned of the danger of woman being 'dragged down from the high pedestal on which I have always loved to see her'.[46] Stout picked up Mill's earlier argument when she suggested that by developing the wider interests of women, enfranchisement had fostered real comradeship between man and wife, and thereby strengthened marriage. But neither side had much evidence on which to base its opinions. Statistics, though, helped the suffragists. Although the birth rate had fallen in New Zealand, this trend pre-dated women's enfranchisement; in any case the rate remained relatively high and even increased after 1900. New Zealand also boasted the highest marriage rate of any European society other than Hungary.[47] As a result the suffragists felt confident about refuting Anti-Suffragist propaganda: 'women sedulously exercise their voting powers without neglecting a jot of their domestic duties,' declared Cockburn, 'and without alteration in the previous relationship of the sexes'. Or, in Bishop Frodsham's words: 'the millennium has not followed.'[48] On balance the Australasian evidence clearly influenced suffragist tactics in helping them to play down the social consequences convincingly; by 1902 Pember Reeves could write that the original apprehensions about domestic discord 'have already almost passed from memory'.[49]

The Anti-Suffragist Response

Conversely, from the perspective of the Antis this colonial experience introduced a wholly unwanted element of empiricism into the debate. R. H. Bakewell reflected this in his petulant attack on the Governor of New Zealand, Lord Glasgow, for failing to refuse the royal assent to the women's bill. Consequently the Antis were forced to fall back on an alternative line of argument consisting in the claim that the experiments conducted in

---

[46] Speech by Seddon, quoted in Dalziel, 'Presenting the Enfranchisement', 52.
[47] 'Adult Suffrage in New Zealand', People's Suffrage Federation, not dated.
[48] 'Women's Suffrage in New Zealand and Australia', NUWSS, 1905; Bishop George Frodsham, 'The Women's Parliamentary Franchise in Practice', *The Nineteenth Century*, 74 (1913), 980.
[49] Pember Reeves, *State Experiments*, 136.

Australasia were not really *relevant* to Britain and thus not to be regarded as a precedent or a guide.

To some extent propagandists such as Edith Grossman and Pember Reeves had played to this view, in as much as they had portrayed New Zealand as a rather Utopian place where British people conducted social experiments with a view to offering a model for the rest of the world. By implication the kinds of innovations that proved easy to assimilate there would not necessarily work in Britain. In any case, the colonies, or so the argument ran, were thinly populated, geographically marginal and polit- ically insignificant societies whose legislatures did not carry the enormous responsibilities for defence and warfare which so dominated the Westminster parliament. 'Should [women's suffrage] fail,' pronounced *The Times* in 1893, 'no serious mischief will have been done.'[50] As the Antis were forced to abandon parts of their case, they strove increasingly to distinguish British politics from colonial experience. As Lord Curzon put it in 1911: 'No precedent exists for giving women, as a class, an active share in the govern- ment of a great Country or Empire, and it is not for Great Britain, whose stake is the greatest, and in whose case the result of failure would be the most tremendous, to make the experiment.'[51] In defiance of all the changes in the role of women since the 1860s Lady Glasgow continued to emphasize the intellectual incapacity of women in external affairs. Women voters, she claimed, would 'practically have the government of the day at their mercy . . . they might force the reduction of our army [and] our navy on the plea of progressing social reform because . . . women are unable to take large views'.[52]

However, by the Edwardian period the suffragists had begun to use colo- nial experience to show that a female electorate had *not* had a debilitating effect on patriotic-imperial sentiment. The Australasian states had loyally backed Britain's cause during the South African War, and contributed badly needed volunteers to compensate for British deficiencies; subsequently New Zealand had financed a battleship to assist the Royal Navy in its rivalry with Germany. This made the colonies seem far less marginal to European power- struggles than the Antis had claimed. In this context the Conservative suf- fragists played a vocal and useful role, emphasizing that without female membership the imperial and patriotic pressure groups in Britain would hardly have been viable. For the benefit of Tory audiences Anna Stout and

---

[50] *The Times*, 11 Sept. 1893; Grossman, 'The Woman Movement in New Zealand', 44–5.
[51] 'Colonial Statesmen and Votes for Women', WFL, 1911.
[52] *Eastbourne Gazette*, 20 May, 1912.

Sir John Cockburn emphasized how keen the women of New Zealand were about compulsory military training for men, ambulance training for women, and voluntary work on behalf of the Victoria, Navy, and Empire Leagues: 'they recognize that there is a "white woman's" burden as well as a man's'.[53] It is also worth noting in this connection the role of Sir Edward Grey, a Liberal suffragist with impeccable credentials in imperial and foreign affairs. Grey challenged head-on the Antis' fears in a speech to the Women's Liberal Federation in 1911:

Now Australia and New Zealand are not decadent communities, and the race is not degenerate. If these young and robust communities who are developing new countries who have to deal with a struggle for life at least as arduous and as enterprising as anything we have—if they have given votes to women, and if there it has been an admitted success, surely we may take it for granted that the giving of votes to women is not any sign that the race is degenerate.[54]

Grey's line of argument showed suffragists how they might capitalize upon national pride rather than allowing their opponents to make a monopoly of patriotism. It may be significant that in the two European states which enfranchised women before 1914 the women's cause benefited from a close association with the national cause. This arose because both Finland and Norway had for years endured foreign rule. In Finland the rejection of proposals for a female franchise by Russia in 1897 had helped to unite the feminists and the nationalists in a common struggle. In Norway the feminist pressure groups had, since the 1880s, built up links with Radical Liberal and Labour parties which were keen to break away from Sweden. To a lesser extent elements of national pride rose to the surface in Australia, notably in 1902 when the federal vote was granted to women. In effect the campaign for the Australian federation ran simultaneously with the movement for women's suffrage, and since two of its territories had already enfranchised women before 1902, the Commonwealth came under pressure to follow suit if only to ensure fair representation between the component parts of the new state.[55] A sense of pride in the new political system, which followed English practice in some respects but also offered something distinctive, seemed to dictate that the Australian people should take their opportunity to set an example for the rest of the democratic world. In New Zealand such considerations were less evident in 1893, but they subsequently

---

[53] Anna Stout, 'Under the Flag', *Conservative and Unionist Women's Franchise Review*, Feb. 1910, 16; Sir John Cockburn, 'Under the Flag', May 1910, 32; 'Women's Suffrage in New Zealand', CUWFA, not dated.
  [54] *The Times*, 18 Dec. 1911.   [55] Oldfield, *Woman Suffrage*, 59–65.

assumed some importance. Politicians like Seddon certainly glowed with pride when visiting Britain: 'Today it was admitted that New Zealand was the brightest, the happiest and the most prosperous part of the Empire,' he claimed, 'and the women had had a great deal to do with bringing about that desirable result.'[56] No doubt this was the hyperbole of a man flattered to receive honorary degrees from British universities; but in a country that placed a high value upon the colonies such sentiments could not be easily brushed aside.

What conclusions may be drawn from the successes of suffragists abroad? In the first place they helped to add an element of novelty to a debate otherwise in some danger of growing stale. Secondly, they went some way to discrediting some of the wilder claims of the Antis, and thus forcing them to retreat to a less compelling argument to the effect that the vote would be especially inappropriate in Britain. Finally, the accumulation of experience from abroad was very good for morale; indeed, by the early 1900s it had created a sense of momentum and inevitability in suffragist circles. By 1913 even *The Times*, a consistent opponent, printed a flattering account of the enfranchisement of 600,000 women in California in 1911, which accepted that the high participation rate indicated that women really did want the vote and that one in six of all votes cast in Presidential elections now came from states in which women had become eligible.[57]

However, some qualifications must be made. Visits by Australasian witnesses during the Edwardian period coincided with the climax of the militant suffragette campaign which to some extent reduced their impact by diverting attention. Moreover, although the British suffragists managed to capitalize on colonial experience in their propaganda, it is less clear whether they learned any lessons from it. The Australasian successes confirmed the efficacy of constitutional methods, but also underlined the value of working with Liberal and Labour politicians.[58] Cooperation had also been easier where the reformers were able to start from a position of full adult suffrage for men. Once this hurdle had been cleared, it seemed less problematic to grant an equally democratic franchise to women, though since they constituted a minority of the population this was less of a challenge to the status quo than it would have been in Britain at this time. In both New Zealand and Australia the original proposals for female enfranchisement had been based on a property qualification which was quickly abandoned.[59] Yet the British suffragists

[56] Quoted in Grimshaw, *Women's Suffrage*, 120.
[57] Grossman, 'The Woman Movement in New Zealand', 45; Grimshaw, *Women's Suffrage*, 61; Oldfield, *Woman Suffrage*, 30–8.
[58] *The Times*, 31 Dec. 1913, 13.   [59] Oldfield, *Woman Suffrage*, 17.

showed themselves reluctant to draw the obvious conclusions from all this. Their Australasian counterparts had avoided too close an association with the cause of single women, and recognized what their political allies saw as essential, namely that the incorporation of wives would simultaneously democratize the electorate and help to reassure sceptical politicians.

5

Conservatism: The Unexpected Ally

BY tradition the movement for women's enfranchisement has appeared to be a pre-eminently Liberal cause. Throughout nineteenth-century Europe feminists identified their chief enemies in the forces of Conservatism entrenched in state and church. Consequently the vicissitudes of the suffragist movement in Britain have largely been seen in terms of a debate within the Radical-Liberal-Socialist side of politics. Scholars have identified Liberal or equal rights feminism, Socialist Feminism, and Radical Feminism, but not *Conservative* feminism.[1] In the process Conservatism has been regarded as a more or less fixed obstacle. This is unfortunate because it is only by taking account of the fluctuating relationship between the suffrage cause and Conservatism that one can adequately explain both the setbacks and, more significantly, the advances enjoyed by the movement in Britain.

It is easily forgotten that although the early male champions of the cause were typically Liberals like Mill and Bright, many of the *female* leaders of suffragism were Conservatives: Frances Power Cobbe,[2] Lilias Ashworth Hallet,[3] Helen Blackburn, Emily Davies,[4] Isabella Tod, Louisa Twining, and Sophia Jex Blake.[5] In addition, others, though associated with Liberalism by family of origin or marriage, moved sharply to the right during their campaigning for the vote, notably, Lydia Becker who was described on her death as a Conservative 'at least in her late years', and Millicent Fawcett who became a Liberal Unionist.[6] In both cases the change of loyalty reflected not only their

---

[1] But see Joan K. Kinnaird, 'Mary Astell and the Conservative Contribution to English Feminism', *Journal of British Studies*, 19 (1979).

[2] Caine, *Victorian Feminists*, 125–6.

[3] Ashworth Hallett went so far as to promote a pro-suffragist Liberal candidate in order to split the vote of an anti-suffragist Liberal at Bath in 1873; see *Women's Suffrage Journal*, 1 Nov. 1873, 158.

[4] Caine, *Victorian Feminists*, 57–60, 85, 97.

[5] Twining was one of the organization's Vice-Presidents; *Conservative and Unionist Women's Franchise Review*, Feb. 1910.

[6] *Women's Suffrage Journal*, Aug. 1890 (the memorial issue on Becker's death); Rubinstein, *Before the Suffragettes*, 117–19.

exasperation with Gladstone's prevarication over the suffrage, but also a wider and more fundamental disillusionment with popular political participation, a phenomenon which was crystallised by the controversy over Irish Home Rule. Emmeline and Christabel Pankhurst travelled even further from their ideological roots on the left, as their association with Radical Liberalism and the Independent Labour Party under the influence of Dr Richard Pankhurst gave way to an increasingly pro-Conservative stance during the Edwardian period; this was more than simply a matter of passing irritation with Liberal governments, for in 1918 Christabel stood for parliament as a 'Couponed' candidate of the Coalition Government on a platform to the right of the average Tory, while her mother actually became an official Conservative Party candidate in 1927.[7]

The Conservative Rationale

In explaining Conservative suffragism two questions arise: how far did they share attitudes in common with Liberal suffragists, and to what extent did they develop a distinctively Conservative rationale for women's enfranchisement? From the outset of the campaign an element of self-interest was apparent in the speed with which some Tories appropriated the conventional Liberal arguments: 'the axiom that tax and representation should go hand in hand is a Constitutional and Conservative one'.[8] 'It was not so much a question of the rights of women', commented one Tory member, 'as of the rights of property.'[9] This was an understandable reaction in the aftermath of the 1867 Reform Act which, under what now appeared the reckless machinations of Disraeli, had initiated the enfranchisement of huge numbers of comparatively poor workingmen. Some Conservatives, anxious to avoid any further lurch in this direction, now argued that it would be wrong to deny property its right of representation under the Constitution merely because it happened to be partly in female hands.[10] Consequently, during the 1870s many Conservatives contemplated the possibility of deriving a party advantage from a carefully restricted measure of female enfranchisement, much to the suspicion of the Liberals.

However, while taking note of cynical calculations about the electoral implications, one should not overlook the more reputable Conservative

---

[7] Pugh, *Women's Movement*, 44–6.
[8] *Women's Suffrage Journal*, 1 Jan. 1873, 2, quoting a letter in *The Standard*, 2 Dec. 1872.
[9] *Hansard, HC Deb.*, 3rd Series, CCI, 4 May 1870, c. 234–5.
[10] *Hansard, HC Deb.*, 3rd Series, CCXI, 1 May 1872, c. 66.

rationale for votes for women. This involved two main elements, first, a distinctive idea about the vote itself, and, second, an appreciation of the nature of the female gender. Conservatives naturally refused to consider the question primarily as a matter of abstract or individual rights; for them the vote seemed less to do with rights than with *duties*.[11] Frances Power Cobbe expressed the case for the vote in terms of strengthening the state; suffragists, she urged, must demonstrate how enfranchisement would 'tend to the stability and prosperity of the State and to the maintenance of social order and religion'.[12] Similarly John Buchan claimed that since anyone who bore the burdens of the state was entitled to be a full citizen, it was logically impossible for a Conservative to exclude anyone merely on grounds of their sex.[13] Explicitly repudiating the liberal view, Lord Robert Cecil declared: 'I have never argued for women's franchise on the grounds of the interests of women.... The important thing to consider in the suffrage question is ... what good it will do to the Kingdom and the Empire at large.'[14] According to Cecil women possessed a stronger sense of public duty than men and ought, in any case, to place whatever special knowledge they had at the service of the state.

The other feature of the Tory view consisted in a belief in the inherently conservative nature of women. 'I confess I have always thought that the female part of the population showed a great reverence for law and order, and was more deeply imbued with religious feelings', observed one of the early Tory suffragists. This thesis became the core of Lord Salisbury's influential speech in 1886 in which he claimed that women were as qualified for the vote as men in terms of their knowledge, training, and character, and that 'their influence is likely to weigh in a direction which, in an age so material as ours, is exceedingly valuable—namely in the direction of morality and religion'.[15] Millicent Fawcett exploited this opportunity to pander to the fears of right-wing politicians in her articles and speeches: 'there can be little doubt, as questions approach which threaten the stability of public order, and with the advance of Socialism and the "red" tinge, [that] the vast majority of women will rally to the side of the maintenance of the authority of the law'.[16]

---

[11] See e.g. A. J. Balfour's reply to Christabel Pankhurst, 23 Oct. 1907, Balfour Papers, BL, Add. MS 49793.

[12] Cobbe in Stanton (ed.), *Woman Question*, p. xvi.

[13] John Buchan, 'Women's Suffrage: A Logical Outcome of the Conservative Faith', *Conservative and Unionist Women's Franchise Review*, Jan. 1911, 84.

[14] Lord Robert Cecil, 'Women's Sphere', *Conservative and Unionist Women's Franchise Review*, Nov. 1910, 65.

[15] *Hansard, HC Deb.*, 3rd Series, CCVI, 2 May 1871, c. 114; Salisbury's speech, 29 Nov. 1886.

[16] *Englishwoman's Review*, 15 Oct. 1890, quoted in Rubinstein, *Different World*, 139; Millicent Fawcett, 'Women's Suffrage: A Reply', *The National Review*, 11 (1888), 45.

Addressing the annual Conservative conference in 1891, she asked: 'what new forces were they prepared to bring against the anarchy, socialism and revolution which were arrayed against them?'[17] This theme had originally become fashionable in the context of the Irish nationalist agitation, but it continued to figure prominently in right-wing rhetoric in the Edwardian period as a result of industrial militancy and the rise of the Labour Party. It led the Tory suffragists into increasingly bold claims about the female temperament as fundamentally antagonistic not only towards Socialism but to any novel or extreme ideas; Socialism was held to be a threat to marriage and family life because it would encourage the state to encroach upon parental duties towards their children.[18] By portraying women as inherently anti-Socialist the Tory suffragists directly challenged the current Anti-Suffragist propaganda which presented women as highly susceptible to Socialism on account of their political ignorance and gullibility. After 1906 the Antis assumed that as a result of what they saw as the growing influence of Socialists on the Liberal Government, complete adult suffrage had become much more likely. But the suffragists countered by arguing that a bill to enfranchise one and a half million female householders would offer a *safeguard* against adult suffrage. Any subsequent extension of the male electorate would inevitably raise the issue of sex equality; but since the inclusion of all adults would create a female majority in the electorate, to which virtually all politicians remained opposed, the preference would be for maintaining the status quo.[19]

On the other hand, Tory suffragists also attempted to minimize the issue of votes for women by presenting it as something the party could take in its stride: 'the intelligent Conservative', commented Fawcett, 'looks facts in the face'. They drew upon the Party's record of reform to justify their current stance. In an article entitled 'Women's Suffrage: A Logical Outcome of the Conservative Faith', John Buchan insisted that the Party had an honourable history of promoting evolutionary reform. 'Any competent political historian will agree with me,' claimed Lord Robert Cecil, 'that the Conservative Party has consistently advocated the extension of the franchise to all those who belong to the same position ... as those that already possess it.'[20]

However, over time the Conservative case for female enfranchisement became much less distinctive. This emerges from the evolution of

[17] *The Times*, 25 Nov. 1891, quoted in Rubinstein, *Different World*, 39.

[18] Gilbert Samuel, 'Women's Franchise: A Safeguard Against Socialism', *Conservative and Unionist Women's Franchise Review*, May 1910, 31.

[19] Ibid. 30.

[20] Quoted in Buchan, 'Logical Outcome', 84; Millicent Fawcett Oct. 1911, 148; Address by Lord Robert Cecil, CUWFA, 1908, 6.

A. J. Balfour's attitude. He had accepted that once the agricultural labourers had been enfranchised in 1885 it became 'quite ludicrous to attempt a distinction of principle between one set of adults and another'.[21] But Balfour went further when he argued that government by consent implied that no significant class of people should be left feeling that they had been denied a legitimate share of influence. Similarly Lord Lytton pronounced that the purpose of the electoral machinery was to return a House of Commons 'representative of all interests in the country which will be affected by the laws that Parliament passes', and, therefore, to tax or to legislate without women's consent was 'straining the theory of our Constitution'.[22] These were impeccably *Liberal* arguments. In his correspondence with Christabel Pankhurst, Balfour also followed the feminists' rationale when he admitted that parliament had increasingly involved itself in the regulation of labour, and that as a result 'it may be productive of injustice to allow one sex to legislate for the other. I think this argument, so far as it goes, quite unanswerable.'[23] His logic here was reminiscent of Mill's in his famous speech in 1867. Since that time many Conservative ladies had been radicalized by the social changes affecting women in Britain. One Dame of the Primrose League, for example, complained about the exclusion of women from certain forms of employment which she denounced as grandmotherly legislation detrimental to women's interests.[24] Her views were reflected by the Conservative and Unionist Women's Franchise Association which advocated the vote partly on the grounds that many women had to take up professions because they were obliged to support themselves and their dependent relatives.[25] Other Tory suffragists chose to emphasize changes in the agenda of politics, much as Liberals and Socialists did. Lady Castlereagh pointed out that since the state had already invaded the home it had become anomalous to exclude women from national politics; in any case there was no evidence that political participation undermined their femininity or domesticity. Cecil expressed the same view when he observed that women could scarcely be held competent to discuss the rates but not to hold views on the taxes.[26] In effect, by the Edwardian period Conservative suffragism had become largely subsumed within the broader case propounded by Liberals and feminists.

[21] A. J. Balfour to Christabel Pankhurst, 23 Oct. 1907, Balfour Papers, BL, Add. MS 49793.

[22] Lord Lytton, 'Votes for Women', 1909, 3.

[23] A. J. Balfour to Christabel Pankhurst, 23 Oct. 1907, Balfour Papers, BL, Add. MS 49793.

[24] Mrs Mitchell, 'Women's Place in Politics', 1903, 11.

[25] 'Why Conservative and Unionist Women Want the Vote', CUWFA, not dated.

[26] Edith Castlereagh, 'The True Meaning of Women's Suffrage', *Conservative and Unionist Women's Franchise Review*, Feb. 1910, 14; Lord Robert Cecil, 'Women's Sphere', 64.

The Leadership's Influence

No doubt the significance of the Conservative case for enfranchisement must be qualified by the absence of any official party policy on the subject. For many years the Anti-Suffragist cause was vigorously upheld by leading Tories including Henry Chaplin, Sir Michael Hicks Beach, Walter Long, Austen Chamberlain, and Lord Curzon. However, this was much less damaging than it appeared at first sight because of the consistent support for women's votes given both by the Party organization and by a succession of Leaders. Disraeli, Sir Stafford Northcote, Lord Salisbury, A. J. Balfour, and Bonar Law all with varying degrees of enthusiasm and qualifications declared in favour of the cause. Naturally these party leaders were fully alive to considerations of party advantage: would women vote Conservative, how far was it expedient to encourage Conservative women to participate in electoral work, and could the suffrage issue be exploited so as to embarrass the Liberals without exacerbating divisions in their own party? A good example of this last tactic occurred in 1884 when ninety-five Tory members suddenly turned out to vote for a women's amendment to the Liberal reform bill, which Gladstone had strongly condemned.

In spite of this, however, the leaders' attitude cannot be satisfactorily explained in terms of parliamentary manoeuvring. In the case of Disraeli, for example, his sympathy for female enfranchisement pre-dated by many years both his own leadership of the party and any realistic expectation of electoral advantage.[27] In fact Disraeli approached the question relatively unencumbered by conventional ideas about the separate spheres; if, as seems likely, he was bisexual, it is less surprising to find him unimpressed by Victorian notions about masculinity, and thus more willing to recognize that women's qualities and talents were as appropriate in the world of politics as men's.[28] At all events, by the 1860s the suffragists regarded him as an uncomplicated supporter of the enfranchisement of propertied women, despite his failure to speak or vote in favour of Mill's amendment in 1867. In 1873 in an attempt to capitalize on his sympathy, they presented him with a memorial signed by eleven thousand women thanking him for his support. They hoped to elicit some further indication of his views, and Disraeli duly obliged; if the parliamentary vote could be extended to male householders, he replied, it could

---

[27] *Hansard, HC Deb.*, 3rd Series, XCIX, 20 June 1848, c. 950; he argued that women were already involved in Church and State as churchwardens, landowners, peeresses, and monarchs, so that there appeared no obvious grounds for excluding them from the vote.

[28] Robert Blake, *Disraeli* (Methuen, 1966), 13–17.

hardly be withheld from female householders: 'as I believe this anomaly to be injurious to the best interest of the country, I trust to see it removed by the wisdom of Parliament'.[29] Lydia Becker endeavoured to flatter him, perhaps partly with a view to embarrassing the Liberal Leader: 'Mr Disraeli writes a simple, straightforward letter, and we know what he means,' she complained, 'we do not know exactly what Mr Gladstone means.'[30] In fact, Disraeli meant little more than that he had no fears about enfranchising a limited number of women who possessed a property qualification; but his support remained personal and in no way committed his party. On his return to office in 1874 he gave no further help to the suffragists, leaving the issue to his backbenchers as before.

Yet Disraeli turned out to be less eccentric over women's suffrage than contemporaries supposed. Much the most unlikely suffragist was his successor, the third Marquess of Salisbury. In view of the disparaging attitude he had adopted over the enfranchisement of male householders in 1867, Salisbury might have been expected to have been a virulent Anti-Suffragist on the grounds that women would simply accelerate the deterioration of the electorate by increasing the numbers of ignorant and gullible voters. However, during the 1870s and 1880s Salisbury gradually acquired a more mature view of democratic political systems, as it emerged that even the propertyless elector could be led to vote for traditional institutions and causes including the empire, the monarchy, the established church, religious education, and the Union with Ireland. This was demonstrated strikingly at the general election of 1886 when Irish Home Rule suffered a heavy defeat at the hands of a recently expanded electorate. According to Lady Frances Balfour, loyalist Irish ladies played their part in the defence of the Union in 1886 by appearing on platforms in England to render first-hand accounts of terrorism in Ireland.[31] By the 1890s thousands of Primrose League ladies regularly participated in election campaigns, in the process becoming an integral part of the party's organizational machinery.[32]

Salisbury also showed himself aware of the wider implications of the women's claim to the vote. Always quick to see when Radical policies lacked a popular mandate, he could hardly fail to notice that there was little or no organized demand for one-*man*-one-vote. While he had no intention of initiating or accelerating the enfranchisement of women, Salisbury appreciated

---

[29] *Englishwoman's Review*, July 1867, 199; Disraeli to Gore Langton, MP, 29 Apr. 1873, *Englishwoman's Review*, July 1873, 218.

[30] *Women's Suffrage Journal*, 1 Feb. 1874, 18.

[31] Lady Frances Balfour, *Ne Obliviscaris*, i. 116.

[32] Martin Pugh, *The Tories and the People, 1880–1935* (Oxford: Blackwell, 1985), 70–93.

that it might be a useful expedient for obstructing the Liberals when, as seemed inevitable, they demanded complete male suffrage. At that stage the Conservatives would be able to argue that over the years women had demonstrated a far more genuine demand for the vote than the unenfranchised men; this would justify incorporating them into a bill as a counter-weight to the additional working-class males.[33] The advantages for the Conservatives in a compromise of this kind had been demonstrated in 1885 in the deal between the Tory-dominated House of Lords and the Liberal government. Meanwhile, as prime minister after 1886 Salisbury suffered little or no pressure to initiate legislation for women's suffrage. The Primrose League abstained from adopting a policy on the question, while the National Union of Conservative and Constitutional Associations, though pro-suffragist, had no pretensions to determine party policy. Thus, by expressing his sympathy for the cause, Salisbury managed to conciliate his own female suffragists while leaving the Liberals to bear the brunt of suffragist pressure.

Happily for the Conservatives these tactics continued to be expedient throughout the Edwardian period both because the election of 1906 raised expectations which Liberal prime ministers refused to fulfil, and because the Pankhursts conveniently adopted a militantly anti-Liberal policy. But the suffragism of Balfour, who succeeded Salisbury in 1902, became more than merely tactical, even if his manner of expressing his views was more convoluted than that of most politicians. He had spoken for the cause in the 1892 debate, but admitted thereafter his reluctance to take the initiative over constitutional reform; he simply believed that if and when further reforms were undertaken, women ought to be included. Yet for some time he remained unconvinced that any widespread sense of grievance existed among women; and in view of the divisions over the issue between his colleagues, not to mention his own precarious position as party leader, he declined to offer any firm lead.[34] In time, however, Balfour lost some of his caution; in 1911, for example, he was photographed at a by-election signing a women's suffrage petition.[35] Both Balfour and his successor, Bonar Law, voted for the Conciliation Bills in 1910 and 1912. As early as 1902 Bonar Law had agreed to serve as a Vice President of his local Women's Suffrage Association in Glasgow, and when tackled by Lord Cromer on behalf of the Antis he insisted that he considered himself pledged to support the Conciliation Bill.[36]

[33] In taking this view Salisbury was simply being consistent; Rover, *Women's Suffrage*, 106, misinterprets his speech of 15 Oct. 1891 as a retreat from earlier support.

[34] A. J. Balfour to Christabel Pankhurst, 23 Oct. 1907, Balfour Papers, BL, Add. MS 49793.

[35] *Votes for Women*, 28 Apr. 1911, 490.

[36] Glasgow and West of Scotland Association for Women's Suffrage, minutes, 25 Oct. 1902; Lord Cromer to Lord Curzon, 18 Jan. 1912, Curzon Papers, BL, F112/35.

The significance of these expressions of support by successive Tory leaders must not be exaggerated. They evidently played a waiting game, leaving the Liberals to tear themselves apart over the issue; and when in office they studiously avoided giving any assistance to the suffragists in parliament. Nonetheless, the fact that the Conservatives aroused lower expectations than the Liberals should not obscure their contribution to the gradual advance of the cause. In effect the sympathy of the leaders deprived Anti-Suffragism of the firm hold it might otherwise have had on what was, after all, its most natural body of supporters. From the earliest days it became perfectly respectable for backbench Tories to take up women's suffrage bills, as was done by William Forsyth in 1874, Baron Dimsdale in 1888, Sir Albert Rollit in 1892, C. Madona in 1895, F. Faithfull Begg from 1896 onwards, Colonel Denny in 1903, and Sir James Agg-Gardner in 1912. Initially, they were a beleaguered minority within the party, but by the mid-1880s circumstances had conspired to make fresh converts among the Conservative rank and file.

The Breakthrough for Tory Suffragism

Not the least of the reasons for regarding the late 1880s as a turning-point for the suffragist cause was the reaction by the Antis to what appeared to be a sharp deterioration in their own position within the Conservative ranks. This was epitomized by the shrill complaints of Professor Goldwin Smith in 1888 when he accused the Conservatives of 'political fatalism' and 'political cowardice'. He warned the party leaders against attempting to repeat the tactics used by Disraeli in 1867, that is, appealing to one class or section in order to outvote another, and thereby outmanoeuvre the Liberals; 'this shallow Machiavellianism prevailed', he claimed, 'and the floodgates of democracy were opened by Conservative hands'.[37] He therefore urgently called on Conservatives to take a stand against Socialism and demagoguery, and 'be the means of saving the nation from dismemberment'.

But what had provoked this outburst? The immediate trigger may have been the women's suffrage debate at the party's annual conference, though this was simply the culmination of a process that had been going on since at least 1883 when the Primrose League had been founded. In establishing this organization neither Lord Randolph Churchill nor his associates had intended to create opportunities for female participation in politics; they simply envisaged a livelier and more effective organization than the official

---

[37] Goldwin Smith, 'Conservatism and Female Suffrage', *The National Review*, 10 (1888), 73–7.

one, and in particular a means of generating the volunteers who had suddenly become essential as a result of the restrictions imposed upon local election expenditure in 1883. Quite unintentionally the founders tapped a rich vein of female activism and aspiration among titled ladies including the Duchess of Marlborough, the Marchioness of Londonderry, Lady Jersey and Lady Knightley of Fawsley. For such women the transition from acting as political hostesses among the elite to coordinating propaganda and entertainment for the masses proved to be remarkably smooth. Indeed, many of these ladies demonstrated more skill and appetite for popular politics than their husbands for many of whom it had often been a tiresome duty.[38] Consequently, many aristocratic women joined the Primrose League without thought for the long-term implications for their sex, while others from lower down the social scale followed their example once respectability had been conferred upon female participation by titled ladies. Eventually women comprised around 49 per cent of the League's huge membership, and one in four of all the Habitations in England and Wales was led by a female Ruling Councillor. Middle and upper-class women enjoyed a key advantage because of their abundant leisure time, which, once placed at the disposal of the Primrose League, made them in due course an indispensable element in the popular organization of Conservatism.[39] By the 1890s the League had become an advertisement for the political talents of women, trumpeted by feminists and ruefully conceded by the Liberals. For while the Dames of the Primrose League devoted much effort to purely social events, they also proved successful at extending the Party's organization into unpromising urban and working-class districts once thought to be Radical strongholds. Their reputation grew perhaps fortuitously as a result of their role in the crucial election of 1886 when, to the relief and delight of the Conservatives, the Home Rule cause received a decisive rebuff. In the process the ladies had taken on the work of canvassing, conveying voters to the polls, locating 'removals' amongst the electors, and speaking from public platforms; they were, in short, far from merely decorative appendages of the machine. 'I consider women the best canvassers', declared Meresia Nevill, 'in as much as they are used to district visiting.'[40] In this way conventional notions about the separate spheres began to become blurred; and by the 1890s party agents and candidates had begun to acknowledge the extent to which they relied upon female assistance to retain their seats in parliament.

The implications of these developments for women's suffrage were very

---

[38] Pugh, *The Tories*, 47–8.   [39] Ibid. 49–51.
[40] *Primrose League Gazette*, 1 Oct. 1898; for similar examples, see 9 Jan. 1892 and 10 June 1893.

considerable, especially as they were taking place within those sections of society which considered it their duty to uphold conventional ideas and behaviour. Experience in the Primrose League helped to modify the attitudes of many Tory women and effectively set the foundations for the party's twentieth-century reliance on women's voluntary work. One Dame, writing in the Edwardian period, recalled the time when it had been considered 'an outrageous thing for a woman to make a speech', but pointed out that once Lady Londonderry had done it, the example was soon followed.[41] Even in the 1880s several ladies, emboldened by their success and flattered by politicians' praise, presumed to draw wider conclusions: 'It is not an age when "men must work and women must weep". . . . Women need not neglect their homes because they share the aims and aspirations of their husbands and fathers or brothers . . . the more women interest themselves in subjects of universal importance, the happier their homes are likely to become.'[42] Lady Knightley, a highly conventional Conservative lady, found herself transformed into a suffragist by her experience; in 1885, after months of hard campaigning to save her husband's seat, she watched him enter the local polling station on election day, and then: 'I felt—for the first time personally—the utter anomaly of my not having a vote.'[43] The fact that the Primrose League members abstained from adopting policies on such subjects as female enfranchisement was of comparatively little significance; if anything their loyalty and patience almost certainly strengthened their case in the eyes of Tory politicians. In fact many of the women active in the local habitations did debate the suffrage issue; and some, including the Scottish Grand Habitation in 1892, passed pro-suffrage resolutions; others quietly took it for granted that their work made enfranchisement inevitable in the long run. After the turn of the century they became increasingly active in suffrage organizations; Lady Knightley, for example, acted as President of the Conservative and Unionist Women's Franchise Association.

Female involvement in the party's electoral machinery placed Anti-Suffragist Conservatives in the embarrassing position of virtually apologizing for their role. 'I hardly consider it a woman's place to address a large meeting such as this,' protested Lady Londonderry on one occasion; even the redoubtable Anti, the Countess of Jersey, had to admit: 'women, whether they like it or not, are born members of the State . . . therefore it seems to us a matter of common sense that they should try to understand what is good for

[41] Mrs Mitchell, 'Women's Place in Politics', 1903.
[42] *Primrose League Gazette*, 29 Oct. 1887.
[43] Lady Knightley's Diary, 27 Oct. 1885, Northamptonshire CRO, Knightley Papers.

the State'.[44] This, of course, was precisely the line of argument previously used by suffragists; on such precarious foundations was Edwardian Anti-Suffragism based. Ironically, one of the reasons for the absence of an organized Anti-Suffrage movement during the 1890s was that so many leading Anti-Suffragist women were too busy with their political work!

No doubt there was another side to this coin. How many of the female activists were diverted from feminism through their eagerness to seize the opportunities offered by the party organizations, and how far did the male politicians merely take advantage of their efforts? However, it is easy to be misled by undue cynicism. Many of the women, especially on the Conservative side, were *not* feminists until their experience of political work opened their eyes; others, more on the Liberal side, had deliberately pioneered women's party organizations as a means of furthering their own aims. As for the male reaction, any assessment must allow for the passage of time. Many Tory politicians began to recognize that female participation in politics held few of the terrors claimed by Anti-Suffragists; women appeared genuinely appreciative of Conservative causes, showed a readiness to put national interests before sectional ones, and often proved more capable of withstanding the pressures of democratic politics than the men. As the Party slipped into the habit of dependence upon women's support during the 1890s, this inevitably began to be reflected in the official party organization. As early as November 1887 the National Union had adopted a resolution to the effect that 'the time has now arrived when the Parliamentary franchise may with perfect safety be extended to women householders'.[45] Subsequently annual conferences reaffirmed this view in 1889, 1891, 1894, 1907, and 1910, as did the party in Scotland in 1887, 1889, 1892, and 1896. Significantly, when Lord Salisbury uttered his celebrated speeches in support of women's suffrage in November and December 1888 he was *following* the initiative already taken at the party conference. Although his remarks may be read merely as an expression of gratitude for the work done by the ladies in campaigning against Home Rule, Salisbury went further than was strictly necessary when he declared: 'I can conceive of no argument by which [women] are excluded [from the franchise].' Though nothing in this constituted a formal party policy, it set the seal of approval on the suffragism of the National Union of Conservative and Unionist Associations. This is corroborated by the angry reaction of the Antis who decided that they must try to halt the trend towards suffragism by publishing their petition in the *Nineteenth Century* in 1889.[46]

---

[44] *North Star*, 4 Nov. 1895; *Primrose League Gazette*, 25 May 1890.

[45] *Women's Suffrage Journal*, 1 Dec. 1887, 39.

[46] According to Goldwin Smith, 'Salisbury is going to take hold of the skirts of the women to

However, if the opponents of the women's cause hoped to deter Salisbury from legislating they were aiming at the wrong target, for a government bill was not on the agenda. Their real problem—the gradual drift of rank and file Conservatives towards the women's cause—proved to be more intractable. By the Edwardian period it had become commonplace for prominent Tory ladies such as Lady Betty Balfour, the Countess of Selborne, and Lady Knightly to campaign either as members of or in cooperation with the non-militant suffragist societies, while the equally well-connected Constance Lytton achieved notoriety as a suffragette prisoner. Although friction between suffragists and politicians was associated largely with the Liberals, it is clear that some Tory women also withdrew active support from Anti-Suffragist candidates.[47] By 1914 the Conservative members appears to have become at least as pro-suffrage as their Liberal counterparts. Striking evidence of this trend survives in some of the surveys conducted by the regional organizations of the NUWSS amongst local Tory activists during 1912. For example, in the north-west of England they found thirty-eight of the fifty-one members of the Bootle Conservative Association Executive willing to sign a suffrage petition, in addition to thirteen of seventeen in St Helens, seventy-eight of the one hundred and one in Ormskirk, and all seventeen of those in Chester.[48] A similar pattern emerged in constituencies in the south-east of England; in Brighton sixty-four of the ninety executive members signed, while in Surrey, thirty-five out of forty-four in Reigate and thirty-nine out of forty-two in Dorking did so.[49] This consistent pattern corroborates the impression gained by the League for Opposing Women's suffrage which had begun to find the Conservative constituency associations most un-cooperative by this time. Lord Cromer complained that his organizers could 'get nothing done by the Unionist Agents', and that 'the apathy and want of intelligence amongst the Unionists generally is past all belief'.[50] Cromer had finally recognized the effects of twenty-five years of political activism by women within the Conservative Party.

save himself from falling', letter to Albert Grey, 1 Apr. 1889, in Arnold Haultain (ed.), *Goldwin Smith's Correspondence* (T. Werner Laurie, 1913), 221.

[47] Pugh, *The Tories*, 63–4.

[48] *Annual Report*, 1912, 19, 20, 31, West Lancashire, West Cheshire, and North Wales Federation NUWSS.

[49] *Annual Report*, Surrey, Sussex, and Hampshire Federation NUWSS, 1912–13; other Surrey branches also showed a consistent pro-suffrage majority: South Park (20 of 24); Meadowvale (9 of 13); Earlswood (25 of 28); Horley (24 of 32); Oxted (10 of 14); Limpsfield (19 of 24); Lingfield (20 of 33); and Godstone (6 of 8).

[50] Lord Cromer to Lord Curzon, 5 Feb. 1912, and 8 Feb. 1912, Curzon Papers, BL, F112/35.

Converting the Politicians

This long-term evolution at the grass-roots level enables the historian to make sense of the shift in favour of votes for women in the House of Commons during the 1890s. For the key element in that trend consisted in changes of attitude amongst Tory members. The magnitude of this can hardly be overestimated. When Mill introduced his amendment for female enfranchisement in 1867, 91 per cent of those Conservatives who voted were against him. During the period from 1867 to 1883 the Tory suffragists comprised a modest minority, usually between 15 and 35 per cent, of all Conservatives voting. However, the years between 1884 and 1908 effectively reversed the earlier pattern. In the seven divisions that took place, a majority of Conservatives supported women's suffrage on each occasion with the exception of November 1884. In 1897, 55 per cent of them backed the women's bill, and 59 per cent in the 1904 division.[51] Several qualifications must be made about this pattern. In some divisions, such as that in 1911, fewer than half the members actually voted; but when, as in 1897, a majority did participate, the suffragists remained ahead of their opponents, which means that the results cannot be explained on the basis that they won only when the Antis stayed away. It is also true that after 1908 the voting pattern became less consistent. In March 1912, for example, a majority of Tories opposed the Conciliation Bill, though largely as a temporary reaction to the resumption of militancy by the Women's Social and Political Union. Nor were most Tories as yet prepared to accept a reform that led to adult suffrage, which explains their heavy vote against W. H. Dickinson's Bill in 1913 a measure which, by incorporating wives, threatened to impose a female electorate of six million.

Of course the pro-suffrage surge amongst Conservatives reflected the fact that as they started from a very low level there was plentiful scope for improvement. However, even a modest shift in their favour damaged morale among the Antis; and the gradual conversion of the Conservative members must be counted the greatest achievement of the constitutional suffragists before 1900.

The Edwardian years saw an acceleration of the campaign with the formation of the Conservative and Unionist Women's Franchise Association (CUWFA) in November 1908. This reflected the fact that Conservative women had become just as frustrated as their Liberal counterparts by the

---

[51] This includes the votes of Liberal Unionists who were officially merged with the Conservative Party in 1912.

patronizing prevarication of male politicians. But several immediate pressures were also responsible for this initiative. 1908 saw the establishment of the Men's and the Ladies Leagues for Opposing Women's Suffrage, which were, to a large extent, run by Conservatives, and thus threatened to push the Party back into the Anti-Suffragist camp. Another factor lay in the political situation. The return of a huge Liberal–Labour majority in 1906 made women's enfranchisement appear, if not imminent, at least inevitable, and it was therefore important for Conservatives to avoid being outflanked on the issue; party interest dictated that when the vote was eventually granted, Conservatives, rather than being purely obstructive, should exert some influence on the extent and nature of the measure. The more the House of Commons supported women's bills, the more the House of Lords, with its overwhelming Tory majority, loomed as the ultimate obstacle; in the long run it would only damage the Party's standing with women if Conservative ladies were seen to follow the men in flocking into the Anti-Suffragist organizations.[52]

At Millicent Fawcett's suggestion the Conservative women, who had been active in the National Union of Women's Suffrage Societies for some time, carried their own banner in the Union's procession in June 1908. At their invitation Lady Knightley became President of the new organization until 1910 when Lady Selborne took over. The CUWFA soon produced a catalogue of aristocratic Vice-Presidents and patrons to rival those of the Antis.[53] Their objects were to use constitutional methods to promote the return of Conservative candidates favourable to the enfranchisement of 'all duly qualified women', and to prepare women to exercise the franchise in the near future—a warning to the Party that it might be dangerous to die in the last ditch on this issue.[54] The Association's tactics involved questioning candidates and distributing propaganda; but it strongly denied the accusation made by *The Times* that it intended to withhold electoral assistance from MPs who opposed the Conciliation Bill.[55] Above all the Tory suffragists attempted to turn the parliamentarians' fears about adult suffrage to their advantage by warning that as Asquith was being edged gradually towards a manhood suffrage bill, it was becoming urgent for the Conservatives to

[52] See Lady Knightley in *The Queen*, 29 Aug. 1908.

[53] Including the Duchess of Sutherland, the Countesses of Huntingdon, Galloway, Meath, and Fingal, Lady Castlereagh, Lady Rayleigh, Lady Willoughby d'Eresby, Lady Betty Balfour, and Lady Robert Cecil.

[54] *Sunday Times*, 8 Nov. 1908; *The Queen*, 28 Nov. 1908.

[55] *The Times*, 3 July 1910; Lady Betty Balfour did resign from her local association in protest over the opposition of the MP for Chertsey; *The Common Cause*, 10 June 1909, 119.

create a new equilibrium which would avert this danger: 'the extension of the Franchise to women is . . . a distinctly Conservative measure'.[56]

The chief value of the CUWFA probably lay in spiking the guns of the Antis who naturally expected to recruit extensively among Conservatives. When Mrs Humphry Ward accused Tory suffragists of being false to their party she was rebuked magisterially by Lady Selborne—a daughter of Lord Salisbury and thus a woman of impeccable political credentials; as she observed, suffragism in the party went back at least to Disraeli's time and thus pre-dated the organization of the Antis by decades.[57]

On the other hand, the Antis exploited any opportunity to embarrass the Tory suffragists by highlighting their association with disreputable elements in both the labour movement and the militant campaign. This was especially a problem after 1911 when militancy reached its most extreme forms. 'It shakes the very foundation on which society exists,' admitted Lord Robert Cecil, one of the staunchest Tory suffragists, 'it is in the nature of a rebellion.'[58] However, the hostile reaction provoked by militancy should not be exaggerated; it did not deter the annual conference from continuing to pass pro-suffrage resolutions for example. The social and political prominence of the Conservative militant, Lady Constance Lytton, probably went some way to mitigating the outrage felt in party circles. While her brother, the Earl of Lytton, described suffragette methods as 'inexpressibly painful and distressing', he vigorously defended their use on the grounds that after forty years of effort the suffragists had to find some means of dispelling the inertia of the parliamentarians.[59] Both Cecil and Lytton hoped to find a way through the parliamentary impasse via the Conciliation Bill, but after its failure in 1912 the split amongst leading Tories became increasingly public. At the end of 1911 *The Times* had published rival letters, one from Austen Chamberlain, Walter Long, and F. E. Smith urging the abandonment of the Conciliation Bill strategy, and another signed by Alfred Lyttleton, George Wyndham, George Cave, Hugh Cecil, and Robert Cecil among others, advocating continued support.[60] Unfortunately, the breakdown of the Bill in 1912 forced the Tory suffragists to face what they had hoped to avoid, namely, the marked preference of their Liberal allies for a more democratic measure that would enfranchise married women. Cecil objected that this would incorporate

---

[56] 'Adult Suffrage or Woman Suffrage: Which Is It To Be?' CUWFA, not dated; Editorial, *Conservative and Unionist Women's Franchise Review*, Feb. 1910, 11.

[57] Lady Selborne, *Conservative and Unionist Women's Franchise Review*, Jan.–Mar. 1912, 183.

[58] Speech to the Actresses Franchise League, *Votes for Women*, 10 Nov. 1911.

[59] Lord Lytton, 'Votes for Women', 1909, 6.

[60] *The Times*, 5 Dec. 1911, and 8 Dec. 1911.

many who could not qualify under the existing system by residence or by property ownership, and thus, in effect, accelerate the introduction of adult suffrage.[61] However, although this view was backed up by the CUWFA, the Tory suffragists failed to maintain an agreed policy.[62] Though preferring a limited measure, Lady Selborne saw no real danger in creating a vote for married women. Her husband argued persuasively that 'as a party the Conservatives would reap most benefit from the enfranchisement of wives. As a rule they would vote with their husbands, thus giving the married men much greater power at the polls than the single men. And surely the family is the foundation of Conservatism.'[63] In their willingness to come to terms with a more democratic reform the Selbornes were shrewd though somewhat ahead of the field; their attitude heralded their party's acceptance of the proposals made by the Speaker's Conference in 1917.

Meanwhile, despite these complications, the cause continued to prosper in the Conservative ranks during the last two years of peacetime. This view is corroborated by the private correspondence of the Anti-Suffragists. Arnold Ward, for example, admitted to Lord Curzon that the suffragists were still making converts among leading Tories. In a private conversation with Cecil, Walter Long, who has been incorrectly assumed by historians to have been a wartime convert, indicated that he had come to favour granting the vote to what he called 'municipal women'.[64] Cromer attributed the difficulties of the Antis to the refusal of Bonar Law to help them which, he claimed, had 'produced a very considerable effect upon the subordinate ranks and has more or less hypnotised the Unionist Agents'.[65] But Law himself had been outstripped as a suffragist by his predecessor, Balfour. In a conversation with Hannah Mitchell at a WSPU meeting in 1908 the then Tory Leader not only expressed his admiration for their campaign but also put a 'generous donation into the collecting box'.[66] Whereas in his 1907 correspondence with Christabel Pankhurst, Balfour had expressed himself doubtful whether women generally desired the vote, by 1911 he had accepted that the demand really existed and concluded that it must be met.[67] This helps to explain why

[61] Lord Robert Cecil to Maud Arncliffe-Sennett, 19 Jan. 1912, Arncliffe-Sennett Papers, BL, C 10.245; Lord Robert Cecil, *Conservative and Unionist Women's Franchise Review*, Oct. 1911, 145.

[62] *Conservative and Unionist Women's Franchise Review*, Jan.–Mar. 1912, 168.

[63] Lady Selborne, *Conservative and Unionist Women's Franchise Review*, July–Sept. 1912, 214, and Lord Selborne, Jan.–Mar. 1913, 258.

[64] Arnold Ward to Lord Curzon, 5 Feb. 1913, Curzon Papers, BL, F112/36; Lord Robert Cecil to Lady Selborne, 23 July 1914, Bodleian Library: Selborne Papers D 422.

[65] Lord Cromer to Lord Curzon, 5 Feb. 1912, Curzon Papers, BL, F112/35.

[66] *Labour's Northern Voice*, Nov. 1952, in Mitchell Papers, Manchester Central Library, M220/4/30.

[67] A. J. Balfour to Lady Betty Balfour (copy), Apr. 1914, Fawcett Letters, FL, 89/2/50.

speculation had arisen by 1911 as to whether the Party was about to adopt a formal policy for female enfranchisement.[68] Although this seems unlikely, it was clearly taken seriously by the Antis, judging by their private correspondence during 1913 and 1914.[69] So confident were Lytton, Cecil, and Lady Selborne by 1912 that they engaged in negotiations with Catherine Marshall of the NUWSS in order to try to establish the form in which women's enfranchisement would be most acceptable as Conservative policy; a referendum seemed to them a probable ingredient at that stage.[70] Although no agreement was reached in these talks, the political value of the exercise lay in the very fact that leading Conservatives were now considering adopting a policy. For by this time the NUWSS had also secured a firm commitment from the Labour Party. This made a deal with the Conservatives extremely desirable. On the one hand, the suffragists wished to avoid alienating any of their members who disliked the link with Labour. On the other hand, Conservatives wanted to check any drift of female activists towards Labour. Above all, the prospect that the National Union might reach agreement with both Labour *and* the Conservatives threatened to place the Liberals in an embarrassingly isolated position, and to undermine still further Asquith's standing in his own party. By the time war broke out in August 1914 no official change had been made in the Conservative position; but it is impossible to avoid the conclusion that Anti-Suffragism had become a fading force within the party by that time.

[68] *Pall Mall Gazette*, 7 May 1911.
[69] Arnold Ward to Lord Curzon, 5 Feb. 1913, Curzon Papers, BL, F112/36.
[70] 'Absolutely Confidential' Memorandum, not dated, Catherine Marshall Papers, Cumbria CRO; see also Lord Selborne to Lord Robert Cecil, 30 May 1914, Bodleian Library: Selborne Papers 79, fo. 189.

6

Liberalism: The Unexpected Enemy

IN the context of party politics women's suffrage was one of the outstanding paradoxes of the late Victorian era: a pre-eminently liberal cause which was persistently thwarted by influential Liberals. After the initial, and largely Liberal, launch of the suffrage campaign in the 1860s, a number of the supporters who had been attracted to the cause, partly by sheer respect for John Stuart Mill, retracted, and, as a result, the debate over votes for women became to a large extent an argument within the ranks of Liberalism. What made the relationship between Liberalism and suffragism so complicated were the inconclusive attempts by Liberals to weigh the significance of the growing support for the cause expressed by Conservatives; in the process questions of principle became hopelessly entangled with considerations of party advantage.

Why, then, was votes for women so strongly supported by some British Liberals and yet so stubbornly resisted by many of them right up to 1914? For the parliamentary reformers of the 1860s the enfranchisement of women initially appeared as a logical extension of their Radical Liberal faith. After all, the purpose of Liberalism was to abolish artificial restrictions on individual liberty; they assumed that to maintain unearned privileges and advantages for any section of the community must be contrary to the public interest as well as placing a check on the realization of individual talent. Opposition to the women's vote was, in Henry Fawcett's words, 'based on the fallacy that man possessed a superior kind of wisdom which enabled him to decide what was best for the other half of the human race.' Liberal intellectuals challenged the separate spheres ideology on the basis that until women had gained real freedom no one would know what they were actually capable of; at present, as Mill argued, 'what is called the nature of woman is essentially an artificial thing—the result of forced repression in some directions, unnatural stimulation in others'. For Liberals, women's interests were bound to suffer under the political status quo because, to quote Jacob Bright: 'Representation always means protection; protection is more necessary for the weak than for the strong.'[1]

Viewed as a question of principle, then, the women's case exercised an overwhelming appeal to many Liberal writers, academics, and intellectuals of the mid-Victorian era, and it is thus hardly surpri...ng that 62 of the 73 MPs who supported Mill's suffrage amendment in ... as Liberals. However, Mill appreciated that parliament as a w... ...ided major issues in terms of abstract arguments. In an... ...ry Liberal Party of the 1860s continued to be d... ...sons of peers and gentlemen of leisure ... ...ptions of their Conservative or... ...ls had killed a very mod... ...nd the elect- orate for ... ...' to natural rights in fa... ...trating at some length. ... ...because they lacked a... ...'ic life would be bene... ...ien's case to the conv... ...ed representation up... ...'- uals; following this... ...sec- tion of society, espec... ...physical facts such as gender. T... ...claim that con- tributions to taxation a... ...Professor Thorold Rodgers, a Liberal memb... ...e franchise could logically be refused to women. Th..., g...ted that franchise on the payment of rates.'[4] Mill virtually appropriated the language used by Gladstone in his famous pale-of-the-constitution speech in which he had argued that only those who were personally unfit or a political danger should be formally excluded from the electorate; for good measure Mill threw in the reminder that during the recent controversy over Gladstone's reform bill, women, unlike men, had not held 'great meetings in the parks or demonstrations at Islington'.[5]

Thus, in its initial stages the women's campaign in parliament relied

---

[1] *Hansard, HC Deb.*, 3rd Series, CLXXXVI, 20 May 1867, c. 835; J. S. Mill, *The Subjection of Women* (Longmans, 1869); *Hansard, HC Deb.*, 3rd Series, CCI, 12 May 1870, c. 622.

[2] B. L. Kinzer, A. Robson, and J. M. Robson (eds.), *A Moralist In and Out of Parliament* (Toronto: University of Toronto Press, 1992), 91, 130; Joseph Hamburger, *Intellectual in Politics: J. S. Mill and the Philosophic Radicals* (New Haven: Yale University Press, 1965), 81.

[3] *Hansard, HC Deb.*, 3rd Series, CLXXXVI, 20 May 1867, c. 828.

[4] Quoted in *Women's Suffrage Journal*, 2 June 1873, 103.

[5] *Hansard, HC Deb.*, 3rd Series, CLXXXVI, 20 May 1867, c. 818–19.

heavily on a small but dedicated band of Liberal members: Mill, Henry Fawcett, Sir Charles Dilke, Leonard Courtney, James Stansfeld, Professor James Stuart, Peter Taylor, Duncan MacLaren, and William Woodall. The virtue of their contribution lay in the fact that these politicians were actually prepared to take risks to promote women's interests. Even those who served in government defied the whips over women's suffrage legislation from time to time. For example, Fawcett, who was Postmaster General, twice failed to vote with the rest of the Liberal cabinet.[6] Stansfeld became best known as a consistent champion of Josephine Butler's campaign to repeal the Contagious Diseases Acts.[7] Though Gladstone tolerated Stansfeld's views when he served as a minister during 1871–4, he noticeably failed to include him in the 1880 government; in effect he had sacrificed a promising ministerial career for the women's cause. Another rising Radical, Dilke, also experienced difficulties of this sort before his career was eventually destroyed by a divorce scandal. In 1869 he had been the original instigator of the proposal to incorporate women into the municipal electorate, though it was Jacob Bright's amendment that was actually adopted.[8] In June 1884, although a member of Gladstone's cabinet, Dilke refused to respect the agreed policy which was to oppose William Woodall's amendment designed to include women in the government's franchise bill. Dilke fully anticipated having to surrender his office over this; indeed, Lord Hartington attempted to force his resignation, but was frustrated by an intervention by Gladstone who suggested that Dilke might be allowed to continue 'if his colleagues concurred'.[9]

To some extent rebellion was comparatively easy in this period due to the ineffectiveness of whipping in the House of Commons, though party control grew tighter partly because of the expansion of government business and because of the development of constituency organizations and pressure from the local activists. This is not, however, a complete explanation. The survival of Dilke and Fawcett owed a good deal to Gladstone's indulgence towards them on an issue with which he did not particularly sympathize. It seems likely that however troublesome these Radicals were to him, he felt reluctant to dispense with them altogether. His own position as Leader rested partly on his peculiar ability to act as a bridge between the rival wings of Liberalism,

---

[6] See the discussion in Lawrence Goldman (ed.), *The Blind Victorian: Henry Fawcett and British Liberalism* (Cambridge: Cambridge University Press, 1989).

[7] J. L. Hammond and Barbara Hammond, *James Stansfeld: A Victorian Champion of Sex Equality* (Longmans, 1932).

[8] Notes for an Autobiography, Dilke Papers, BL, Add. MS 43931, fos. 33–5; Notes on the Municipal Franchise, Dilke Papers, BL, Add. MS 43909, fo. 116.

[9] Sir Charles Dilke to Mrs Paterson, 16 Jan. 1885, Dilke Papers, BL, Add. MS 43906, fos. 94–5; Notes for an Autobiography, Dilke Papers, BL, Add. MS 43938, fos. 174–8.

and his cabinets already listed markedly towards the traditional, Whiggish elements. Thus, though reluctant to concede more than minor offices to men like Stansfeld, Dilke, and Joseph Chamberlain, he nonetheless found their inclusion in the cabinet as representatives of rank-and-file Liberalism essential. Moreover, Gladstone could not escape the fact that from the outset women's suffrage attracted support well beyond the ranks of middle-class Radicalism; it enjoyed the backing of several well-connected Liberal families including Lord Amberley, the son of Lord John Russell, whose wife, Kate, so enraged Queen Victoria by advocating female enfranchisement from a public platform in 1870, also the Earl and Countess of Aberdeen, and Rosalind, the Countess of Carlisle. Although women such as Lady Aberdeen and Lady Carlisle remained loyal to the Liberal Party, they refused to be browbeaten into abandoning their work for the women's vote.[10] Their social standing combined with their political connections conferred a measure of respectability on the cause especially in the early stages when it was still a novelty.

The Waning of the Radical Impulse

Against this background of Liberal enthusiasm, how are we to account for the embittered relationship that developed between the Party and women's suffrage? To some extent it reflected the dashing of the high expectations originally entertained in the late 1860s. 'I do not believe that the Liberal Party as a party cares a straw for the interests and wishes of women,' concluded Lydia Becker, 'their profession of Liberalism and desire for government founded on popular consent . . . sound a mockery.' Frances Power Cobbe chose to blame Gladstone whom she variously described as 'the evil genius of our sex', 'our ruin', and 'our arch enemy'.[11] Even the veteran Radical, John Bright, came out in opposition to female enfranchisement in 1876 which Millicent Fawcett described as 'a great blow to the movement'.[12] As late as 1906 the suffragettes still complained about the 'great Liberal betrayal of 1885' by way of justification for the adoption of militancy.[13]

[10] Marjorie Pentland, *A Bonnie Fechter: The Life of Ishbel Marjoribanks, Marchioness of Aberdeen and Temair* (Batsford, 1952), 100; Charles Roberts, *The Radical Countess: The History of the Life of Rosalind, Countess of Carlisle* (Carlisle: Steel Brothers, 1962), 114–18.

[11] Blackburn, *Women's Suffrage*, 41; Frances Power Cobbe to Lydia Becker, 5 Aug. 1885, 26 Nov. 1885, Becker Papers, Manchester Central Library, M50/1/2.

[12] *Westminster Review*, 122 (1884), 189.

[13] Teresa Billington-Greig, 'The Militant Policy of the Women Suffragists', 12 Nov. 1906, Fawcett Library, Billington-Greig Papers, Box 404, file 3.

To some extent the suffragists' frustration was borne out by the Liberals' parliamentary record on the issue. Despite the promising start in 1867, the MPs as a whole proved stubbornly resistant to suffragist persuasion. In eleven parliamentary divisions between 1867 and 1883 the total number of Liberals actually voting for female enfranchisement fluctuated between 61 and 103; although they comprised the bulk of the suffragist vote at this stage, they represented only a minority of the Party. On six of the eleven occasions more Liberals voted against than for women's suffrage, and in the other five the pro-suffrage margin was modest. In short, though the campaign had achieved a solid base in the party, by the early 1880s support seems to have reached a plateau. This may be attributed in part to the hostility shown by the Liberal leadership, and also by the politicians' perception of the cause as lacking popular support in the country. In any case, the initial enthusiasm shown by some Liberals was misleading, for the success of the activists in pushing the issue regularly onto the agenda in the 1870s eventually provoked their opponents, who had kept quiet, into declaring themselves now that the matter had to be taken seriously.

But why were so many hostile? Of course, many Liberals simply shared the assumptions and prejudices of their sex and their class about women's abilities and their role in society. But some features of Liberal Anti-Suffragism do seem distinctive to Liberalism. The influence of Positivist thinking on several staunch Anti-Suffragists, including Joseph Chamberlain, Henry Labouchere, and Randall Cremer, led them to take the conventional emphasis on family life to extremes; they believed that unless women stuck to their domestic role the whole institution of the family would be destroyed.[14] Also, many Radicals, of whom John Bright, John Morley, and Randall Cremer were typical examples, saw women through the perspective of anti-clericalism. On the assumption that women were naturally prone to emotionalism, they were thought to be highly susceptible to the influence of the clergy and to the appeal of ritualism. 'No doubt many of them are priest-ridden,' wrote Goldwin Smith, 'and female suffrage would give a vast increase of power to the clergy.'[15] This was an entirely natural fear for those Radicals who wanted to promote a secular system of education in the face of entrenched Catholic and Anglican opposition. Similar concerns in France, Belgium, and Australia inhibited Liberals and Radicals from supporting votes for women. As late as 1911 when the Asquith cabinet was attempting to resolve its differences on

---

[14] See the discussion in Harrison, *Separate Spheres*, 40.
[15] 'Female Suffrage', *Macmillan's Magazine*, 30 (1874), 145; Howard Evans, *Sir Randall Cremer: His Life and Work* (T. Fisher Unwin, 1909), 342.

the issue, the Party's organization delivered a damning piece of advice: 'religious bigotry will find a ready response among the women'.[16]

However, though influential with vocal minorities of Liberals, these fears were probably of less importance than long-term changes in the party political system. During the 1860s and 1870s the Liberal Party was still in the process of evolving from a multitude of provincial interests and radical pressure groups each clamouring for its chosen cause, and each anxious to use the national party as a vehicle for achieving sectional objects. The emergence of the women's movement in the form of a series of single-issue pressure groups during the late 1850s and 1860s must be seen in this context. Many of the feminists emerged from impeccably Liberal backgrounds; they and their male relatives had participated in earlier campaigns for temperance, anti-slavery, peace, and the repeal of the Corn Laws. They continued this tradition often with conspicuous success, achieving a reform of the divorce law (1857), the municipal franchise (1869), several Married Women's Property Acts (1870–82), the repeal of the Contagious Diseases Acts (1886), and the appointment of female inspectors for the poor law (1872) and factories (1892). But from the perspective of the party managers, and especially Gladstone, these Liberal connections were precisely the problem: by pursuing single-issue tactics the feminists exacerbated the incoherence which already afflicted Liberalism. This manifested itself in a lack of discipline in parliament, and also played into the hands of the Conservatives by encouraging them to accuse the Liberals of representing sectional not national interests. Feminist campaigners in the Ladies National Association for the Repeal of the Contagious Diseases Acts also antagonized the party leaders by employing tactics used by the temperance reformers, that is, interventions at by-elections with a view to splitting the vote of candidates who refused to adopt their policy.[17] This history of friction between parliamentarians and pressure groups helps to explain the extreme hostility shown by the Liberal organization towards the Pankhursts when they intervened in by-elections after 1906.

Several prominent Liberal suffragists, notably Mill, Fawcett, and Courtney, also exacerbated concerns about the party's tendency towards fragmentation by their advocacy of proportional representation at this time. During the late Victorian era proportional representation was not generally seen—as it came to be during the twentieth century—as a means for ensuring fair representation for parties, but rather as a device for allowing the intelligent and informed voter to save independent-minded politicians who disagreed

---

[16] Bishop George Frodsham, 'The Women's Parliamentary Franchise in Practice', *The Nineteenth Century*, 74 (1913), 984; J. Renwick Seager, Nov. 1911, PRO CAB 37/108/148.

[17] Josephine Butler, *Personal Reminiscences of a Great Crusade* (Horace Marshall, 1898), 151, 178.

with their party from being eliminated from parliament by the party machine. By promoting the return of independents the reform thus threatened to institutionalize the Liberal tendency to disintegration which so irritated the party managers; it suggested the nightmare of a party effectively comprising single-issue Radicals like Fawcett whom Gladstone once castigated as 'totally unable to work in concert with others'.[18] For Gladstone proof of the dangers of 'faddism' came in the shape of the shocking Liberal defeat—the first since 1841—at the general election of 1874.

That setback also highlighted the concern among Liberals about the steady expansion of the *male* electorate in the late Victorian period; for the more mixed their reactions to mass democracy in general, the more hesitant their attitude towards women voters was bound to become. A watershed was reached in the mid-1880s when the third reform act extended the county electorate by two-and-a-half million to produce a total of 5.7 million voters. Though the immediate result of this was a Liberal victory in the election of 1885, it fell somewhat short of expectations because Liberal gains in the counties were balanced by Conservatives gains in the towns; then followed the disastrous defeat over the Home Rule Bill at the 1886 election which, despite a narrow victory in 1892, excluded the party from effective power for the next twenty years. These events delivered a severe blow to Liberal confidence. 'There is no more unwelcome fact for Liberals', commented one MP, 'than that popular institutions have not always and not everywhere been a success.'[19] Consequently, by the mid-1880s many Liberal intellectuals were already in full retreat from the buoyant radicalism they had displayed in the 1860s. Their disillusionment over the popular electorate reflected not simply the party's electoral setbacks, but also a repugnance for the changes *within* the party in the shape of the greater pressure to conform which came from rank and file members as well as from the parliamentary leadership. This had major implications for women's suffrage in that several of Mill's original supporters, including Professor Goldwin Smith, A. V. Dicey, Professor Thorold Rodgers, and James Bryce, shared these misgivings and became vocal Anti-Suffragists. Some flatly repudiated the rhetoric they had previously employed. 'It is not because men pay rates and taxes, or even occupy property, that they have votes,' insisted Edward Leatham, MP, 'but because they are men.'[20] Violet Markham, whose father stood as a Liberal candidate and whose brother was a Liberal MP, became a prominent opponent of the cause

---

[18] Quoted in Goldman, *The Blind Victorian*, 86.

[19] *Hansard, HC Deb.*, 3rd Series, CCLXXXIX, 12 June 1884, c. 102.

[20] Ibid., c. 103, 166; see also Christopher Harvie, *The Lights of Liberalism* (Croom Helm, 1976), 195.

partly as a result of her general distaste for electoral politics: 'Liberal though I am,' she admitted, 'there are times when the ignorance, the apathy, the utter lack of discrimination in the class to whom we have handed over the governing power fill me with despair.'[21]

In a sense the original rationale about the link between citizenship and taxation, used so freely by Liberals, had worked rather too well by encouraging Conservatives to see women as a means of extending the representation of property within the electorate. No doubt some Liberals had always hidden their purely partisan motives about the vote behind conventional arguments about the role of women in society. Osborne Morgan, MP, admitted that he 'believed Thackeray was right when he said that every woman was a Tory at heart'.[22] As Conservative suffragism began to strengthen, deeply prejudiced Liberals such as Henry Labouchere found it only too easy to damn the cause by association: 'I thought that a Liberal should pause before going into such company.'[23] Though female Conservatism had been a matter of mere speculation in the 1870s, during the 1880s the conspicuous success of the Conservatives in recruiting thousands of women into the Primrose League appeared to substantiate Labouchere's warnings. They gained further credence when Lord Salisbury—in Liberal eyes an arch-reactionary who had resigned from the Tory government in 1867 in protest against its reform bill—endorsed female enfranchisement in 1888. Nor were these fears groundless. In both 1866–7 and 1884–5 the Conservatives had taken advantage of Liberal initiatives on the franchise so as to modify the legislation in ways that conferred long-term advantages on their party. It increasingly appeared to Liberals that Salisbury intended to repeat this manoeuvre by inserting a carefully contrived measure of female suffrage into some future bill with a view to frustrating the reformers by giving additional weight to property-owners.

The Gladstone Factor

However, for contemporary suffragists all these problems paled into insignificance beside the anti-suffragism of W. E. Gladstone, the party leader. Gladstone started from the conventional separate-spheres approach to the subject: 'A vast difference of type has been impressed upon women and men

---

[21] Violet Markham's diary, 24 Jan. 1898, BLPES: Markham Papers 17/4.

[22] *Hansard, HC Deb.*, 3rd Series, CCXI, 1 May 1872, c. 55; this was countered by Sir Wilfred Lawson who pointed out that voting in Wyoming suggested that women divided along party lines as men did: *Hansard, HC Deb.*, 3rd Series, CCLXXXIX, 12 June 1884, c. 175.

[23] Ibid., c. 172.

respectively by the Maker of both ... the fear I have is lest we should invite her unwittingly to trespass upon the delicacy, the purity, the refinement, the elevation of her own nature.'[24] However, Gladstone, who had begun his career as 'the rising hope of the stern unbending Tories', changed his mind over many issues during his long life; and he certainly gave repeated signs of doing so over votes for women. At the very least his attitude was far more complicated than his critics acknowledged. As we have already seen, in his capacity as party leader Gladstone naturally regarded the women's movement as an unwanted complication; but equally he felt obliged to meet the claim for the vote half-way just as he had done earlier in dealing with the challenge of the National Liberal Federation. What really infuriated feminists was the ease with which the Liberal Leader adopted inconsistent positions on the vote, and raised hopes only to dash them. In part this may have been because he wished to avoid alienating politically active women and feared being outflanked by Disraeli, while on the other hand he shrank from allowing a handful of enthusiasts to push him into a policy which was still dangerously in advance of public opinion. Keeping on terms with both sides in any controversy was almost essential to Gladstone's strategy for maintaining Liberal unity, however irritating it seemed to the partisans.

Yet Gladstone's inconsistency arose from more fundamental causes, notably the sheer intellectual pleasure he derived from forcing his mind around all the arguments and counter-arguments involved in each issue. As a result it often proved difficult to know whether he was speaking as prime minister, as party leader, or as the tutor in an academic seminar. Suffragists tried in vain to read his mind on its tortuous path through successive suffrage debates. When, for example, in 1870 Jacob Bright's bill unexpectedly won a second reading majority by 124 to 91 votes, the Home Secretary, H. A. Bruce, indicated that the government was neutral on the issue; but when the bill went into Committee Gladstone intervened and used the whips to secure its rejection by 220 to 94 votes.[25] Yet in the following year he raised hopes by giving a sympathetic speech in which he emphasized that the impropriety of ladies attending polling stations was 'an objection of great force'; since Gladstone was proposing to remove this obstacle by introducing the secret ballot, which he successfully did in 1872, it looked as though he was preparing to adopt women's suffrage.[26] In addition he approved of the recent admission of women to school board elections and accepted that Bright had thereby

---

[24] W. E. Gladstone to Samuel Smith, 11 Apr. 1892.

[25] Blackburn, *Women's Suffrage*, 106–7.

[26] *Hansard, HC Deb.*, 3rd Series, CCVI, 3 May 1871, c. 90–1; *Women's Suffrage Journal*, 1 Aug. 1872, 105.

established 'a presumptive case' for granting the parliamentary franchise. He also criticized the leading Anti-Suffragists for failing to see beyond the interests of the upper classes who did not need the vote themselves. Gladstone particularly drew attention to the growing number of women who supported themselves and assumed the responsibilities for dependants which men were generally assumed to carry; this seems to indicate that he had become fully aware of the shortcomings of the separate spheres approach. Gladstone even agreed with Bright that women not only faced greater difficulty in the labour market than their male competitors but were often denied employment in occupations in which they could perform as well as or better than men. Finally, he cited the divorce law of 1857, in which he had taken an active part, as an illustration of the 'gross inequality' in the treatment accorded to the sexes by parliament.

In spite of all this Gladstone declined to vote for Bright's bill! Yet his words were suggestive: 'If it should hereafter be found possible to arrive at a safe and well-adjusted alteration of the laws as to political power, the man who shall attain that object . . . will, in my opinion, be a real benefactor to his country.'[27] Enigmatic as these words sound, they express just the kind of convoluted and qualified sympathy for reform which he had uttered on the subject of votes for *men* in the 1860s. Lydia Becker had some grounds for describing his speech as Gladstone's 'half-conversion'.[28] Unhappily, when he next intervened in 1874 it was to oppose the suffrage bill! By that time Becker and her colleagues had heard enough Gladstonian equivocation to convince them that he was guilty of calculated obfuscation.[29] The sorry process of alienating women from the Liberal Party was now underway.

Like most radicals Becker found it hard to appreciate that Gladstone's mind functioned like an oil-tanker—its capacity was huge and it proved very slow to turn itself around. But for all that it was in motion, and Gladstone continued to show himself tantalizingly alive to the political potential of women. In his famous speeches in the Midlothian Campaign in 1879–80 he went out of his way to appeal to them. In an address to a ladies demonstration at Dalkeith, for example, he argued that the current controversy over the 'Bulgarian Atrocities' committed by the Turks involved *female* interests; he declared: 'in appealing to you to . . . play your own part in this political crisis we are making no inappropriate demand, but are beseeching you to fulfil the duties which belong to you, which, so far from involving any

[27] *Hansard, HC Deb.*, 3rd Series, CCVI, 3 May 1871, c. 92–5.
[28] *Women's Suffrage Journal*, 1 Jan. 1873, 2.
[29] Ibid., 1 Feb. 1874, 18.

departure from your character as women, are associated with the fulfilment of that character'.[30] In effect he was here rebutting one of the central tenets of Anti-Suffragism, namely the incapacity of women to comprehend major issues of foreign and imperial policy. But in the short run nothing came of this. Gladstone again disappointed suffragist hopes in 1884, only to come up with the suggestion of allowing women to vote by means of a proxy in 1885; Becker, who by now should have known better, hailed this as the 'removal of the last formidable obstacle'.[31]

In retrospect the suffragists' chief grievance against Gladstone was his intervention in 1884 when he killed what some regarded as their best chance of success. This was because his bill to extend the householder and lodger franchises to the counties was a *government* measure, and thus almost certain to pass. A backbencher, William Woodall, proposed to add a women's amendment, but with the prime minister's approval the Liberal Chief Whip then circulated a memorandum to MPs threatening that the passage of Woodall's amendment would result in the abandonment of the bill and the resignation of the government.[32] Gladstone subsequently insisted that 'the cargo which the vessel carries is, in our opinion, a cargo as large as she can safely carry'.[33] This was a nautical way of saying that as the House of Lords was already anxious to reject the bill—which it did initially—the addition of a women's suffrage clause would be regarded as a perfect excuse by the peers. This interpretation gained further credence when Tory members suddenly rallied in Woodall's support; Viscount Folkestone, hitherto an Anti-Suffragist, mischievously urged support for the amendment while admitting he would not vote for it again.[34] The immediate effect of the prime minister's intervention was that 104 Liberal members who had previously pledged their support for female enfranchisement voted against Woodall; though some 32 Liberals defied Gladstone by supporting him.[35] However understandable, Gladstone's action probably did as much damage to the Liberal Party as to women's suffrage for it encouraged leading campaigners like Fawcett and Becker to focus more on the Conservatives, and it exacerbated the ill-will which was to culminate in the confrontations between the Pankhursts and successive Liberal Home Secretaries during the Edwardian period.

[30] Quoted in *Women's Suffrage Journal*, 1 Jan. 1880, 7.
[31] *Women's Suffrage Journal*, 2 Feb. 1885, 19–20.
[32] H. C. G. Matthew, *The Gladstone Diaries*, xi. *1883–6* (Oxford: Clarendon Press, 1995), 144.
[33] *Hansard, HC Deb.*, 3rd Series, CCLXXXIX, 10 June 1884, c. 1959.
[34] Ibid., 12 June 1884, c. 121–2.
[35] Blackburn, *Women's Suffrage*, 165.

Gladstone also dominated the politics of the 1880s through his adoption of Home Rule for Ireland in 1886 which split his party by driving out both the Whigs and Joseph Chamberlain. This, too, had major indirect implications for the women's cause. Most immediately it decimated Gladstone's supporters and excluded the Liberals from office until the end of 1905 apart from a brief interval from 1892 to 1895. The results were mixed however. On the one hand, by weakening the party which had hitherto provided most of the parliamentary supporters for women's suffrage, Home Rule enhanced the significance of the Conservatives as a source of fresh recruits for the cause. On the other hand, by excluding the Liberals from office it helped to relieve the pressure on the party to adopt a policy on votes for women; and by modifying the relationship between Gladstone and the party in the country to the detriment of the former it proved helpful in the long run.

The withdrawal of a majority of the anti-reform Liberals in 1886 also promoted a rapprochement between the parliamentary Liberal Party and the National Liberal Federation (NLF); even Gladstone recognized the higher status now enjoyed by the NLF. Unfortunately for the suffragists this development failed to yield any short-term dividends because women had not been very prominent in the NLF before 1886. As a result the organization determined its priorities largely without female influence. Successive annual conferences endorsed a comprehensive set of electoral reforms including the abolition of plural voting, one-day polling, a reduced qualifying period for voters, and successive occupation for electors who moved into new constituencies. All this was calculated to help restore the party's electoral fortunes. But votes for women did not appear to be part of the solution; when Woodall and Stansfeld attempted to include the proposal in the NLF programme in 1889 they were heavily defeated.[36]

Home Rule also led to the creation of a new party, the Liberal Unionists, which comprised most of the Whigs and a handful of Radicals. Lord Hartington (later Duke of Devonshire) who led the Whigs, treated the subject of women's suffrage with a mixture of hostility and condescension, while Joseph Chamberlain, for all his Radicalism, loathed the idea; he once referred to the *Women's Suffrage Journal* as 'a truly awful periodical... he never rose from its perusal without a most depressing sense of inferiority'![37] Not surprisingly the Liberal Unionists as a group were the most hostile towards women's suffrage of any political party. However, the purge at least had the advantage of leaving Gladstonian Liberalism more amenable to reform after

---

[36] *Annual Report*, National Liberal Federation, 1889, 137.
[37] Gleefully quoted in *Women's Suffrage Journal*, 1 Feb. 1874, 25.

1886, though the full effects would not be felt until the party regained its former strength.[38] Unfortunately Liberal Unionism proved to be more complicated, for while its male leaders proved highly unsympathetic, the party
attracted a number of prominent female suffragists. The split helped to crys-
tallize the underlying conservatism of erstwhile Liberals such as Becker,
Fawcett, Kate Courtney, and Lady Frances Balfour whose resentment
towards Gladstone had been steadily increasing. In 1887 Fawcett refused to
join the Women's Liberal Federation executive, and she fought to prevent
political organizations from affiliating to the National Society for Women's
Suffrage for fear of giving it a pro-Liberal bias. From 1888 onwards she
attended Liberal Unionist meetings and by the 1890s was much in demand as
a speaker at Conservative and Unionist functions. Though skilful at expressing the case for female enfranchisement in terms acceptable to Conservatives, Fawcett played into the hands of Liberal Anti-Suffragists who wished to
damn the women's movement as a Tory front; her own meetings were sometimes interrupted by Liberals angered by her betrayal of the progressive
cause.[39]

The Women's Liberal Federation and the New Liberalism

Although in the short term Gladstone succeeded in imposing his Irish policy
on his party, the long-term significance of the split of 1886 lay in the way in
which it undermined his influence in the declining years of his career. His
retirement in 1894 owing to disagreements with the policies of his own cabinet underlines the point. The effect is obvious in the shift by John Morley,
originally a loyal Gladstonian and an opponent of votes for women, who had
emerged as a pro-suffragist by the turn of the century. The electoral defeats
of the 1880s and 1890s helped to end the careers of many older-generation
Liberals, leaving opportunities for younger men who had grown up with different assumptions about women's role in politics. By the 1890s Liberalism
had begun to change both intellectually and at the organizational level. The
gradual spread of the ideas of New Liberalism, which placed a greater
emphasis on state intervention, began to narrow the gap between national
politics and women's politics. More immediately, the emergence of the
Women's Liberal Federation in 1887 opened up a new front in the suffrage
campaign.

---

[38] *Annual Report*, National Liberal Federation, 1889, 137.
[39] Rubinstein, *Different World*, 117–19.

By the mid-1880s it had become evident that the Liberals were losing their traditional advantage over the Conservatives in terms of local organization and membership. The rapid expansion of the Primrose League after 1883 and its acknowledged contribution to the Tory victory of 1886 was relentlessly exploited by suffragist propaganda: 'now it is recognized that women are an element of strength in politics', claimed Becker.[40] But it was not until 1887 that the Liberals responded by establishing their own organization for women, a delay which reflected Gladstone's misgivings. Ever since 1877, when Chamberlain set up the National Liberal Federation with a view to radicalizing the party's programme and policy, Gladstone had devoted much of his efforts to limiting its influence. He was therefore fully alive to the threat posed by a similar organization for women. However, electoral decline had weakened his position by making the improvement of the organization an urgent necessity. In any case, local associations for women Liberals were being set up spontaneously; it therefore seemed wiser on balance to accept the inevitable and attempt to control it.

Thus the WLF began life in 1887 with Mrs Catherine Gladstone—no feminist—safely ensconced as President.[41] But in contrast to the ladies of the Primrose League, the Liberal women enjoyed effective control of their own organization from the outset, with their own council, executive, annual conference, programme, and publications. Their activity was ostensibly designed simply to equip the Liberals with the volunteer activists needed to compete with the Conservatives.[42] But it also provided a convenient means of bringing the wives, mothers, sisters, and daughters of Liberal politicians into regular contact with feminist ideas and recruiting activists for suffragism.

TABLE 6.1. The Women's Liberal Federation, 1887–1895

	1887	1889	1890	1891	1892	1895
Branches	63	96	133	177	367	448
Membership	16,500	33,500	45,350	51,734	77,014	82,000

Source: Annual Reports, WLF.

Not that the women failed to demonstrate their loyalty to orthodox Liberalism; their conferences endorsed Irish Home Rule, disestablishment of the

---

[40] *Woman's Suffrage Journal*, 1 June 1886, 76–7.

[41] She was no friend of women's rights; see Pat Jalland, *Women, Marriage and Politics 1860–1914* (Oxford: Oxford University Press, 1986), 200.

[42] On its work, see Emlyn Boys to Millicent Fawcett, 26 Sept. 1892, Fawcett Papers, Manchester Central Library, M50/2/26/29.

Welsh Church, Sunday Closing, and Local Option. Yet within a few years the priorities of the Federation had changed. Almost from the start the organization became the scene of a protracted struggle to foist votes for women upon the Liberal Party. In 1889 the suffragists attempted to include it in the objects of the WLF on the grounds that it was illogical for women to work for Liberal measures but not to try to secure direct political influence for themselves.[43] In 1890 the initiative was seized by the Countess of Carlisle who had declined to join the WLF in 1887 because it was not pledged to women's suffrage. Her 1891 resolution instructing the executive to campaign for the women's vote was lost by 266 to 201 votes.[44] But in the same year the Scottish WLF took the lead by adopting a constitution which defined its aims as 'to secure just and equal legislation and representation for women, especially with reference to the Parliamentary Franchise, and the removal of all legal disabilities on account of sex'.[45] Meanwhile Gladstone, perhaps uncertain of his reception, refused Lady Aberdeen's requests to address the annual conferences. The year 1892 proved to be the turning-point. A major increase in local branches, boosted by the approach of a general election, helped to tip opinion in favour of the suffragists. As a result the WLF accepted Lady Carlisle's proposal that the executive should promote votes for women but stop short of making it a test question for Liberal candidates; local branches were encouraged to organize deputations to their members and candidates to seek their support.[46] The Liberals' success at the subsequent election accentuated dissatisfaction because it left many women feeling that they were being taken for granted by the party; and they reacted angrily when many Liberal members voted against the suffrage bill introduced by Sir Alfred Rollit in that year. Gladstone only exacerbated matters by tactlessly writing a letter, which was circulated by the Anti-Suffragists, in which he rehearsed most of the traditional arguments against enfranchisement.[47] Yet Gladstone found himself conceding two of the suffragists' claims; it was, he admitted, 'impossible to deny that there have been and are women individually fit for any public office, however masculine its character'. He also accepted that 'as legislators [we] have been most unfaithful guardians of [women's] rights to moral and social equality. And I do not say that full justice has in all things yet been done.' In short, while adopting the Anti-Suffragist line Gladstone appears to have been

[43] *Annual Report*, Women's Liberal Federation, 1889, 4.   [44] Ibid., 1891, 5.

[45] Scottish Women's Liberal Federation, executive minutes, 5 May 1891.

[46] *Annual Report*, Women's Liberal Federation, 1893; Scottish Women's Liberal Federation, executive minutes, 21 Apr. 1892 (the executive decided by only seven votes to five not to make it a test question).

[47] W. E. Gladstone to Samuel Smith, 11 Apr. 1892.

preparing the ground for a strategic retreat, but still taking refuge in the plea that public opinion was not yet ripe. His conversion to women's suffrage was probably not far off; but after years of equivocation his comments only antagonized the suffragists, and by this stage he was losing his ability to prevent further reform not only on women's issues but on the wider Radical programme.

By 1893 the WLF had formally declared that 'the time has now come when the extension of the Parliamentary Franchise to women should be included in the programme of the Liberal Party, seeing that this measure is one which is based on essentially Liberal principles'.[48] As a result Mrs Gladstone withdrew from the Presidency, to be replaced by the loyal but pro-suffragist Lady Aberdeen; she, however, quickly departed when the Earl was appointed Governor-General of Canada. If this was a ploy by Gladstone to get the Aberdeens off the scene it backfired, for it allowed Lady Carlisle to move up from the Honorary Secretaryship to the Presidency. At this stage a minority withdrew from the WLF to form the Women's National Liberal Association, taking around 10,000 members and 50–60 branches, because it felt unwilling to antagonize the party leadership over female suffrage. This of course left the WLF even more militantly pro-suffrage and accentuated its pressure on the party. From 1895 a debate took place nearly every year, initiated by Eva MacLaren and Mrs Cobden Unwin, on whether the Federation should withhold assistance from Anti-Suffrage Liberal candidates. Though initially rejected by margins of more than two-to-one, the sanction was eventually adopted in 1902.[49] In fact some local branches had already imposed women's suffrage as a test question; delegates from Hull justified their action thus: 'we are not Liberals first and suffragists afterwards; we are Suffragists because we are Liberals'.[50] To many activists it seemed they were wasting time by passing annual resolutions; increasingly they wished to concentrate on the vote to the exclusion of all else—a sentiment which, ominously for Liberals, heralded the outbreak of the suffragette campaigns.

During the later 1890s the feminists effectively used the WLF to promote the cause within the wider Liberal Party. In 1897 the general committee of the National Liberal Federation, meeting at Derby, adopted a women's suffrage policy, a decision which was reaffirmed in 1899.[51] But the cause was now benefiting from more than just the decline of Gladstonianism; for by this time

---

[48] *Annual Report*, Women's Liberal Federation, 1893, 10–11.
[49] Ibid., 1896, 38; 1898, 40; 1899, 17–28; V. Munro-Ferguson to Millicent Fawcett, 12 Feb. 1896, Fawcett Letters, Fawcett Library, 89/1/20.
[50] *Annual Report*, Women's Liberal Federation, 1899, 17.
[51] Ibid., 1898; Women's Liberal Federation, *News*, Dec. 1899.

feminists were working with the grain of Liberal thinking. The WLF programme encompassed not just the vote but a range of feminist social reforms
including the removal of protective legislation, equal pay for women, equality in the divorce law, abolition of the state regulation of vice, and the entry
of women into the police forces.[52] The Liberal women now showed a general
bias in favour of state intervention and a sympathy for trade unions which put
them on the left of the party.[53] They were one of several movements leading
the party towards the 'New Liberalism' around the turn of the century.
Women's contribution to this process was an empirical as much as an ideological one, reflecting their involvement in experiments at municipal level
designed to relieve poverty and improve living conditions. In 1894 for example, the Federation reported that at least 240 of its members had been
elected to local authorities that year, and the organization clearly functioned
as part of the broader campaign to promote female participation in local
government.[54]

   This trend towards interventionism also explains why suffragists like
Fawcett, who adhered rigidly to a laissez-faire ideology, found Conservative
politics more congenial in this period. Some Radicals had always anticipated
that women's suffrage and social reform would advance together; according
to James Stansfeld female enfranchisement would 'have the effect of concentrating the mind of the public and our legislators upon the great social
reforms'.[55] The truth of this was to become apparent after 1906 when a Liberal government embarked upon a series of major innovations from school
meals to old age pensions and maternity allowances. At that stage it was hard
to deny that women had a contribution to make; social reform became the
bridge between local and national politics across which women could
advance without posing a fundamental threat to conventional thinking about
gender.

Edwardian Suffragism and Liberal Decline

As a result of the WLF's decision in 1902 every by-election candidate found
himself subjected to a scrutiny of his views not only on votes for women but
also on the state regulation of vice. The first candidates to be rejected for
failing to meet these criteria were T. A. Brassey (Devonport) in November

   [52] *Annual Reports*, Women's Liberal Federation, 1892, 5–6; 1893, 11–13; Women's Liberal
Federation, *News*, May 1894, 5–6.
   [53] Women's Liberal Federation, *News*, 1893, 3.
   [54] *Annual Report*, Women's Liberal Federation, 1895, 12.   [55] Ibid., 1889, 137.

1902 and Colonel Seeley (Isle of Wight).[56] The minutes of the Scottish WLF show that the same policy was followed north of the border, though few candidates were proscribed, probably because Scottish Liberals had been more generally converted, and the SWLF tactics were to bargain rather than force a confrontation; even Winston Churchill, a notably wayward suffragist, appears to have won their endorsement at Dundee in 1908.[57] Altogether, in twenty by-elections during 1904–5 the WLF granted its support officially to only 13 candidates, often after extorting written pledges; it formally repudiated five.[58]

At a time when the party was attempting to heal the divisions between Liberal Imperialists and 'Pro-Boers' arising out of the South African War and also implement a new electoral pact with the Labour Representation Committee, the suffragists' sanctions represented an unwanted complication. The friction between the Federation and the politicians throws some light on the party's extraordinarily hostile reaction to the Women's Social and Political Union whose members sought pledges on votes for women prior to the general election of 1906. The refusal to answer questions at public meetings and the violence used by stewards to eject suffragette interruptors appear both illiberal and counter-productive; but the politicians' behaviour is explicable in the context of developments since 1902. In effect, Mrs Pankhurst, who had herself contemplated joining the executive of the WLF in 1892, was extending the pressure already being applied to the party by its female members. Though the Liberal leaders found the non-cooperation of Liberal women highly embarrassing, they could hardly prevent a tactic which had been democratically adopted by an autonomous Liberal organization. They therefore vented their anger on the Pankhursts who were presented as stooges of the Tories.

Despite this friction between the parliamentarians and the suffragists, political trends during the Edwardian period conspired to raise the expectations of the Liberal suffragists. At its conference in May 1905 the NLF overwhelmingly carried a women's suffrage resolution which it reaffirmed in 1907 and 1908.[59] Though this did not commit a Liberal government, it effectively obliged even a stubborn opponent of votes for women like H. H. Asquith, who became prime minister in 1908, to allow his cabinet ministers

---

[56] Women's Liberal Federation, *News*, Nov. 1902, Apr. 1904; for other refusals, see Women's Liberal Federation, executive minutes, 30 June 1911, 31 Oct. 1911.

[57] Scottish Women's Liberal Federation, executive minutes, 20 Dec. 1905, 1 Feb. 1909, and 2 Apr. 1914 for opposition to Asquith.

[58] Women's Liberal Federation, *News*, 1905, 3.

[59] *Annual Report*, National Liberal Federation, 1905, 66.

to speak freely on the issue; by now Asquith was in a minority in his cabinet, in parliament, and in the party organization.

The Liberal landslide at the 1906 election boosted the cause by returning four hundred Liberal and 29 Labour members. When Charles MacLaren, MP, took a deputation to see the new prime minister, Campbell-Bannerman, the response was decidedly friendly. Though making no promises about legislation, Campbell-Bannerman acknowledged that the traditional arguments against women's suffrage had lost their force as a result of female participation in local government, parliamentary elections, and royal commissions; and he agreed that current political issues such as fiscal reform, education, housing, and temperance fell well within their sphere: 'In my opinion, therefore, you have made out before the country a conclusive, irrefutable case.'[60]

In view of this it was bad tactics for the suffragettes to heckle the Liberal Leader during 1905–6. When Lady Aberdeen wrote to dissociate the WLF from such actions he merely replied: 'no cause can be benefited by what is nothing more than a composition of vanity and bad manners'.[61] But in acrimonious debates at the NLF some delegates argued that it was simply unreasonable to expect the government to enfranchise women while the WSPU subjected it to regular attack.[62] The significant thing is that many women Liberals refused to be embarrassed by suffragette tactics. Eva MacLaren thought they were 'effecting a revolution which neither the Women's Suffrage Society nor the Women's Liberal Associations have ever achieved'; and Lady Carlisle rebuked Liberal politicians for overreacting to interruptions at their meetings: 'we must not be so thin-skinned'.[63]

The suffragists' impatience was well founded, for as a result of the election the balance had shifted sharply in their favour; a House of Commons division in 1908 recorded 273 votes for enfranchisement and only 94 against. The exact loyalties of Liberal members, however, remained unclear because of abstentions and some switching of votes. After the election of December 1910 the WLF calculated that 195 of the 272 Liberals elected supported votes for women, based on assurances given to their local associations. However, this appears optimistic by comparison with a National Union of Women's Suffrage Societies estimate in 1913 which suggested that the Liberals comprised 153 suffragists, 78 Antis, and 31 doubtful members.[64] The

[60] Dated 19 May 1906, Report in Arncliffe-Sennett Papers, BL, C 10.245.

[61] Pentland, *Bonnie Fechter*, 151–2.

[62] *The Times*, 22 Feb. 1908.

[63] Lady Carlisle to Charles Trevelyan, 28 Apr. 1906, Newcastle University Library: Trevelyan Papers 16; *Daily Chronicle*, 21 Jan. 1908.

[64] *Annual Report*, Women's Liberal Federation, May 1911, 27; for the National Union's figures, see House of Lords Record Office: Lloyd George Papers C 317/3/26.

uncertainty arose partly from the fact that while many candidates had honestly declared their support for the principle of women's suffrage, they did not regard it as a priority especially for the new government during 1906–8. After being out of office for several decades the Liberals had a crowded timetable, which was exacerbated by the repeated emasculation of their legislation by the peers.

The progress of the cause was further hindered when the sympathetic Campbell-Bannerman resigned through ill-health in 1908 to be succeeded by Asquith who had been a consistent Anti-Suffragist since the 1880s. Asquith's stubbornness requires some explanation since he persisted to the point where his opposition had begun to damage both the party's interests and his own standing as Leader. Though sometimes portrayed as aloof from party politics, Asquith was in reality a narrowly partisan figure, ever fearful of conceding an advantage to his opponents. Moreover, despite his relatively humble origins he had acquired an elitist outlook, lacked sympathy with those he regarded as mediocre or ill-educated, and lost touch with his provincial origins in his enjoyment of Balliol College, the law, and London society. He therefore found it difficult to understand why ordinary women wanted the vote so badly. This bias was reinforced by Asquith's own experience which led him to treat women essentially as amiable companions and uncritical supporters. His two wives, in their different ways, confirmed this. Helen had no interest in politics, while Margot showed far too much! Asquith so feared Margot's interference and wild indiscretions that he tried to keep her in ignorance of high politics altogether.[65]

Apart from the accident of Asquith's rise to power, the advance of suffragism was also thrown out of kilter by the protracted controversies generated by Lloyd George's famous 'People's Budget' of 1909. Its summary rejection by the House of Lords forced the Liberals into a general election in January 1910 thereby creating a new priority and an agenda which dominated politics until 1914. Although the Liberal women accepted the need to secure the budget, they resented the prime minister's tendency to take it for granted that they would work on its behalf, especially as women were excluded from the meetings of the Budget League on the grounds that they might be suffragettes.[66] However, in 1910 Asquith did offer to find time in the new parliament to debate a women's suffrage bill.[67] Since the result of the election was the return of the Liberals but without an overall majority, the parliamentary

[65] Roy Jenkins, *Asquith* (Collins, 1964), 55–9.
[66] *The Times*, 17–18 Nov. 1909; *Annual Reports*, Women's Liberal Federation, 1910, 19–20.
[67] *Annual Report*, Women's Liberal Federation, 1910, 15.

supporters of the cause decided to modify their tactics by forming a Conciliation Committee representing all four parties in February 1910. The Conciliation Bill which they promoted obtained a majority of 109 in July, and,
under pressure from his cabinet colleagues, a majority of whom favoured
female enfranchisement, Asquith agreed to offer the facilities demanded by
the Committee. It was a sign of the seriousness of the disagreement that the
cabinet debated the issue at three meetings before reaching a decision.[68]
Since a further general election intervened in December 1910, the Conciliation Bill was not reintroduced until May 1911 by Sir George Kemp, when it
won by the huge margin of 255 to 88. However, this division gave a misleading impression of the strength of suffragism, partly because comparatively
few Conservatives took part, and also because many of the Liberals who
backed Kemp made it clear that they would be reluctant to vote it into law
unless it was amended so as to include a more democratic measure of enfranchisement.[69] Nonetheless, the cabinet could scarcely ignore so emphatic a
verdict, and after another heated discussion they agreed to offer a week of
parliamentary time to the Conciliation Bill.[70]

However, this decision provoked a crisis within the Liberal Party. The
Conciliation Bill proposed to enfranchise about one million women who
were heads of households or who possessed a ten pound occupation qualification. The latter provision was dropped from the bill in deference to fears
that it would encourage 'faggot voting', that is, the endowment of pieces of
property on women with the sole aim of manufacturing extra votes. Despite
this concession, prominent Liberals condemned the bill as fundamentally
detrimental to the party's interests. Churchill claimed it gave 'an entirely
unfair representation to property as against persons'; Lloyd George complained that it would 'on balance add hundreds of thousands of votes to the
strength of the Tory Party';[71] and when ministers asked the chief whip to consult the various regional Liberal federations they largely backed up this diagnosis with dire warnings: 'suicidal to pass the Bill ... would wipe out Liberal
representation ... nobody wants it and [everybody] dreads its advent'.[72] None
of this excitable comment should be taken as proof of the impact of the Bill;
but nor can it be ignored as a partial explanation for what subsequently happened. The fears expressed by the local Liberal organizers did not entirely

[68] PRO CAB 41/32/61, 62, 63, held on 8, 15, and 23 June 1910.
[69] *Annual Report*, Women's Liberal Federation, June 1912, 23–4.
[70] PRO CAB 41/33/15, 17 May 1911.
[71] *Hansard, HC Deb.*, 5th Series, XIX, 5 May 1911, c. 224–7; Lloyd George to the Master of
Elibank, 5 Sept. 1911, National Library of Scotland: Elibank Papers 8803.
[72] J. Renwick Seager, memorandum, 16 Nov. 1911, PRO CAB 37/108/148; see also *Liberal Agents'
Journal*, No. 51, 52, 56.

lack foundation. The existing system was biased in favour of the wealthy in the shape of half a million plural voters in a total electorate of 7.9 million. Moreover, the 1910 elections underlined the danger of taking any unnecessary risks, for the two main parties were now fairly evenly balanced in terms of the vote, even though the Conservatives were well behind in terms of seats.

This political situation, combined with the conspicuous divisions within the suffragist camp, put Asquith in a stronger position than he appeared to enjoy. Though in a minority, he was seen to be reflecting the party's interests in resisting the Conciliation Bill. For all its efforts the Conciliation Committee had failed to produce a credible compromise because its formula leant too far towards the Conservative view of women's suffrage. By November 1911 the cabinet had resolved its dilemma in what at first appeared to be a neat way. A surprised delegation from the People's Suffrage Federation received the news that the government now intended to introduce a bill of its own to reform the registration of parliamentary electors; though this would not include women's suffrage, it would be open to amendment by suffragists in the Commons. This expedient had a number of short-term results. The prospect of achieving votes for all men reassured the Liberal Party. The WLF were evidently satisfied that a government bill, which was what the Pankhursts themselves had always demanded, offered an excellent prospect, and they concentrated on promoting an amendment to it.[73] Conversely, the Pankhursts were provoked into a dramatic resumption of militancy which played into Asquith's hands. Finally, the prospect of a more democratic measure of women's suffrage attracted some Liberals away from the Conciliation Bill, and this, combined with politicians' reactions to the renewed suffragette violence, led to a narrow defeat for that bill in 1912.

All this, however, simply raised the stakes for both sides. As Lloyd George had observed: 'the Liberal Party ought to make up its mind as a whole whether it will either have an extended franchise which would put the workingmen's wives on to the register as well as spinsters and widows, or that it will have no female franchise at all'.[74] Rather ominously the WLF executive expressed its gratitude to the *Labour* Party for its consistent support for women's suffrage, and warned the government that were they to enact a reform bill without including votes for women, 'it will become extremely difficult and perhaps impossible to sustain the present amicable relations between the members of the WLF and the Liberal Party'.[75] Since any further

[73] *Annual Reports*, Women's Liberal Federation, 1912, 23–4; 1913, 11.

[74] D. Lloyd George to the Master of Elibank, 5 Sept. 1911, National Library of Scotland: Elibank Papers 8803.

[75] *Annual Report*, Women's Liberal Federation, 1912, 55.

failure threatened to be severely embarrassing for both non-militant suffragists and for the pro-suffrage ministers, these two groups were forced by the cabinet's initiative to coordinate their efforts for one final push. Millicent Fawcett held confidential talks with Sir Edward Grey, the foreign secretary, in December 1911 to arrange for him to introduce what was known as the 'Norway' amendment to the new bill, that is, the enfranchisement of the *wives* of all householders, a formula well-calculated to reassure Liberal and Labour members.[76] In order to build the momentum behind this proposal the WLF organized a major rally addressed by the two leading Liberal suffragists, Grey and Lloyd George. 'I want the household to be represented by husband and wife', declared the foreign secretary. Lloyd George, as usual, went slightly over the top by enthusiastically announcing: 'Our success next year, I think, is assured. I do not see what there is to prevent it.'[77] On the other hand, their high-profile role had the effect of driving other Liberal ministers, notably Reginald McKenna and Lewis Harcourt, into attending an Anti-Suffragist rally at the Albert Hall. According to a mildly hysterical Margot Asquith, this put the prime minister into a 'hopeless and even ridiculous' position by revealing his inability to avert the disintegration of his cabinet![78] In the event the whole enterprise was upset by the Speaker of the House of Commons, James Lowther, who unexpectedly ruled that because the original bill was a purely registration bill it would be out of order to alter its character by including women's suffrage amendments.[79] As Lowther's interpretation contradicted all previous rulings by speakers, it came as a shock; but Asquith naturally bore the chief blame for the fiasco. The government bill was swiftly abandoned; the Conciliation Bill had been wrecked; and the only other attempt to enfranchise women by Willoughby Dickinson in 1913 also met with defeat. To the suffragists all this was proof of Asquith's duplicity.

Inevitably these events took a severe toll on the morale of the Liberal women. 'I think the conviction has been growing that there is nothing to hope for from the Liberal Party even when Home Rule and Welsh Disestablishment are out of the way,' wrote Catherine Marshall, 'I am becoming rather discredited as a false prophet because I have so often predicted better things of Mr Lloyd George than he has performed.'[80] As a result some women Liberals endorsed the new strategy of the NUWSS by working to help Labour candidates even in opposition to Liberals at by-elections (see Chapter 10).

[76] Confidential memorandum, Fawcett Library: Fawcett Letters, 89/2/58.
[77] *The Times*, 18 Dec. 1911.
[78] Margot Asquith to the Master of Elibank, 14 and 28 Jan. 1912, National Library of Scotland: Elibank Papers 8803.
[79] Martin Pugh, *Electoral Reform in War and Peace, 1906–1918* (Routledge, 1978), 41–2.
[80] Catherine Marshall to F. D. Acland (draft), 4 Nov. 1913, Cumbria CRO: Marshall Papers.

Others simply began to drop out altogether. This temptation had been grow-ing for several years as frustration mounted. As one woman complained in 1909: 'We have been hewers of wood and drawers of water for the Liberal Party too long.'[81] During the last two years of peace the process accelerated. According to one organizer, 'women are leaving us in shoals ... every bright and clever woman in my Liberal society has left us'.[82] One estimate suggests that between 1912 and 1914 sixty-eight local branches of the WLF folded and 18,000 members were lost; according to the Federation's annual reports, in 1911–12 thirty-six associations lapsed and eight withdrew, in 1912–13 thirty lapsed and twenty withdrew, and in 1913–14 thirty-nine lapsed and nineteen withdrew.[83] Helena Swanwick later claimed 'this was the beginning of the disintegration of the Liberal Party'.[84] Though the effects are impos-sible to measure, there can be little doubt that the demoralization of local organization especially amongst women Liberals formed a major reason for the party's protracted decline during the post-war period.

Conversely, there are some indications that by 1913–14 even Asquith had recognized the dangers of his position. While he prevaricated, two pincers had begun to close around him. On one side, his electoral pact with Labour was being prised apart by the NUWSS scheme to promote extra Labour can-didates; on the other, some Conservatives were preparing to fight the next election on a promise to introduce an 'equal terms' bill for women.[85] Yet when the prime minister received a deputation led by Fawcett in August 1913 he continued to be evasive, taking refuge behind the weary excuse that women would get the vote if they persuaded the people of their cause. 'How is that judgement to be obtained?' demanded Fawcett, to which Asquith merely replied that some people favoured a referendum.[86] On the other hand, the last deputation before the war in June 1914 was treated more sympathet-ically, perhaps because it comprised working-class women from London's East End led by Sylvia Pankhurst. Asquith apparently approved of them because he felt they were more representative than the usual deputations, and because they had dissociated themselves from what he called 'criminal

[81]   *The Common Cause*, 7 Oct. 1909, 329; see similar comments in 'Mr. Asquith at Aberdeen', *Votes for Women*, Jan. 1908, 58, Feb. 1908, 62, Mar. 1911, 429.
    [82]   Mrs L. Bulley to Margaret Lloyd George, 25 Oct. 1913, House of Lords Record Office: Lloyd George Papers C/10/1/68.
    [83]   *Annual Reports*, Women's Liberal Federation, 1912, 1913, 1914; see also Claire Hirshfield, 'Fractured Faith: Liberal Party Women and the Suffrage Issue in Britain, 1892–1914', *Gender and History*, 2/2 (1990), 179.
    [84]   H. M. Swanwick, *I Have Been Young* (Gollancz, 1935), 222.
    [85]   Catherine Marshall to Lady Selborne (copy), 13 Nov. 1913, Cumbria Record Office: Marshall Papers.
    [86]   *Manchester Guardian*, 9 Aug. 1913.

methods'. This seems a little odd in the light of the fact that Sylvia Pankhurst was drilling a private army in the East End at that point! However, the prime minister concluded with the words: 'I have always said ... if the change has got to come we must face it boldly and make it thoroughly democratic.'[87] This could be interpreted as an endorsement of Lloyd George's formula, but whether it marked a change of heart is impossible to say. Evidently some observers thought it did. Philip Snowden understood Asquith to mean that if a majority of the Liberals returned at the next general election were pledged to women's enfranchisement, he would accept this as the verdict of the party and the country.[88] However, the outbreak of war meant that Asquith had left it too late to climb down without lasting damage.

Despite this, the prolonged confrontation between his government and the suffragists had not been wholly barren of results. It had established what ought to have been accepted earlier, that votes for women could not be treated simply as a question of principle but had to be translated into a form acceptable to the governing party. Dickinson's bill of 1913 which was designed to include some six million women including wives, actually embodied the solution which was to be adopted in the successful measure of 1917 which enfranchised 8.4 million women. Beyond that, the vital achievement of Asquith's administration lay in the removal of the ultimate obstacle to the women's vote—the veto powers of the House of Lords.

---

[87] *Manchester Guardian*, 22 June 1914.
[88] Manchester Society for Women's Suffrage, executive minutes, 5 Mar. 1913, including Memorandum/Appendix C, Manchester Central Library M50/1.

7

The Failure of Anti-Suffragism

ONE learns a good deal about any political movement by investigating its opponents; adversaries often make recruits from rival organizations, they emulate each other's methods, capitalize upon each other's mistakes, and implicitly corroborate their claims to success. Certainly the opponents of female enfranchisement enjoyed an almost symbiotic relationship with suffragism. Until the suffragists fanned it into life, Anti-Suffragism had no cause or rationale, and without the stimulus provided by the steady conversion of politicians to the women's cause, not to mention the 'outrages' committed by Edwardian suffragettes, they would have found great difficulty in sustaining a campaign at all. In some sense, then, the Antis offer a barometer of the fluctuating fortunes of suffragism. They themselves appear to have appreciated the complexity of their relationship with their opponents; tactless speeches by male Antis aroused the sense of grievance among inactive women, while the more the female Antis became drawn into active campaigning the more they demonstrated that women were, after all, capable of playing a role in politics. Their peculiar aim, therefore, was somehow to quell the suffragist campaign and retire from public life before anyone had realized how effective they had been! In effect they sought not so much to defeat their opponents as to promote the circumstances in which the public and the politicians would become bored with the whole question. Consequently, the Anti-Suffragists showed themselves all too eager to interpret any period of calm as proof of their success; in 1909 they claimed to detect a subsidence of interest in the suffragette campaign: 'we cannot hope better for our cause than that this lack of interest should extend also to ourselves for this will mean that the nation has made up its mind, at any rate for the present'.[1] Yet a strategy that relied upon stirring up apathy required more subtlety than most Anti-Suffragists possessed. In any case premature assumptions about the

[1] *Anti-Suffrage Review*, July 1909, 4.

defeat of the suffragists led inevitably to diminished activity and funding for the Antis, and hence to an episodic campaign rather than to the continuous effort of their rivals.

Female Anti-Suffragism

Much of the opposition to votes for women reflected an instinctive defence of entrenched privilege combined with a deep-seated fear of the female sex. In the early days before politicians had begun to take suffragism seriously, they felt uninhibited about speaking their minds and admitting to self-interested motives. At an election meeting in North Northamptonshire in 1877 Lord Burghley contemptuously rejected women's claims thus: 'you want me to give women the same rights as men; I don't. I married an heiress myself and I do not want her to have as many rights as I have. I like her to stop at home, and give me counsel when I ask for it.'[2] Not surprisingly, Lydia Becker gratefully seized upon such rash comments; but even in the 1870s the confidence and arrogance betrayed by Burghley rarely put its head above the parapet. Such blatant hostility to women would have played into the hands of the suffragists. It seemed politic for the Antis to adopt more subtle tactics, praising the female sex for its positive attributes rather than simply emphasizing flaws of intellect or temperament. Above all, to escape the charge of being a vehicle for self-interest, the movement had to be more than merely male. At the very least the existence of a substantial and vocal body of female Antis bestowed respectability on the cause and undermined the credibility of the feminists. It is, however, difficult to know how far the men simply took advantage of the phenomenon and how far they were genuinely influenced by female opposition to the vote. Professor Goldwin Smith claimed that though he had supported Mill's amendment in 1867 'we soon bolted when we saw whither he was leading . . . we found that the best women of our acquaintance were against it'.[3] In reality his antagonism towards women was only part of a wider reaction against the effects of the 1867 Reform Act on British politics; his views on the female intellect were symptomatic of a deeper prejudice based on class as much as on gender assumptions.

Some female Antis pandered to male prejudice by cultivating the notion that they lacked political aptitude and experience. Janet Courtney referred to the 'ladylike incompetents' in the Anti-Suffrage campaign, while even

---

[2] 'Election Intelligence', *Women's Suffrage Journal*, 1 Sept. 1877, 156.
[3] Haultain, *Goldwin Smith*, 172.

Gladys Pott, a redoubtable activist, claimed 'I did not know how' when first invited to speak in public.[4] This was an almost calculated misrepresentation characteristic of many able women of the late Victorian and Edwardian era. Gladys Pott, Mary Ward, and the Duchess of Atholl, to name but three prominent Antis, quickly mastered the arts of platform oratory and committee work. In any case, Antis such as the Countess of Jersey *already* enjoyed extensive political experience in the Primrose League which exposed them to ridicule in their later role as critics of female enfranchisement. 'What is [Lady Jersey] doing in the Primrose League if she is incapable of political judgement?', Lord Robert Cecil demanded to know.[5]

Both the skills demonstrated by these ladies and the zest they showed for politics make the historian's task of explaining their hostility to votes for women a formidable one. No doubt the attitude of the aristocratic ladies is less of a mystery. 'What earthly good will it do to any woman to have a vote?' asked Lady Salisbury.[6] In her privileged position a woman enjoyed a vicarious sense of power exercised through her male relations and as a hostess and confidant to cabinet ministers, in addition to the challenge of electioneering if her tastes ran in that direction.[7] The addition of a mere vote seemed unlikely to add much to her influence.

Even women who started life with fewer advantages often interpreted their personal success in achieving a satisfying role in public life as proof that the grievances expressed by feminists were merely indicative of their own inadequacies. For example, Octavia Hill gained the status of an authority on housing for the poor through her work for the Charity Organisation Society and her skill in putting urban property on a sound financial footing. But her disapproving view of those who were less able or disadvantaged carried over into the political sphere in that she regarded ordinary people as inadequate as voters.[8] In the 1860s Florence Nightingale considered the claims about women's rights to be absurd because women failed to take up the opportunities already open to them.[9] Invited by Mill to lend her name to a suffrage petition, she grandly claimed to command as much political influence as a parliamentary borough! However, Nightingale is a reminder of the instability of female Anti-Suffragism, for, despite her evident lack of sympathy, she did

[4] Harrison, *Separate Spheres*, 113.

[5] Address by Lord Robert Cecil, CUWFA, 1908, 8; Pugh, *The Tories*, 47–56.

[6] Lady Salisbury to Lady Frances Balfour, 11 Feb. 1897, Balfour, *Ne Obliviscaris*, i. 148.

[7] Pugh, *The Tories*, 42–56; for the earlier period, see K. D. Reynolds, *Aristocratic Women and Political Society in Victorian Britain* (Oxford: Oxford University Press, 1998).

[8] Octavia Hill, *Anti-Suffrage Review*, Aug. 1910, 5.

[9] Florence Nightingale to M. Mohl, 13 Dec. 1861, in E. Cook, *The Life of Florence Nightingale* (Macmillan, 1913), ii. 14.

subsequently agree to support the cause. Similar remarks apply to Beatrice Potter (later Webb) who for many years remained unconvinced about the need for a women's movement. Potter who aspired to both a career and marriage, found the latter the more difficult to attain; the former was accomplished through her work for Charles Booth and the Charity Organisation Society. Her success in building a life as an emancipated woman gave Beatrice Potter the satisfaction and self-confidence that led her to regard the women's movement as an irrelevance; this revealed itself in her dismissive attitude towards working-class women and her reluctance to focus her research on women's working conditions. As a result she had little compunction about signing the Anti-Suffrage petition in 1889. 'At the root of my anti-feminism', she wrote, 'lay the fact that I had never myself suffered the disabilities assumed to arise from my sex.'[10] She probably signed without giving the matter much thought; at all events, by 1906 she had come to appreciate the illogicality involved in being both a public figure and an Anti-Suffragist.

Female Anti-Suffragism appears to have been on firmer ground with Gertrude Bell, Violet Markham, and Mary (Mrs Humphry) Ward. Yet they, too, were full of contradictions. Though Bell ostensibly accepted the conventional view of the woman's sphere, in practice she paid it scant regard, enjoying a liberated lifestyle, the advantage of an enlightened Liberal family, and the satisfaction of a public role as an expert comparable to that of Nightingale, achieved by means of her travels in the Middle East. She chose to see this as proof of her personal talent and enterprise and thus tended to look scornfully on the shortcomings of the female sex in general.[11]

Violet Markham, a key figure in Edwardian Anti-Suffragism, also enjoyed the advantages of financial independence and a Liberal family background; her brother, Arthur, was a pro-suffrage MP. Elected to a school board in 1897, Violet Markham embarked on a life filled with public work and sustained by a sense of achievement.[12] Her opposition to the vote must thus be seen in terms of personal success combined with a disdainful attitude towards the poor and ill-educated of *both* sexes. Like many other late Victorians she shrank from the trend towards democracy, believing that Britain had too

[10] Beatrice Webb, *My Apprenticeship* (Longman Green, 1971), 354; Barbara Caine, 'Beatrice Webb and the Woman Question', *History Workshop Journal*, 14 (1982), 31.

[11] H. V. F. Winstone, *Gertrude Bell* (Cape, 1978), 80.

[12] See the chapter on Markham in Jane Lewis, *Women and Social Action in Victorian and Edwardian Britain* (Edward Elgar, 1991); Helen Jones (ed.), *Duty and Citizenship: The Correspondence and Papers of Violet Markham* (The Historians' Press, 1994); Violet Markham, *Return Passage* (Oxford: Clarendon Press, 1953). Interesting light is thrown on Markham's Anti-Suffragism by her collection of press cuttings which concentrate on tariff reform, the 1909 budget, and all the major issues of the day; this seems to indicate a woman who felt no inhibitions about the 'male' sphere in national politics.

many ignorant voters already; her conservatism was as much a reflection of class as of gender. Indeed, as a keen advocate of employment for women and an enthusiast for women's work in local government, Markham appears to be another closet feminist entrenched within the Antis' organization.

In the case of Mrs Humphry Ward even her biographer has admitted that 'no one, least of all herself, has convincingly explained why [she] was so hostile to the cause of women's rights'.[13] In fact Mrs Ward helped to promote the Association for the Education of Women and acted as secretary for Somerville College in 1878. She fought her way up as a journalist and an immensely successful and prolific novelist during the 1880s and 1890s, which is why the Antis regarded her as so great an asset in connection with the petition of 1889 which they published under her name. Though in some ways predisposed towards feminism, Mrs Humphry Ward got blown off course during the 1880s when she turned away from Liberalism over Irish Home Rule which she somehow associated with feminism.[14] It undoubtedly flattered her to be asked by powerful politicians to lend her reputation to their cause, and, having committed herself, her pride was at stake; she reacted to the House of Commons vote in favour of the 1897 suffrage bill almost as though a personal affront had been offered to her.[15] Yet Mrs Ward's position as a figurehead for Anti-Suffragism remained uncomfortable: 'there is something a little comic', observed Lord Robert Cecil, 'in the energy and the ability and the eloquence with which a writer like Mrs Humphry Ward proclaims to the world that she ought not to be trusted to exercise the franchise'.[16] Though enjoying her acclaim as an Anti-Suffragist speaker, she clearly shrank from the role, partly because it diverted her from her writing.[17] For she was not just a career woman; by the 1900s she operated under enormous pressure to keep writing in order to maintain the two inadequate men in her life—her husband and her son.

Organizing the Antis

Not surprisingly the first signs of organized parliamentary opposition to votes for women appeared in reaction to the bills repeatedly introduced in

[13] John Sutherland, *Mrs Humphry Ward* (Oxford: Oxford University Press, 1990), 200.

[14] Ibid. 78, 199–200.   [15] Ibid. 200.

[16] Address by Lord Robert Cecil, CUWFA, 1908, 6.

[17] In 1909 she confessed to withdrawing to Italy to 'escape the suffrage debate for a time in the interests of my work': Mrs Ward to Millicent Fawcett, 23 Apr. 1909, Fawcett Library: Fawcett Letters, 89/1/38; Janet Trevelyan, *The Life of Mrs Humphry Ward* (Oxford: Clarendon Press, 1923), 230.

the early 1870s. In June 1875 a Committee for Maintaining the Integrity of the Franchise emerged under the leadership of two Tories, E. P. Bouverie and Lord Randolph Churchill, and a Liberal, Sir Henry James. 'We cannot say that we are greatly alarmed,' scoffed Lydia Becker.[18] The Committee canvassed members and appointed eight whips, but lapsed around 1878 ostensibly on the grounds that the suffrage movement had declined.[19] Thereafter no concerted effort seems to have been made until June 1889 when James Knowles, the editor of *The Nineteenth Century*, printed a famous petition signed by 104 women and accompanied by an article by Mrs Ward summarizing the Antis' case.

Why did the Antis deem it necessary to take a fresh initiative after years of inactivity? Knowles gave a clue:

The difficulty of obtaining a public expression, even of disapproval, about such a question from those who entirely object to mixing themselves up in the coarsening struggles of party political life, may easily become a public danger. Their silence will be misinterpreted as indifference or consent to designs they most dislike and thus help to bring them about.[20]

Mrs Ward also underlined the danger in her rather odd-sounding comment: 'we believe that the emancipating process has now reached the limits fixed by the physical constitution of women'. Behind these remarks lay a realization that since 1869 women had slowly but surely been raising their profile in elective local government, and winning male approval in the process. 1889 brought further innovation in the shape of Lord Salisbury's bill for elective county councils, a ploy intended to spike the Radicals' guns, but which extended to women an additional vote and, it was initially if erroneously assumed, the right to be elected as county councillors. This was regarded as a half-way step to national politics for women. In short, Mrs Ward's petition must be understood in the context of what appeared to be a rapidly deteriorating situation for the opponents of female enfranchisement, especially among the Conservatives. During the previous six years women had flocked into the Primrose League, thereby earning the endorsement of Salisbury for their fitness to vote in parliamentary elections. Hence the tetchy complaint in the petition: 'meanwhile pledges to support female suffrage have been hastily given in the hopes of strengthening existing political parties'.[21] In this

---

[18] *Women's Suffrage Journal*, 2 Aug. 1875, 107; Blackburn, *Women's Suffrage*, 140.

[19] Conservatives: Henry Chaplin, A. J. Beresford Hope, Charles Russell, J. H. Scourfield; Liberals: E. A. Leatham, Sam Whitbread, Henry James, E. A. Knatchbull-Huguessen.

[20] James Knowles, *The Nineteenth Century*, 209 (1889), 788.

[21] Mrs Humphry Ward, 'An Appeal Against Women's Suffrage', *The Nineteenth Century*, 209 (1889), 748; also Smith, 'Conservation and Female Suffrage'.

light it would be a mistake to interpret the 1889 petition primarily as a demonstration of the *strength* of opposition to the women's vote; rather it was symptomatic of the Antis' fear that the initiative had begun to slip away from them. In the twenty years since 1869 a generation of men and women had begun to take for granted a degree of female participation in public affairs; nothing could undo that process whatever efforts were subsequently made by the Anti-Suffragists.

Even in the short term the significance of the petition seems questionable. Though it purported to be a genuine manifestation of female opinion, the editor's role in orchestrating it and appealing for further signatures could not be concealed. 'That [Knowles] should have got together a fanfaronade of empty titles is characteristic enough,' scoffed the *Pall Mall Gazette*, '[the ladies] have inherited wealth, or name or position . . . their lives are full and comfortable; they have what they want.'[22] Knowles claimed that his readers' opinions 'might certainly be taken as a fair sample of the judgement of the educated women of the country'. But as Millicent Fawcett cuttingly observed, the list contained 'a very large preponderance of ladies to whom the lines of life have fallen in pleasant places. There are very few among them who have had to face the battle of life alone to earn their living by daily hard work.'[23] Certainly the list was dominated by titled women such as Lady Frederick Cavendish-Bentinck, Lady Wimborne, and Lady Revelstoke, by the wives of prominent politicians including Margot Asquith, Mrs Goschen, Lady Randolph Churchill, and Mrs Mundella, and by the wives of writers and academics such as Matthew Arnold, Arnold Toynbee, J. R. Seeley, Walter Bagehot, and T. H. Green. Apart from Beatrice Potter, Eliza Lynn Lynton, and Mrs Ward, hardly any had achieved a reputation through their own efforts or talents.[24] By contrast Fawcett flourished the names of suffragist women notable for their contributions to education, philanthropy, social work, and medicine.

In spite of this attempt at discrediting them, the Antis concluded that the 1889 petition had succeeded in its object of alerting both the public and the politicians to the fact that any decision on women's suffrage would be premature. The very fact that many of the ladies were obscure or inactive could be taken, in their view, as an indication that they were more typical of female opinion than the suffragist campaigners.[25] These and the other names which

---

[22] Quoted in *Women's Suffrage Journal*, 1 July 1889, 91.

[23] Millicent Fawcett, 'The Anti-Suffrage Petition', *The Nineteenth Century*, 209 (1889), 89.

[24] Indeed the next list defied Fawcett by leading with four duchesses, nine countesses, and seven viscountesses, 357–84.

[25] Louise Creighton, 'The Appeal Against Female Suffrage: A Rejoinder', *The Nineteenth Century*, 209 (1889), 347–8.

Knowles soon gathered, might have provided the basis for a standing organization of Anti-Suffragists during the 1890s. But no such organization
appeared for the next eighteen years. 1889 thus appears as an isolated intervention in the debate rather than as the start of a sustained campaign.
Mrs Ward herself seems to have remained inactive during the 1890s and was
evidently surprised as well as angered by the comfortable majority won by
the suffrage bill in 1897. Even then no initiative was taken. The Antis had set
too high a valuation on their own influence in 1889, and were lulled into a
false sense of security by the relative infrequency of women's suffrage bills
during the 1890s. For years they refused to treat the evidence of a shift in parliamentary opinion seriously. As late as 1912 Sir Herbert Maxwell declared
that it would have been absurd to have organized opposition to women's
suffrage in the earlier period—only the emergence of a 'revolutionary movement' had made it necessary. Lord Curzon endorsed this diagnosis, claiming
that 'people had been disposed to think that the anti-suffrage cause might be
left to look after itself, and that the pro-suffrage cause was a chimera'.[26] As a
result, when the opponents of votes for women did pick up the threads of
their organization in the Edwardian period they found themselves even
further behind their rivals both at Westminster and in the country.

The Problem of Feminism

It is a sign of the complacency amongst Anti-Suffragists that it was not until
1908 that they again attempted to put their cause on a regular footing. In July
of that year Lady Jersey presided at a meeting to establish the Ladies League
for Opposing Women's Suffrage, in December John Massie, MP, and Lord
Cromer formed a Men's League, and in December 1910 the two amalga-
mated into a National League for Opposing Women's Suffrage.[27] One does
not have to look far for the explanation for these developments. The general
election of 1906 had greatly strengthened the existing parliamentary support
for suffragism by the return of four hundred Liberal and 29 Labour members.
During 1906 and 1907 Sir Charles Dilke, Keir Hardie, and W. H. Dickinson
introduced women's bills, and when a division was taken on Henry York
Stanger's Bill to enfranchise both single and married women in February

    [26] 'The Historic Scottish Anti-Suffrage Demonstration', 1 Nov. 1912, Curzon Papers, BL,
F112/38.
    [27] *The Times*, 4 Dec. 1908.

1908 the suffragists won by 273 votes to only 94.[28] This alerted the Antis to the short-term erosion of their support; but the recantation by Beatrice Webb in 1906 was a more telling symptom of long-term changes in British society.[29]

The new Leagues relied heavily on Conservative and Liberal Unionist peers, politicians, and writers for their support.[30] They published a monthly *Anti-Suffrage Review* and rapidly began to catch up with the suffragists in forming local branches. At first they avoided publishing membership figures for fear of unfavourable comparison with their opponents; but by 1913 they claimed a healthy total of 33,000 and 42,000 by 1914.[31] It seems that the majority of members were women, and that they undertook most of the work of running branches and recruiting; 'they are far more efficient than the men', admitted Lord Cromer.[32] Indeed, the role of the male leaders was almost decorative; they provided a list of prominent names to grace the notepaper and the platforms of Anti-Suffragism, but their chief measurable contribution lay in fund-raising. The correspondence between Cromer and Curzon during 1910 shows their absorption in this task in which they were successful to the tune of £20,000 raised between July and September alone.[33] Cromer appealed to political allies for donations and also issued a circular request to companies.[34]

TABLE 7.1. National League for Opposing Women's Suffrage branches, 1908–1913

Dec. 1908	26	Oct. 1910	104
Jan. 1909	48	1912	243
June 1909	98	1913	270

Source: Anti-Suffrage Review.

[28]	Liberals	Conservatives	Irish	Labour
For	185	34	21	33
Against	48	30	14	2

[29] *The Times*, 5 Nov. 1906, 8.

[30] Lord Cromer, the Duke of Northumberland, Lord Dunraven, Lord George Hamilton, Austen Chamberlain, Henry Chaplin, Lord Haversham, Lord Weardale, Lord James of Hereford, A. V. Dicey, Heber Hart, St Loe Strachey, Leo Maxse, Charles Oman: *The Times*, 4 Dec. 1908.

[31] *Anti-Suffrage Review*, July 1914, 114.

[32] Lord Cromer to Lord Curzon, 18 July 1910, Curzon Papers, BL, F112/33; Harrison, *Separate Spheres*, 128, notes that in 1913, 16,148 out of 18,978 members were female as reported by 145 branches.

[33] Memorandum by Curzon (copy), 27 Nov. 1912, Curzon Papers, BL, F112/35.

[34] See copy, 27 Oct. 1910, in Fawcett Library: Fawcett Letters 89/1/47; *Conservative and Unionist Women's Franchise Review*, Apr.–June, 1913, 282–3, lists some of the 293 contributors: N. M. Rothschild (£3,000); Lord Ridley, Lord Glenconner, W. W. Astor, Lord Iveagh, Sir Ernest Cassel, and Lady Wantage each gave £1,000; Lord Joicey and David Davies, MP, gave £500.

However, even this success is chiefly of interest for the way it exposes the *weaknesses* in Anti-Suffragism. Their lordships met with many rebuffs from, for example, Arthur Steel-Maitland, Lord Derby, Lord Londesborough, Donald MacMaster, and (initially) William Waldorf Astor, ostensibly on financial grounds. Lord Londonderry refused to contribute 'as the budget has so crippled me'.[35] But other respondents thought Curzon wrong or misguided; for example, Charles Stewart suggested that women were likely to improve parliamentary work, the Duke of Bedford felt women would simply vote as men did, and J. G. Crompton warned him against making the same error as the doctors who had once fought to exclude women from their profession only to discover that their admission was not at all damaging.[36] Astor and W. Bromley Davenport frankly told Curzon that he ought to be concentrating on fighting *Socialism* not women's suffrage.[37] Even those who agreed to contribute often emphasized that they did not fully share the apprehensions of Cromer and Curzon about the effects of enfranchising women. The general impression is that by 1910 a large section of the Establishment had lost its fears about women. While the Antis had endlessly argued that women did not feel strongly about getting the vote, the private correspondence suggests that many of their opponents were similarly lukewarm about preventing them.

The decision to amalgamate the men's League with the women's seems shrewd in some ways; it was calculated to embody the philosophy underlying Anti-Suffragism by demonstrating how the two sexes could cooperate by playing distinct roles while contributing to a common cause. In practice, however, the experience only revealed the complications, and, on balance, amalgamation was probably a mistake. It largely broke down over feminism, and to a lesser extent over party politics. From the outset the attitude of the leading men—an unattractive mixture of fear and condescension—made for uncomfortable relations. Curzon and Cromer insisted on retaining the Presidency in male hands, which made them look ungracious when they refused to accept Lady Jersey's claims on the Chairmanship. Even the office work became the scene of squabbling between the men chosen by Cromer to run the headquarters and the women who largely did the work.[38] Essentially Cromer disliked having to collaborate with independent-minded women at all; he especially resented Mrs Humphry Ward whom he described variously

---

[35] Lord Londonderry to Lord Curzon, 20 July 1910, Curzon Papers, BL, F 112/32.
[36] Stewart, 18 July 1910, Bedford, 21 July 1910, and Crompton, not dated, Curzon Papers, BL, F112/32.
[37] W. W. Astor, not dated, Davenport, 24 July 1910, Curzon Papers, BL, F112/32.
[38] Lord Cromer to Lord Curzon, 28 Sept. 1910, Curzon Papers, BL, F112/33.

as 'a rather disturbing element' and 'that most tiresome woman'.[39] Within a few months relations had become so bad that he regretted having abolished the men's League.[40]

Yet the problem went deeper than a clash of personalities. Previous Anti-Suffrage organization had been so brief and limited that no one had appreciated the complications of working with women, some of whom were actually *feminists*. It was only in the Edwardian period that the female Antis began to emerge as an unstable element in the movement. Beatrice Webb's explanation for her abandonment of the cause in 1906 sounded a warning. She argued that the advance of state legislation into the traditional sphere of women meant that women's entry into national politics would simply reflect 'a desire to more effectually fulfil their functions by sharing control of state actions in these directions'.[41] It is difficult to see any *fundamental* distinction between Beatrice Webb's views and those of Violet Markham and Mrs Ward; the former now believed women should have the vote as a result of the overlap between local and central government, while the latter based their opposition to enfranchisement on the strength of women's contribution to local government. Ward and Markham fully appreciated the danger of a purely negative resistance to the vote. If women were denied an outlet in the form of wider participation, they would steadily succumb to the appeal of suffragism; consequently they felt they could counter suffragist propaganda best by showing that the parliamentary vote was an unnecessary extension of women's existing role.

However, female Antis felt embarrassed when speaking in public because of the divergence between their own view of the female role and the negative attitudes of many male leaders.[42] Perhaps understandably, the men regarded local government as the thin end of a very dangerous wedge. It seems probable that one of Cromer's objects in merging the two Leagues had been to check the 'Forward Policy' of the leading ladies, which involved promoting female candidates in local government and trying to establish a women's council representing women in elective local authorities. Decades of practical work with children, the poor, and the elderly had led many ladies to regard their own enfranchisement simply as a way of strengthening their existing efforts, and to this extent social reform had taken root even in the ranks of the Conservative Party. Some of the men seem to have been out of

---

[39] Lord Cromer to Lord Curzon, 5 Dec. 1912, Curzon Papers, BL, F112/35.
[40] Lord Cromer to Lord Curzon, 12 Oct. 1910, Curzon Papers, F112/33.
[41] *The Times*, 5 Nov. 1906, 8.
[42] Editorial, *Anti-Suffrage Review*, July 1910, 2; C. Moir to N. Ormsby-Scott (copy), 6 Dec. 1912, Manchester Central Library: Manchester Branch NLOWS, M131/3/2.

touch with or frightened by these developments. Cromer loftily dismissed all suggestions of a connection between tackling social issues and female enfranchisement. John St Loe Strachey scornfully attacked Markham and Ward's proposals: 'recent events have shown the extreme danger of women acting together . . . they seem to suffer from a kind of moral and intellectual contagion of a very dangerous sort'.[43]

Such patronizing comments, which were partly a reflection of male reactions to suffragette militancy, merely provoked Ward and Markham who went ahead and established a Local Government Committee within the NLOWS.[44] Since this involved promoting female candidates who were, in some cases, pro-suffragists, and also meant criticizing political parties for failing to nominate enough women, the strategy inevitably exacerbated the friction within the League.[45] In February 1912 Cromer insisted that the Committee's work was incompatible with opposition to the parliamentary vote for women; and he denounced Ward and Markham as extremists because they urged women to vote for female candidates 'merely on account of [their] sex'. Though chastened by his rebuke, Violet Markham refused to be intimidated and she reminded Cromer that the intrusion of party politics into local government often put 'the most impossible people'—presumably men—onto local authorities.[46] But after a confrontation with members of the executive (Heber Hart, Charles Mallet, Gertrude Bell, and Mitchell Innes), Mrs Ward accepted the necessity to separate her Committee from the League; her sarcastic references to 'the flood of fury on dear Lord Cromer's part' and to the Director, Captain Creed, as 'wholly illiberal and bigoted' suggest a deep rift in the organization.[47] In fact the female Antis considered re-establishing the original women's League which would have made the cause a laughing stock.[48]

The controversy forced Violet Markham to face up to the inconsistency of her position. In a revealing letter to Elizabeth Haldane she admitted:

[43] Lord Cromer to Violet Markham, 10 Mar. 1909, BLPES: Markham Papers 26/30; St Loe Strachey to Violet Markham, 11 Oct. 1910, BLPES: Markham Papers 26/30.

[44] Violet Markham to Lady Jersey, 23 Sept. 1909; Mrs Ward to Violet Markham, 29 Sept. 1909: BLPES: Markham Papers 26/30; 'Aims of the Local Government Committee', Markham Papers 29/30; Mary Ward to C. Moir, not dated, 1911, Manchester Central Library: Manchester Branch NLOWS M131/3/3.

[45] Mrs Ward to Violet Markham, 7 Feb. 1912, BLPES: Markham Papers 26/30.

[46] Lord Cromer to Violet Markham, 9 Feb. 1912; Violet Markham to Lord Cromer, 10 Feb. 1912, BLPES: Markham Papers 26/30.

[47] Mrs Ward to Violet Markham, 14 Feb. 1912; Mrs Ward to Violet Markham, 11 Feb. 1912, BLPES: Markham Papers 26/30.

[48] Violet Markham to Mrs Ward, Mar. 1912, BLPES: Markham Papers 26/30.

I have felt and feel my alienation on [women's suffrage] from three parts of my friends and fellow workers more keenly than I can well describe ... Obviously there is so much to be said for the Suffragist position ... I feel so very strongly about the spiritual aspects of life for which women ought to stand in their public work and I can not see how that spiritual quality could survive the obligation to take part in the rough and tumble [of parliamentary elections] on even terms.[49]

Though sometimes seen as a wartime convert to women's suffrage, Markham had clearly reconsidered her views before 1914 and for quite different reasons.

The growing incompatibility between male and female Antis was exacerbated during 1912 by the publication of the notorious letter by Sir Almroth Wright in *The Times*. In this he offered an insulting analysis of the suffragette phenomenon portentously fortified with scientific authority:

The recruiting ground for the militant suffragettes is the half million of an excess female population ... a class of women who have all their life been strangers to joy, women in whom instincts long suppressed have in the end broken into flame. These are the sexually embittered women in whom everything has turned to gall and bitterness of heart and hatred of men ... Next there file past the incomplete. One side of their nature has undergone atrophy with the result that they have lost touch with their living fellows, men and women.[50]

Now in view of the fact that suffragette window-breaking was provoking widespread outrage at this time, Wright would have commanded support for an attack focused solely on the militants. However, he committed a fatal error by extending his analysis, drawing confidently but dangerously on his authority as a doctor to generalize about the entire female sex:

For man the physiology and psychology of woman is full of difficulties. He is not a little mystified when he encounters in her periodically recurring phases of hypersensitiveness, unreasonableness and loss of the sense of proportion. He is frankly perplexed when confronted with the complete alteration of character in a woman who is child-bearing ... he sees serious and long-continued mental disorders developing in connection with the approaching extinction of a woman's reproductive faculty ... no doctor can ever lose sight of the fact that the mind of woman is always threatened with danger from the reverberations of her physiological emergencies.

Although this outburst appears to have been a spontaneous reaction to the Pankhursts' campaign rather than part of a concerted effort by Anti-Suffragism, it immediately damaged the cause by exposing to public view

[49] Violet Markham to Elizabeth Haldane, 6 Mar. 1912, National Library of Scotland: Haldane Papers 6023, fos. 103–6.
[50] *The Times*, 28 Mar. 1912.

both the extreme opinions of some Antis, and the divisions within their organization. Letters poured into *The Times* scornful of Wright's views, including
those from men and doctors such as Sir Victor Horsley who refuted any
claims by Wright to represent medical opinion: 'every one of us regards the
letter as an insult to women, but . . . Sir Almroth Wright has also insulted his
profession and his sex'.[51] Other correspondents mocked Wright for his sheer
eccentricity: 'we also know him as an irresponsible humourist who tells us
that personal cleanliness is a danger, physical exercise of no value to health,
and open windows a blunder'.[52]

But by far the most telling responses came from women. Eleanor Cecil
challenged Mrs Humphry Ward to say whether she endorsed 'the misogyn-
istic and retrogressive view of women expressed by Sir Almroth Wright'.
After a week Violet Markham offered a dignified criticism of Wright for failing to show 'that calm and dispassionate judgement which we look for from a
man of science'. She suggested he had shown himself foolish for generalizing
about women from a few examples and for throwing fuel on the flames of the
sex war. Finally Mrs Ward repudiated 'the bitter and unseemly violence
which [Wright's] letter displays'; and she observed that 'if the suffragist
movement contained only the elements he allows, it would long ago have
spent itself in disaster'.[53] Despite this the League compounded the offence in
women's eyes by succumbing to the temptation to circulate the original
letter as a pamphlet to members of both Houses of Parliament.[54] There can be
little doubt that the letter was counter-productive, for it carelessly revealed
crude prejudices which, though widely held by male Antis, were usually confined to their private correspondence and their gentlemen's clubs. By exposing them to public view at a time when Ward and Markham's controversy
inside the League had reached its height, Wright unwittingly exacerbated the misgivings amongst the leading female opponents of female
enfranchisement.

Clearly the Antis suffered from internal divisions as serious as those
afflicting the suffragist camp. They, too, found the non-party approach complicated. For example, Cromer and Curzon felt irritated by Mrs Ward's
readiness to support female candidates who happened to be Liberals.[55] This
was only to be expected in view of the violent partisan emotions aroused by
the 'People's Budget' of 1909, the reform of the House of Lords in 1911, and

  [51] *The Times*, 30 Mar. 1912.   [52] Stanley Leathes, *The Times*, 1 Apr. 1912.
  [53] *The Times*, 2 Apr. 1912; 8 Apr. 1912; 10 Apr. 1912.
  [54] Ethel Williams in *The Standard*, 17 Apr. 1912.
  [55] Violet Markham to Lord Cromer (copy), 10 Feb. 1912; Violet Markham to Mrs Ward,
Mar. 1912, BLPES: Markham Papers 26/30.

the re-emergence of Irish Home Rule in 1912. Not surprisingly, no Labour or Socialist Antis appear to have been associated with the NLOWS. Even the Liberals showed considerable reluctance to be prominently involved, no doubt for fear of exposing themselves to criticism in their constituencies and local parties. However, this left the League apparently dominated by right-wing Tories and Liberal Unionists. The leading Liberal Antis, Lewis Harcourt and Lord Crewe, were handicapped as members of the government; they cooperated privately with Curzon, donated to the funds and acted as go-betweens for him and Asquith.[56] But they felt constrained by the damage such contact could do to their standing in the Liberal Party, and by the need to avoid provoking a split in the cabinet. J. A. Pease, another who professed himself vehemently opposed to votes for women, declined to be associated with the cause at all; and this extended to several wives such as Mary Harcourt who refused to join the committee.[57] Even Asquith, whom Curzon persistently tried to attract onto the League's platform at the Albert Hall, refused to allow his name to appear in the list of subscribers.[58]

To become a Conservative-dominated pressure group would have been less worrying for the League if the Tory Party itself had been more reliable. But, as we have seen, by the 1900s suffragism had made major advances in that quarter. Lord Lytton, the Earl of Selborne, Lord Robert Cecil, and Alfred Lyttleton campaigned uninhibitedly for women's suffrage, while Balfour allowed himself, allegedly under the influence of his female relations, Lady Betty and Lady Frances Balfour, to be drawn closer into the suffragist camp. The leading Antis, Austen Chamberlain and Walter Long, seemed reluctant to sign Anti-Suffragist petitions for fear of provoking Balfour into a counter-declaration.[59] Nor did the leadership coup of 1911 which replaced Balfour with Andrew Bonar Law improve matters, for the new Leader told Cromer that he considered himself pledged to support the Conciliation Bill.[60] Moreover, the lack of cooperation at the top had, according to Cromer, 'produced a very considerable effect upon the subordinate ranks and has more or less hypnotised all the Unionist Agents'. He complained bitterly that 'the apathy and want of intelligence amongst the Unionists generally is past all belief'.[61]

[56] Lord Cromer to Lord Curzon, 7 July 1910; Lord Crewe to Lord Curzon, 19 July 1910; Lewis Harcourt to Lord Curzon, 7 July 1910, Curzon Papers, BL, F112/33.

[57] J. A. Pease to Lord Curzon, 3 Jan. 1913; Mary Harcourt to Lord Curzon, 5 Aug. 1910, Curzon Papers, BL, F112/33.

[58] H. H. Asquith to Lord Curzon, 26 July 1910; Lord Cromer to Lord Curzon, 27 July 1910, Curzon Papers, BL, F112/33; Lord Cromer to Lord Curzon, 15 Dec. 1911, Curzon Papers, BL, F112/34.

[59] Arnold Ward to Lord Curzon, 19 July 1910, Curzon Papers, BL, F112/33.

[60] Lord Cromer to Lord Curzon, 18 Jan. 1912, Curzon Papers, BL, F112/35.

[61] Lord Cromer to Lord Curzon, 5 Feb. 1912, 8 Feb. 1912, Curzon Papers, BL, F112/35.

This was not entirely attributable to conversions to suffragism amongst Conservatives; for many of the ladies chose to devote their efforts to promoting tariff reform or opposing Home Rule, because the vote was simply not the important issue.[62] But whatever the reason, the Anti-Suffragist cause was dwindling in the party in which it ought to have been strongest.

Anti-Suffragist Tactics

To a large extent the Antis were parasitic upon their opponents for tactics and ideas; they felt obliged to emulate them by gathering petitions, intervening at by-elections, and canvassing members of parliament. This was unavoidable for an organization that had entered the field relatively late in the day. Despite this the Antis caught up with their rivals in several respects. By 1910 they had established a campaign committee comprising ten MPs including A. MacCallum Scott, Neil Primrose, and Hilaire Belloc from the Liberals and J. W. Hills and Arnold Ward for the Conservatives. The Committee attempted to dissuade members from supporting Kemp's Conciliation Bill in May 1911 by emphasizing the failure of the suffragists to obtain a popular mandate for votes for women. To this end the Antis produced their own petitions signed by 337,000 people in 1908, by 254,000 in 1909, and by 329,000 in 1911.[63] However, at the parliamentary level they were now clearly pulling against the tide. An analysis conducted by Gladys Pott in 1910 put the Anti-Suffrage members at only 189 by comparison with 283 pro-Suffragists and 175 whose views remained unknown or uncertain.[64] They campaigned in the 1910 general elections but struggled to find any strategy beyond offering support to those candidates who were basically unsympathetic to enfranchisement but were constantly looking over their shoulders at their constituents.[65] They also attempted to pressurize MPs into receiving local deputations from Anti-Suffragists, and tried to embarrass prominent suffragists such as Sir George Kemp by confronting them with canvassing returns showing opposition to votes for women in their own constituencies.[66] In some

---

[62] C. Moir to Mr Rylands, 9 Jan. 1913, Manchester Central Library: Manchester Branch NLOWS M131/10.

[63] Memorandum, May 1911, Manchester Central Library: Manchester Branch NLOWS, M131/3/2.

[64] G. S. Pott, Analysis of Information, Dec. 1910, Curzon Papers, BL, F112/33.

[65] Editorial, *Anti-Suffrage Review*, Jan. 1910.

[66] N. Ormsby-Scott, circular letter, 6 Jan. 1912; C. Moir to the secretary (copy), 13 Apr. 1911; Lucy T. Lewis, circular letter, 12 May 1911, Manchester Central Library: Manchester Branch NLOWS, M131/3/2.

cases they successfully exposed the lack of conviction amongst members supposedly committed to women's suffrage. Montagu Barlow admitted to being pledged to the Conciliation Bill, but assured the Antis he was 'not greatly moved by the suffrage question at all'. This was frustrating, as is suggested by their comment on Sir William Aitken (Ashton-under-Lyne): 'like the bulk of our invertibrate, jelly-fish senators . . . he is sitting on the fence at the present moment wondering how he has *got* to vote'.[67]

While these efforts confirmed what the suffragists already knew—that many members were vacillating and lukewarm—it also underlined the need for the local organization which impressed the politicians. In this respect the social-geographical distribution of Anti-Suffragism proved a handicap. Of the original 26 branches, 18 were in London and the south of England; and by October 1909 no fewer than 75 of the 104 were concentrated in this area.[68] This almost certainly reflected a heavily middle- or upper-class membership. Yet one finds local organizers claiming that 'the working classes are solidly with us'.[69] This is not altogether surprising as the canvassing notes prepared by the Antis show a shrewd appreciation of the working-class woman's perspective. The tactic was to flatter her domestic role and skills, and appeal to her pride in being 'only' a housewife. Faced with the classic evasive response to the effect that the housewife had insufficient time to think about votes for women, the canvasser was primed to reply: 'Well! That is just what we say! If women do their work, they have *not*, most of them, time to go to meetings and study politics. . . . Now the Suffragists are saying that all the women who stay at home and do their work are on their side. Are you?'[70] It is difficult to evaluate such material. It shows an awareness of the latent Anti-Suffragism amongst housewives who felt vaguely threatened by feminism, but in view of the uneven distribution of local organization this may well have remained a largely untapped resource. When the North Berkshire branch recruited 88 working-class members it received due publicity, which suggests this was a rare achievement, and it probably reflected groups of dutiful servant girls following their employers' known wishes.[71] One would need a breakdown of the League's membership to show what proportion paid a guinea to be on the council, or five shillings for regular membership as opposed to the one shilling to be an Associate.

[67] C. Moir (copy) to the secretary, 13 Apr. 1911, Manchester Central Library: Manchester Branch NLOWS, M131/3/2; J. Broadbent to C. Moir, 22 Jan. 1913, M131/10.

[68] *Anti-Suffrage Review*, Dec. 1908, 2; Oct. 1909.

[69] C. Moir to Lord Alston, 9 Jan. 1913, Manchester Central Library: Manchester Branch NLOWS, M131/10.

[70] 'Arguments for Use in Poor Districts', *Anti-Suffrage Review*, Jan. 1911, 13.

[71] *Anti-Suffrage Review*, June 1910, 5.

Where the source material does permit a closer look at grass roots Anti-Suffragism a gloomy picture emerges. The Manchester-based branch of the League, for example, attempted to propagate the message throughout Lancashire and Cheshire, a region characterized by a radical tradition and an underlying Conservatism. By the summer of 1910 the local Antis admitted to lacking the local presence necessary to pressurize MPs over the Conciliation Bill. In August the secretary conceded privately that 'the branch does not seem to make any headway'. By October membership had fallen from 349 to 270, and in Liverpool it comprised a mere twenty.[72] This may have been a sign of demoralization caused by the large majority in favour of the Conciliation Bill; but it also reflected the social composition of the movement. For the active participants in Manchester Anti-Suffragism lived ten to twenty miles from the city in salubrious parts of Cheshire; this meant that their urban organizations were often outposts in hostile territory. Consequently, the committee felt reluctant to hold a rally at Manchester's Free Trade Hall for fear of being humiliated if the meeting was swamped by pro-suffragists. By November 1910 Cromer even contemplated winding up the branch altogether.[73] In the event membership expanded to 720 by the summer of 1911, though the organization continued to suffer from lack of funds and commitment; even in middle-class districts the members were admitted to be 'absolutely apathetic!'.[74] As a result, Anti-Suffragist speakers invariably got defeated when they held debates with their opponents, and the League avoided holding meetings in such places as Oldham and Rochdale for fear of being outnumbered. In Warrington they claimed it was unnecessary to intervene as the suffragists themselves were relatively inactive! In December 1911 the organizer in Manchester continued to advise against a Free Trade Hall meeting: 'the only people interested are suffragists and they have large and strong organisations extending over a wide area'.[75] This dismal cycle continued through 1913 and 1914. The truth is that the Antis felt happiest in drawing-room meetings rather than in public campaigning. Their strength lay amongst the senior politicians entrenched in the House of Lords and the Commons; but the latter had become increasingly unreliable because

[72] Lucy T. Lewis to Miss Q. Hogg, 11 June 1910; the Secretary to T. Lewis (copy), 3 August 1910; Mrs Simon to Jack Scott, 7 Oct. 1910, Manchester Central Library: Manchester Branch NLOWS, M131/4/1.

[73] Secretary to T. Lewis, 28 Nov. 1910, Manchester Central Library: Manchester Branch NLOWS, M131/4/11; Lord Cromer to Mr Hamilton, 29 Nov. 1910, M131/3/1.

[74] C. Moir to N. Ormsby-Scott, 10 Nov. 1911, Manchester Central Library: Manchester NLOWS, M131/3/2.

[75] W. Martin, report to headquarters, 6 Dec. 1911; C. Moir to N. Ormsby-Scott, 27 Dec. 1911, Manchester Central Library: Manchester Branch NLOWS, M131/3/2; C. Moir to Mr Rylands, 9 Jan. 1913, M131/10.

members were vulnerable to trends in public opinion which the Antis' local weakness made them largely unable to reverse.

By contrast the Antis demonstrated much more originality and skill in their tactics at the national level. For example, they exploited the divisions in the suffragist camp by focusing on the threat of adult suffrage.[76] A good opportunity presented itself in the shape of Geoffrey Howard's Adult Suffrage Bill in 1909 which proposed to reduce the residence qualification for voters to three months and to abolish plural voting. This was rejected by the Pankhursts, Millicent Fawcett, and, predictably, by Lady Knightley on behalf of the Conservative suffragists.[77] Despite this, the Bill won by 159 to 124 votes, though significantly the Tory members opposed it by 78 to 1 thus neatly driving a party political wedge into the suffrage majority. When the suffragists responded with the Conciliation Bill in 1910, which was obviously designed to maintain Conservative support, the Antis countered by arguing that the policy of the Labour Party since 1904 had been adult suffrage, and thus *any* bill to enfranchise women would accelerate progress in that direction. The belief that young women would be highly susceptible to Socialism, however implausible in the light of later evidence, remained deeply engrained on the right; as late as 1927 the *Daily Mail* regularly regaled its readers with editorials on 'Why Socialists Want Votes for Flappers'.[78] In 1912 this claim gained some plausibility when the National Union of Women's Suffrage Societies formed an alliance with the Labour Party. Following the defeat of the Conciliation Bill in that year many left-wing suffragists decided to focus on a more democratic measure of women's suffrage, a shift which put the Conservative suffragists under pressure.

Faced with a suffragist majority in the Commons the Antis' shrewdest innovation lay in a systematic canvass of the existing female local government electors, which aggravated the politicians' long-standing suspicion that votes for women remained the cause of a minority of enthusiasts. The findings invariably suggested that these women opposed parliamentary enfranchisement by a margin of around four to one. Thus 'the very class in whose interests the Conciliation Bill is framed, do not desire Woman Suffrage'.[79] Naturally this evidence was wholly contradicted by canvasses carried out

---

[76] This did not stop them from using the opposite argument—that the proposal was too narrow: 'The wife of the poor man would hardly ever find herself in a position to secure a vote.... The suffragists are not demanding votes for women, but votes for wealthy women': 'What Woman Suffrage Means', WNASL, No. 7, 1908.

[77] *Anti-Suffrage Review*, Apr. 1909, 1.

[78] Pugh, *Women's Movement*, 77–8, 113; *Daily Mail*, 20, 23, 28 Apr. 1927.

[79] See reports in *Anti-Suffrage Review*, Nov. 1910, Dec. 1910, May 1911; *The Times*, 13 Mar. 1911, 2 May 1911, 9 Jan. 1912.

by the suffragist organizations who challenged the methods employed by the League (see Chapter 9). However, the accuracy and reliability of the canvass was beside the point. Neither side could prove its claims; but by producing evidence of female opinion the Anti-Suffragist propagandists succeeded in forcing their opponents onto the defensive. However dubious, their findings fuelled the misgivings amongst many nominally suffragist MPs whose votes had boosted the majority behind the Conciliation Bills in 1910 and 1911.

The Antis' other tactical initiative followed logically from the canvass. If ordinary people really did remain unconvinced by decades of suffragist propaganda, then the resort to a referendum might administer the *coup de grâce*. This must, however, be seen as a desperate step on the part of the Antis, justified only by the apparent shift of parliamentary opinion to the suffrage side between 1906 and 1911. Though alien to the British political system, the referendum had become increasingly fashionable in right-wing circles since Lord Salisbury had developed the idea of the mandate as an expedient for justifying the peers' rejection of reforming legislation. The referendum simply extended and formalized Salisbury's logic. Since the Tory leaders had accepted it as an expedient for defusing the unpopularity attached to tariff reform, it was scarcely surprising that Bonar Law felt inclined to adopt a referendum for women's suffrage.[80] In the cabinet Winston Churchill energetically promoted the referendum during late 1911 and early 1912 but purely as a means of obstructing the reform.[81]

However, the referendum proved to be too complicated an expedient to command the general backing of the Antis. Who should be eligible to vote in a referendum? The logic of Anti-suffragist thinking pointed to men alone. In the words of one of their more excitable leaflets: 'Men of England, your interests and those of your families and the welfare of the country are in danger. . . . A large number of amiable but short-sighted MPs are willing to grant this demand *without getting your permission*.'[82] However, it was obvious that the rejection of women's suffrage by a vote of men would have resolved nothing. Conversely, to allow women to participate in a referendum seemed patently illogical; it would have made the Antis' position ridiculous, and might even have opened the way to complete adult suffrage. In any case Curzon regarded a referendum as unnecessary as long as the House of Lords could be

---

[80] Lord Cromer to Lord Curzon, 18 Jan. 1912, Curzon Papers, BL, F112/35.

[81] Winston Churchill to the Master of Elibank (copy), 18 Dec. 1911; H. H. Asquith to Winston Churchill, 23 Dec. 1911; Lord Curzon to Winston Churchill, 20 Jan. 1912, Randolph Churchill, *Winston Churchill* (Heinemann, 1969), ii/3, 1473, 1477, 1481–2.

[82] 'Votes for Women—Never', NLOWS, not dated.

relied upon to delay a suffrage bill for two years: 'we Antis want a Referendum only if the Government uses the Parliament Act to force a bill on the House of Lords'.[83] The whole scheme looked even less realistic in the light of the cabinet's attitude. Sir Charles Hobhouse assured Curzon that ministers had looked carefully at a referendum as a means of testing the support for the Conciliation Bill, but were most unlikely to adopt it because that would 'wreck the Liberals for a long time to come'.[84] To recognize the principle would have been to render almost any radical reform vulnerable to delaying tactics. Interestingly, when the Antis took a deputation to see Asquith in December 1911 it was Violet Markham not Curzon who urged the use of a referendum. The prime minister, perhaps mischievously, appeared to encourage her, only to emphasize how ineffectual an expedient it would be if confined to men: 'I do not believe you would allay agitation by any verdict so pronounced.'[85] One senses that the Antis found Asquith almost as frustrating as the suffragists did.

Consequently, the referendum failed to emerge as a realistic means of breaking the deadlock. Indeed, the significance of the issue lies largely in what it tells us about the plight of the opponents of women's suffrage during the last years of peace; their failure to stem the drift of the MPs towards suffragism drove them to resort to an appeal over the heads of the politicians to the public. This interpretation is corroborated by the refusal of the suffragists to be drawn by the referendum option. Always committed to playing the parliamentary game, by 1911 they appeared to have all but won it; anything else represented a delay and a diversion at best, and at worst a setback for the cause.

Conclusions

It would be wrong to minimize the role of the opponents of the women's cause simply because we know that they were on the losing side. They exploited some of the flaws in suffragism very effectively, even if they relied too heavily on their opponents to create their own momentum. When they denounced the 'mock-heroic imprisonment' of suffragettes in 1908 and

[83] 'Memorandum by Lord Curzon and Women's Suffrage and the Referendum', Mar. 1914; Memorandum by Curzon, 22 Feb. 1913, Curzon Papers, BL, F112/39; Lord Curzon to Lord Cromer (copy), 19 Jan. 1911, Curzon Papers, BL, F112/34.
[84] Lord Cromer to Lord Curzon, 20 Jan. 1912, Curzon Papers, BL, F112/35.
[85] Violet Markham in the *Westminster Gazette*, 27 Dec. 1911; *Votes for Women*, 22 Dec. 1911, 2.

claimed that attempts to rush the House of Commons had provoked 'a wave of angry laughter' amongst the public, they were not entirely wrong.[86] The weakness lay in the Antis' heavy reliance upon their opponents to commit further outrages as a means both of deterring the politicians from granting the vote and also of covering up their own internal divisions. They also continued to set an unrealistic valuation on their own efforts. As late as 1912 they declared that their rally at the Albert Hall had 'sounded the death-knell of the agitation in favour of votes for women'.[87] In reality the Antis themselves faced as great a crisis as the suffragists by that stage. They were finding it difficult to obtain speakers and to maintain local branches; defection and disillusionment especially among female members weakened the organization; and even the defeat of the Conciliation Bill could not obscure the minority status of Anti-Suffragism in the Commons. According to Arnold Ward even *The Times*, hitherto the staunchest of allies, was in retreat from Anti-Suffragism.[88]

Inevitably this deteriorating situation generated friction within the League which led to the resignation of Colonel Lewis as chairman and of Captain Creed as director in 1912. Curzon then attempted to reduce expenditure and to reorganize by appointing the formidable Gladys Pott, one of the few women of whom he and Cromer had a high opinion, as secretary in 1913–14. Pott hoped to achieve a greater concentration on the press and propaganda, and more effective coordination between the League and its parliamentary supporters. But however well organized, by this stage the Antis were rowing against the tide in the shape of long-term political and social changes. Their local activists had noticed the difficulty in recruiting younger women which they attributed to the spread of higher education amongst the middle and upper classes during the previous two decades. 'Most of the younger generation ... are taught by their school teachers to demand votes for women much in the same way that they might be taught to accept the ten commandments,' complained one worker.[89] There was no more telling symptom of shifting attitudes than the way in which Mrs Humphry Ward fell victim to anti-Victorianism. By the early 1900s her views on women, as expressed in her anti-divorce novel, *Marriage a la Mode* (1908), had begun to antagonize her readers especially in the United States.[90] When she debated with

[86] *Anti-Suffrage Review*, Dec. 1908, 1.   [87] *Morning Post*, 29 Feb. 1912.
[88] Arnold Ward to Lord Curzon, 5 Feb. 1913, Curzon Papers, BL, F112/36; see also *The Times*, 31 Dec. 1913.
[89] Alfred D. Seares to C. Moir, 27 Feb. 1914, Manchester Central Library: Manchester Branch NLOWS, M131/4/12.
[90] Sutherland, *Ward*, 104.

Millicent Fawcett in 1909, Ward was shocked and angry to find herself defeated by 235 votes to 74. Even more ominously when she visited Newnham and Girton Colleges to speak on female enfranchisement she found herself subjected to the indignity of heckling and hostility from the students.[91] To add insult to injury, Somerville severed relations with her altogether. Yet Mrs Ward's rejection by young educated women should not have come as such a surprise to her. Aged 50 by 1909, she had become enough of a Victorian figure to attract the fashionable scorn of the educated and sophisticated; but in becoming out of touch Mrs Ward gradually ceased to be the asset to Anti-Suffragism that she had been in the 1880s. In this period the Antis' natural reservoir of support in the Conservative Party had dwindled as a consequence of women's participation in electoral, municipal, and philanthropic work which had modified assumptions and made women seem more relevant to the whole question of National Efficiency than they had appeared to be in the 1870s. Curzon and Cromer could not realistically expect to unravel this pattern of change whatever tactics they used or arguments they adopted.

This perspective underlines the importance of the 1890s as the stage at which the Antis allowed their case to go by default; they never really recovered the ground they had lost. Yet the leaders seemed slow to recognize their situation. As late as 1913 Curzon stubbornly refused requests to release the remainder of the funds which he and Cromer had raised on the grounds that it was hardly worth preventing the Commons from passing a women's bill. He reasoned that the real crisis would not come until the MPs had thrice passed the bill under the Parliament Act; during the two-year period that must elapse the Antis would throw their resources into a campaign to persuade the country of the folly of enfranchising women.[92] He evidently contemplated something equivalent to the protracted struggle waged by the Unionists over the Irish Home Rule Bill. This, however, illustrates Curzon's misplaced confidence in his own party, for he had scarcely grasped how far the battle had gone against him amongst the Conservatives. On the eve of war Lord Selborne's suffrage bill was defeated by the peers—but by only forty votes. This heralded the crumbling of resistance in the Lords during 1917.[93] In effect by 1914 the League had been reduced to the increasingly desperate belief that suffragette outrages would curb the suffragist tendencies of the MPs; meanwhile Asquith and his die-hard colleagues could be relied upon to prevaricate almost indefinitely.

[91] Ibid. 305–6.
[92] Arnold Ward to Lord Curzon, 5 Feb. 1913; Typed memorandum by Curzon, 27 Nov. 1912, Curzon Papers, BL, F112/36.
[93] Pugh, *Electoral Reform*, 151–3.

Part III

Edwardian Climax

8

The Anatomy of Militancy

THE decision of Emmeline Pankhurst and her eldest daughter, Christabel, to form a new pressure group, the Women's Social and Political Union (WSPU), in October 1903, was one of the heroic initiatives of modern history. Their bravado in proposing to succeed where so many better connected and more experienced suffragists had for thirty-six years failed was remarkable. Not surprisingly, the escapades and the sufferings of the Edwardian suffragettes constitute by far the most familiar aspect of the women's struggle for enfranchisement; but research in the last twenty years has cast doubt on the centrality usually accorded to militancy. Traditional accounts tend to take the form of narratives which inevitably sacrifice analysis to the wealth of detail and anecdotage and to the appeal of the human drama. The aim here is to focus on the key questions and issues raised by militancy with a view to putting the campaign into a truer perspective and thus evaluating its significance.

Why Militant?

The Pankhursts' own rationale for the adoption of militant methods involved a mixture of shrewdness and single-mindedness, on the one hand, with a lack of judgement and a measure of pretentiousness, on the other. In essence they sought to cut through to the heart of the suffragists' problem: since the government of the day was responsible for women's votelessness it was logical to pressurize them and them alone. This implied direct pressure by embarrassing a Liberal Government for failing to live up to its liberal pretensions, and indirect pressure by mobilizing the mass of the people against it. For a small family group based in Manchester this represented a highly ambitious objective. It meant appealing to the public to intimidate a government elected in 1906 with a huge overall majority in parliament. As the Home Secretary,

Herbert Gladstone, put it, to compromise with such a group would be 'an exhibition of weakness in the face of these threats'.[1] But the suffragettes gambled that the public would accept that after so long a campaign their new tactics were justified. In any case, the use of militancy, including violence, represented no more than a continuation of a tradition sanctified by decades of practice and by success. 'When men show that they can get reforms without militancy then they can blame women,' wrote a Scottish suffragette in 1913, 'need I say what history has taught us all along the line?'[2]

Several foolish cabinet ministers including Herbert Gladstone (in 1908) and Sir Charles Hobhouse (in 1912) effectively endorsed this view by suggesting that the women had produced nothing to compare with the violence generated by men's demand for the vote in 1832 and 1867; in so doing they provoked further militancy and deprived themselves of the moral high ground on which they claimed to stand. On her visits to the United States Emmeline Pankhurst made great play with this historical rationale: 'Nothing has ever been got out of the British Parliament without something very nearly approaching a revolution', she told her audiences whose forefathers had taken up arms for the principle of no-taxation-without-representation.[3]

It is worth emphasizing that this interpretation commanded wide assent. Lord Lytton defended militancy on the basis of forty years of neglect by the politicians; and Lord Robert Cecil felt that the Liberals had no right to criticize the WSPU since they themselves had taught people to use violence in politics. In the early years of the campaign even Liberal newspapers such as the *Daily News* accepted that militancy was the best means of getting the vote; and the pro-Conservative *Daily Mirror* argued: 'Parliament has never granted any important reform without being bullied.'[4] One elderly Liberal, Dr George Cooper, who sat for Bermondsey, drew approvingly on his experiences of 1867 when the Reform League had stormed the platforms of the politicians who opposed reform and prevented them from speaking: 'I own it is a rough weapon, but cabinet ministers do not recognise antagonists using any other.'[5]

Yet despite this, the Pankhursts' historical analogies were seriously flawed. The acts of arson committed before the 1832 Reform Act hardly provide an adequate explanation for the passage of the bill; neither then nor during the

---

[1] Herbert Gladstone to Lady Frances Balfour (copy), 29 June 1908, Fawcett Library: Fawcett Letters 89/1/33.
[2] Jean Lambie to Roland Muirhead, 11 July 1913, Mitchell Library: Muirhead Papers Box 1/37.
[3] Speech in New York, 21 Oct. 1913.
[4] *Votes for Women*, 10 Nov. 1911; *Daily Mirror*, 2 Mar. 1907.
[5] Quoted in *Votes for Women*, Dec. 1907, 30.

subsequent campaigns in which thousands of Chartists agitated for political reforms did the government back down. When the supporters of the Reform League broke the Hyde Park railings in 1866 and 1867, the authorities, though worried, saw no revolutionary intent in the agitation; they were more influenced by their experience over two decades which suggested that the vote might safely be conceded to certain groups of workingmen. Thus when the Pankhursts invoked the spectacle of John Bright urging the crowds to intimidate parliament in 1867 and Joseph Arch threatening to march 100,000 agricultural labourers to London in 1884, they were striking a rhetorical note not giving a history lesson. In fact, the key to success for the earlier agitators lay in their relationship with the parliamentary forces rather than in their ability to coerce them from outside. Gladstone had put himself at the head of the popular movement and thereby given it a link with the system. This is what Millicent Fawcett doutbtless had in mind when she observed that the English 'are not naturally a revolutionary people; they only condone revolutionary methods when all other courses are blocked'.[6] By contrast, Asquith and the Edwardian Liberal leaders suffered from a failure of imagination and an inability to offer the leadership Gladstone had given; hence the dangerous vacuum which the Pankhursts filled with militancy.

The suffragettes also put the politicians on the defensive by highlighting the inconsistencies in their attitude towards political protest. 'You are full of sympathy with men in Russia,' Mrs Pankhurst pointed out, 'you are full of sympathy with nations that rise against the domination of the Turk.' But above all it was the example of Ireland that appears to have influenced the Pankhursts, both the older Nationalist campaigns and the current resistance of the Ulster Unionists to the Liberal Government. In a speech urging attacks upon property, George Lansbury reminded his audience that Liberal governments had responded to pressure from the Irish.[7] According to this analysis the Home Rulers had gone into decline after 1906 because they had allowed the Liberals to win an election without extracting a pledge to legislate for a Dublin Parliament.[8] However, this was a misleading analogy partly because the Irish already enjoyed the advantage of being voters and sent eighty Nationalist members to Westminster in addition to their command of thousands of Catholic electors in the English urban constituencies on which the Liberals depended. Although the Pankhursts also intervened in by-elections with a view to splitting the Liberal vote, it was consequently almost

[6] Millicent Fawcett to D. Lloyd George (copy), 2 Dec. 1911, Fawcett Library: Fawcett Letters 89/1/54.

[7] *East London Observer*, 19 Apr. 1913; T. M. Kettle in *Votes for Women*, 14 May 1909, 661.

[8] Editorial, *Votes for Women*, 7 May 1908, 146.

impossible for them to demonstrate their ability to make the same impact as
the Irish (see Chapter 9). In any case the Nationalists had actually used a
judicious mixture of agitation and parliamentary pressure to gain their
object. After 1906 they had the favourable majority they required in the
House of Commons, reinforced after 1911 by a new means of overcoming the
resistance of the House of Lords under the Parliament Act; in these circumstances mass agitation became redundant for the Nationalists.

The example of the Ulster Unionists, who used the period between 1912
and 1914 when the Liberals were pushing their Home Rule Bill through
under the terms of the Parliament Act, moved the Pankhursts to even greater
indignation. This was partly because they began to squeeze the suffragettes
out of the headlines and because Asquith showed himself reluctant to punish
Unionist leaders for advocating violence while using the full force of the law
against the women. Christabel insisted: 'The Liberals can no longer say that
the Government will not yield to violence because [they] are doing so.
Unionists . . . can no longer say that violence is not legitimate when used by
women because they have threatened it themselves.' She certainly struck a
chord with Liberal members who felt uneasy about legal proceedings instituted against suffragettes and striking trade unionists while Sir Edward
Carson, Walter Long, and other Unionist politicians freely made inflamma-
tory statements. But Asquith simply denied that the two cases were parallel.[9]

While these claims provided a *rationale* for militant tactics, the immediate
cause for their adoption requires a different explanation. For all their rhetoric
the Pankhurst family actually enjoyed a considerable history of working
along constitutional lines through the Women's Liberal Federation, the
North of England Society for Women's Suffrage, and the Independent
Labour Party (ILP). In 1903 Mrs Pankhurst believed, perhaps naively, that
the Labour Representation Committee (LRC), recently formed, would be
the key to a breakthrough for female suffrage. Accordingly during 1904–5 the
WSPU devoted its efforts largely to addressing meetings of ILP branches,
trade unions, Labour Churches, and Clarion Clubs with a view to making the
vote a priority for Labour at the forthcoming general election.

However, these calculations proved to be unrealistic especially as the
Pankhursts were so impatient for results. As the election approached the candidates of the LRC focused increasingly on free trade, the Taff Vale ruling
and other issues which they regarded as central but which left suffragism
marginal and the women resentful. 'Not one per cent of [Labour's] advocates

⁹ *The Suffragette*, 10 Jan. 1913; Christabel Pankhurst to Janie Allan, 15 Mar. 1914, Janie Allan
Papers, National Library of Scotland, Acc. 4498/3; *Hansard, HC Deb.*, 5th Series, LXII, 14 May 1914,
c. 1279.

were interested in winning women's suffrage' according to Teresa Billington-Greig, 'our bellicose emergence was an unwelcome complication.' Christabel, whose attachment to the ILP had never been as close as her mother's, also became sceptical: 'workingmen are as unjust to women as are those of other classes'.[10] They refused to recognize that the LRC had been established with different priorities in mind; it was engaged in a struggle to win the votes of skilled workers from their traditional Liberal loyalties, and it was in any case suspicious of interference by external organizations like the WSPU which appeared to wish to use the movement for their own purposes. Moreover, though Labour made a breakthrough in 1906 by returning 29 MPs, this was achieved largely by means of an electoral pact with the Liberals who gave many of their candidates a free run; by insisting that the new party should adopt a position of wholesale opposition to the Government, the Pankhursts were asking Labour to saw off the branch on which it sat. Relations would have been easier if franchise reform for men had been more of a priority for the Labour Party, and if the party had not entertained doubts about the limited form of female suffrage being promoted at this time. Fearful of simply extending votes to propertied women, many Socialists opted for the adult suffrage policy which, to the intense irritation of Emmeline Pankhurst, was endorsed at the party conferences in 1904 and 1907. Even leading Labour women such as Mary MacArthur and Margaret Bondfield preferred adult suffrage to a limited women's bill.

The split between the WSPU and the Labour Party which arose from this disagreement was the product of different class and ideological perspectives, dangerously exacerbated by personality clashes. The Pankhursts were far from being alone in finding it difficult to work within the Labour Movement; Isabella Ford, who was middle-class, and Selina Cooper, who was working-class, struggled to make Socialist men give a higher priority to women's interests. But they managed to avoid a total breakdown. Suffragettes were often less patient. Teresa Billington-Greig, a teacher by profession, took a very condescending attitude towards Labour politicians who, she considered, had 'no historical background to inform them'. She described the 'semi-educated type of male always anxious to cling to his one area of mastership'.[11] Friction was easily sparked by the prickly personalities on each side. The ILP Chairman, John Bruce Glasier, who bore the brunt of the Pankhursts' demands in the early 1900s, felt provoked by what he called 'a weary ordeal of chatter about women's suffrage', which led him to denounce the 'miserable sexist

---

[10] Teresa Billington-Greig, Notes, Fawcett Library: Billington-Greig Papers 397 A/6; Christabel Pankhurst, Aug. 1903, quoted in Rosen, *Rise Up Women*, 29.

[11] Teresa Billington-Greig, Notes, Fawcett Library: Billington-Greig Papers 397 A/6.

individualism' of the two women. In a revealing outburst in 1904 he lamented: 'Really the pair are not seeking democratic freedom, but self-importance ... Christabel paints her eyebrows grossly and looks selfish, lazy and wilful. They want to be ladies, not workers, and lack the humility of real heroism.'[12] These remarks encapsulate an important part of the explanation for the eventual failure of militancy. The Pankhursts consciously set out to dress in a very feminine way with a view to disarming critics, and they sought to tap the resources of well-to-do ladies and gentlemen for the cause; but it inevitably proved difficult to reconcile this with an appeal to the working-class movement, for outward signs such as dresses and cosmetics were apt to be interpreted as symptomatic of social climbing which was fatal to their credibility. Even before the suffragettes had become notorious, men like Glasier refused to take them at their own valuation. Though skilful and effective with some audiences, the Pankhursts proved to be counter-productive with others. As a result, during 1903 to 1906 relations between Labour and the WSPU followed the same cycle as those between the earlier suffragists and the Liberals, but much more rapidly. In the Pankhursts' disillusionment with Labour one has the proximate explanation for the adoption of militant tactics once the 1906 election had pushed the suffrage question down the political agenda. But at the time it was not clear that this split was to become a serious flaw in the entire campaign.

The Pankhurst Autocracy

No analysis of the suffragette campaign can overlook the question of leadership. The WSPU began in 1903 as an essentially *family* organization, a quality it retained, despite its enormous expansion, down to 1914; the sibling rivalry between Sylvia, the neglected sister and Christabel, the dominant one, not to mention Mrs Pankhurst's desire to retain the affection of her eldest daughter, all left their mark on the implementation of the militant strategy. Despite the antagonism they provoked amongst colleagues and allies, the two leading Pankhursts also aroused deep admiration and unquestioning loyalty amongst many women. Teresa Billington-Greig, though later a critic of their methods, painted a telling picture of the ability of the Pankhursts to overcome the reservations of older suffragists by their brash enthusiasm and over-confidence. They chattered absurdly about Emmeline becoming prime

[12] Quoted in Lawrence Thompson, *The Enthusiasts: A Biography of John and Katharine Bruce Glasier* (Gollancz, 1971), 136; see also, Martin Pugh, 'Labour and Women's Suffrage', in K. D. Brown (ed.), *The First Labour Party* (Croom Helm, 1985).

minister and Christabel, fresh out of law school, sitting on the Woolsack. But Billington-Greig recognized that this pretentiousness was leavened by intelligence and tactical skill; on acquaintance their minds, she wrote, 'revealed more than crude family megalomania'.[13]

As a result of its origins as a family group the WSPU operated initially on an informal basis. But as it expanded this inevitably generated friction. By the summer of 1906 Fred and Emmeline Pethick-Lawrence had agreed to finance the organization and to arrange a new headquarters at St Clement's Inn in London, while Billington-Greig and others were building up branches in the capital. Christabel and her mother then left Manchester to take control, dispatching Annie Kenney to organize branches in the West of England and a disgruntled Billington-Greig to distant Scotland. By February 1907 the organization had grown to 58 branches and, thanks to the Pethick-Lawrences, was financially secure. Yet it still lacked a formal constitution, a situation which suited Emmeline and Christabel but naturally looked suspect to new members especially those who came from a background in the ILP and other left-wing groups.[14] Herein lay the origins of the first major split of 1907. Our account of this comes largely from a biased source—Billington-Greig who became embittered in later life at being marginalized by the Pankhursts and thus deprived of the fame which they enjoyed through the eventual triumph of the cause. However, her account of the split was corroborated by Mrs Pethick-Lawrence and was not disputed by the Pankhursts themselves; they simply felt justified in insisting on a free hand.[15] After repeated prevarication a draft constitution was drawn up for approval at the annual conference in September 1907 only to be 'dramatically torn up and thrown to the ground'.[16]

No doubt the Pankhursts appreciated that the combination of newly recruited members and a democratic constitution would weaken or even destroy their control. Yet although the arguments were couched in terms of democracy, the underlying cause of this split lay in differences over *politics* as is evident from the fact that the leading figures in the breakaway group, Charlotte Despard, Marion Coates Hansen, and Edith How Martyn held left-wing opinions and were loyal to the Labour Party. The same problem contributed to the later expulsions from the WSPU—the Pethick-Lawrences who stood as Labour candidates, and Sylvia who remained a Socialist and became a Communist after the war.

[13] Teresa Billington-Greig, Notes, Fawcett Library: Billington-Greig Papers 397 A/6.
[14] 'The Birth of the WFL', Fawcett Library: Billington-Greig Papers 397 A/6.
[15] E. Pethick-Lawrence, *My Part*, 176–9.
[16] 'Autobiographical Fragments', Fawcett Library: Billington-Greig Papers, 397 A/6.

In view of the origins of the WSPU in the North of England it was hardly surprising that many rank and file members regarded it originally as a female wing of the ILP. In Middlesborough, for example, Marion Coates Hansen, who established the WSPU branch, was also organizing secretary of the local ILP.[17] Consequently, many women who joined in this period became confused and antagonized by Christabel's insistence on moving to the right. After a by-election at Cockermouth in 1906 where she appeared to support the Conservatives, even though a Labour candidate was standing, there were moves to expel her from the ILP; and it is certain that her anti-Labour stance would have been challenged if not actually overruled if the WSPU's policy had been subject to an annual debate at a representative conference. The fact that the non-militant National Union of Women's Suffrage Societies, which repeatedly proclaimed its non-party policy, also suffered internal disputes arising partly from the partisan loyalties of its members, only underlines the point that party politics was at least as divisive as militant tactics for the Edwardian suffrage movement.

In addition to this, it seemed somehow inconsistent to many suffragists that a movement dedicated to winning democratic rights should deny freedom of debate to its own members, and over the years many of those who worked with Christabel and Emmeline Pankhurst eventually recoiled from their dictatorial style. Helena Swanwick, one of the earliest to reject them, considered Christabel 'cynical and cold at heart. She gave me the impression of fitful and impulsive ambition and of quite ruthless love of domination.' Mary Stocks compared her to Hitler, a point reiterated in an admittedly extreme passage by Cicely Hamilton who depicted the campaign as:

the first indication of the dictatorship movements which are by way of thrusting Democracy out of the European continent. Not the Fascists but the militants of the WSPU first used the word 'leader' as a reverential title ... Emmeline Pankhurst was a forerunner of Lenin, Hitler and Mussolini—the leader whose fiat must go unquestioned, the leader who could do no wrong.[18]

Such hostile comment by women is so widespread that it has to be taken into account in any analysis of the movement. However, it raises several questions. First, is such a view exaggerated to the point of absurdity? Second, to the extent that the Pankhursts *were* autocratic, was this advantageous rather than a flaw as is presumed by the critics?

<hr />

[17] Claire Eustance, 'Daring to be Free: The Evolution of Women's Political Identities in the Women's Freedom League, 1907–1930', Ph.D. thesis (University of York, 1993), 46–7.

[18] Swanwick, *I Have Been Young*, 188; Mary Stocks, *My Commonplace Book* (Peter Davies, 1970), 70; Cicely Hamilton, *Life Errant* (J. M. Dent, 1935), 68.

From 1907 onwards the WSPU was effectively run by a small coterie comprising Emmeline, Christabel as organizing secretary, Fred Pethick-Lawrence as treasurer, and a few paid organizers and others invited by the Pankhursts. In practice, as Mrs Pankhurst spent much time away on tours or in prison, Christabel retained effective leadership. They ruthlessly expelled Fred and Emmeline Pethick-Lawrence in 1912 and Sylvia in 1913, and a whole series of minor withdrawals punctuated the life of the WSPU. As with most autocrats however, the Pankhursts exercised their power most conspicuously over individuals and appointments, for which there was considerable scope once the paid staff had expanded to over a hundred. When Janie Allan, their Scottish organizer, tried to negotiate a deal to suspend militancy during a royal visit to Perth in 1912 in return for the cessation of forcible feeding in the local gaol, they promptly sacked her, saying simply that one could not bargain with the enemy.[19] Christabel was belived to suffer especially strongly from a propensity for personalizing all issues and regarding both colleagues like Sylvia and opponents like Lloyd George as threats to her personal position. On the other hand, it must be recognized that the disputes with Janie Allan, Mrs Despard, the Pethick-Lawrences, and Sylvia all involved issues of tactics or principle notwithstanding the personal element.

Yet if the Pankhursts sometimes behaved autocratically, their policy did not lack some justification: 'Those who cannot follow the general must drop out of the ranks.' This militaristic language was not just empty rhetoric. Once the movement had adopted illegal activities, it had to be able to operate in ways similar to a guerilla force, moving rapidly so as to evade the superior forces ranged against it. This situation inevitably limited the scope for discussing strategy. In the absence of a formal constitution the WSPU leaders could switch tactics quickly so as to respond to or anticipate changing conditions. This flexibility is well illustrated by the adoption of the truce in 1910, its abandonment in 1911, and above all by the events of August 1914 when the Pankhursts seized the opportunity presented by the outbreak of war to reverse their entire relationship with the authorities by suspending the campaign. By contrast the NUWSS embarked upon a series of agonized debates before its official attitude towards the war could be established, and even then a split was not to be avoided; the Pankhursts deserved credit for swiftly appropriating the mantle of patriotism for women's suffrage.

However, such key decisions and the dramatic schisms in their organization give a misleading impression of the Pankhursts' effective authority. They

[19] Helen Crawfurd, MS Autobiography, 110–11, Marx Memorial Library.

found it easier to manipulate personnel than to determine policy. Indeed, they frequently found themselves being led by spontaneous initiatives taken by their followers. It was Mary Leigh who first broke the windows in Downing Street after Asquith's refusal to meet a deputation in June 1908; hunger-striking began on the initiative of Marion Wallace Dunlop in July 1909.[20] When the suffragists began the boycott of the Census in 1911, the WSPU leaders initially spurned the idea, but they soon found it was too popular amongst the members to ignore and so they adopted it too. To some extent their readiness to compromise in 1911 reflected their uncertainty about their own strategy at that stage. Perhaps the greatest freelance suffragette was Emily Wilding Davison who began to set fire to letter boxes in December 1911 on her own responsibility and committed suicide under the King's horse on Derby Day in 1913. In any case, when Christabel fled to Paris in March 1912 she retained only the most tenuous grip on the movement for the next two and a half years despite the regular visits by the loyal Annie Kenney and her own articles in *The Suffragette*. In that period the activists operated as scattered individuals and the whole suffragette movement lost momentum and coordination.

Thus, there can be no simple conclusion about the impact of the Pankhursts' approach to leadership. It clearly suffered from a serious drawback in its tendency to provoke splits, though this was also a feature of the non-militant side. Indeed, splits were a congenital weakness in the whole movement from the 1860s onwards; the recriminations they involved helped to discredit the cause and also diverted the energies of the activists into internal rivalry rather than into external propagation of the cause. On the other hand, the multiplication of women's suffrage organizations did bring some advantages; it extended the appeal to those with differing ideas about tactics, to different sections of society, to men, to the various political parties, to the churches, and to several occupational groups. This variety also maximized the scope for developing fresh ideas and tactics, the best example being the Women's Freedom League which was the result of the split of 1907. The League pioneered some more subtle variations on the theme of militancy; it also facilitated collaboration between suffragists who favoured militancy and those who inclined towards constitutional methods, and to that extent actually *mitigated* the divisions within the movement. In fact the formal divisions which loomed so large amongst the leaders, proved to be of far less significance for the women's movement at the grass roots.

---

[20] Though Mary Allen claimed to have been the first to do so in 1908: Mary Allen, *Lady in Blue* (Stanley Paul, 1936), 20–1.

The Relationship between Militancy and Non-Militancy

Traditionally the suffrage movement has been regarded as fundamentally divided by the foundation of the WSPU in 1903. However, research into the local and regional campaigns and the experience of less prominent activists has gone a long way to undermining that view by revealing the common ground that existed between the different organizations and the innumerable variations within militancy itself. This is not to ignore the initial challenge faced by the constitutional suffragists whose patient efforts were frankly derided by the Pankhursts. Indeed, by 1906 the NUWSS found it necessary to define its position: 'confusion having arisen in the public mind'.[21] The National Union emphasized that it was strictly non-party, did not oppose Liberal candidates on principle like the WSPU, and relied upon 'ordinary constitutional methods of agitation'. Unhappily for the National Union, its activists often suffered when members of the public vented their anger towards the suffragettes on them.[22] Confusion was inevitable especially as some women in Manchester, Newcastle, and elsewhere had resigned from existing suffrage societies to form new WSPU branches.[23]

The NUWSS found itself in an impossible position; it was either too hostile or too sympathetic to the suffragettes. When Millicent Fawcett offered public support to the WSPU following the incident at the Manchester Free Trade Hall in 1905 she attracted an immediate rebuke from Margaret Ashton on behalf of both the non-militants in Lancashire and the Liberal women in the region on the grounds that those who had interrupted the meeting represented a small clique which had been disowned by the North of England Society.[24] This reminds us that the rank and file often disagreed with their leaders over politics as much as over tactics. In both North-West and North-East England suffragists sometimes insisted on supporting Liberal candidates when their London headquarters sent down organizers to oppose them.[25]

---

[21] 'The Policy of the NUWSS', not dated, 1906; they found it irritating when newspapers such as the *Daily Mail* and the *Daily Mirror* reported the National Union's 'Mud March' of Feb. 1907 as the work of the suffragettes.

[22] On meetings broken up, see *Daily Express*, 6 Dec. 1907.

[23] *Annual Report*, North of England Society, 1905, records resignations of executive members; David Neville, 'The Women's Suffrage Movement in the North East of England, 1900–1914', M.Phil. thesis (University of Northumbria, 1991), 44.

[24] Liddington, *One Hand Tied Behind Us*, 194–5.

[25] In Chorley all the Liberal members of the Suffrage Society resigned in 1913 when the NUWSS failed to back the Liberal candidate in a by-election: *Annual Report*, W. Lancashire, W. Cheshire, and N. Wales Federation, 1913, 33.

Yet despite the rivalry created by the new organization, leading non-militants were undoubtedly appreciative of and conciliatory towards the suffragettes, at least during the early years. Even Lady Knightley, who disapproved of militancy, acknowledged that they were helping the cause by 'their pluck and determination'. Mrs Fawcett wrote in 1909: 'I feel that the action of the [suffragette] prisoners has touched the imagination of the country in a manner which quieter methods did not succeed in doing.'[26] Following the release of some suffragettes in December 1906 Fawcett had joined in a luncheon in their honour, an action which exposed her to attack by Gladys Pott of the Anti-Suffrage League for condoning violence.[27] But the National Union continued to support the suffragettes to the extent of protesting when they were not treated as political prisoners.[28]

Quite apart from understandable feelings of sympathy, some non-militants argued that their own organizations benefited indirectly from suffragette activities in terms of the extra funds and support engendered. Mary Stocks even described the National Union as 'parasitic' upon the WSPU at least up to 1912: 'the fire kindled by Mrs Pankhurst's organisation helped to heat the furnaces of Mrs Fawcett's'.[29] This verdict appears to be corroborated by the growth in National Union membership during 1907 to 1911 (see Chapter 10). But the relationship was complex, for the non-militants benefited not just from the extra publicity won by militancy, but also from the effect the suffragettes had in encouraging the National Union itself to undertake mass demonstrations for the first time. An early example was the so-called 'Mud March' by several thousand non-militants in very inclement weather in February 1907. This attracted very sympathetic reporting and comment; 'the militant element was conspicuously absent', noted the *Daily Graphic*, thereby underlining how the two organizations complemented one another; by drawing criticism upon themselves the suffragettes helped the constitutional suffragists to be better appreciated by the press and the politicians.[30] This effect is also noticeable locally in the work of the Glasgow and West of Scotland Society which had begun sedately in 1902 with drawing-room meetings patronized by titled ladies such as the Countess of Aberdeen and dignitaries such as the Lord Provost, but later organized public demonstrations, ran by-election campaigns and pressurized MPs. The suffragettes intrigued many respectable women and thereby led them to reconsider their own role. In June 1909 Lady Frances Balfour and her sister-in-law, Lady

[26] *The Queen*, 29 Aug. 1909; E. Pethick-Lawrence, *My Part*, 171.
[27] *The Times*, 8 Mar. 1912.   [28] *The Common Cause*, 29 July 1909, 207.
[29] Lady Frances Balfour in the *Evening Standard*, 18 Feb. 1907; Stocks, *Commonplace Book*, 66.
[30] *Daily Graphic, Daily Chronicle, Daily Mail*, 11 Feb. 1907.

Betty, both staunch constitutionalists, treated themselves to a night out with the militants. They followed them from the Caxton Hall to Victoria Street, Parliament Square, and Whitehall. 'The women showed extraordinary courage in the rough rushes of the crowd round them,' Lady Frances reported, 'there is a fine spirit, but whether it is not rather thrown away on these tactics remains a doubt in my mind.'[31] The experience left the ladies personally committed to non-militancy but appreciative of both the suffragettes and the police.

Yet just as opinions about tactics varied amongst the non-militants, so even within the WSPU itself militancy ranged from the total dedication of a few to a largely nominal or symbolic endorsement on the part of many ordinary members. Local reports of WSPU branches suggest that they relied on 'At Homes' and drawing-room meetings as much as the constitutionalists.[32] Mary Stocks recalled two of her aunts who joined the WSPU only to attend meetings and walk in processions and avoided militant action altogether. Elizabeth Robins defended militancy but never committed an act of militancy herself. Cicely Hamilton admitted that her own militancy was 'of the slightest', and she felt that the whole approach suffered from a 'lack of logic'. Another variation on militant participation has been identified by Leah Leneman who has identified some Scottish suffragettes who were reluctant to practise militancy at home but ready to venture to London to make the experiment. Helen Crawfurd, also a Scots activist, recorded that while determined to break the windows of a government minister she also wanted to return home as quickly as possible afterwards.[33]

The account left by Margaret Haig (later Lady Rhondda) is very revealing of attitudes among the rank and file of the WSPU. She decided to set fire to a letter box as this seemed an easy form of militancy; but after an unsuccessful attempt she received a one-month sentence, was released after five days, and never tried to repeat her offence. When she explained the episode to her local WSPU branch in Newport, she found they were far from keen to follow even her modest example; as a result she scrapped all the materials supplied for tackling letter boxes.[34] Such examples help to put the suffragette campaign in a truer perspective. Many of its members were either non-militant or

---

[31] Lady Frances Balfour to Millicent Fawcett, 29 June 1909, Fawcett Library: Fawcett Letters 89/1/40.

[32] See e.g. *Votes for Women*, 14 Jan. 1909, 266–8.

[33] Stocks, *Commonplace Book*, 70; Hamilton, *Life Errant*, 65–6; Angela V. John, *Elizabeth Robins: Staging a Life 1862–1952* (Routledge, 1995), 94, 151; Helen Crawfurd, MS Autobiography, 89, Marx Memorial Library.

[34] Lady Rhondda, *This Was My World* (Macmillan, 1933), 151, 156–61.

faint-hearted militants, and as a result militancy tended to be concentrated in London and a few regional capitals; it was not necessarily a central part of local WSPU activity and the dramatic events that captured the headlines were largely the work of a handful of itinerant activists who travelled out to the provinces when a visit by a leading politician offered a suitable target.

This pattern of activity also modifies our perspective on the suffrage movement as a whole. Far from being rigidly divided into hostile factions, it was a series of overlapping circles in which women continually crossed back and forth according to their changing views or local circumstances. In some places where branches of the NUWSS, the WFL and the WSPU existed in close proximity, it was not uncommon for suffragists to take multiple membership or at least to cooperate over meetings, demonstrations, and deputations. Alternatively, as WSPU branches dwindled, suffragettes sometimes joined the WFL or even National Union locally for want of an alternative. Some prominent individuals repeatedly shifted their loyalty. Cicely Hamilton quickly dropped the WSPU to join the WFL and the Actresses Franchise League. Elizabeth Garrett Anderson, sister to Mrs Fawcett, left the WSPU at the end of 1911 believing that miltancy had become too extreme and counter-productive. Maud Arncliffe-Sennett joined the London Society for Women's Suffrage (strictly constitutional), resigned from its *executive* in 1909 but maintained her membership while also participating in the WSPU which she left in 1912 before founding a new group, the Northern Men's League. Janie Allan, another wealthy woman who could please herself, joined the WSPU in 1909 while retaining membership of the constitutional society in Glasgow. In North-East England Mona Taylor quit the WSPU in September 1912, also alienated by extreme militancy and by the expulsion of the Pethick-Lawrences.[35] These examples suggest that the main traffic was away from militancy, though they underline the common ground amongst suffragists especially in the period up to 1911.

In this situation the role of the Women's Freedom League as a half-way house between militants repelled by the Pankhursts and constitutionalists looking for something livelier is especially interesting. However, Claire Eustance has argued that even within the WFL members were less involved in militancy in the provinces than in London, and that after 1909 the League retreated somewhat from militancy under pressure from its rank and file.[36] The WFL aspired to develop a militant strategy that was non-violent and

[35] Hamilton, *Life Errant*, 65–6; E. Garrett Anderson to Millicent Fawcett (copy), 3 Dec. 1914, Fawcett Library: Fawcett Letters 89/2/56; Glasgow and West of Scotland Association for Women's Suffrage, minutes, 10 Feb. 1909.

[36] Eustance, 'Daring to be Free', 91, 162–3.

would thus avoid the drawbacks of the WSPU's approach. Though difficult to put into practice, this at least facilitated common action with the WSPU at by-elections, and also led to tactics such as the boycott of the Census in 1911, tax resistance, and refusal to pay dog licences in which non-militants were often happy to participate.[37] In 1911 the National Union even helped rescue the WFL from its financial difficulties by donating £100 to its funds.[38]

The conclusion is unavoidable that the tactical issues which proved so divisive amongst the leadership and in London were much less relevant at local level. However, even this generalization is subject to regional qualification. For example, the London Society for Women's Suffrage, which was always inclined towards caution, took a severe attitude to militancy and even changed its rules in 1909 so as to facilitate the expulsion of any members whose actions were 'prejudicial to the objects and methods of the Society'. In Glasgow, too, the suffragists were keen to maintain their distance from the WSPU in the early years, even to the extent of declining expressions of sympathy for suffragette prisoners and refusing invitations to collaborate which were made by Helen Fraser, the WSPU's local organizer.[39] However, the Glasgow executive came under pressure from its members who were impressed by the WSPU speakers and felt that joint meetings would be advantageous. In 1907 the executive voted by eight to six to cooperate with WSPU speakers, and both the Glasgow and Edinburgh Societies agreed to support a WSPU procession in Edinburgh.[40] However, it is clear that the Glasgow suffragists remained rather divided partly because many of them were staunch Liberals who regarded the WSPU as a Tory front organization. Scotland attracted the Pankhursts because it was well-endowed with Liberal cabinet ministers (and golf courses), but the WSPU failed to retain significant strength there, being reduced to only three branches by 1912.

On the other hand, in Leeds the suffragists showed mutual appreciation and managed to collaborate. Isabella Ford, for example, became enthused at a by-election in which the WSPU 'behaved splendidly—there were no rows', she reported, 'I see more and more their policy [at by-elections] is far more workable than ours.' Mary Gawthorpe, though well-known as a

---

[37] For example the Manchester Society members discussed tax resistance at Margaret Ashton's suggestion, and apparently agreed to it in principle, though it was left to individuals to practice it: *Annual Report*, Manchester NSWS, 1907, Sandra Stanley Holton, *Suffrage Days: Stories from the Women's Suffrage Movement* (Routledge, 1996), 167.

[38] Eustance, 'Daring to be Free', 64–5.

[39] See Special Council Meeting, 17 Jan. 1909, Fawcett Library: Fawcett Letters 89/1/42; Glasgow and West of Scotland Association for Women's Suffrage, minutes, 8 May 1906, 17 Oct. 1906, 29 Nov. 1909, 11 Dec. 1909.

[40] Glasgow AWS, minutes, 17 Jan. 1907, 28 Feb. 1907, 3 July 1907.

suffragette, belonged to the NUWSS in Leeds and also joined the Women's Labour League which was hardly consistent with the Pankhursts' views.[41] Welsh suffragists stood at the opposite end of the spectrum in being loyal to Liberalism and thus inclined to regard the WSPU as the enemy; as a result militancy remained fairly weak in Wales and it had to be fortified by missionary work from England. Political loyalties also determined the pattern in North-West England where the Liberal suffragist Margaret Ashton grew steadily disillusioned with her party, and in North-East England where Dr Ethel Bentham, Dr Ethel Williams, and Mona Taylor all cooperated with militancy because they reacted so strongly against Liberal anti-suffragism. The North-East thus saw joint activities by the two wings of suffragism which became especially close during the truce of 1910–11.[42] However, as in Wales and Scotland cooperation amongst the North-East suffragists was easier because of the comparative weakness of the WSPU in the region. It had only a handful of branches compared to 26 for the NUWSS; and by 1912 suffragists like Taylor had withdrawn in reaction to extreme militancy, while Bentham and Williams embraced the alliance with Labour in total opposition to the Pankhurst line.

Provincial suffragettes were usually ready to cooperate either because they felt rather isolated or because they were less than wholly committed to militancy and were effectively beyond the control of the leaders. Conversely, in WSPU strongholds in London and the South-East its branches were more likely to remain separate. When Fawcett invited WSPU cooperation in a demonstration to support the Conciliation Bill in June 1910—on the basis that they guaranteed to restrain their followers from militant actions—they 'declined absolutely'.[43] Fawcett concluded that as the feeling against the suffragettes began to harden, the interests of the constitutional societies pointed to complete separation.[44] Cooperation certainly seems to have dwindled from 1911 onwards. The WFL regarded the breaking of the truce by the Pankhursts in that year as a mistake; Mrs Despard condemned the subsequent attacks on ministers and found cooperation with the WSPU to be virtually impossible. The National Union also felt that by this stage the suffragettes were seriously hampering their own efforts by playing into the

    [41] Isabella Ford to Millicent Fawcett, 14 Feb. 1908, Fawcett Library: Fawcett Letters 89/1/31; Holton, *Suffrage Days*, 120–2.
    [42] By 1908 Taylor and Williams were trying to persuade the National Union to oppose Liberal candidates like the WSPU: Glasgow AWS, minutes, 18 Jan. 1908; Neville, 'Women's Suffrage Movement', 38, 52–3.
    [43] NUWSS circular, Fawcett Library: Fawcett Letters 89/1/46.
    [44] Millicent Fawcett to Maud Arncliffe-Sennett, 16 June 1909, Arncliffe-Sennett Papers, BL, C 10.245.

hands of hostile politicians. 'You can hardly realise what the feeling is even amongst members of Parliament who have hitherto been steadiest in their support of Women's Suffrage,' Lloyd George told Mrs Fawcett in November 1911 after Asquith had been shouted down at a meeting at the City Temple. Fawcett unhesitatingly replied: 'I regret and deplore, condemn also . . . the disgusting scenes of November 21 and 29 as much as you do.'[45] The National Union believed the suffragette actions were not simply alienating their support at Westminster, but were also undermining the campaign in the country. 'It is impossible for anyone who has not worked in N. Wales to realise the strength of the antagonism which is aroused by militant outbreaks and the revulsion of feeling which they cause,' as one local report put it.[46] By 1913 many suffragists had concluded that the suffragettes had become the biggest single obstacle to the success of the cause.

These shifts over time make any balanced conclusion about relations between the various campaigners elusive. It is clear that for much of the period splits over tactics assumed far less significance locally than in London, because women's approach was fairly flexible, and that the cause prospered regardless of disputes amongst the leading figures. In some sense the efforts of the rival organizations complemented each other in that the WSPU attracted publicity; this brought extra resources which in turn helped the constitutionals to capitalize upon their links with the politicians. After 1911, however, the latter were handicapped by extreme militancy and had to overcome the problem by in effect displacing the WSPU as a campaigning movement especially after 1912 when they made an election pact with the Labour Party.

Mild Militancy

Although the methods adopted by the suffragettes have been endlessly described over the years, they have rarely been subjected to evaluation. This is unfortunate because the tactics were far more subtle and varied than is usually appreciated. Not only did militancy develop over time from the mild heckling of 1905 to the arson attacks of 1913, but the Pankhursts also shifted from militancy to non-militancy, and even managed to combine the two methods for several years. As we have seen, they began by using essentially

[45] Lloyd George to Millicent Fawcett, 30 Nov. 1911; Millicent Fawcett to Lloyd George (copy), 2 Dec. 1911, Fawcett Library: Fawcett Letters 89/2/53–4; *The Standard*, 1 Dec. 1911; *The Times*, 5 Dec. 1911.

[46] *Annual Report*, W. Lancashire, W. Cheshire, and N. Wales Federation, 1912.

constitutional methods during 1903 and 1904. After December 1905, when Balfour resigned as prime minister, they moved into a phase of mixed tactics until 1907; while confronting politicians in public, Christabel cultivated a private correspondence with the Tory leader in these years and she used her new recruits among wealthy women to invite politicians to their homes for friendly discussions about women's suffrage.[47] By 1908 the campaign was reaching its first peak; during 1909 it began to lose impact, and it was over-taken in 1910 by the adoption of a truce designed to promote the Concili-ation Bill. By the end of 1911 militancy had been resumed; it reached new heights in 1912 and in the last two years of peacetime the strategy had deteri-orated from an attack on the government into an indiscriminate campaign against members of the general public. Though brilliantly successful in cap-turing the headlines, in creating a sense of urgency about the vote, and in giving an example of sacrifice to thousands of women, militancy suffered from a loss of novelty value and from the competition from controversies over strikes, the People's Budget and the drift towards civil war in Ireland; this drove the activists to find ever more shocking expedients in order to retain the initiative and to maintain the flow of funds. The result by 1912, in the words of Cecil Chesterton, was that 'nothing less than the mutilation of a Cabinet Minister will induce an editor to give sixpence for a paragraph con-cerning [the suffragettes]'.[48]

In the early stages of militancy the most favoured tactic was the interrup-tion of ministers at public meetings which Christabel claimed to have used systematically in 1906 after the new prime minister, Sir Henry Campbell-Bannerman, told her that his cabinet was largely opposed to female enfran-chisement.[49] Her timing proved to be inept politically, for even when the Conservatives had still been in office the suffragettes had made a point of tackling *Liberals* alone. Despite this, Christabel's exuberant claims for the success of the interruptions had some basis.[50] The publicity given to suf-fragette heckling by the press deflated the politicians' pride because it diverted attention from the subject of their speeches. 'It was greatly to be regretted that anyone should seek to interrupt a Minister of the Crown', complained Augustine Birrell, 'when he was endeavouring to make a grave statement on matters which he declared to be of public urgency.' There was

[47] Christabel Pankhurst to Maud Arncliffe-Sennett, 22 June 1907, Arncliffe-Sennett Papers, BL, C 10.245.

[48] Cecil Chesterton in Huntly Carter (ed.), *Women's Suffrage and Militancy* (Frank Palmer, 1912), 10.

[49] E. Pethick-Lawrence, *My Part*, 155.

[50] Christabel Pankhurst, 'Why We Protest at Cabinet Ministers' Meetings', WSPU, not dated, 1908.

no one so pompous as a newly-appointed cabinet member! In assessing reactions to heckling one must distinguish between committed party members who were antagonized, and the general public for whom it often constituted part of the entertainment. As a result men in the audiences sometimes felt aroused by the violence meted out to suffragettes by the stewards to intervene on their behalf.[51] Heckling was, after all, a tradition which the Liberals themselves happily encouraged when Conservatives were on the receiving end.[52] In any case, the more skilful orators used their interruptors to sharpen their wit and humour. 'We have waited for forty years,' one suffragette shouted at Lloyd George, 'I must say the lady rather looks it,' he replied to general merriment.[53]

The object in these exchanges was to secure the moral high ground. In many ways leading Liberals were foolish in exposing their intolerance so readily. Grey's refusal to answer Christabel's question at Manchester in 1905 was repeated by many speakers even when the ladies politely sent written questions up to the platform.[54] When the stewards pounced on an individual and threw her out this could be seen as threatening the civil liberties of men, too, and consequently the overreaction often attracted criticism from Liberal supporters. At a meeting in Aberdeen in 1908 addressed by Asquith, one local newspaper described the ejection of hecklers as 'methods of Barbarism', the phrase famously coined by Campbell-Bannerman to denounce Lord Kitchener's use of concentration camps during the Boer War; the problem, the paper went on, was 'not to be solved by Russian methods of conducting public meetings', one of the worst insults for a Liberal at this time.[55] At one of Winston Churchill's meetings in Manchester ladies were obliged to apply for tickets only with the authority of a male member of the Liberal Federation who in effect gave a guarantee of their good behaviour; again the local press described these expedients as 'quite Russian in their severity'. It also antagonized Liberals like Margaret Ashton who asked 'Is the party really trying to get rid of its women members?'[56] This reminds us that the strength of the Pankhursts' tactics lay in the fact that they commanded some support *within* the Liberal Party despite the embarrassment caused.

On the other hand, interventions at public metings were of limited value, and in any case suffered from many drawbacks. Young men, especially medical

---

[51] *Daily Chronicle*, 12 Nov. 1907.   [52] *Votes for Women*, 7 Jan. 1910, 233.

[53] *Daily Chronicle*, 7 Dec. 1908.

[54] Undated paper on Churchill, 1908 Manchester Central Library: Mitchell Papers 220/4/6.

[55] Reported in 'Mr Asquith at Aberdeen', *Votes for Women*, Jan. 1908, 59; see also Mona Caird, 'Militant Tactics and Women's Suffrage', *Westminster Review*, 170 (1908), 526.

[56] *Votes for Women*, 4 June 1909, 753.

students and articled clerks, who traditionally disrupted Radical meetings, swiftly turned the tables on the WSPU by ringing bells, rattling cans of dried peas, and releasing boxes of live mice at their own demonstrations. At by-elections where the Pankhursts wanted to gain a sympathetic hearing for their cause, this proved highly disadvantageous. It is also questionable whether the WSPU applied the tactics with enough skill and discretion. To make indiscriminate targets of all members of the government including friends of women's suffrage was unwise. It is noticeable that Richard Haldane, Walter Runciman, Augustine Birrell, Lloyd George, and Winston Churchill all attracted heavy attention from the suffragettes during 1906–8 despite being *pro-suffragists.* As a result Churchill became largely alienated from the cause: 'For the last five years you have disturbed or tried to disturb almost every meeting I have addressed . . . if I have been returned [to Parliament] on three occasions it has been in spite of every effort on the part of the militant suffragettes to prevent me.'[57] This may sound a little petulant. The truth is that Churchill and Lloyd George enjoyed and attracted publicity, which helps to explain why Christabel so frequently targeted them. Yet it is easy to forget how vulnerable ministers were to physical attack despite enjoying police protection. With no gates Downing Street stood open to the crowds and ministers to assault. However, for many contemporaries the repeated attacks on these ministers seemed not unfair so much as perverse; had the suffragettes focused on opponents of women's enfranchisement on both Liberal *and* Conservative front benches they would have avoided much of the resentment they aroused.

Moreover, as the initial novelty of the interruptions wore off the tactic deteriorated, so that instead of heckling or sending in written questions, the women organized continuous interruption designed to make it impossible for a speech to be delivered. At a meeting addressed by Reginald McKenna in 1907 twelve women interrupted one at a time, each creating a period of uproar drowned by the playing of the organ and culminating in her ejection; in effect the entire meeting was disrupted. Fred Pethick-Lawrence admitted that the organizers deliberately issued numbers to activists so that each one would remain silent until her predecessor had been dealt with, so as to maximize the period of disorder.[58] The culmination came at a demonstration at the Albert Hall in 1908 organized by the Women's Liberal Federation to *promote* women's suffrage; at this Lloyd George was subjected to two hours of

---

[57] Winston Churchill to H. N. Brailsford (copy), 12 July 1910, Randolph Churchill, *Churchill,* ii/3, 1437.

[58] *Daily Chronicle,* 12 Nov. 1907; F. W. Pethick-Lawrence, *Fate,* 83.

interruptions and fifty women were carried out.[59] However, this proved counter-productive, for a Conservative MP, Lord Robert Cecil, himself a strong pro-suffragist, introduced a Public Meetings Bill which imposed penalties on anyone creating disorderly conduct in order to prevent the transaction of business at a meeting, and allowed the organizers to maintain control by using their own stewards. With government support the Bill passed rapidly with very little discussion—a sign that many left-wing members had concluded that the WSPU had been abusing the rights of free speech.[60] Pethick-Lawrence rightly observed that the Act failed to deter suffragette interruptions and did not result in prosecutions. However, this was missing the point. It effectively gave the advantage in law to the party stewards to use violence to eject interruptors.[61] Even without this the politicians had learnt to control their indoor meetings by issuing tickets which could be refused to women. Although some managed to frustrate this by hiding themselves in large halls twenty-four hours in advance, the fact remains that by becoming trapped in a confrontation with politicians the suffragettes had to some extent killed the dialogue and begun to turn the women's issue into a debate about law and order.[62] Within a few years this tactic had been exhausted.

However, heckling was complemented by other activities designed to demonstrate that the suffragettes commanded public sympathy while the politicians were losing credibility. Many of these techniques became common to suffragist organizations, including non-militant ones, because they did not involve violence except insofar as the women sometimes attracted attack from the crowds. Christabel decided to revive the traditional Radical tactic of intervening at by-elections with a view to securing the defeat of the government's candidates. Since huge numbers of by-elections occurred in this period the WSPU enjoyed excellent opportunities to win publicity for the cause, especially when high-profile ministers such as Churchill had to face the electorate; moreover, their message—to reject the Liberal—had the advantage of simplicity and clarity by contrast with the more qualified and complicated stance adopted by the NUWSS. However, whether the

---

[59] *Daily Chronicle*, 7 Dec. 1908.

[60] The Bill's supporters argued that it safeguarded the traditional right to heckle; *Hansard, HL Deb.*, 4th Series, CXCVIII, 18 Dec. 1908, c. 2206–7; *HC Deb.*, 4th Series, CXCVIII, 19 Dec. 1908, c. 2336.

[61] *Votes for Women*, 30 Apr. 1909, 596; in the long run the Act proved to be more significant in enabling the British Union of Fascists' stewards to inflict violence at their rallies with the force of the law behind them.

[62] Billington-Greig, for example, concluded that the tactics became largely counter-productive: 'The Militant Suffrage Movement', 1911, Fawcett Library: Billington-Greig Papers 397 A/6.

Pankhursts had any significant impact on the voters is a complex question, not hitherto analysed (see Chapter 9). To some extent the whole idea had become obsolescent since the mid-Victorian period because the electorate was so much larger and party machines more efficient. Nonetheless, many results still turned on a few hundred votes, and the Liberals held scores of vulnerable seats which, having been won in exceptional circumstances in 1906, could scarcely be defended against the mid-term unpopularity of the government. Nonetheless, the by-election policy suffered from several drawbacks, the most obvious of which was that as women possessed no votes, an appeal had to be made to male chivalry; the danger was that an aggressive approach would merely threaten male pride. Also, the campaign easily got out of hand. In a notorious incident at Bermondsey in October 1909 an elderly suffragette poured acid into a ballot box containing 83 ballot papers in order to invalidate the poll.[63] Such freelance interventions were embarrassing; they led the authorities to take precautions at the 1910 general elections, though this turned out to be unnecessary. The more typical problem was that the various suffrage organizations gave conflicting advice at the same by-election, or that local members refused to oppose the candidate who had been proscribed by headquarters in London. To some extent the candidates also frustrated the suffragists by issuing very similar, but slightly vague, statements which made it difficult to justify distinguishing between them. Above all, many left-wing members of the WSPU felt reluctant to antagonize Labour and Liberal candidates whom they regarded as their best supporters in the long term; where the result of suffragette intervention appeared to be the return of an *anti-suffragist* Conservative the whole tactic was rather discredited. Teresa Billington-Greig, who accepted the validity of the policy at by-elections, felt it to be mistaken at general elections.[64] In 1910 when the Liberals gave a promise to make parliamentary time available for a women's bill, it seemed suicidal to attack them, more especially as no undertakings had been obtained from the Conservatives. Whether the return of a Tory government would have advanced the women's cause appeared doubtful to many suffragists, especially in view of the presumed opposition of the House of Lords. Christabel simply argued that as long as the peers kept their opinions quiet it was best to concentrate on the House of Commons.[65] This, however, merely confirmed Liberal suspicions about the WSPU as a Tory front.

[63] *Southwark and Bermondsey Recorder*, 20 Oct. 1909, 5.

[64] 'The Militant Suffrage Movement', 1911. She was shrewd here; the Irish supported the Liberals at general elections but frequently withheld their votes at by-elections during 1906–9 to punish the government for neglecting Home Rule.

[65] Christabel Pankhurst to Maud Arncliffe-Sennett, 22 June 1907, Arncliffe-Sennett Papers, BL, C 10.245.

Mass meetings and processions offered a less complicated means of intimidating recalcitrant politicians. By 1908 the WSPU enjoyed the resources and organization to undertake impressive public displays; and the appointment to the premiership of Asquith who insisted that he would never concede the vote without evidence that women generally demanded it, provided an incentive to force him to live up to his words. In February 1908 the WSPU organized a Women's parliament at the Caxton Hall, a major demonstration at the Albert Hall in March, and a mass gathering in Hyde Park in June, each of which proved to be highly successful as public spectacles. In organizing these events the Pankhursts showed themselves very conscious of comparisons with the Reform League which had famously attracted 67,000 people to Hyde Park in 1867 when the park railings had been broken down. They felt confident of doubling that figure. Flora Drummond, now known as 'The General' and dressed in cloak, epaulettes, and peaked cap, persuaded the police to remove a quarter of a mile of railings in advance to avoid damage.[66] In the event, observers, including suffragists, thought that the crowds were curious and indifferent rather than sympathetic, but the size of the event exceeded all expectations. Even the hostile *Times* estimated the crowds at anything between 250,000 and 500,000. Asquith, however, stubbornly declined to be drawn over the evidence of such spectacles; Christabel used this to justify a reconsideration of her tactics. The prime minister's refusal to meet a deputation after Hyde Park provoked Mary Leigh to take stones to Downing Street to smash the windows. In effect the WSPU was reaching the limit of constitutional methods.

For contemporaries the most shocking aspect of militancy was the eagerness with which suffragettes engaged in direct physical confrontation with politicians and the police both at their homes and in attempts to enter the precincts of parliament. In these encounters the two sides were involved in a struggle for the moral high ground. The suffragettes made a symbolic challenge to male territory and sought to show themselves as victims of state brutality used by politicians who refused to listen to them. The authorities sought to show that they were simply applying the law in the face of increasingly irrational attacks by women determined to extract publicity from a bogus martyrdom. Despite some notorious examples of violence inflicted by the police, it is clear that in the early stages they avoided heavy-handed treatment of the women, either because they found handling middle-class ladies an embarrassing novelty, or because they were under instructions to be lenient for political reasons. During 1906 and 1907 the suffragettes were evidently

---

[66] F. W. Pethick-Lawrence, *Fate*, 78.

allowed to spend long periods banging on the doors of Campbell-Bannerman and Asquith's private homes as well as in Downing Street itself before being arrested.[67] Though charged with a breach of the peace, they were invariably frustrated in their object because the ministers requested that no proceedings be taken against them. As the London police became familiar with their adversaries, relations became almost friendly and cooperative; however, even in the early years the police were sometimes criticized for using unnecessary force, though this usually occurred when men had been transferred from outside the area to handle a situation with which they were unfamiliar. At the famous demonstration in Parliament Square in June 1909 which was witnessed by MPs, the police simply barred Mrs Pankhurst's way into Parliament Yard. Even the account in *The Common Cause* noted that when *eventually* the police decided to clear the square they were 'almost without exception kind and courteous but firm in their handling of the crowd'.[68] Lady Frances Balfour reported that when the rushes of the crowd knocked the women over the police helped to pick them up and walled them in; only when a stone was thrown did they seize the suffragettes.[69] Many suffragettes endorsed Mary Allen's verdict that 'the police were our protectors far more than they were ever our adversaries', and were 'altogether kinder and more lenient than the general public'.[70] Indeed, some newspapers complained that the police treated the women more lightly than they treated men and accused the suffragettes of trying to have it both ways: 'If woman is to be the equal, mental and political, of man, she must be prepared to accept the consequences.... Among these are the liability to be punished for rioting in the streets.'[71]

To this extent the authorities appear to have retained the advantage at least initially. Herbert Gladstone, as Home Secretary, wanted the police to make arrests on fairly minor charges such as obstruction which, at worst, would attract only a few days in prison. The magistrates, whether under his influence or not, endeavoured to damp down the offences even further by avoiding custodial sentences; they invited suffragettes to agree to be bound over to keep the peace for a year, thereby putting the onus on them to go to prison if they refused.[72]

However, the suffragettes managed to frustrate these aims by opting for

---

[67] PRO MEPOL 2/1061 (Suffragette Disturbances 1906–7).

[68] *Daily Mirror*, 15 Feb. 1907; *The Common Cause*, 1 July 1909, 159.

[69] Lady Frances Balfour to Millicent Fawcett, 29 June 1909, Fawcett Library: Fawcett Letters 89/1/40.

[70] Allen, *Lady in Blue*, 22.   [71] *Daily Dispatch*, 17 Feb. 1907.

[72] E. Pethick-Lawrence, *My Part*, 186; Ian Fletcher, 'A Star Chamber of the Twentieth Century: Suffragettes, Liberals and the 1908 "Rush the Commons" Case', *Journal of British Studies*, 35/4 (1996), 509–10.

prison and by repeating their offences which inevitably resulted in longer sentences. In the process they began to gain the moral high ground. Liberal opinion naturally felt uneasy over the imprisonment of women who were asking for an essentially liberal reform, especially as in these early years suffragette offences were not regarded as especially threatening. Therefore the demand that the prisoners should be placed in the First Division attracted wide sympathy, and as early as March 1906 Gladstone conceded the point. Foolishly, however, he failed to stick consistently to this policy, arguing that much depended on the individuals concerned and on the specific offences committed. Consequently, some suffragettes continued to be put in the Second Division which prolonged the controversy and seemed to many people to put the government in the wrong. When Churchill became Home Secretary in 1910 he introduced a long list of concessions including allowing prisoners to wear their own clothes, have their hair cut, obtain food from outside, receive books, and converse with other prisoners while exercising.[73]

The authorities were also exposed as heavy-handed by Christabel's brilliant handling of the court case in October 1908 resulting from the attempt to rush the House of Commons. On that occasion several ministers and other members had watched the proceedings which enabled Christabel to summon Lloyd George and Gladstone as witnesses and subject them to cross-questioning. She succeeded in demonstrating that they had not in fact felt threatened by the demonstration, and that Gladstone's earlier speeches were tantamount to encouragement of the tactics that had been used. Moreover, one lady, a Mrs Travers Symons, who was employed as a secretary by Keir Hardie, had actually managed to enter parliament while the demonstration was taking place, but had escaped any punishment at all.[74] Consequently the sentences imposed on the suffragettes merely served to put the government in an oppressive and illiberal light, while making the Pankhursts appear justified in their actions.

The Truce

There is, thus, much validity in the conventional view that during 1906 to 1908 militant tactics were, on balance, successful in forcing the issue of

---

[73] For the list of concessions, see National Library of Scotland: Emrys Hughes Papers, Deposit 76 Box 2/2. In her MS Autobiography, 91, Helen Crawfurd gave a first-hand account of prison experience in which she wrote that the rules were not enforced by the wardresses who felt unable to discipline ladies so far above them in the social scale.

[74] See National Library of Scotland: Emrys Hughes Papers, Deposit 76 Box 2/2.

female enfranchisement higher up the agenda, attracting funds and members to the campaign, and in putting the politicians on the defensive. As we have seen, even non-militant suffragists often endorsed this view. However, by the start of 1909 a turning-point had been reached. Although the WSPU continued to keep itself in the newspapers at by-elections and in clashes with the police, the novelty had already begun to wear off. Moreover both the party organizers and the police were coping more effectively, while Asquith showed little sign of backing down. In this situation how was the momentum to be maintained? The spontaneous resumption of stone-throwing without authorization at the end of June 1909 suggests that Christabel felt uncertain what to do next. This explains why she seized so quickly on the example set by Marion Wallace Dunlop who undertook a hunger-strike in prison in July. After ninety-one hours the authorities released her, and Christabel immediately pronounced that the government had been decisively beaten, for they would not in future dare to keep women in prison for more than a few days. However, this proved to be over-optimistic, for after thirty-seven prisoners had been released, the authorities resorted to forcible feeding. A political judgement had been made that it would be regarded as more defensible to save prisoners from starvation, even at the cost of dangerous and humiliating treatment in gaol, than to allow them to take the consequences of their actions. This, however, presented a gift to WSPU propaganda which graphically portrayed the sufferings of prisoners subjected to forcible feeding. Their claims received endorsement from doctors who protested to the prime minister about the 'unwise and inhumane' practice.[75]

On the other hand, if forcible feeding had been the decisive breakthrough for which Christabel hoped, she would hardly have been so willing to suspend the militant campaign early in 1910. Later in life she admitted that she welcomed the opportunity for a truce because 'mild militancy was more or less played out'.[76] A lull in the campaign, ostensibly to give a fair chance to the Conciliation Bill by removing the pressure on the politicians, enabled the suffragettes to re-evaluate their tactics with a view to resuming hostilities with greater impact in due course.

Meanwhile the Pankhursts used the period from 1909 to 1911 to experiment with various alternatives. For example, it was in October and November 1909 that Emmeline embarked on a visit to the United States; she was to make the trip again in the autumn of 1911 and the autumn of 1913, and Sylvia also went in January 1911. These excursions had several advantages. They

---

[75] 'Fed by Force: Statement of Mrs Mary Leigh', WSPU, 1909; *Votes for Women*, 1 Oct. 1909, 2; 8 Oct. 1909, 19.

[76] Christabel Pankhurst, *Unshackled* (Hutchinson, 1959), 153–4.

offered the leaders a respite from the pressure of hunger strikes and forcible feeding and the pleasure of a recuperative voyage. More importantly they boosted morale. Emmeline's reception in America demonstrated that she had become a figure of international stature. Audiences that had expected an aggressive feminist were charmed and fascinated on finding her frail and distinctly feminine.[77] As a result Americans contributed generously to WSPU funds; the 1913 trip raised £3,684. From the outset Emmeline proved adept at appealing to anti-British sentiment in her speeches which must have added to the pleasure of defying the home authorities. Christabel made similar use of Paris as a refuge from March 1912 to August 1914, a period when the WSPU leaders were being prosecuted for conspiracy; although she continued to promote what were by that time illegal activities from Paris, she was never subject to extradition by the French authorities.

The Pankhursts also found themselves obliged by the pressure from the rank and file to experiment with tactical variations. A large proportion of their members had left to found the Women's Freedom League (WFL) in 1907, some of whom continued to operate as militants especially during 1908 and 1909. The WFL's diagnosis was that militancy as practised by the Pankhursts was losing its impact, and they therefore tried to find a more subtle form of militancy, in effect passive resistance, which would retain public sympathy by avoiding violence. By far the most dramatic idea to emerge was a scheme to promote birth control amongst *working-class* women, advocated by Nina Boyle but not in the end adopted by the WFL.[78] Tax resistance attracted a much greater response, especially the refusal to pay dog licences which offered a symbolic challenge to the government but not a sufficiently great one to attract severe retribution. To withhold taxes on income and property involved more risks and was therefore less widely adopted. Only suffragists who were sufficiently well-to-do to withstand the protracted process of having their moveable property distrained by bailiffs embarked on this course. For example, the Duchess of Bedford opted to make her protest by refusing property tax on the Prince's Skating Rink; following non-payment by the Princess Sophia Dhuleep Singh she forfeited a diamond brooch which was promptly bought by another suffragette who returned it to her.[79]

Perhaps the greatest success for WFL strategy was non-cooperation with the Census of 1911 which brought virtually no personal risk and helped unify the movement by attracting participation by both NUWSS and the WSPU members. The organizers printed dummy Census returns on which was

---

[77] *The Common Cause*, 4 Nov. 1909, 382; *Votes for Women*, 5 Nov. 1909, 85.
[78] *Annual Report*, Women's Freedom League, 1914, 61–3.   [79] *The Times*, 8 March 1913.

written: 'If I am intelligent enough to fill in this Census Form, I can surely make X on a ballot paper!'[80] This placed the minister, John Burns, in a dilemma. He clearly contemplated prosecuting the offenders, but eventually decided to take no action on the grounds that evasion of the Census had been 'altogether negligible' and he could count the omissions anyway![81] Yet if the suffragists were correct in claiming that tens of thousands had participated, it would have been impractical for Burns to take legal reprisals against them.[82] The success of the Census campaign casts more general light on the suffrage movement; it demonstrated the feasibility of combining the rival factions and, more importantly, it underlined the need to implement the WSPU strategy on a wider scale if it was to succeed in intimidating the authorities.

For the Pankhursts, however, none of these activities resolved their dilemma. Their decision to suspend militancy in February 1910 *pre-dated* the Conciliation Bill and must therefore be attributed chiefly to their desire for a breathing space and to the impact of the general election in January which had polarized British politics over the issue of House of Lords reform.[83] Nonetheless, when the Conciliation Bill, introduced by David Shackleton, won a majority of 109 they did not wish to be responsible for jeopardizing what appeared to be a good chance of success. The suffragists capitalized on the public mood tactfully by organizing a Coronation Procession in honour of the new King, George V. In June 1911 ten thousand women marched from the Victoria Embankment to the Albert Hall with forty bands and seven hundred banners amid friendly, cheering crowds and a barrage of compliments from the press on both the beauty and the organization of the spectacle.[84] Although the WSPU was suspicious about the intentions of the cabinet, they became unusually conciliatory and kept to the truce apart from a brief lapse in November when they intervened in two by-elections.[85] This appeared to be justified when Asquith, under pressure from his pro-suffrage cabinet colleagues, offered to provide facilities for the Conciliation Bill, an undertaking which was to extend into the next parliament. After the Liberals' success in retaining office at the election in December, a second debate took place on the Conciliation Bill introduced by Sir George Kemp in May 1911, when it again triumphed by the large margin of 255 to 88 votes. In June the prime

[80]   *Votes for Women*, 31 Mar. 1911, 1.

[81]   John Burns to Winston Churchill, 28 Mar. 1911, Randolph Churchill, *Churchill*, ii/3, 1471; *Hansard, HC Deb.*, 5th Series, XXIII, 5 Apr. 1911, c. 2194.

[82]   Lawrence Housman, *The Unexpected Years* (Cape, 1937), 287–9; Henry Nevinson, 'Complete Success of Census Protest', *Votes for Women*, 7 Apr. 1911, 440.

[83]   See Editorial, *Votes for Women*, 18 Feb. 1910, 34; 11 Mar. 1910, 372; 23 Mar. 1910, 409.

[84]   *Daily Telegraph*, 20 June 1911; *The Standard*, 20 June 1911.

[85]   See Editorial, *Votes for Women*, 19 Aug. 1910, 766; 3 Feb. 1911, 292.

minister specified that a week of parliamentary time, or more if necessary, would be made available to debate the Bill. Since Asquith's pledge seemed unequivocal, the WSPU became very optimistic at this stage; it would have been foolish to have excluded themselves from what seemed to be the best chance of success available to the women's movement. For a brief interlude the WSPU joined with the NUWSS in throwing its efforts behind the Bill. Its literature stressed that the measure involved 'no dangerous innovation' because it simply enfranchised around a million women already exercising the local government vote.[86]

However, as the enactment of the Bill appeared imminent, the politicians inevitably scrutinized the details more carefully. In cabinet Churchill argued that wealthy men would be able to manufacture extra votes by bestowing property on their female relations. In order to try to meet this point the Conciliation Bill was amended so as to prevent husbands and wives being registered as voters in the same parliamentary borough or county division. However, this still left the substantive argument about the qualification of single women and widows as heads of households. The WSPU's claim that the Bill was fair to the working class and was accepted by the Labour Party was far from wholly convincing. In order to allay fears, the ILP had conducted canvasses of the existing female municipal electorate in Bangor and Caernarvon (Lloyd George's constituency) where they claimed that 75 per cent were either working-class wives with no servants or wage earners, and in Dundee (Churchill's constituency) where 89 per cent lived in one or two rooms and could thus be presumed to be working class. Overall the ILP calculated that 82.5 per cent of the 59,220 women in the areas it had surveyed were working-class women.[87] However, one historian has dismissed the surveys as 'worthless' on the grounds that the findings were drawn from only fifty out of three hundred branches and that, in any case, ILP branches were not representative of the whole country.[88] Though true, this hardly made the findings worthless, for it was precisely the social composition of the kinds of seats represented by Liberal and Labour members that mattered. A greater weakness lay in the rather erratic definitions used by the ILP which seems to have equated 'working women' with working-class women. Yet a survey of municipal voters in London published in *The Nation* showed a similarly high proportion of women involved in manual occupations. Even assuming that the 24,000 women not included were housewives and women of leisure, it does appear that the critics of the Conciliation Bill were exaggerating the advantage likely to be given to the middle and upper classes.

[86] 'Votes for Women: The Conciliation Bill Explained', WSPU, 1911.
[87] Keir Hardie, 'The Citizenship of Women', 1905, 13.   [88] Rosen, *Rise Up Women*, 34–5.

TABLE 8.1. Female municipal electors in London

Occupation	
Charwomen, office helpers, laundresses	30,334
Dressmakers, milliners	14,361
Shirt and blouse makers, seamstresses	6,525
Waitresses and matrons	5,595
Tailoresses	4,443
Lodging and coffee-house keepers	4,226
Medical women, nurses, midwives	3,971
Teachers	2,198
TOTAL	71,653
TOTAL ELECTORS	94,940

Source: *The Nation*, 9 July 1910.

However, the result of the December 1910 election had been so close in terms of the vote that ministers felt loath to risk giving even a slight advantage to the Conservatives. In October Christabel claimed that 'a conspiracy of wreckers and reactionaries' in the cabinet was trying to kill the bill, a warning apparently vindicated in November when the government announced its intention of introducing a franchise and registration bill of its own which would be open to amendment by supporters of women's suffrage. Though this left the Conciliation Bill technically unaffected, Christabel interpreted this initiative as a plot by Lloyd George to negate the government's pledges: 'the whole crooked and discreditable scheme is characteristic of the man'.[89] He foolishly corroborated her charge by gleefully boasting that the Conciliation Bill had been torpedoed.

As a result the WSPU announced the resumption of militancy with the breaking of windows at government ministries, the National Liberal Club, newspaper offices, and shops on the 21 November, which led to the arrest of 223 women. On the 28th they howled down the prime minister who was forced to abandon his speech at the City Temple. Though the abandonment of the truce in this way is understandable in view of the political machinations during the summer and autumn of 1911, it was still an irrational response. Christabel argued that the new government bill could not be enacted with a women's amendment because the Conservatives would oppose it, as would 66 Anti-Suffrage Liberals.[90] But it is important to avoid making assumptions based on hindsight. The Pankhursts had all along demanded a *government* bill as the only kind worth having; and now that the

[89] *Votes for Women*, 6 Oct. 1911; 10 Nov. 1911, 88.
[90] Christabel Pankhurst, Memorandum, 20 Feb. 1912, Fawcett Library: Fawcett Letters 89/2/61.

House of Lords veto had been removed by the Parliament Act, the prospects of such legislation, however controversial, were greatly enhanced. In the anger of the Pankhursts' response one detects an element of pride, for the enactment of a broader reform bill would to some extent have deprived them of the credit for the passage of a bill wholly concerned with female suffrage. In any case, Lloyd George's manoeuvres only provided an excuse for the abrupt change of tactics which the WSPU was already keen to make. The truce had already lasted too long and the prospect of extending it through 1912 to accommodate the new government proposal was very unwelcome; it threatened to marginalize the Pankhursts and deprive the WSPU of momentum and funds.

As a result the debate on Sir James Agg-Gardner's Conciliation Bill took place amid a wave of attacks on West End shops in which 190 women were arrested. No fewer than 120 of the MPs who had previously supported the bill signed a letter of protest, and the Anti-Suffragists invited them to teach the suffragettes a lesson when they voted. One minister, Sydney Buxton, announced that he was switching his vote so as to prevent the militants from claiming a success for their methods.[91] The bill went down to a narrow defeat by 222 to 208, a dramatic reversal of the 1911 majority. This outcome was widely attributed to the reaction against militancy. 'The window-smashers have smashed themselves,' exulted the *Pall Mall Gazette*. 'What really upset the Conciliation Bill,' wrote Sir Edward Grey, 'was the resentment caused by the senseless window-breaking.'[92] In fact militancy was far from being the major factor. The reversal of the Irish members who had previously voted by 31–9 in favour of the bill but were against it by 35–3 in 1912 was a reflection of their dedication to Home Rule and to Asquith rather than a sign of their views on militancy. However, three Conservatives, and twelve Liberals who had voted for the bill in 1911 opposed it in 1912. Much larger numbers of previous abstainers now turned out to vote against, while some of the bill's previous supporters now chose to abstain.[93] No doubt many members who had been lukewarm used the renewal of militancy as a convenient excuse for changing their position. Clearly the huge majority won in 1911 would have been reduced regardless of the WSPU campaign; but militancy accentuated the shift and can thus be held responsible for the very narrow defeat. Whereas

---

[91]   *The Times*, 12 Mar. 1912; 16 Mar. 1912; 22 Mar. 1912; 23 Mar. 1912.

[92]   *Pall Mall Gazette*, 29 Mar. 1912; Sir Edward Grey to Millicent Fawcett, 5 Apr. 1912, Fawcett Library: Fawcett Letters 89/2/67.

[93]   Conservatives: I. H. Benn, R. A. Cooper, A. H. Paget; Liberals: A. W. Black, Sydney Buxton, H. Carr-Gomm, J. A. Dawes, R. Edwards, Sir H. Havelock-Allan, R. Lambert, Sir W. Menzies, A. C. Murray, R. Pearce, E. Wason, Sir T. P. Whitaker; *Annual Report*, W. Lancashire, W. Cheshire, and N. Wales Federation, 1912.

both the WFL and the NUWSS were prepared to wait and see whether Asquith's promises would be honoured, the WSPU had abandoned the truce precipitately, thereby dissipating some of the goodwill amongst MPs. When the government's bill collapsed in January 1913 after the Speaker's ruling, the prime minister found himself covered with abuse by the newspapers for his opportunism, incompetence, and dishonesty. 'Mr Asquith has been tripped up in the meshes of his own cleverness,' scoffed *The Standard*.[94] But he would have been far more vulnerable in 1913 but for the fourteen months of extreme militancy which had preceded the fiasco; in effect the suffragettes had played into his hands.

The Decline of Militancy 1912–1914

In the spring of 1912 the suffragette campaign entered its final, climactic phase involving window-breaking, attacks on letter boxes, and arson. The rationale for this was twofold. First, it enabled the women to avoid the increasingly rough treatment at the hands of the police; 'Black Friday' on 18 November 1910 when police from the East End of London had used violence and sexual intimidation instead of making arrests, had convinced Christabel of the need to focus on attacks upon property from which suffragettes could withdraw quickly. Certainly the arsonists proved difficult to apprehend, though window-breakers in shopping centres were often seized by members of the public. The second justification implied the virtual abandonment of any attempt at persuasion: 'Women will never get the vote except by creating an intolerable situation for all the selfish and apathetic people who stand in their way.'[95] However unrealistic this seems, the WSPU leaders appeared to be convinced that their letter box campaign heralded a breakthrough; in December 1912 Mrs Lamartine Yates advised that Christmas was an especially good time for this tactic.[96] According to the Postmaster General, Herbert Samuel, 5,000 letters were damaged between 1 October and 4 December 1912, but none completely destroyed; between January 1913 and April 1914, 237 pillar boxes and 4,014 letters suffered damage of which 114 letters were destroyed.[97] The extent of the fires and explosions in private buildings may well have been exaggerated as a result of actions by owners anxious to

---

[94] *The Standard*, 27 Jan. 1913; *The Globe*, 25 Jan. 1913; *Pall Mall Gazette*, 24 Jan. 1913; *Daily Telegraph*, 27 Jan. 1913; *The Times*, 27 Jan. 1913.

[95] *The Suffragette*, 12 Dec. 1912, 1.

[96] Speech at Wimbledon, 9 Dec. 1912, PRO HO45/10695/231366.

[97] PRO HO144/1268/238 215.

dispose of well-insured property, rather than of suffragette attacks. There also remains some doubt about famous events such as the 'bombing' of Lloyd George's house at Walton Heath; the WSPU initially declined to claim responsibility for it, and Emmeline Pankhurst's subsequent decision to accept responsibility was evidently a calculated political act.[98]

In the process a qualitative change occurred in the suffragette campaign. Despite claims about the precautions taken, it seems indisputable that the new forms of militancy were life-threatening rather than simply targeted on property; moreover, actions were now directed indiscriminately at members of the public rather than at politicians. For example, Mary Leigh and Gladys Evans set fire to a crowded Dublin theatre; signals at railways stations were tampered with; and a number of parcels addressed to Asquith, Lloyd George, and Burns, which contained volatile chemicals, burst into flames when collected or examined by Post Office employees.[99] In December 1912 a Miss Gilliat made a notorious speech at Wimbledon in which she suggested it would not be difficult to kill a cabinet minister: 'Attend their political meetings', she advised, 'and you will find out for yourselves what an easy matter is their destruction.'[100] As a result the authorities feared that the death of a suffragette after forcible feeding would provoke an attempt to assassinate a leading politician.

This escalation generated a bitter dispute between Christabel, on the one hand, and the Pethick-Lawrences, Lawrence Housman, and Henry Nevinson, on the other. According to Emmeline Pethick-Lawrence, Mrs Pankhurst often said 'I want to be tried for sedition'; this reflected a desire to discredit the government though her own martyrdom and her growing obsession with the Ulster Unionists whose defiance was being studiously ignored by the authorities. However, the critics felt that by 1913 Christabel had wrecked the WSPU partly by alienating public opinion at a time when it had come round to the suffragists' view, and partly by removing herself to Paris.[101] That the Pankhursts were now careless about taking risks with public opinion is underlined by Emmeline's defiant remark: 'the argument of the broken pane of glass is the most valuable argument in modern politics'.[102] As a result shopkeepers whose windows fell victim to the suffragettes received explanatory

[98] Helen Crawfurd, MS Autobiography, 99, Marx Memorial Library; *The Suffragette*, 21 Feb. 1913, 92.

[99] *Daily Herald*, 8 Aug. 1912; *The Times*, 30 Jan. 1913; 1 Dec. 1913; Reports on Suffragette Activities 1912–13, PRO HO45/10695/231366.

[100] Report, 9 Dec. 1912, PRO HO45/10695/231366.

[101] E. Pethick-Lawrence, *My Part*, 277–8; F. W. Pethick-Lawrence, *Fate*, 98–100; Housman, *Unexpected Years*, 282.

[102] *Votes for Women*, 23 Feb. 1912, 319.

leaflets urging them not to be angry with the suffragettes but to blame the government and to use their political clout to force the cabinet to back down. Though apparently tactless, this message was not wholly misguided in that repeated attacks were likely to encourage owners to demand a resolution of the problem by the government. 'You can get on very well without Mr Asquith and Mr Lloyd George,' ran the argument, 'but you can't get on without women who are your good friends in business.'[103] Here was an echo of the old Chartist tactic of exclusive dealing; even the WFL had contemplated a commercial boycott during the 1910 general elections. It may be significant that despite the destruction of windows, the suffragette journals retained their advertising from West End shops. Helen Crawfurd also claimed that the insurance companies began to support votes for women at this time as a result of the large sums of money paid out in claims arising out of suffragette attacks.[104] More compelling was the propagandist literature designed to highlight the physical suffering of women subjected to forcible feeding. Since 1909 the WSPU had published graphic accounts of the experiences of women such as Mary Leigh.[105] Reginald McKenna, as Home Secretary from 1910, frankly accepted that some suffragettes were fanatical enough to risk death and thus martyrdom which would be politically disastrous for the government. By 1913 the WSPU was propagating the idea that Mrs Pankhurst was already at death's door, and they reminded workingmen that the methods used against her could be turned on them if the government chose to regard them as a threat to public order.[106] In June 1913 Emily Wilding Davison succeeded in frustrating McKenna's calculations through her own death at the Epsom races. Although she had previously declared that 'a tragedy was wanted', the question arising from her death is less about her motives than about its impact.[107] Reactions to the tragedy were so mixed as to make assessment difficult. The spectacle of her funeral was a very moving one, and Lawrence Housman noticed that the crowds in Hyde Park took off their hats as a sign of respect at the mention of her name. Conversely Mary Stocks, an admittedly hostile observer, believed her action was regarded as irrational; and Maud Arncliffe-Sennett was shocked to hear the crowds shouting 'The King's 'orse', apparently reflecting greater feeling for the animal which had had to be destroyed and possibly anger at the insult offered

---

[103] 'Window Breaking: To One Who Has Suffered', WSPU, 1912.
[104] Helen Crawfurd, MS Autobiography, 99, Marx Memorial Library.
[105] 'Fed by Force: Statement by Mrs Mary Leigh', WSPU, 1909.
[106] 'The Case of Mrs Pankhurst: A Victim of the Cat and Mouse Act', WSPU, 1913.
[107] Her words to the prison doctor after attempting suicide in Holloway in June 1912: PRO PCOM/8/174.

to the King.[108] Since Davison's death occurred *outside* prison the political impact was inevitably limited; press comment acknowledged her bravery, but argued that society could not afford to yield to what was a form of terrorism.[109]

One deduces from the consistency with which the government stuck to its methods of handling the suffragettes that it never felt that public opinion had turned in the suffragettes' favour. 'I am not condemning militancy morally,' said Lloyd George, 'I am condemning it tactically. Militancy has set public opinion against you at the moment.'[110] On the other hand, ministers came under pressure from some surprising quarters. King George V left the Home Secretary in no doubt of his unease: 'His Majesty cannot help feeling that there is something shocking, if not almost cruel, in the operation to which these insensate women are subjected.'[111] The King clearly *believed* the accounts given by suffragettes and wanted the government to abandon forcible feeding. The significance of this royal intervention lay not in its influence—McKenna had already decided to introduce the Prisoners' Temporary Discharge Bill—but as an indication of sympathy aroused in one who was basically hostile to votes for women. Conversely, many pro-suffragists adopted a disparaging attitude. Helena Swanwick, for example, referred to the 'policy of martyrdom' as 'dishonest and cynical'.[112] When the Men's League for Women's Suffrage tried to gain support from Philip Snowden over its protest about Mrs Pankhurst's treatment under the 'Cat and Mouse Act' in 1913 it received a stern rebuff:

You and I read public opinion very differently if you are right in saying public sympathy is with her. For every one who is in the least concerned about her treatment I find twenty who are indifferent or hostile to her. . . . She is punishing herself because she will not take the punishment imposed upon her for outrages which no community can allow anyone to perpetrate.[113]

While Snowden's hostility may have reflected his party political position, the same cannot be said of others much closer to the WSPU who also felt that extreme militancy had damaged the cause. Henry Harben frankly told Christabel that she had alienated most of the able suffragettes and 'from the leader of a great movement you are developing into the ringleader of a little

---

[108] Housman, *Unexpected Years*, 295; Stocks, *Commonplace Book*, 66; Martha Vicinus, *Independent Women* (Virago, 1985), 278.

[109] *Daily Sketch*, 28 May 1914, 6.   [110] *Manchester Guardian*, 23 Nov. 1911.

[111] Lord Stamfordham to Reginald McKenna, 27 Mar. 1913, Harold Nicolson, *King George V: His Life and Reign* (Constable, 1952), 212.

[112] Swanwick, *I Have Been Young*, 189.

[113] P. Snowden to J. Drummond, 26 June 1913, John Rylands Library: Manchester Men's League for Women's Suffrage Papers.

rebel rump'. Another activist, Beatrice Harraden, challenged Christabel over her apparent readiness to pursue militancy even at risk to her mother's life. In her view the sacrifice would have been futile because by 1914 the WSPU had lost its grip on public opinion; it was folly for Christabel to remain in Paris out of touch with events at home while WSPU branches were becoming comatose for lack of activity.[114]

Such internal criticism was echoed in press comment even in hitherto supportive newspapers like the *Daily News* which argued that WSPU methods had 'neither historical nor moral sanction . . . they have no right to appeal to force because they enjoy the freedom to persuade'.[115] This diagnosis seems to have spread beyond the editors and politicians. By the spring of 1912 attempts by the WSPU to hold public meetings and to open new suffragette shops and offices attracted hostile crowds eager to pelt them with eggs, fruit, and bags of flour.[116] This pattern continued throughout 1913. Following the collapse of the government's bill in January 1913, Flora Drummond and Sylvia Pankhurst attempted to force an entry into the House of Commons and smashed the windows of official and business premises; but press reports demonstrated how badly their position had deteriorated:

The attitude of the crowds towards the suffragettes was so menacing at times that the women had to seek the protection of the police. . . . Mrs Drummond whose arrest was loudly cheered by the crowd, broke down and wept . . . the demonstration ended . . . in the curious spectacle of demonstrators imploring the assistance of the police while they hurried away from the crowd to places of safety . . . [in Whitehall] some half a dozen women wearing the colours of the WSPU were . . . jeered and booed, and the people surging around them shouted and gesticulated wildly . . . a posse of police arrived to protect them, escorted them up Whitehall, pursued by the crowd, and put them on a bus.[117]

In effect the WSPU was being driven off the streets even in London. In March 1913 Mrs Drummond and others spent three successive Sundays trying to keep the flag flying by speaking in Hyde Park, but even though encircled by police they were showered with fruit and lumps of turf and forced to abandon their meetings.[118]

Against this background one can understand why the Home Secretary managed to get away with a policy designed to suppress the WSPU. During 1912 Scotland Yard kept the organization under surveillance with a view to

---

[114] Quoted in Rosen, *Rise Up Women*, 225; Beatrice Haraden to Christabel Pankhurst, 13 Jan. 1914 (copy), National Library of Scotland: Janie Allan Papers Acc. 4498/3.
[115] *Daily News*, 20 Feb. 1913.   [116] *The Standard*, 11 Mar. 1912.
[117] *Daily Graphic*, 29 Jan. 1913; *The Times*, 29 Jan. 1913.   [118] *Daily Mirror*, 17 Mar. 1913.

obtaining proof of incitement to violence and criminal conspiracy. Evidence was readily available in the speeches delivered by Mrs Drummond, Annie Kenney, Mrs Pankhurst, and Mrs Yates as well as by George Lansbury who advocated acts of arson and destruction of property.[119] When the police raided suffragette headquarters in March 1912 with warrants for the arrest of the Pethick-Lawrences and Christabel on conspiracy charges, Christabel was by accident absent and took the opportunity to flee to Paris; but the others including Emmeline, were found guilty and sentenced to eight months in prison.[120] Over the next two years the full force of the law was used to suppress the campaign. With a view to stopping publication of *The Suffragette* proceedings were instituted against its printers, and customs officials were alerted to intercept copies entering from the Continent. Sydney Drew, the manager of the Victoria House Printing Company was prosecuted and eventually gave undertakings not to publish illegal material again.[121] This was politically dangerous for the government, for in May 1913 printing was transferred to Manchester and the presses of the National Labour Press. Within a week its manager had been arrested, but the threat to free speech attracted the anger of Ramsay MacDonald who offered to act as the manager of the press on the assumption that the authorities would always shrink from prosecuting fellow politicians.[122] In spite of all this publication did continue, though *The Suffragette* sometimes appeared with eloquent blank sections.

During May and June 1914 the police raided a suffragette flat in Maida Vale where they seized a half hundredweight of stones, three hammers, a chopper, and documents. They took possession of WSPU headquarters in Lincoln's Inn and in Kingsway to gather more material for prosecution of the activists. McKenna evidently intended to keep the police in occupation of these premises even after the search had been completed—against the advice of the Attorney General.[123] He also signed a warrant to allow police to divert the WSPU's mail and to cut off the telephone lines.[124] By the eve of war he had managed to identify forty leading subscribers with a view to taking legal proceedings against them in the name of the National Gallery to seek compensation for the attack on the Velazquez 'Venus' by Mary Richardson.[125] The Liberal backbencher, Josiah Wedgwood, protested against these actions as unconstitutional and a threat to civil liberties.[126] However, the remarkable

[119] See Reports of Suffragette Activities 1912–13, PRO HO45/10695/231366.
[120] PRO HO45/10700/236173.
[121] PRO HO144/1268/238215.   [122] *Daily Herald*, 14 May 1913.
[123] Reginald McKenna, 30 May 1914: PRO HO144/1318/252288.
[124] *The Times*, 10 June 1914.   [125] PRO HO45/10725/252949.
[126] Josiah Wedgwood to Reginald McKenna, 23 Mar. 1913: PRO HO45/10700/236973.

thing is that such voices were comparatively few; by 1913 the authorities could apparently suppress the organization safe in the belief that public outrage against the suffragettes made their actions appear justified.

The second weapon in McKenna's strategy was the Prisoners' Temporary Discharge Bill, known subsequently as the Cat and Mouse Act, which was passed in April 1913. He had arrived at this expedient in July 1912 when all forty-five of the current hunger strikers had been released from prison before completing their sentences. Now that sentences were growing longer and the health of the women was deteriorating, forcible feeding had become too dangerous. Consequently, suffragettes were to be released under the Act, on medical advice, usually for periods of a few weeks, with instructions to report back to the authorities on a specific date to continue serving their sentences.

Although the application of the Cat and Mouse Act is one of the most notorious aspects of the suffragette campaign, it has rarely been examined especially from the perspective of the authorities. Historians have often assumed that the refusal of many prisoners to report when required, and their attempts at eluding arrest, made a mockery of the legislation.[127] Yet such a conclusion is scarcely borne out by the mass of evidence in the Public Record Office. According to the Home Secretary, 163 suffragettes were imprisoned during 1913, and 23 during January to March 1914, of whom only 42 were in fact discharged under the new legislation. This begins to put the problem in perspective. Most prisoners appear not to have been in need of temporary release. Of those that were, the authorities clearly succeeded in rearresting many of them repeatedly to continue their terms.[128] Even more striking is the evidence in the detailed files on suffragettes such as Harriet Kerr, Phyllis Brady, and Harry Johnston, which show that after repeated release and rearrest they eventually agreed to sign statements undertaking to abandon militancy in return for the remission of the remainder of their sentences.[129] Others like Ethel Slade and Agnes Lake were released because the Home Secretary judged that they were unlikely to commit any further offences.[130] In effect the Cat and Mouse Act was steadily whittling away the number of active militants by securing promises of good behaviour. This practice pointed the way towards the well-known truce offered in August 1914 on the outbreak of war. It appears that at that point McKenna effectively accelerated a policy already in operation for some time.

---

[127] Rosen, *Rise Up Women*, 215; Vicinus, *Independent Women*, 254.
[128] See *Daily Mail*, 1 May 1913; *Evening Dispatch*, 12 Jan. 1914; both thought the Act was working.
[129] PRO HO144/1275/239581; PRO HO144/1261/236533; PRO HO144/1274/239318.
[130] Letter dated 1 July 1914: PRO HO144/1236/2300251; PRO HO144/1275/239582.

TABLE 8.2. Prisoners released under the Cat and Mouse Act, 1913–1914

	Temporarily discharged	Number of offences	Times released	Times recaptured
42 prisoners of which:				
	1	7	5	5
	1	4	5	4
	1	3	3	2
	5	2 of which :		
		2	3	2
		2	2	2
		1	1	1
	34	1 of which :		
		17	1	0
		2 paid fines		
		3	1	3
		3	2	1
		6	3	2
		1	4	3
		2	5	4
		1	6	5
		1	7	6

Source: Hansard, House of Commons Debates, 5th Series, LIX, 18 Mar. 1914, c. 2068–9.

Of course, some of the released prisoners took refuge in safe houses to evade recapture, but in so doing they effectively dropped out of the campaign. In the case of the most prominent figures rearrest was difficult, but, as Mrs Pankhurst's case shows, the authorities refused to be deterred.[131] In March 1914 when she appeared at the St Andrew's Hall in Glasgow on a platform surrounded by barbed wire and an armed guard of suffragettes, the police used great force to arrest her; but McKenna had no hesitation in defending their actions on the grounds that it was their duty to take a prisoner convicted of felony and illegally at large.[132] In response the WSPU was threatening to create a private armed guard in July 1914 to protect Mrs Pankhurst. In fact, in the East End of London Sylvia Pankhurst and George Lansbury had been at work since the autumn of 1913 drilling a 'citizens' army' for the same purpose. How they reconciled this with their pacifism is unclear. 'The government is so cowardly that even the appearance of force will make it give way,' Sylvia claimed.[133] However, she had little idea how to train and organize such a force. Under the captaincy of Nora Smythe some eighty to one hundred people met each week at the Bow Baths, and Sylvia

[131] PRO HO144/1254/234646.
[132] *Hansard, HC Deb.*, 5th Series, LIX, 16 Mar. 1914, c. 1689.
[133] Quoted in Barbara Winslow, *Sylvia Pankhurst* (UCL Press, 1996), 57.

spoke about marching on Downing Street. Yet the police seem to have been undeterred, and one concludes that there was a large element of bluff in the scheme; as so often the Pankhursts were imitating the example set by the Ulster Unionists.[134]

Amid the drama of the Cat and Mouse Act, it is easy to miss the mundane reality of the situation reached by 1914. The Act was *working* both directly through the recapture of prisoners and indirectly through the withdrawal of suffragettes from militancy. The government persisted with its highly illiberal methods in the confidence that opinion had turned against the WSPU's campaign at least for the time being. In the process the organization was driven steadily underground and lost contact both with the public and much of its membership; by 1913 subscriptions had begun to fall and some members withdrew into other suffrage societies.[135] Thus, when the Pankhursts grasped the Home Secretary's offer of a truce involving release of the prisoners in return for a cessation of the campaign in August 1914, they were effectively recognizing the need to extricate themselves from the spiral of decline in which they had become trapped.

Militancy as a Mass Movement

At the heart of the suffragette campaign lay a gamble: that enough people would support militancy to convince the politicians that the dangers of continuing to neglect the women's claim exceeded the inconvenience involved in tackling their grievance. Herbert Gladstone rather crassly recognized this when he referred to the mobilization of tens of thousands of people in the 1830s, the 1860s, and the 1880s to demand the vote: 'it is not expected that women could assemble in such masses', he observed.[136] In the obvious sense the suffragettes proved Gladstone to be completely wrong. Yet while they unquestionably succeeded in antagonizing the Edwardian politicians, it is doubtful whether they ever came near to intimidating them, which was the sense of Gladstone's remarks. Although the suffragette movement expanded greatly from 1906 onwards, the militant part of it remained a minority. The core of the WSPU consisted in four or five thousand individuals at the peak; and by 1912 the membership stabilized before commencing its fall in 1913–14. Estimates are hampered by the failure of the WSPU to publish full

---

[134] Winslow, *Pankhurst*, 59–60.

[135] New subscriptions fell from 4,459 in 1909–10 to 2,380 in 1912 and 923 in the first eight months of 1913 at which point the WSPU stopped publishing figures.

[136] Feb. 1908, quoted in Rover, *Women's Suffrage*, 135.

membership figures, and the subscribers' lists are not a complete record.[137] In 1909 the Anti-Suffragists estimated that the WSPU had 8,374 members. [138] Any attempt to put the militants in the context of the whole movement is also complicated by the phenomenon of multiple membership which was extensive, and became more so as new organizations constantly appeared. One Edwardian suffragist, Edy Craig, the daughter of Ellen Terry, apparently belonged to eight different suffrage societies: 'when one considers all the cause means, one cannot belong to too many', she remarked.[139]

TABLE 8.3. WSPU subscribers, 1906–1914

1906–7	405	1910–11	4,519
1907–8	1,448	1911–12	4,633
1908–9	1,777	1912–13	4,831
1909–10	3,918	1913–14	4,134

Source: WSPU, *Annual Reports.*

We do, however, learn a good deal from the regional distribution of WSPU branches. In 1907, in a total of 65 branches, 23 were in London, 4 in Southern England, 22 in Northern England, 4 in the Midlands, 10 in Scotland, and 2 in Wales. Over time the regional imbalance was accentuated. The breakaway of the WFL in 1907 carried off most of the Scottish branches, leaving the WSPU to expand chiefly in London and the Home Counties in middle-class, residential districts. The analysis of 1913 underlines the strong metropolitan bias of the organization, and also demonstrates its modest size in relation to the non-militant organization; even the combination of the WSPU and the WFL, which was only partly militant, represented only about a quarter of the total suffrage organization. It would therefore be misleading to describe

TABLE 8.4. Distribution of suffragist branches in 1913

	WSPU	NUWSS	WFL
London	34	47	18
England	50	328	28
Scotland	3	58	10
Wales	3	27	5
TOTAL	90	460	61

Source: A.J.R. (ed.), *The Suffrage Annual and Women's Who's Who*, 1913.

[137] In view of the large headquarters staff this probably indicates a reluctance to reveal how small it was by comparison with other suffrage organizations.

[138] E. L. Somervell, *The Times*, 13 Oct. 1909.

[139] Lis Whitelaw, *The Life and Rebellious Times of Cicely Hamilton* (The Women's Press, 1990), 80.

TABLE 8.5. Suffragette prisoners, 1908–1913

	Prisoners	Arrested	Hunger Strike	Forcibly fed
1907–8[a]	130			
1908–9[a]	60			
1909–10[a]	163	294	110	36
1910–11[b]	113 women; 3 men			
1911–12[b]	182 women; 6 men			
1912–13	311	367	131	89
1913–14	95	169		5

Sources: [a] WSPU, *Annual Reports*; [b] *Hansard, House of Commons Debates*, 5th Series, LI, 7 Apr., 1913, c. 813t.

the suffragettes as a mass movement even at the peak around 1908–12. In any case only a minority of WSPU members were personally involved in militant acts. Mary Richardson thought there had been about a thousand 'actual front line militants' and fewer than that after the introduction of the Cat and Mouse Act in 1913. The official list of suffragette prisoners for 1905–14 comprised 1,097 names, though since some arsonists were not caught this is presumably an underestimate of participants.[140] When the figures are broken down into annual totals, the scale of the phenomenon becomes clearer; at the height of the campaign around three hundred suffragettes were in prison in a year, though in most cases only for days or weeks at a time. Another measurement of the problem facing the police was the arson campaign during 1913–14. While the financial costs of these attacks attracted enormous publicity, the number of incidents each month was small and reflects the work of small groups and scattered individuals who were able to escape detection and so repeat their attacks.

Taken as a whole these pieces of evidence about the campaign point to the conclusion that militancy failed to achieve its potential impact on the government largely because participation was fairly limited. However shocking the attacks launched by middle and upper-class ladies, they could never have the effect that extensive *working-class* involvement would have had. The role of individual working-class women including Annie Kenney, Hannah Mitchell, and Minnie Baldock, is well known, and some writers have reacted indignantly to the traditional view of the suffragettes as a largely middle-class movement. However, they have made no attempt to provide the

---

[140] Mary Richardson, *Laugh a Defiance* (Weidenfeld and Nicolson, 1953), 189; 'Roll of Honour: Suffragette Prisoners 1905–14', Manchester Central Library: Mitchell Papers M220/2/2/4.

analysis of the social composition of the movement that might substantiate their claim.[141] A study of thirteen branches of the WFL—which was of course much more sympathetic to working-class women than the WSPU and much closer to the Labour Movement—found only one with a substantial working-class membership.[142]

TABLE 8.6. The arson campaign 1913–1914

		Number of incidents	Costs of damage (£)
1913	March	5	7,000
	April	8	14,000
	May	11	36,475
	June	10	54,000
	July	3	23,100
	August	5	10,250
	September	5	51,800
	October	5	10,500
	November	4	9,200
	December	8	54,490
1914	January	3	8,200–12,200
	February	8	62,000
	March	5	25,900–27,000
	April	6	53,000–57,000
	May	4	41,000–63,000
	June	7	5,000–12,000
	July	3	21,250

Source: Andrew Rosen, *Rise Up Women! The Militant Campaign of the Women's Social and Political Union 1903–1914* (1974).

This is not difficult to explain if one considers the dilemmas facing the working-class woman. Even a minimal involvement in militant activities was likely to lead her to neglect her responsibilities to her family and household.[143] Helen Crawfurd reflected this reluctance when she recalled her intention of having a quick fling so that she could return to her home as soon

---

[141] For example, in an article apparently intended to challenge the view of the WSPU as middle-class, June Purvis produced no evidence of class composition except to identify the occupations of certain suffragettes as businesswomen, nurses, teachers, actresses, and artists—all rather middle-class! ('The Prison Experiences of the Suffragettes in Edwardian Britain', *Women's History Review*, 4/1 (1995), 14). In 'No Surrender! The Militancy of Mary Leigh, a Working-Class Suffragette', Maroula Joannus and June Purvis (eds.), *The Women's Suffrage Movement: New Feminist Perspectives* (I. B. Tauris, 1998), Michelle Myall bases the claim on a single individual who turns out to have been a teacher—not obviously working-class.

[142] Eustance, 'Daring to be Free', 123.

[143] The WFL believed that members could not reasonably be militant if they did not live in London, or had paid employment or family responsibilities: Eustance, 'Daring to be Free', 63.

as possible.[144] Working women such as actresses felt loath to risk breaking their contracts. In any case, not every woman could afford the uniforms on which the Pankhursts were so keen. As a result of such considerations, militancy was often regarded as an indulgence beyond the resources of many women; a woman required either a private income, the support of her parents, or subsidies from sympathizers before embarking on a career of militancy.

Nor were material factors the only deterrent. Traditions of working-class respectability also influenced some women's attitude. For a securely upper-middle class family this may not have been a serious problem. But those who were attempting to maintain their status at the top of the working class or in the lower middle class showed themselves sensitive to threats of this sort; for such people a prison sentence for militancy was a social disaster comparable to entry into the workhouse. This helps to explain why the Women's Co-operative Guild reacted against militancy. As Eva Gore-Booth put it, clashes with the police deterred 'the average working woman whose dignity is very real to her'.[145] Some of the Lancashire women regarded the imprisonment of suffragettes as a stunt rather than as a courageous sacrifice; they accused the Pankhursts of the 'crooked course, the double-shuffle between revolution and injured innocence'. Class-based scepticism was also evident in Ramsay MacDonald's dismissive verdict on the suffragettes: 'I have the strongest objection to childishness masquerading as revolution.'[146]

This was unfortunate because the Pankhursts had originally been closely involved with the campaign in Lancashire, and they always retained an appreciation of the material interests of working women in using the vote to help them remove the evil of low pay. Yet they had made a very deliberate decision to sacrifice that connection by quitting Manchester for London in order to move their campaign up the social scale and tap the money and influence of the well-to-do. By 1906 Christabel had concluded that the WSPU had become 'too exclusively dependent for the demonstrations upon women of the East End', and that parliament was 'more impressed by the feminine bourgeoisie'. Though this did not prevent participation by working-class women, they certainly found it discouraging.[147] Drawing-room gatherings were not congenial and, in any case, occurred at inconvenient

---

[144] Helen Crawfurd, MS Autobiography, 89, Marx Memorial Library.

[145] Liddington and Norris, *One Hand Tied Behind Us*, 204–5.

[146] Ibid. 218; David Marquand, *Ramsay MacDonald* (Cape, 1977), 148.

[147] *Daily Mail*, 11 Feb. 1907; Pankhurst, *Unshackled*, 67–8; in 1907 the secretary of the Canning Town WSPU resigned because the leaders were 'not keeping their promises to the working women': Winslow, *Pankhurst*, 32.

times of day. Even Billington-Greig, who felt herself to be distinctly superior to the working classes, confessed to being taken aback by the 'At Homes' organized by the Pankhursts at the Clement's Inn headquarters: 'we found the place full of fashionable ladies in rustling silks and satins'; and she feared that this would play into the hands of those who suspected suffragism as essentially a movement for the upper and middle classes.[148]

None of this made a working-class suffrage movement impossible; but it did mean that the militants failed to exploit the potential that existed. The conditions for a successful appeal were not just social but ideological. When the Scottish suffragette, Helen Crawfurd, campaigned in the mining villages of Lanarkshire she found the miners willing to take collections and offer her free use of their halls. They admired the women's fight, but also responded to the nature of her appeal—a mixture of Socialism and Christianity which was familiar to them but far removed from the ideology of the Pankhursts.[149]

Much the most conspicuous departure from the ideology and strategy of the WSPU was the campaign led by Sylvia Pankhurst in London's East End. There she reverted to the original alliance with the ILP whose members were drawn into the East London Federation (ELF). For her pains Sylvia was expelled from the WSPU in January 1914. From Christabel's perspective, the ELF was objectionable because it was based on the working class, closely involved men, advocated complete adult suffrage, and went beyond feminism to embrace Socialist and even Syndicalist views. Though Sylvia denied that she had formed an alliance with the *Daily Herald* League, she certainly cooperated with George Lansbury and James Connolly on public platforms to support the Dublin workers' strikes and the protests against the imprisonment of Jim Larkin. She argued that this enabled her to get the women's message across to audiences at a time when the WSPU had been largely driven underground, and also generated some physical protection against the police. Even Asquith extended a sympathetic hearing to a deputation from the ELF in 1914 on the basis of its working-class character. Not that Sylvia had solved the problem of creating a mass movement; the membership of the ELF has been put at sixty. The workers of the East End had already demonstrated their hostility to female suffrage at the Bow and Bromley by-election in November 1912 (see Chapter 9), though Sylvia was justified in feeling that by working with local figures she would be able to erase the impression created by the WSPU. Even when accompanied by Ben Tillett and Lansbury, she found herself the victim of unfriendly crowds who stoned

[148] Notes, Fawcett Library: Billington-Greig Papers 397 A/6.
[149] Helen Crawfurd, MS Autobiography, 95–6, Marx Memorial Library.

her and seized the platform from beneath her feet.[150] Ultimately the ELF enjoyed too short a period before the outbreak of war to be able to demonstrate how effectively it would work. But by keeping alive the idea of a working-class alliance it underlined the miscalculation that lay at the heart of militancy.

How Radical Was the Suffragette Movement?

As historians have unearthed more evidence about the participants in the suffragette movement, they have indirectly invited a long-overdue reconsideration of the nature of the challenge it presented. For contemporaries the methods and the language used by the Pankhursts seemed to justify an interpretation of the WSPU as a thoroughly subversive organization which has survived down the decades. Even as staunch a suffragist as Lord Robert Cecil maintained that militancy 'shakes the very foundations on which society exists. . . . It is in the nature of a rebellion.'[151] This diagnosis was consciously fostered by Emmeline Pankhurst who, at the height of the struggle in 1912, urged her followers to 'attack the secret idol of property so as to make the Government realise that property is as greatly endangered by Woman Suffrage as it was by the Chartists of old. . . . I incite this meeting to rebellion.'[152] By this time the Metropolitan Police and the legal advisers at the Home Office were only too willing to take her words at face value in order to justify the suppression of the agitation. However, the security services are notoriously poor judges of political ideology, and the historian must look sceptically at the rhetoric of both the critics and the allies of the suffragette movement. In the heat of the struggle it was understandable that the nature of the challenge it presented should have been misunderstood by some and misrepresented by others. The traditional focus on the *methods* adopted by the Pankhursts has had the effect of obscuring the fact that in many ways they and their followers were distinctly conventional in aims and attitudes. In reality, though the suffragettes attacked and disparaged the parliamentary politicians, they desired to join the system rather than to overthrow the *status quo*. This is scarcely surprising because both their social class and their political connections placed many suffragettes comfortably within the British Establishment. The scholarly argument about how far the movement was working class as opposed to middle class misses the point, for the key feature

---

[150] See Victoria Park meetings reported in *Daily Chronicle*, 26 May 1913; *The Times*, 26 May 1913.
[151] Speech to the Actresses Franchise League, 3 Mar. 1911, *Votes for Women*, 10 Nov. 1911.
[152] Speech at the Albert Hall, *Votes for Women*, 25 Oct. 1912.

of the WSPU was its extensive *upper-class* element in the form of wealthy and titled women whose male relations enjoyed considerable political influence and social standing. Among the well-connected were Lady Constance Lytton, the sister of the Earl of Lytton, Charlotte Despard, whose brother was General Sir John French, Britain's Commander-in-Chief on the Western Front in 1914, and Anne Cobden Sanderson, a daughter of Richard Cobden, a hallowed name among Edwardian Liberals.[153] Constance Lytton's prison experience has usually been cited as an illustration of the class prejudice of the authorities, but this is to miss the point that people like the Lyttons were able to associate prominently with militancy without jeopardizing their status in society.

One learns a good deal about attitudes towards militancy from respectable families such as that of Margaret Haig (later Lady Rhondda) whose father, D. A. Thomas, was an extremely wealthy industrialist and a Liberal MP, a connection which ought to have guaranteed the maximum of social and political embarrassment. Evidently this was not the case. Thomas's wife and daughters, not to mention assorted cousins and aunts, all became involved in the suffragette agitation. 'The truth is', wrote Margaret Haig, 'that it was almost the done thing in our family to go to prison.'[154] For a time a brief sentence for suffragette activity became a fashionable middle-class offence which carried no especial stigma and did no real damage to one's position. Indeed, the very fact that so many militants were well-connected bestowed a certain cachet or measure of respectability upon their actions.

The social composition of the WSPU had other more tangible implications. The Pankhursts had been shrewd in perceiving the advantages of making the transition from Manchester to London in terms of funds as well as status. A list of their prominent subscribers underlines their links with titled families and wealthy business interests. According to Emmeline Pethick-Lawrence the practice when canvassing a new district of London was to devise a list of all the well-to-do ladies, get them involved, and then ask them for money.[155] A single rally at the Albert Hall in March 1908 yielded £7,000 for the funds. Perhaps because of the traditional emphasis on the role of the Pankhursts as an inspiration to women and as brilliant propagandists, their talents as fund-raisers have not been sufficiently recognized. Certainly the huge rise in resources, which produced an annual income of almost £47,000

[153] French, however, was not very gallant about his sister's arrest: 'If she insists on joining in with these people she must expect it', *Daily Mirror*, 15 Feb. 1907.

[154] Rhondda, *This Was My World*, 161.

[155] Emmeline Pethick-Lawrence to Maud Arncliffe-Sennett, 11 July 1907, Arncliffe-Sennett papers, BL, C 10.245.

TABLE 8.7. Major WSPU subscribers

F. W. and E. Pethick-Lawrence	Lady Sybil Smith	Mrs D. A. Thomas
Mrs Joseph Fels	Maud Arncliffe-Sennett	Lady Isobel Margesson
Lady Weetman Pearson	Viscountess Harberton	Mrs Dacre Fox
Muriel, Countess de la Warr	Mrs Bernard Shaw	Miss Janie Allan
Princess Sophia Dhuleep Singh	Mrs Hertha Ayrton	Lady Ernestine Hunt
Lady Brassey	Lady Wolsely	Lady Lely
The Hon. Mrs Haverfield	Mrs Brackenbury	Dr Ethel Smythe
Mrs Elizabeth Garret Anderson	Beatrice Harraden	Mrs Saul Soloman
Mrs F. Cavendish-Bentinck	Miss Mary Blomfield	Lady Blake
The Hon. Mrs Hamilton Russell	Lady Byron	Mrs Douglas Hamilton
Miss Una Dugdale	Mrs Fahey	Lady Barclay
Lady Parsons	Lady Constance Lytton	Lady Maud Perry
Miss Joan Wickham		

Sources: WSPU, *Annual Reports*; Self-Denial Week *Report*, 1908; *Daily Graphic* article in the Janie Allan Papers Acc. 4498/6.

TABLE 8.8. WSPU, annual income, 1906–1914

1906–7	£2,959	1910–11	£29,000
1907–8	£7,545	1911–12	£33,980
1908–9	£21,213	1912–13	£35,710[a]
1909–10	£33,027	1913–14	£46,875[b]

[a] £10,000 of this represented balance carried forward.
[b] £7,200 of this represented balance carried forward.

Source: WSPU, *Annual Reports* and Balance Sheets.

by 1914, was the foundation of the WSPU's success after 1906, for it allowed the movement to develop a formidable machine. In February 1908 it employed 34 staff (20 in London and 14 organizers in the country), 75 by February 1909 (45 in the office and 30 organizers), and no fewer than 110 by February 1911. But at a total cost of £7,175 in 1911–12 the bill for salaries made only a modest dent in the total income. WSPU funds can be put into perspective by comparison with other Edwardian organizations. In 1908 the Labour Party enjoyed a pitifully small income of £9,674, and its pre-war maximum in 1909 was £15,606. Even the Liberal Party's total central expenditure in 1906 was only £133,000. Clearly the Pankhursts had become serious competitors with the parties, which is why they represented such a threat when they intervened at by-elections. On the other hand, the fall in WSPU income in 1910–11, presumably a reflection of the effect of the truce, underlines their vulnerability; it was necessary to keep finding novel forms of militancy in order to retain their prominence and thus maintain both momentum and income.

However, individual donations represented only part of the WSPU's financial success. The organization developed an extensive commercial dimension, becoming in effect a *business* in the form of shops which sold a wide range of merchandise including suffragette jewelry, china, soap, handkerchiefs, Christmas cards, postcards, tablecloths, and party games such as 'Panko' and 'Pank-a-Squith'.[156] Mrs Pankhurst's own unsuccessful attempts to run shops earlier in life doubtless helped her to see that many women would find this a congenial way of contributing to the movement.

Even more remarkable was the close relationship between the WSPU and the fashionable West End stores which sold expensive dresses, coats, hats, furs, and drapery to wealthy women. Debenham and Freebody, Peter Robinson, Derry and Toms, Swan and Edgar, Marshall and Snellgrove, Burberrys, Dickins and Jones, and Waring and Gillow were among the shops that advertised regularly in *Votes for Women*; from 1909 onwards many of them took half or full-page advertisements. This helped to make the paper profitable and boosted another WSPU business venture, The Woman's Press which was founded in 1908. But what were the advertisers' motives? If they had hoped to protect themselves against the danger of broken windows they were obviously mistaken. The fact is that at its height *Votes for Women* sold over forty thousand copies weekly. These shops would scarcely have bothered to take space so regularly if they had not regarded the readers of suffragette papers as their natural customers.[157] They presumably entertained no fears about alienating their respectable clientele by association with the militant movement. On the contrary, they appear to have gone out of their way to highlight it in all kinds of ways. Charles Lee of Wigmore Street offered a new suffragette coat in green and purple 'cunningly blended'; a West End taylor announced special terms for WSPU members and the Men's League; Lilley and Skinner shoes put on a window display in WSPU colours; Derry and Toms even sold tricolour underwear in purple, white, and green ; a manufacturer of fountain pens inscribed with 'Votes for Women' promised a donation for every pen sold; and in Newcastle the Elswick Cycle Company marketed the Elswick bicycle for ladies enamelled in WSPU colours for ten guineas.[158] Whatever else they were, suffragettes were good business. In response *Votes for Women* often attached articles to the advertisements urging readers to dress in official colours for processions and in general to support its

---

[156] See Diane Atkinson, *The Purple, White and Green* (Museum of London, 1992).

[157] By contrast the pages of *The Common Cause*, the NUWSS journal, were largely free of such advertising, though some appeared in 1912–14.

[158] 'Dress in the Colours', *Votes for Women*, 26 Mar. 1909, 483; 30 Apr. 1909, 594; 14 May 1909, 675; Atkinson, *The Purple*, 21.

advertisers at every opportunity. 'These firms are helping us to fight the battle, and you are helping by patronising them.'[159] In one such piece no fewer than thirty-seven shops were recommended in addition to twenty well-known products including Colman's Mustard: 'Remember, the above list of reliable names is YOUR shopping list.'[160] Another article went so far as to advise dealing exclusively with the advertisers, which echoed a tactic used by the Chartists in order to coerce shopkeepers into supporting the cause.[161] Quite apart from the financial advantages of this commercial relationship, Christabel placed much importance on the use of suffragette colours in public demonstrations which she felt made a strong impression as well as making for ease of identification in crowds.[162] In effect the emphasis on dress maximized the appeal to women but also brought the advantages of a political uniform to the WSPU.

Perhaps surprisingly, the shops were by no means immune to attacks on their windows. The spate of assaults in March 1912 led to a protest meeting of indignant West End proprietors demanding to know what steps the authorities were taking to prevent disorder.[163] A report of their meeting suggests that they were actually more worried about marches by poor people from the East End affected by the coal strike than by the suffragettes. At all events they continued to advertise in *Votes for Women*. According to *The Times* the window-breaking of March caused £5,000 of damage which was paid by the insurance companies who had reaped a rich harvest in extra business.[164] It seems likely that the only ultimate loser in all this was Fred Pethick-Lawrence from whose estate the shopkeepers managed to recover £5,000![165]

What does this close relationship between the suffragettes and commercial interests tell us about the militant strategy and ideology? Despite its attacks on property the WSPU appears to have maintained its financial strength right up to 1914. Although the campaign aroused strong feelings which were at least in part directed against the government as the WSPU had intended, it was not interpreted as a sign of hostility towards property or wealth as such, let alone as reflecting a desire to overthrow the institution of private property. The real danger, as is suggested by the shopkeepers' meeting, lay in setting an example which the lower classes might emulate. In fact, suffragette targets—club and shop windows, letter boxes, golf greens, churches, private houses—were quite marginal in economic terms. Although the damage resulting from arson attacks attracted headlines and

[159] 'Dress in the Colours' *Votes for Women*, 26 Mar. 1909, 483; 'White Sales', 27 Jan. 1911, 282, 284.
[160] *Votes for Women*, 27 Jan. 1911, 284.   [161] *The Suffragette*, 10 July 1914.
[162] Christabel Pankhurst, *Votes for Women*, 7 May 1909, 632.   [163] *The Times*, 12 Mar. 1912.
[164] *The Times*, 14 June 1912.   [165] F. W. Pethick-Lawrence, *Fate*, 102.

ran into tens of thousands of pounds each year, no important industrial target was ever tackled. Thus the campaign cannot be equated with, say, a general strike; it was neither intended to paralyse the economy and thus undermine the political system, nor did it involve an ideological hostility to capitalism. This of course is consistent with the failure to mobilize working-class partici-pation on any great scale. To have done so would have enabled the suf-fragettes to mount an extensive threat to property and the economy rather than sporadic attacks, and it would have been interpreted as genuinely subversive in intent.

The implication is that the methods used by the Pankhursts offer a poor guide to their political ideology. They had begun their careers advocating some radical social and economic policies. But between 1906 and 1914 this became a more marginal element in their propaganda; and the vote tended to become a goal in itself, as is understandable for those of the ladies who had few personal grievances. In this context the steady movement of the leading militants to the right after 1906, a process which was accelerated by the Pankhursts' enthusiastic adoption of a patriotic, pro-government stance dur-ing the war, seems less of an aberration. The original move from left to right around 1906 may have been largely tactical, though Christabel had never felt any great loyalty to the ILP. But the consistent hostility shown towards Labour right up to 1914 seemed to indicate a genuine growth of Conserva-tive sentiment. During the war the suffragette leaders developed an extreme hostility towards trade unions and they toured the industrial districts urging the workers not to be seduced by Socialists and Communists into taking strike action. The natural culmination of this phase was Christabel's insist-ence on fighting Labour in a working-class constituency as the candidate of the Lloyd George Coalition in 1918. By this time women's issues had been effectively abandoned in favour of an extreme right-wing appeal based on anti-German, anti-Bolshevik, and anti-trade union propaganda.

However, the Women's Party perished quickly with Christabel's defeat at the election, taking with it her own interest in parliamentary politics. The setback accentuated the disillusionment which was now widespread among former suffragettes. Whether by temperament or through experience, many of the women had found it difficult to cooperate with conventional political organizations and became rather isolated from parliamentary politics.[166] The suffragettes were not the only figures who felt let down by politicians in the post-war world. Mrs Pankhurst was galvanized, as were others on the right,

---

[166] See the valuable analysis in Brian Harrison, 'The Act of Militancy: Violence and the Suffragettes', in *Peaceable Kingdom* (Oxford: Oxford University Press, 1982).

by the General Strike of 1926, which led to her brief re-emergence as a Conservative candidate in 1927. Flora Drummond formed the Women's Guild of Empire which dedicated itself to resisting strikes and Communism. Even more striking was the eventual reappearance of some ex-suffragettes such as Mary Allen, Mary Richardson, Norah Elam (Mrs Dacre Fox), and Miss Mercedes Barrington, in the British Union of Fascists (BUF).[167]

This connection can be explained in terms of common style and organization rather than in terms of ideology. Like the WSPU, the BUF operated in a semi-militaristic fashion, advocated the wearing of a uniform, offered its members the excitement of street confrontations and the satisfaction of belonging to a tightly-knit group. Richardson said that she saw in the Blackshirts 'the courage, the action, the loyalty, the gift of service and the ability to serve which I had known in the Suffragette movement'.[168] Above all, Sir Oswald Mosley satisfied the deeply-felt need among many ex-suffragettes for a strong leader to whom one could give total loyalty. The path towards the BUF had led these suffragettes through the war which had at first provided a fresh object in life, but left them without a purpose. While Emmeline and Christabel succeeded brilliantly in creating a new role for themselves, others struggled to fill the gulf often by entering one of the uniformed services now open to women. Mary Allen found the experiment with Women Police Volunteers a congenial experience, but it was snatched away in the post-war reaction against female employment. In 1923 she founded the Women's Auxiliary Service as a substitute body. It was easy to feel let down by the political system in this period.

Yet there were also ideological links between the suffragette movement and fascism. Mosley himself established an impressive record as a supporter of feminist causes in the 1920s which was recognized by the Six Point Group. Moreover, the corporate state treated woman as full citizens, which meant, among other things, equal pay for female workers. Also, the ex-suffragettes, who had always been sceptical about party politics, showed an acute sense of alienation from conventional institutions after the war; consequently they were bound to feel the attraction of an organization that disparaged parliamentary politics. They professed to regard the post-war women's movement as decadent because of the widespread collusion of its members with the political parties.[169] Many of them had failed to find a satisfying role in the

---

[167] See Martin Durham, 'Women and the British Union of Fascists 1932–40', in Tony Kushner and Kenneth Lunn, *The Politics of Marginality* (Cassell, 1990); Martin Durham, 'Gender and the British Union of Fascists', *Journal of Contemporary History*, 27 (1992); Julie Gottlieb, 'Women and Fascism in Inter-War Britain', Ph.D. thesis (University of Cambridge), 1998.
[168] Ibid. 154, from *Blackshirt*, 29 June 1934.   [167] Ibid. 159.

existing system, which accentuated their profound conviction that British society was suffering from an enfeebled form of politics and from a collapse of moral values. The BUF came as close as any movement could to satisfying the needs that had originally led these women into the WSPU. But their divergence from the broader evolution of the women's movement underlines the extent to which militancy was an untypical strand within the suffrage campaign.

9

Women's Suffrage and Public Opinion

FROM the very start the women's cause had been dogged by claims that it lacked a genuine popular mandate. Commenting editorially in January 1913 *The Times* predicted that female enfranchisement would not be settled on its merits but by wider political considerations, in particular when it was 'decided by a genuine and incontestable majority of the British people that they ought to have it'.[1] Since *The Times,* like the prime minister, continued to take comfort in the belief that 'no such majority has been proved to exist', the comment may be dismissed as routine Anti-Suffragist prevarication. However, both sides were conscious that in the end public opinion was likely to be decisive in determining the timing of enfranchisement; they expected the cause to follow the pattern of 1832 and 1867 in which after a prolonged period of education and propaganda followed by a more concentrated phase of agitation, parliament would accept that the issue had become too urgent to be ignored any longer.

Yet Edwardian politicians were handicapped in discovering what the public really wanted. No daily opinion polls recorded the shifts in loyalties and priorities. Many MPs visited their constituencies infrequently and relied on their agents or their relations to keep them in touch. Members who represented small boroughs or rural seats often saw little or no evidence of local interest in women's suffrage. Frontbenchers' lives were dominated by Westminster, Whitehall, and the narrow world of the London clubs; what purported to be a national press was largely absorbed with London and with the affairs of the Balkans, Turkey, and far flung parts of the Empire rather than with the English provinces, Scotland, or Wales.

On the other hand, politicians were not entirely wrong in regarding the many pressure groups with which they dealt as small articulate minorities who spoke largely for themselves; behind the enthusiasts stood millions of

---

[1] *The Times,* 21 Jan. 1913.

indifferent or apathetic men and women. It is easily forgotten that by 1910 these remarks were just as applicable to the *opponents* of women's suffrage as to the supporters. But this offered no great comfort to the suffragists because the onus lay on them to demonstrate the popularity of reform rather than on the upholders of the status quo to prove the reverse. For analytical purposes it is helpful to distinguish three levels of opinion: first the parliamentarians with whom the ultimate decision rested; second, the political activists, pressure groups, and the press; and third, the wider public that was not directly involved but could be intermittently stirred by political issues. In common with most pressure groups the women's suffragists were more effective in converting the first two sections of opinion than the third; the trick lay in convincing the politicians that the point had arrived when the views of the activists really did represent those of the population at large.

On the Stage and in the Press

While comparatively large numbers of Edwardians attended public meetings, which were still an important form of mass entertainment, they derived their political ideas from several alternative sources. That these were often light-hearted and superficial may make them difficult to assess, but this hardly justifies neglecting them. For example, the *Daily Mirror* which had been founded in 1903 as a picture paper for ladies, frequently filled its front page with photographs of suffragist activities.[2] The paper's attitude towards the vote—rather neutral—was almost irrelevant; it could hardly avoid promoting the cause because it depended heavily upon the visual material generated so freely by the campaign. Similar remarks apply to the large quantity of postcards, cartoons, and music hall songs of the period which often presented women's suffrage in a humorous or hostile form, but which nonetheless forced the issue into public consciousness.

Ever since Ibsen's play, *A Doll's House,* had been performed in Britain, actresses had felt drawn towards feminism both because he articulated the woman's dilemmas effectively and because he created challenging roles for women. The Actresses' Franchise League (AFL), formed in December 1910 with the backing of Ellen Terry, Cicely Hamilton, and Evelyn Sharp, soon recruited a thousand members.[3] They were potentially a great asset to the movement; as experienced public performers actresses were in demand at

[2] See *Daily Mirror,* 11 Feb. 1907, on the 'Mud March'.

[3] Julie Holledge, *Innocent Flowers: Women in the Edwardian Theatre* (Virago, 1981); John, *Elizabeth Robins*, 53–4; Whitelaw, *Cicely Hamilton*, 77–84.

suffragist meetings and also for training other speakers. However, most of the AFL actresses worked in theatre not music hall, which limited their audience, and as working women they could not usually afford to campaign, let alone risk punishment for militant activities. One exception to this was Kitty Marion who sacrificed her career for the WSPU. But as a rule members kept the AFL informed of their touring schedules so that it could coordinate them with the programmes of the regional suffrage societies and enable the actresses to fit in meetings between performances.

However, their most important contribution to popularizing the cause lay in presenting the women's case on the stage. Several actresses wrote plays themselves, including Elizabeth Robins (*Votes For Women*), Cicely Hamilton (*How the Vote Was Won* and *Diana of Dobsons*), and Eva Moore (*Her Vote*); as did Beatrice Harraden, Lawrence Housman, J. M. Barrie, and George Bernard Shaw. Although produced by serious-minded suffragists these plays shrewdly appealed to the taste for humour and satire. The Anti-Suffragist women presented an easy target; they were portrayed as confused and brainless in H. M. Paul's *The Other Side,* and in Beatrice Harraden's *Lady Geraldine's Speech.* In *Votes for Men* Mary Cholmondely took the attack into the enemy camp with a play set in a society in which men had been disenfranchised. In 1909 the popular farce, *How the Vote Was Won,* centred around a general strike by women in which the prime minister was obliged to make his own bed. Perhaps the most successful was Shaw's *Press Cuttings* which portrayed the prime minister, 'Balsquith', in drag for fear of being attacked by suffragettes and attempting to impose a two-mile woman-free zone around Westminster. However, the impact of these plays is easily exaggerated. Shaw was exceptional in getting press attention and a West End launch. On the whole the suffrage plays did not enjoy a London run. Most of the performances took place in exhibitions or demonstrations by suffrage societies rather than in a commercial setting where the audience was drawn from the general public.[4]

Unfortunately, as the AFL was not interested in music hall, this more popular audience lay wide open to Anti-Suffragist entertainment. 'In the songs of the populace, in their caricatures, in their jokes, in their whole attitude towards the movement,' declared Hilaire Belloc, 'the populace dislikes [votes for women].'[5] This, however, was an oversimplification. Since music hall invariably attacked anything novel or unconventional, it saw the suffragettes' challenge to gender roles as an irresistible target. Characteristically it depicted men emasculated by feminism, as in *Put Me Upon an Island*:

---

[4] Holledge, *Flowers,* 59, 67–8.
[5] In July 1910, quoted in Harrison, *Separate Spheres,* 138.

All the boys are longing to be put among the girls,
Bless their darling curls, they're all like other girls
When they keep themselves as girls, but very sad to state
That some of them have got into a fighting mood of late.
So when the woman of today comes near, let me be miles away.
Put me upon an island where the girls are few
Put me among the most ferocious lions in the zoo,
Put me upon a treadmill and I'll never fret,
But for pity's sake, don't put me near a suffragette!

The destruction of family life by women who neglected their husbands for the thrill of participating in suffragette campaigns featured prominently in postcards and cartoons, and was set to music in *The Suffer-a-Gee*:

I'm a down-hearted man as you'll easily see,
The wife's been and gone and done it for me,
She's joined what is known as the Down-with-Men Club,
And so most of my time I wash and I scrub.
We used to be happy when first we were wed,
She trusted me then and she called me 'Dear Ned'.
But now I'm a monster, I'm just a mere man,
And to end my existence, she's done all she can.

The aggressive feminist appeared regularly in Anti-Suffragist postcards haranguing the working-class housewife without success. This is the impression given in one of the most famous Edwardian records of popular attitudes, *Seems So! A Working-Class View of Politics* (1911). In this the housewife adopted a dismissive view of the whole issue: 'I reckon they suffragettes wants half-a-dozen kids.... That'd steady 'em.'[6] The working-class woman who took pride in her domestic role could easily be made to feel inadequate by feminism, and thus tempted to regard the suffrage campaign as a hobby for the unmarried or leisured. In this respect male and female sentiment often coincided: 'I tell 'ee what, 'tis sweethearts they wants. There's nowt like it for a girl as is kicking up a buzz.'[7] However, some qualifications are required here. The opinions in *Seems So!* were purportedly drawn from the Devonshire working class for whom the whole idea of female emancipation must have seemed a remote and unsettling one; Mrs Pankhurst encountered one of her most hostile receptions in the Dartmoor town of Ashburton after her intervention in the 1908 by-election there. It does not follow that workers in the large urban

    [6] Stephen Reynolds, Bob Wooley, and Tom Woolley, *Seems So! A Working-Class View of Politics* (Macmillan, 1911), 15.
    [7] Ibid. 15.

centres in northern England, long familiar with radical and suffragist campaigns, regarded it in quite the same way. Moreover, on closer inspection
even the attitudes in *Seems So!* reveal a more balanced view. They showed
sympathy for the suffragettes over their treatment in prison, and enjoyment
of their skill in harrassing the government and authority in general; often on
the receiving end of official policies, they felt some sense of common cause
with the suffragettes.[8] Even the music hall songs were far from being wholly
hostile. For example, *The Suffragette,* performed by Arthur Aiston, began with
the usual mockery: 'My name is Mrs Pancake and me object's Votes for
Women'; but it then moved into a lengthy monologue which invited sympathy for women's life of drudgery and asked why men should continue to
have everything their own way:

Man can get up and speak of politics at a public meeting and get money for it . . . if a
woman speaks of politics at a public meeting what does she get? Fourteen days . . .
fourteen days in Holloway . . . why should a man be allowed to air his views in public
while we are at home airing the beds? . . . while we are at home putting down our
irons, men are in public houses putting down pints. . . . Oh girls! Stand up for your
rights . . . even if you get knocked down for your impudence. . . . Man? I wouldn't
pump the very air he breathes into me bicycle tyres!

This is a reminder that appeals to the sense of fair play could be just as
resonant with the music hall audience as attempts to pander to masculine
pride, especially if well mixed with humour.

The Edwardian press presents a more complex source of opinion because,
though like the music hall, it aspired to entertain and to make money, these
motives were often subordinated to the ambitions of proprietors and editors
to influence opinion rather than to reflect it. There seems no reason to doubt
that after the comparative neglect of the women's issue prior to 1905, the
press helped to promote the cause both by reporting and by editorial comment from 1906 onwards. Yet there was another side to the coin. The suffragettes became very dependent upon newspaper coverage, and their
leaders complained bitterly that the press had imposed a boycott on them in
1907, 1909, and 1911.[9] Coverage was bound to fluctuate according to competition with other issues and also variations in suffragist tactics. In the aftermath of the 1906 election which had focused on free trade and tariff reform,
women's activities had great novelty value; but during 1909 they were to
some extent eclipsed by the controversies over the budget and the House of

    [8] Reynolds, *Seems So!,* 16–17.
    [9] 'How the Press Deceives the Public', WSPU, 1907; F. W. Pethick-Lawrence, 'Is There a Press
Boycott of Woman Suffrage?', *Votes for Women,* 25 June 1909; Christabel Pankhurst, 'The Boycott of
the Press', 3 Feb. 1911; 17 Mar. 1911.

Lords. The suffragettes' truce during 1910–11 diminished their news value until they began non-cooperation with the Census which broke the alleged boycott in the press. In fact, even during the truce *The Times* discussed the suffrage question frequently in editorials, but reported on the campaign less often.

The key questions about the press were how far it was biased against the cause, how far this pattern changed over time, and whether the focus on tactics diverted attention from the substantive case for the vote. Hostile editorial comment, especially in the early years, was by no means an unqualified drawback for it aired the issue and attracted correspondence. One might suppose that editorial bias alone led *The Times* to print twice as many antisuffrage letters as pro-suffrage ones; but it is likely that this simply reflected the views of its readers. More worrying for suffragists was the tendency to misrepresent the movement by exaggerating the militant side of it. Millicent Fawcett complained in 1912 that in reporting her *The Times* omitted her condemnation of militancy at a time when the Antis were trying to discredit suffragists by association with the WSPU.[10] However, even *The Times* gave useful publicity to the cause by printing maps and lists of speakers in connection with major suffrage demonstrations. In any case, once the battle lines had been drawn it seems likely that many readers discounted the opinions of their newspaper.

The newspapers comprised a minority which held firm and often extreme views about votes for women, and a majority with either less pronounced or inconsistent opinions. The heart of the opposition to the cause lay in the *Morning Post* and *The Times* which represented London clubland and imperialist masculinity. At the opposite end of the spectrum the most enthusiastic supporters were the *Manchester Guardian*, the *Daily News*, and the *Daily Herald*. *The Common Cause* argued that up to the start of 1911 most of the London newspapers had been rather vague over the issue, but had adopted a definite position by 1912. On the basis of a survey conducted by the journal in January of that year they claimed to enjoy the backing of a majority of daily papers and weekly journals. The list surprisingly omitted the *Daily Mail* whose attitude had usually been hostile, though subject to the whims of Lord Northcliffe. It is not entirely clear why the National Union regarded the year from 1911 to 1912 as a period of growing support. Possibly the emphatic majority won by the Conciliation Bill in May 1911 led the press to regard the issue as imminent and thus encouraged them to adopt a firm view. However, although the 1911 debate was fully reported, it attracted little comment in the press partly because it was overshadowed by other issues; in the days immediately

[10] *The Times*, 9 Mar. 1912.

TABLE 9.1. The national press in 1912

Pro-Suffrage	Anti-Suffrage	Neutral
Manchester Guardian	The Times	Daily Mirror
Daily Telegraph	Morning Post	Illustrated London News
Daily Express	Guardian	Church Times
Daily Chronicle	Morning Advertiser	Ladies Pictorial
Daily News	Saturday Review	TP's
Daily Graphic	Spectator[a]	Outlook
Morning Leader	Pall Mall Gazette[a]	Hearth and Home
Star	Truth[a]	Throne
Western Gazette		Onlooker
Financial News		World
The Labour Leader		
Christian Commonwealth		
The Nation		
The Tablet		
Queen[a]		

[a] No reply from the editor, but classified according to the tone of the leading articles.

Source: The Common Cause, 4 Jan. 1912, 677.

prior to the debate the Parliament Bill had completed its Committee Stage in the Commons, and once this had been accomplished the commentators switched their attention to Lloyd George's National Insurance Bill. In July a huge march by 40,000 suffragists representing twenty-eight societies attracted virtually unanimous approval in the newspapers. In the *Daily Chronicle's* words: 'With sure and certain steps the cause of women's suffrage is marching to victory ... Saturday's remarkable procession in London served as a prelude to the inevitable triumph. This beautiful pageant was one of the most impressive demonstrations that London has ever witnessed.'[11] Such comment does indeed suggest that a turning-point had been reached around 1911. Yet these newspapers proved to be very fickle and easily influenced both by party considerations and by changes in suffragist tactics. Only a month before the 1911 procession the *Chronicle* had played down the significance of the Conciliation Bill and had noticeably failed to express any support for it in an editorial. In view of the paper's loyalty to Asquith this was not surprising. Like most of the press it was antagonized by the resumption of the suffragette campaign later that year. At the climax of another well-behaved march, the Pilgrimage of July 1913, the *Chronicle* failed to express any support for or confidence in the success of the cause.[12] Another sympathetic paper,

[11] 16 June 1911; this is one of a large collection of press comments on this procession in the Arncliffe-Sennett Papers, BL, C 10.245.

[12] *Daily Chronicle*, 5 May 1911, 1, 6; 27 July 1913, 1.

The Standard, devoted a daily page to reports of suffrage activities during 1911–12, but it, too, was alienated by renewed militancy. It denounced the six-month sentence passed on Mary Richardson for slashing the Rokeby 'Venus' in the National Gallery as 'absurdly lenient', and concluded that 'her special mania altogether unfits her for liberty'.[13] However, condemnation of the suffragettes did not necessarily mean repudiation of the principle of female enfranchisement. Even the *Daily Mail* claimed in 1913 that it had always supported the enfranchisement of the female municipal electors, yet it continued to pour cold water over the Pilgrimage in July and advised women that they would have more impact if they devoted themselves to remedying other female grievances instead of concentrating on the vote.[14] The *Mail*'s proprietors claimed to be unconvinced that public opinion wanted votes for women; and it was not until 1916 when Lord Northcliffe decided that the vote had become inevitable that he jumped on the bandwagon at the last minute.[15] Amongst all the equivocation in the press, the *Daily Herald* stood out for its forthright views: 'It is supremely pretentious and arrogant on the part of men to desire to keep the franchise to themselves.'[16] As the mouthpiece of George Lansbury, who was in close alliance with the Pankhursts, the *Herald*'s unqualified backing for even the most extreme acts of militancy was highly untypical. By 1913 most of the newspapers found themselves badly torn between the issue of women's suffrage and their desire to condemn the methods being used to bring it about.

The By-Election Campaign 1906–1908

The Edwardian by-elections offer the historian significant evidence about public opinion. One of the central parts of the Pankhursts' strategy was their threat to mobilize the country to such an extent that the government would be compelled by the force of opinion to back down. They hoped to demonstrate that reactionary politicians were simply using the absence of popular support for the women's vote as an excuse for their inaction. From 1906 onwards this strategy was implemented through interventions in by-elections designed to persuade the male voters to reject any candidate representing the Liberal Government.

However, the Pankhursts' claims about the efficacy of this campaign have never been systematically examined, perhaps partly because of the difficulty

---

[13] *The Standard*, 13 Mar. 1913.   [14] *Daily Mail*, 20 Jan. 1913; 28 July 1913.
[15] Lord Northcliffe to Lady Betty Balfour, 20 Dec. 1916, Fawcett Library: Fawcett Letters 89/2.
[16] *Daily Herald*, 23 Jan. 1913.

of drawing definite conclusions from the evidence. Certainly the by-elections present major complications. In the first place, they offered an ephemeral verdict on a government suffering from mid-term unpopularity. The capacity of the Liberals to recover many of their losses at the 1910 general elections casts some doubt on the impact of suffragist campaigns. Second, it is extremely difficult to distinguish the impact of any single issue from that of all the others; a multitude of pressure groups descended on the Edwardian by-elections, and one has to allow for the possibility that the suffragettes were simply benefiting from their influence on the voters. It is, however, possible to form an impression of the issues that loomed largest in each campaign. Third, arguments over the vote itself often became entangled with controversy over suffragist *methods*. Indeed, the Pankhursts themselves sometimes became the issue. Some of the constitutionalists argued that after 1912 the suffragettes were having a counter-productive effect on the public, while others insisted that, though unhelpful, their actions had not affected the underlying support for the cause. Fourth, although the by-election technique became associated with the WSPU, it was far from exclusive to that organization. Most suffragist groups participated, but they frequently adopted different, and on occasion contradictory, policies which enormously complicates attempts to assess their impact. Finally it seems certain that the impact of the suffragists fluctuated according to local and national circumstances. In some by-elections there is a *prima facie* case for claiming that suffragism swung votes against the government; but in other cases where the suffragists tried to win a *positive* vote for a pro-suffrage candidate, the poor outcome suggested that their impact was quite limited.

At the general election in January 1906 a pro-suffragist candidate was promoted by the non-militants at Wigan.[17] As in most such cases the circumstances were unusual. Wigan was a traditional Conservative working-class constituency. But as many of the female textile workers in the area paid a political levy to their unions they felt they had some claim to parliamentary representation.[18] The ground had already been prepared by the campaigns of Esther Roper, Eva Gore-Booth, and Selina Cooper in the area. As a result they promoted Thorley Smith as a Labour-and-women's-suffrage candidate. The general anti-Tory swing and the enthusiasm for free trade in Lancashire appeared to enhance his prospects. In the event Smith came second, just ahead of a Liberal; but in a bad year for the Conservatives their candidate

---

[17] The others being Wimbledon in 1907 and Bow and Bromley in 1912.
[18] *Wigan Examiner*, 6 Jan. 1906, 3; 12 Jan. 1906, 5; also Liddington and Norris, *One Hand Tied Behind Us*, 197–9.

held Wigan comfortably with 46.5 per cent of the poll. Much of Smith's vote must have been a Labour one, how far enhanced by his suffragism is impossible to say. The significant thing is that the victorious Conservative had been wholly unapologetic about having voted against women's suffrage bills which he said would only enfranchise rich women.[19] He clearly did not regard anti-suffragism as a liability in this working-class seat, and there are no grounds for thinking he was wrong.

The Pankhursts' campaign got underway in July 1906 at a contentious by-election following the death of the Liberal member for Cockermouth. When the miners decided to run a Labour candidate this posed a dilemma for the Pankhursts who travelled up to Cockermouth eager to inflict a defeat on the new government. At this point they were in transition between their left-wing past and their right-wing future. Although Christabel stayed at the home of a Labour supporter, she declined to support the Labour candidate, thereby precipitating the break with the ILP.[20] During the campaign the Pankhursts boasted that the crowds often abandoned the meetings held by the candidates to listen to the suffragettes. However, they mistook a desire for entertainment as a sign of support. The lady speakers endured much good-humoured heckling from men who usually wanted to know why the suffragettes did not get married. The campaign also generated marked hostility; at a meeting in Maryport Christabel was obliged to stop speaking when the chair on which she stood disappeared from beneath her, and she and her colleagues were hustled back to the railway station to make their escape.[21] The result—a narrow Conservative victory—was entirely explicable in terms of the split in the Liberal vote due to the new Labour candidate, and owed nothing to suffragette intervention.[22] In fact the Pankhursts did themselves more harm than good, for Cockermouth set a pattern of antagonism between them and Labour and working-class audiences.

Less well-known but very revealing of the flaws in the by-election campaign was the contest at Huddersfield in November 1906. Since it was already a three-way Liberal marginal Huddersfield appeared to offer an excellent opportunity to humiliate the government, and it attracted large numbers of suffragettes including Emmeline and Christabel Pankhurst, Mary Gawthorpe, and Annie Kenney (both recently released from Holloway), as well as Esther Rope and Eva Gore-Booth. But confusion arose over the WSPUs advice to electors; Mrs Pankhurst urged them simply to vote against the Liberal, but the suffragettes were also reported to be backing Labour.[23]

---

[19] *Wigan Examiner*, 6 Jan. 1906, 5.   [20] *Carlisle Journal*, 10 July 1906, 5; 13 July 1906, 13.
[21] *Carlisle Journal*, 20 July 1906; 24 July 1906.   [22] *Carlisle Journal*, 7 Aug. 1906.
[23] *Huddersfield Daily Examiner*, 21 Nov. 1906; 23 Nov. 1906.

The probable explanation is that the leaders were still fearful of the reaction of their own members to an anti-Labour stance, or simply that in this tight three-way contest they hoped to be able to claim the credit for *either* a Labour or a Tory victory.

In the event the Pankhursts miscalculated hopelessly. The new Liberal, A. J. Sherwell, was armed with an impeccable record as an advocate of women's suffrage; he reminded his audiences that he had even been approached by Annie Kenney as a prominent suffragist for a donation! In these circumstances the local press regarded the Pankhursts' tactics as illogical.[24] Sherwell's victory in a close contest was a triumph. Since *both* Liberal and Labour candidates had lost a few hundred votes since the general election while the Conservatives gained a few hundred, it appears that the voters had reflected the general political mood by swinging slightly back towards the right; and the conclusion must be that the suffrage issue had failed to become a relevant factor in the by-election.

The WSPU's tactless reaction to the result was also revealing. Having confidently predicted a Liberal defeat, Christabel complained: 'Huddersfield has not done the trick. You have left it to Lancashire ... When we do get [the vote] we shall show you Huddersfield people how to win elections [derisive laughter].' Equally petulant, Mary Gawthorpe berated the audience: 'You ought to be ashamed of yourselves, but we are not beaten. There will be another election next week at Middlesborough and we will be there.'[25] These reactions exposed the hollowness of the Pankhursts' claims to be more in touch with public opinion than the politicians; they had underestimated party loyalty and exaggerated their own influence with their audiences.

However, by 1907 it had become clear that the new government could not satisfy the expectations of its supporters, and the mood of euphoria among radicals generated by the 1906 general election had subsided; the obstruction of legislation in the upper house and the onset of an economic recession made 1907 and 1908 difficult years for the Liberals, and thus created opportunities for the WSPU. In March a by-election in the vulnerable Liberal seat at Hexham demonstrated the confusion still surrounding the by-election strategy. Hexham split the suffragists three ways. The WSPU sent its organizer, Helen Fraser, to support the Conservative candidate. Since the Liberal, Richard Holt, appeared to veer between hostility and neutrality on women's suffrage the leading figures in the NUWSS also refused to work for him; but as no candidate's views were satisfactory their policy was simply to undertake

---

[24] *Huddersfield Daily Examiner*, 21 Nov. 1906; 22 Nov. 1906; 23 Nov. 1906.
[25] Ibid., 29 Nov. 1906.

propaganda.[26] Yet Holt was also reported as favouring women's suffrage at least as part of an adult suffrage bill, and so local members of the North East Society for Women's Suffrage (affiliated to the NUWSS) actively campaigned for him.[27] In effect the WSPU's intervention provoked Liberal women suffragists, who might otherwise not have bothered, into participating, thereby making its policy counter-productive and exposing the divisions within the suffrage camp. Moreover, Holt won in spite of his views.

By contrast, in the Wimbledon by-election in April 1907 the suffragettes decided that there was nothing to be gained by intervening in what was a safe Conservative seat. But in the absence of an official Liberal, Bertrand Russell, who was a Liberal, stood on a women's suffrage platform with the backing of the NUWSS and a thousand female canvassers.[28] Since the Tory, Henry Chaplin, was an unapologetic opponent of votes for women, the WSPU's abstention appeared to be further proof of its Conservative sympathies. In the event Russell polled fewer than half the 1906 Liberal total, while Chaplin won by a three-to-one margin. Russell's campaign was marked by rowdy scenes caused by Anti-Suffragists, though the main issue was tariff reform on which Chaplin was keen. If women's suffrage did not actually lose Russell votes, it clearly failed to help him.

After these depressing results the suffragettes took comfort from two Liberal defeats at Jarrow and Colne Valley in July 1907. As in Hexham, the suffragist forces split in Jarrow. The NUWSS in London regarded the Liberal and Labour candidates as equally pro-suffrage and therefore undertook only propaganda work. But local suffragists were persuaded to support Pete Curran who stood for Labour, while the Pankhursts opposed him. This, however, did not stop them subsequently claiming credit for Curran's narrow victory in a four-cornered contest! One can only surmise that the efforts of the rival suffragists cancelled one another out. Whether the issue was relevant to the outcome seems to be doubtful.[29] The Liberals had comfortably defeated Curran in a straight contest in 1906, and the fall in their 1907 vote was more apparent than real. The unusual decision of the United Irish League to run its own candidate in order to punish the government for neglecting Home Rule, carried off a quarter of the Liberal vote, and the intervention of a Conservative reduced it further. The seat was recovered by the Liberals in 1910.

[26] *Newcastle Evening Chronicle*, 23 Mar. 1907, letter from Ethel Bentham and Lilian Craigie.
[27] *Daily Chronicle*, 15 Mar. 1907; 23 Mar. 1907.
[28] *Daily Mirror*, 24 Apr. 1907; *Daily Chronicle*, 6 May 1907.
[29] See the discussion in A. W. Purdue, 'Jarrow Politics 1885–1914', *Northern History*, 18 (1982); Henry Pelling, 'Two By-Elections: Jarrow and Colne Valley', in *Popular Politics and Society in Late-Victorian Britain* (Macmillan, 1968).

The chief significance of such by-elections was to expose the weaknesses in the NUWSS strategy. Its activists regarded general propaganda not linked to a specific candidate as distinctly unsatisfactory, and they often found themselves being attacked in the streets by crowds who took them for suffragettes.[30] This dilemma was not resolved until 1912.

Colne Valley, another traditional Liberal stronghold which fell vacant through the death of the sitting member, saw an exciting three-cornered contest resulting in the election of Victor Grayson; he was an Independent Socialist though supported by Keir Hardie and Philip Snowden. Again the WSPU claimed the result as a suffragette victory. At the time the *Daily Mirror* attributed the success of the youthful, charismatic Grayson to the enthusiasm he engendered among the local mill girls, though as they obviously had no votes the claim assumes that they influenced their fathers and brothers.[31] But other contemporary comment attributed the result partly to the complacency of the Liberals who had been unopposed in 1906 and allowed their organization to deteriorate, and also to the vulnerability of their candidate as an employer in a district of mills and factories.[32] Growing unemployment at this time also dented the credibility of the free traders and left the Liberals exposed until the government regained the initiative with its social reforms and the budget of 1909. Their recapture of Colne Valley in 1910 suggests that, whatever the causes of defeat in 1907, they were ephemeral. As for the Pankhursts, though they were friends of Grayson and spoke for him, they could not endorse the pure Socialist platform on which he stood. But they shrewdly managed to get onto the winning bandwagon and may have helped Grayson towards his slender 163-vote victory. Together with Jarrow the by-election suggests that their new link with the Conservatives had been a mistake, for they had ditched Labour just at the stage when it had begun to make a dramatic impact, thereby undermining the credibility of their claims to be able to influence public opinion.

1908 proved to be an important year partly because extra by-elections were caused by the replacement of Campbell-Bannerman by Asquith, and partly because the Liberals suffered some major defeats; but it also saw a sharpening of public attitudes towards the suffragettes. In January the by-election at Ashburton or Mid-Devon achieved some notoriety due to the violence inflicted on Mrs Pankhurst after the declaration of the poll. She had claimed credit for the overturning of a Liberal majority of 1,200 by a

---

[30]   Liddington, *Respectable Rebel*, 196.

[31]   *Daily Mirror*, 20 July 1907; in his 'Two By-Elections', 142, Dr Pelling made only a passing reference to the role of suffragism in the by-election.

[32]   *The Times*, 20 July 1907.

Conservative one of 559. However, an examination of the local campaign casts serious doubt on this. In the isolated villages and townships of Mid-Devon the suffragists appeared as an alien intrusion, and at best as a source of entertainment. As a result their entire campaign became the target for disruption and rowdyism by local men. Open-air meetings were literally broken up by crowds who rushed at the wagons which were used as platforms and pushed them around market places and streets.[33] At indoor meetings the suffragettes were subjected to cross-questioning as to whether they were backing the Conservatives, whether they wanted to become MPs themselves, and how many more women than men there were in Britain. One middle-aged man who had no vote himself asked whether he should assist women to obtain the vote before he did.[34] These exchanges help us to understand the problems the suffragettes faced in dealing with ordinary people; as long as they had no convincing answer to the resentments harboured by the unenfranchised males they would find working-class support elusive.

At Ashburton both parties agreed that votes had turned on the increase in the price of bread and coal, on wages and on tariff reform. The regional press also noted that previously the Liberals had held the seat because their member was a resident landowner who enjoyed a personal following but had neglected politics; the carpet-bagger brought in to replace him was inevitably at a serious disadvantage.[35] The WSPUs campaign proved to be an entertaining side-show, which on balance may have made the cause less rather than more popular in the area.

Most of the 1908 by-elections occurred in large urban areas where conditions were very different. For example, at Leeds South reports suggested that the suffrage campaign attracted large audiences and was taken seriously in contrast to those in Derbyshire, Hereford, and Worcester where it fell flat.[36] But the Liberal majority in Leeds, though reduced, remained substantial. A much greater turnover of votes took place in Peckham which fell to the Conservatives in April. The explanation lay in the unpopularity of the government's licensing bill in a constituency where jobs depended on the brewing industry, and also in the reaction of Catholic voters to the Education Bill.[37] By contrast, in Kincardine in Scotland, where the licensing bill did not apply, the Liberal majority was only slightly reduced even though the suffragettes campaigned there too.

---

[33] *Votes for Women*, Jan. 1908, 54; *Western Morning News*, 4 Jan. 1908, 3; 6 Jan. 1908, 2; 10 Jan. 1908, 5.
[34] *Western Morning News*, 10 Jan. 1908, 5.
[35] *The Times*, 20 Jan. 1908; *Western Morning News*, 20 Jan. 1908, 2–3.
[36] *Votes for Women*, Mar. 1908, 85, quoting from the *Daily News*.
[37] *Daily Mirror*, 16 Mar. 1908.

Asquith's elevation to the premiership triggered a series of ministerial by-elections in Dewsbury, NW Manchester, Dundee, Montrose, and East Wolverhampton.[38] In fact the Liberals held four of the five, but the Pankhursts shrewdly focused on the most vulnerable, NW Manchester which was represented by Winston Churchill. So sure were they of their target that even before Churchill's promotion to the cabinet had been announced they rushed up to Manchester and booked all the halls they could find.[39] However, the usual confusion arose amongst the suffragists. The North of England Society for Women's Suffrage, led by Margaret Ashton, who was also President of the Lancashire and Cheshire Women's Liberal Association, wished to support the candidate most favourable to women's suffrage, and Churchill, for all his shortcomings, was better than the Tory, William Joynson-Hicks. After deputations had waited upon the candidates, the NUWSS decided eventually that it could support neither and resorted to general propaganda. But many of the Liberal women worked for Churchill.[40]

The Pankhursts were rewarded for their efforts when Joynson-Hicks won the seat by 429 votes overturning a 1,200 Liberal lead in 1906. By comparison with Devon, Manchester had enjoyed years of suffragist propaganda and had a highly aware electorate; it therefore seems more likely that the Pankhursts' struck a chord with some of the voters, especially now that many women Liberals felt badly torn between loyalty to party and support for the cause. In view of the narrow margin of victory the issue could well have tipped the balance. On the other hand, the result was actually very impressive for Churchill in the circumstances. NW Manchester was, after all, a marginal Conservative seat which he had gained at a point when the threat to free trade gave Manchester Liberals a popular policy with the commercial community. To have lost narrowly when free trade had lost some of its appeal and at the height of the government's unpopularity was hardly surprising. Churchill also faced two crucial complications. As in many urban constituencies Liberal strength depended on mobilizing the votes of the ethnic communities. In NW Manchester some of the Jewish community switched to the Conservatives because they were dissatisfied over the implementation of the Aliens Act.[41] Doubts also developed over whether John Redmond, the Irish Nationalist leader, would recommend the nine hundred Irish electors to support

---

[38] Until the reforms of 1918 and 1926 ministerial appointees were required to resign and seek re-election.

[39] *Manchester Evening Chronicle*, 8 Apr. 1908; 10 Apr. 1908.

[40] Ibid., 8 Apr. 1908; 11 Apr. 1908; 16 Apr. 1908; 24 Apr. 1908; *Annual Report*, Manchester NSWS, 1908, 13.

[41] *Manchester Evening Chronicle*, 11 Apr. 1908; 14 Apr. 1908.

Churchill, and the Liberals expected to lose about half of them.[42] As a result even the local Conservative newspaper concluded that the result had little to do with women's suffrage.[43]

While Christabel had some grounds for regarding Manchester with satisfaction, her attempts to claim all the ministerial by-elections as successes were swiftly undermined.[44] At East Wolverhampton the suffragists again contended with critical audiences. When asked: 'If the Conservatives get in power will they give women the vote?', they offered the lame response: 'Yes, if we make them.'[45] Despite the WSPU's efforts the presence of the ardent Tory protectionist, L. S. Amery, ensured that the by-elction was fought largely over tariffs; the Liberals suffered from the rise in unemployment, but narrowly retained the seat.[46] Meanwhile the Pankhursts continued to harass Churchill who had proceeded to another by-election at Dundee; however, his victory there was so convincing that for once Christabel seemed reluctant to claim any success.[47] The Liberals also held off challenges at Dewsbury, Montrose, and Stirling without much difficulty.

In September, however, another attractive target presented itself in the shape of Newcastle-upon-Tyne. A large two-member borough, Newcastle had fallen to the Conservatives in 1895 and 1900, and been recaptured in 1906 only by means of a united Liberal–Labour ticket. When the Liberal member died, Mrs Pankhurst hurried down from Aberdeenshire to launch her campaign in the city. Although the Labour Party hesitated to break the pact by opposing the Liberal, a Socialist eventually stood and the Liberal seat was lost. It has been suggested that in the North-East Labour and women's suffrage made a united advance in this period.[48] However, this seems impossible to square with the evidence for 1908. Although leading North-East Liberals such as Dr Ethel Williams and Mona Taylor became very dissatisfied with their party's attitude to women's suffrage and consequently withheld support, relations on the Labour side were not much better. The Women's Labour League encountered marked antagonism from workingmen in the region; and the non-militant suffragists pronounced none of the candidates to be worth supporting. When Mrs Pankhurst attempted to hold her first open-air meeting in Newcastle the crowds were so hostile that she was unable to get a hearing and had to resort to a police escort to protect her. At

---

[42] *Manchester Evening News*, 15 Apr. 1908; 16 Apr. 1908; 20 Apr. 1908.
[43] Ibid., 25 Apr. 1908.
[44] *Votes for Women*, 30 Apr. 1908, 118, 127.
[45] *Wolverhampton Chronicle*, 6 May 1908, 7.
[46] *Votes for Women*, 7 May 1908, 150.
[47] Ibid., 7 May 1908, 152–3; 14 May 1908, 158.
[48] Neville, 'Women's Suffrage Movement', 141, 146, 148.

smaller indoor meetings of branches of the engineering union the suffragettes managed to get a more respectful hearing.[49] But they found themselves once again the target of hostile questions about their reasons for never
agitating against Conservative governments, and whether they had any
pledges as to the intentions of a future Tory cabinet on votes for women.
While the local crowds clearly enjoyed the suffragettes' campaign, the issues
of the election were tariffs, licensing, education, and naval rebuilding.[50]
Opinion both locally and nationally attributed the Liberal defeat primarily
to the United Irish League which had advised Catholics to switch votes to the
Tories just for the by-election. In addition the 2,900 votes drawn off the
Liberal–Labour poll by the Socialist probably sealed the Liberal's fate.

A Failing Strategy 1909–1912

After 1908 the by-election strategy had passed its peak. The non-militants
recognized this more readily than the WSPU. At a succession of elections
in East Edinburgh, SW Warwickshire, Sheffield Attercliffe, Bermondsey,
Central Glasgow, Cleveland, Mid-Derbyshire, and High Peak, the NUWSS
found itself unable to support any candidate. In many cases the rival candidates foiled them by adopting a common attitude; sometimes both declared
their opposition to the vote, or both refused to give any promises or commitments; sometimes both claimed to be pro-suffrage but refused to be precise
enough to satisfy the National Union.[51] Only at Dumfriess did they judge the
Liberal, John Gulland, to be sufficiently consistent a suffragist to deserve
active support.[52] Their only alternative was to gather petitions signed by local
electors which were presented to the newly-elected members as a reminder
of the extent of suffragist support in their constituencies.[53] Yet this failed to
satisfy the activists. After the High Peak by-election in August Maude
Royden was 'full of depression at the ineffectiveness of the NU policy'.[54]
However, no way out of this dilemma was found until 1912 when the
National Union decided to support Labour candidates.

   The second reason for regarding the by-election strategy as losing force by
1909 was simply that as the government regained the initiative it appeared to
do better in these contests. Despite suffragette interventions they retained

---

   [49] *Newcastle Evening Chronicle*, 8 Sept. 1908, 5; 9 Sept. 1908, 5; 10 Sept. 1908, 4.
   [50] Ibid., 10 Sept. 1908, 4; 21 Sept. 1908, 5; *Votes for Women*, 1 Oct. 1908, 11, quoting the *Daily News*.
   [51] *The Common Cause*, 29 Apr. 1909; 6 May 1909; 8 July 1909; 22 July 1909.
   [52] Ibid., 22 July 1909.   [53] Ibid., 29 July 1909.   [54] Ibid., 19 Aug. 1909.

seats at Forfar, Hawick Burghs, Cleveland, Dumfriess, High Peak, Mid-Derbyshire, and East Edinburgh. Losses occurred in Glasgow Central in February and Bermondsey in October. The Glasgow seat was similar to NW Manchester in that the Liberals had gained it by only four hundred votes in 1906 because of the popularity of free trade amongst the business community. It was therefore vulnerable, and, as the Liberal candidate was an anti-suffragist, it attracted the WSPU. However, the subsequent Conservative gain was attributed to the reluctance of the Unionist free traders to continue supporting the Liberal on account of his pronounced support for Irish Home Rule rather than his views on votes for women.[55] In Bermondsey the modest Liberal majority became vulnerable when a Labour candidate split the vote; and, again, the result was not attributed to suffragism.[56] In April 1909 a by-election at East Edinburgh saw the Liberals retain the seat with a much reduced majority, a result which produced conflicting interpretations. While the WSPU campaigned against the Liberal, the NUWSS persuaded 2,393 voters to sign a suffragist petition outside the polling stations which was at least a means of keeping the issue in electors' minds when they voted. In addition the Women's Freedom League distributed postcards on which electors declared that they had voted against the Liberal because of women's suffrage. Almost 1,300 of these were returned for transmission to the prime minister. These totals were large enough to be significant for the final result, though one cannot be sure how far the postcards were signed by electors who were already opposed to the Liberals. However, other issues also figured in the by-election. The questions put to the candidates at public meetings focused on Home Rule, the Dreadnought programme, and tariff reform.[57] The local press explained the shift of votes largely as a temporary response by Irish Catholics to the Education Bill and to the cabinet's neglect of Home Rule; naval building scares were also thought to have influenced some voters.[58]

Similarly at Cleveland in July there was evidence that the WSPU campaign made some impact if not enough to determine the outcome. At another ministerial by-election where the incumbent, Herbert Samuel, was opposed to women's suffrage, Cleveland galvanized the WSPU organizers who were

---

[55] *Glasgow Herald*, 18 Feb. 1909, 10; 22 Feb. 1909, 5; 3 Mar. 1909, 8. A disagreement flared up between the National Union which sent its organizer to support the Conservative and the local suffragists who noted that he refused to vote for any suffrage bill: Mitchell Library: Glasgow and West of Scotland Association for Women's Suffrage, minutes, 10 Mar. 1909.

[56] *Southwark and Bermondsey Recorder*, 22 Oct. 1909, 6; 29 Oct. 1909, 2, 5; 5 Nov. 1909, 5; *The Common Cause*, 4 Nov. 1909, 386.

[57] *Edinburgh Evening News*, 13 Apr. 1909; 14 Apr. 1909; 15 Apr. 1909.

[58] Ibid., 17 Apr. 1909.

optimistic about defeating him. *The Times*'s reporter, not sympathetic to the cause, felt that for the first time electors had been really aroused by the women's sense of grievance and that Samuel had lost votes as a result. Samuel counter-attacked by accusing the WSPU of financing its campaign with 'Tory Gold' and he retained his seat fairly comfortably.[59]

Before the Newcastle by-election Mrs Pankhurst had predicted: 'Only a few more by-elections are needed, and Mr Asquith will consent to give votes for women.'[60] In fact the Pankhursts' chief hope was that a general election would be held at which the Liberals would be defeated. However, such a prospect was wrecked by the crisis surrounding Lloyd George's famous budget in 1909 which restored the government's radical credentials and led eventually to two general elections in January and December 1910. As a result the by-election strategy went into an accelerated decline during 1910. The general elections exposed the limitations of the suffragette campaign when set against the political loyalties and resources which were now unleashed. According to *Votes for Women* the WSPU focused their election work on eleven London constituencies and seventeen in the rest of the country, though the Annual Report for 1910 indicated forty amongst which eighteen seats were lost by the government. Either way, this was a limited effort. The basic problem lay in the nature of the election which became almost a refer-endum on the budget and on reform of the House of Lords. In January 30 per cent of candidates mentioned votes for women in their election addresses and 27 per cent in December, which was a higher proportion than in 1906.[61] At the end of the year one Anti-Suffragist challenged the campaigners about their effectiveness: had any single candidate given a prominent place to women's suffrage? Millicent Fawcett claimed that over a hundred had done so. Had any election been influenced by the issue? Fawcett thought that some Liberal Antis had been defeated.[62] But it was impossible to show they had lost because of their Anti-Suffragism, or that they had done any worse than Lib-eral pro-suffragists. In fact, in the aftermath of the January election Christa-bel took comfort chiefly from the fact that the government's overall majority had been destroyed which would make them more vulnerable to future by-elections.[63] But while political opinion remained polarized it was extremely

---

[59] *The Times*, 6 July 1909; *Votes for Women*, 2 July 1909; 9 July 1909; 16 July 1909; the WSPU claimed that one-third of its funds came from Conservative sources: *The Common Cause*, 8 July 1909.

[60] *Newcastle Evening Chronicle*, 5 Sept. 1908.

[61] Neal Blewett, *The Peers, the Parties and the People* (Macmillan, 1972), 317, 326.

[62] *The Times*, 26 Dec. 1910; 21 Jan. 1911; when Arthur Bulley ran as Women's Suffrage candidate at Rossendale (the seat held by arch-Anti Lewis Harcourt) in Jan. he polled a mere 639 votes: Liddington and Norris, *One Hand Tied Behind Us*, 242–6.

[63] Christabel Pankhurst, editorial, *Votes for Women*, 18 Feb. 1910, 324.

difficult for suffragism to make an impact. In April 1910 a Liberal seat at South Edinburgh was defended by Charles Lyell, an unrepentant opponent of the women's vote, who merely declared that he was prepared to consider the idea now that militancy had been abandoned but would not support the Conciliation Bill.[64] He retained the seat with almost the same majority as at the general election; clearly the strength of party loyalty aroused by the struggle with the peers had marginalized suffragism for the time being. By November when ministerial by-elections occurred in South Shields and Walthamstow, the WSPU had decided to resume warfare with the Liberals. But they failed to dislodge either Sir William Robson, an opponent, or Sir John Simon, a supporter, in these contests.

During the spring and summer of 1911 Christabel remained in a relatively conciliatory mood because it seemed likely that the Conciliation Bill would pass, and as a result only two candidates were opposed by the WSPU. In March the working-class constituency of NE Lanarkshire presented an attractive target. Though Liberal it had fallen to the Conservatives in 1901 when Robert Smillie stood for Labour. But experience of three-cornered contests in 1901 and 1906 meant that the Liberals had organized their supporters efficiently. Once again the suffragists' tactics were self-defeating in that while the WSPU urged the rejection of the Liberal, the non-militants supported him.[65] The key issues here were land, mining questions, and the House of Lords; and the Liberals' positive policy on Home Rule helped to keep the local branches of the United Irish League loyal. Consequently they enjoyed an impressive victory despite Labour intervention.[66]

In July SW Bethnal Green tempted the Pankhursts because it was defended by another ministerial Anti-Suffragist, Charles Masterman, who posed as a friend of the cause but had actually voted against the Conciliation Bill. The constituency was inundated with suffragist canvassers and literature, and Masterman came under attack at most of his meetings.[67] The activity of the Men's League for Women's Suffrage and the fact that the Conservative supported votes for women helped to focus this election on the suffrage issue. The reduction in Masterman's majority from 682 to 184 votes might well have been ascribed to his attitude on the question, except that his actual vote remained the same as at the general election. Things were completely different at Keighley in October where the ministerial candidate,

[64] *Edinburgh Evening News*, 21 Apr. 1910; 22 Apr. 1910; 24 Apr. 1910.
[65] *Glasgow Herald*, 24 Feb. 1911; 25 Feb. 1911; 6 Mar. 1911.
[66] Ibid., 27 Feb. 1911; 10 Mar. 1911; Mitchell Library: Glasgow and West of Scotland Association for Women's Suffrage, minutes, 1 Mar. 1911.
[67] *Votes for Women*, 28 July 1911.

Sir Stanley Buckmaster, had such a consistent record of support for women's suffrage bills that the NUWSS gave him strong backing.[68] Even the WSPU avoided Keighley despite the fact that as a three-cornered contest it appeared vulnerable. Buckmaster duly retained his seat.

1912 inaugurated a new phase in the struggle between the suffragists and the government. At this stage the NUWSS finally recognized the futility of its non-party policy and opted for a pact with the Labour Party. This, however, put it even more blatantly at odds with the WSPU which regarded Labour as no better than the Liberals. 1912 was also the year in which the WSPU itself began to retreat from the whole task of converting the general public. The key to this development was the famous contest which took place at Bow and Bromley in November.

When the Labour member, George Lansbury, who had grown increasingly frustrated with his own party's reluctance to back the women, resigned his seat to seek a fresh mandate, the Pankhursts were given the opportunity to demonstrate their claims about public opinion. In the ensuing by-election Lansbury enjoyed exactly the same conditions as at the general election: a straight fight with a Conservative. Moreover, when the Tory, Reginald Blair, announced his opposition to female enfranchisement he enabled the election to become a relatively uncomplicated test of the male voters' attitude to the issue.[69] No government candidate was involved. Amid great enthusiasm the WSPU threw its resources into Bow and Bromley determined to secure a triumph for their ally.

In the event, however, Blair captured the seat with a 10.7 per cent swing to the Conservatives which was very high for this period.[70] What significance is to be placed on this outcome? Two main explanations present themselves. In the first place Lansbury suffered from an inability to appeal effectively to the Labour and Liberal supporters on whom his majority depended. Labour naturally resented the whole idea of an unnecessary by-election conducted merely to appease the suffragettes who were heaping insults on the party. Lansbury had also become increasingly critical of the government despite his acute dependence on Liberal votes. His own position was made more complicated by the inept propaganda of the WSPU which disparaged Asquith as a 'public danger', scorned his 'sham Liberal Government' and generally implied that a vote for Lansbury was a means of getting rid of the Liberals.

---

[68] *Keighley News*, 14 Oct. 1911; 21 Oct. 1911.

[69] Material on the by-election is in Catherine Marshall Papers, Cumbria CRO; for the WSPUs view, see *The Suffragette*, 15 Nov. 1912, 64; 22 Nov. 1912, 78, 84–8, 98.

[70] The worst swings against the Liberals in two-cornered contests were 9.1 per cent at Ilkeston and 8.4 per cent at Linlithgow.

This was, of course, the Pankhursts' usual line of attack, but they evidently failed to appreciate how counter-productive it would be in Bow and Bromley.

The other explanation is that women's suffrage played badly in the constituency. Although the Pankhursts emphasized their desire to enfranchise working women, the overbearing manner in which they descended upon Bow and Bromley and took over the campaign reinforced the impression of the cause as the work of wealthy women, which simply antagonized the male voters. One of the activists told Lansbury, 'it does not help when some [suffragette] canvassers go round saying that they do not agree with your socialism...in fact, frankly they are using you as a tool'.[71] The outcome shocked the WSPU which had confidently predicted Lansbury's return, and it had the effect of alienating the Pankhursts from the political process. Christabel's analysis of the result suggests a retreat from reality: 'a great mass of men are still so corrupted and led astray by party politics that to depend simply on the help of the electors to secure the enfranchisement of women is a grave and fatal mistake'.[72] As a result they largely ceased trying to persuade the public during the last eighteen months of peacetime. It was in any case becoming increasingly difficult to hold public meetings in the face of hostile crowds. A turning-point had been reached for militancy if not for suffragism as a whole.

Thus, between 1912 and 1914 the by-election policy lay increasingly in the hands of the non-militants. They campaigned for Labour candidates in eight by-elections in this period, four of which resulted in a Liberal defeat (see Chapter 10). But many by-elections were not fought by Labour, nor did the National Union support every Labour candidate; in some places it reverted to propaganda, and in a few it backed a Liberal. As a result the 1912 results were rather mixed. The Liberals lost seats at Crewe and Midlothian because of three-cornered contests. On the other hand, they enjoyed a string of victories at NW Norfolk, Bolton, E. Carmarthen, Ilkeston, Hanley (a gain), and Holmfirth. The Norfolk election revolved around the Liberal's advocacy of land reform and the Tory's challenge over Home Rule. Here the NUWSS supported the Liberal while the WSPU urged his defeat despite the fact that the other candidate opposed women's suffrage.[73] In the two-member Bolton seat everything depended on whether the Liberal–Labour pact was maintained. While the National Union contented itself with propaganda, as both candidates favoured votes for women, the WSPU stayed away, perhaps to concentrate on Bow and Bromley. In the event the Liberals enjoyed a straight fight and retained the seat despite the unpopularity of the National

[71] G. S. Jacobs to George Lansbury, 27 Nov. 1912, quoted in Rosen, *Rise Up Women*, 183.
[72] Christabel Pankhurst, *The Suffragette*, 29 Nov. 1912, 98.
[73] *Norfolk Chronicle*, 25 May 1912, 10; 1 June 1912, 4.

Insurance Act.[74] Similarly, at E. Carmarthen the National Union found both candidates satisfactory, while at E. Edinburgh they supported J. M. Hogge, a Liberal whom they had previously opposed because of his advocacy of adult suffrage.[75] But the most telling election occurred at South Manchester where the Liberal, Sir A. Haworth, received the backing of the Manchester Society for Women's Suffrage but lost to a Conservative Anti-Suffragist all the same.[76] This was probably a reflection of the government's unpopularity rather than of attitudes towards votes for women, but it was a further indication of the inability of the campaigners to secure positive endorsements for their cause as opposed to riding on the back of a negative reaction against the government.

This pattern did not change significantly during 1913 when the Liberals lost South Lanark in a three-cornered fight, but retained seats at Keighley, Leicester, Houghton-le-Spring, and Whitechapel. The latter, another East End constituency like Bow and Bromley, saw action by the NUWSS, the WFL, and the WSPU. But they were frustrated by the refusal of both candidates to support women's suffrage, and in the event the election was dominated by the National Insurance Act.[77] In the first few months of 1914 the government scored victories in Poplar and NW Durham but lost at Leith and in a further election in SW Bethnal Green where Masterman's 184 vote majority turned into a deficit of just 24. Local reports suggested that the unpopularity of the Insurance Act and the Shops Act had been enough to tip the balance against him.[78]

What conclusions can be drawn from these attempts to mobilize public opinion from 1906 to 1914? It is clear that the suffragists faced a tough task in that they attempted to influence the votes of men who had no direct interest in the cause. Other pressure groups in the field, notably the Tariff Reform League and the United Irish League, were probably more effective in determining the results especially in urban constituencies. The Pankhursts almost certainly mistook the size and the excitement at their meetings for real influence and support. This is corroborated by the inability of the suffragists generally to mobilize votes in favour of women's suffrage. More fundamentally, they misjudged their strategy. The increasingly right-wing stance of the WSPU resulted in widespread confusion and division at by-elections as suffragists supported rival candidates. Things were simplified when the

[74] *Bolton Evening News*, 12 Nov. 1912; 18 Nov. 1912.
[75] *The Common Cause*, 25 Jan. 1912, 721; 1 Feb. 1912, 729.
[76] *Annual Report*, Manchester NSWS, 1912.
[77] *East London Observer*, 26 Apr. 1913; 3 May 1913.
[78] Ibid., 14 Feb. 1914.

National Union adopted its pro-Labour pact, but the Pankhursts continued to attack the candidates it supported. Above all, the interventions antagonized Liberal politicians without creating enough popular pressure to force them into major concessions. Many of the four hundred seats the Liberals had won in 1906 were obviously vulnerable in by-elections, but by the same token the government could discount losses on a considerable scale. In any case their record was not as bad as suffragette propaganda suggested. In 101 by-elections between 1906 and 1909 the Liberals lost twelve to the Conservatives and four to Labour. Moreover, the by-elections were largely transient phenomena, for the party recovered seven losses from the Conservatives and two from Labour in the 1910 general elections. In the twenty by-elections of 1910 they suffered no losses. In the 66 by-elections from 1911 to 1914 they lost fourteen to the Conservatives but gained two from Labour. They expected to regain many of these at the general election in 1915; this seems likely as their support was recovering by 1914 just as it had during 1906–9.[79]

The fluctuations in voting recorded at by-elections cannot be explained convincingly in terms of the suffrage issue. This examination of local conditions suggests that the most damaging single factor for the government was the incidence of three-cornered contests in seats previously won in a straight fight with Conservatives. The main issues affecting voters appear to have been changes in unemployment and prices which undermined free trade, legislation on licensing, education, and National Insurance, and the neglect of Irish Home Rule in the early period. This is why years such as 1907–8 and 1912 proved so difficult for the Liberals and 1910–11 rather better. So far as one can tell, Asquith's ministers were probably correct in thinking that the Pankhursts had failed to mobilize public opinion. However, they put a somewhat different interpretation on the new by-election tactic adopted after 1912 by the NUWSS which therefore requires a separate analysis.

The Ballot and the Referendum

Parliamentary elections could never be a satisfactory means of demonstrating the state of public opinion on the issue of female enfranchisement partly because the evidence was so inconclusive and partly because it necessarily excluded *women's* views, at least in a direct sense. Both advocates and opponents of the suffrage therefore felt tempted from time to time to canvass the women who already enjoyed a municipal vote (and were therefore

---

[79] P. F. Clarke, 'The Electoral Position of the Liberal and Labour Parties, 1910–14', *English Historical Review*, 92 (1975), 833.

conveniently listed) to ascertain their views. It comes as no surprise to find that the two camps produced wholly contradictory results.

TABLE 9.2. Canvass returns among women conducted by pro-suffragists

Lancashire textile workers, 1904

	Pro-Suffrage	Anti-Suffrage
Bolton	1,236	256
Clitheroe	1,563	128
Colne	2,432	126
Nelson	4,594	881
Hyde	1,027	440
Haslingden	1,364	272

Source: *Women and Citizenship*, Women's Co-operative Guild, 1904.

Female municipal electors, 1910

	Total on register	Pro-Suffrage	Anti-Suffrage	No response/ Not visited
Reading	1,730	1,047	467	
Glasgow Tradeston	2,080	1,462	176	422
Liverpool & Bootle	3,185	1,611	471	1,103

Source: NUWSS figures in A. J. Balfour Papers (BM) Add. MS 49793, fos. 86, 90.

Female municipal electors in Oldham, 1910

Total visited	Pro-Suffrage	Anti-Suffrage	Indifferent	Dead or removed	Out
3,218	1,938	370	190	221	499

Source: *Annual Report*, Oldham Women's Suffrage Society, 1911, Lees Collection D/LEES/141 Oldham Local Studies Library.

Female municipal electors

	Total	Pro-Suffrage	Anti-Suffrage	Neutral or indifferent	Removed	Dead	Out
Bolton	5,750	2,660	610	340	576	93	
Warrington		618	57	157	92	23	155

Source: NUWSS, *Women Municipal Electors and the Parliamentary Vote*, not dated.

It is probably significant that for the suffragists these canvasses were never a major preoccupation. They loomed larger in the Anti-Suffrage strategy especially during 1910 and 1911. The Antis also continued to use mass petitions which had long been disregarded by their opponents.[80] These activities were designed to alert hesitant MPs to the fact that the Conciliation Bill, to which they were giving a majority, enjoyed only minority support among their female constituents.[81]

[80] *Anti-Suffrage Review*, July 1909.
[81] See correspondence, Manchester Central Library: Manchester Branch NLOWS, M131/3/2.

Table 9.3. Canvasses of female municipal electors by the National League for Opposing Women's Suffrage, 1910–1911

	Electors	Anti-Suffrage	Pro-Suffrage	Neutral
Croydon	4,080	1,571	605	30
Southampton[a]	2,243	1,361	147	229
Westminster[a]	1,979	1,036	221	136
Torquay	1,640	467	210	13
N. Berks	1,291	1,085	75	63
C. Finsbury	1,261	535	128	257
Weston-s-Mare[a]	935	380	235	69
Kew	155	96	21	23
Ashbourne	153	107	5	2
Bristol[a]	7,615	3,399	915	2,004
Hampstead[a]	3,084	1,288	405	233
Bath[a]	2,153	1,026	230	21
Oxford	2,145	571	353	22
Cambridge[a]	2,098	1,168	570	271
Reading[a]	1,700	1,133	166	31
Guildford[a]	544	360	60	26
Thames Ditton/LongDitton	187	134	10	8
E.Molesey	136	93	14	20
Cobham	88	61	4	15
Esher	75	52	9	8
Cheam	69	43	11	10
Ashtead	67	25	7	21
S. Kensington	4,728	1,183	671	33
N. Paddington	3,700	1,090	407	98
Chelsea	3,355	617	566	36
Birkenhead	3,338	1,154	861	—
Hastings	2,610	921	425	20
N. Hackney	2,044	961	451	—
East Berks	2,355	603	264	415
Mayfair	2,217	1,114	445	13
N. Kensington	2,160	472	211	2
Brixton	1,826	739	267	8
Mid Bucks	1,389	248	222	47
NW Manchester	1,374	246	198	—
Watford	935	302	178	7
Reigate	906	338	199	23
St Andrews	598	142	96	47
St George's in The East	457	123	81	2
Hampton	277	92	39	4
Basingstoke	273	77	71	6
Berkhampstead	265	88	36	1
Liverpool[a]	8,182	2,189	1,218	—
Fulham[a]	2,971	941	265	830

[a] by house-to-house canvass; otherwise by reply-paid postcards

Sources: *Anti-Suffrage Review*, Nov. 1910, 6; Dec. 1910, 6; May 1911, 9. In Ilkeston in a referendum of 6,000 women, 2,885 voted, 1,811 against and 1,074 for women's suffrage: *Morning Post*, 12 Jan. 1912.

To some extent it is possible to reconcile the conflicting results produced by the rival organizations. They asked different questions, or rather put the question in different ways. Also, they conducted their surveys in different parts of the country; the Antis' work reflected their concentration in the Home Counties and suburban districts. It is not surprising that women in northern textile townships leant more towards the suffrage, though it seems unlikely that the variation was as wide as suggested by the canvasses. Only two towns, Reading and Liverpool, were canvassed by both sides, still with wholly conflicting results.

Are there any grounds for attributing greater weight to one side? Considerable doubt was cast on the Antis' efforts by the methods they employed. Sometimes they used loaded questions such as: 'Do you prefer that the Parliamentary vote should remain as at present in the hands of the men of this country?', which implied withdrawing it from men to give to women. They also used slightly confusing questions such as: 'Do you consider that women should not be given the vote?'[82] In Manchester the Anti-Suffragist ladies resorted to traditional methods by giving tea to large numbers of domestic servants and shop assistants before inviting them to sign their petitions; several claimed to be so confused that they thought they were recording their opposition to militancy rather than to women's suffrage itself.[83] There are also odd disparities in the Antis' returns. For example, in Finsbury 257 out of 1,261 were reported as neutral but a mere thirty out of 4,080 in Croydon, which suggests that the canvassers were influencing the results. The difference between returns from Oxford and those from Bath might be explained by the different methods adopted—the house visit as opposed to the reply-paid postcard. Finally, one must remember that all these surveys focused on a *minority* of women—those who already had a municipal franchise. It is possible that they may have been more favourable to the parliamentary vote as they were already familiar with voting and because some of them had careers. But the reverse is just as likely; they may have been satisfied with the higher status they enjoyed, or even become disillusioned by the experience with the local government vote.

No doubt it would have been possible to resolve the conflicting claims made by the rival organizations by conducting a national referendum. The idea certainly became fashionable at this time partly because the Conservative leaders resorted to it as a way of dealing with their dilemma over tariff reform. By 1911 two Liberal newspapers, the *Daily News* and the *Westminster*

---

[82] *Votes for Women*, 17 Feb. 1911, 318; for a defence of the Antis' methods, see John Massie, *The Times*, 29 Nov. 1911.
[83] *The Common Cause*, 21 Oct. 1909, 350.

Gazette, had taken up the referendum as an expedient for breaking the dead-lock over women's suffrage.[84] Had women voted in favour of enfranchise-ment, it was assumed that even Asquith would have backed down; conversely a rejection by women would have killed the issue in parliament for some years. This was precisely the suffragists' fear, and they could not but be alarmed to find a paper like the *Morning Post* advocating a referendum in January 1912. But this was an indication that many Antis, who in principle detested the idea of a referendum, now contemplated the imminent collapse of their cause in the House of Commons. A referendum was essentially a last ditch expedient to win a further delay; after all, if it were to be based on more than just the existing female municipal voters it would have taken some time even to draw up a list of those entitled to participate.

Yet while the idea of a referendum seems to reflect the declining fortunes of the Antis, it also throws light on the lack of confidence amongst the suffragists about the extent of their support in the country. This is why they had all along avoided the proposal. Privately the NUWSS secretary, Catherine Marshall, admitted she would not fear a referendum from which all the apathetic and the indifferent had been excluded! But, she argued: 'I don't believe you would ever get a majority for *enacting* something new or untried.'[85] Written in 1913 at a time when the suffragists had ostensibly mobilized the support of the working class and the unions, this was a very damning obser-vation. But Marshall was probably shrewd. When the suffragists held debates with their opponents they usually won comfortably, but presumably because the apathetic and the hostile had stayed at home.[86] One level of opinion had been converted, the other remained doubtful. If, as seemed almost certain by 1910, the vote could be obtained through the conversion of the parliamen-tarians and the political activists, then public opinion could be tacitly dis-pensed with. After all, the politicians showed themselves rather cynical about public opinion. They used lack of popular demand as a respectable justifica-tion for neglecting what they wished to ignore, but conversely, the absence of a clear mandate did not deter them from enacting a reform they thought to be in their interests. Speaking of the agricultural labourers' vote in 1884 even Gladstone had insisted: 'I am not concerned whether they want it or not; the State wants it for them.'[87]

---

[84] *Westminster Gazette*, 27 Dec. 1911; *Daily News*, 23 Jan. 1912.

[85] Catherine Marshall to Lord Robert Cecil (copy), 24 Nov. 1913, Cumbria CRO: Marshall Papers.

[86] In 1910 five Manchester wards were opposed by three to one: Report, Manchester Branch NLOWS 1909–10, Manchester Central Library, M131/3/1.

[87] Quoted in Harrison, 'Women's Suffrage at Westminster', 109.

Nonetheless, the suffragists had no choice but to attempt to deprive the politicians of any excuse about lack of popular demand. This is why they reacted with such dismay to the resumption of militancy in 1912. At that stage the Pethick-Lawrences judged that they had largely got the public on their side and that government attempts to suppress the WSPU would only engender more sympathy for the cause, but they believed that the advantage was being thrown away by extreme forms of militancy.[88] The leaders, however, adamantly rejected this interpretation. Flora Drummond reportedly declared that she 'cared not what the opinion of the public was as regards destroying letters'; Annie Kenney asked: 'what do we care whether we have public opinion with us or not'; and Mrs Pankhurst summed up the rationale by saying: 'If the general public were pleased with what we are doing, that would be proof that our warfare is ineffective.'[89] Yet these tactics played into the hands of the politicians rather than increasing the pressure on them. Ministers, including Grey and Lloyd George, insisted that by 1913 the militants had made the cause so unpopular in the country that nothing could be done.[90] This of course must be seen for what it was—a convenient alibi. Yet it cannot *simply* be dismissed as an excuse, for the politicians' views appeared to be corroborated by the widespread attacks on the WSPU activists in public places. The question as to what the public really wanted remained unresolved.

[88] E. Pethick-Lawrence, *My Part*, 277–8; NUWSS memorandum on the deputation, July.

[89] CID Reports, 3 Dec. 1912, 4 Feb. 1913: PRO H045/10695/231366.

[90] To a deputation led by Fawcett in July 1913: Memorandum, Fawcett Library: Fawcett Letters 89/2/83.

10

The Revival of Non-Militant Suffragism, 1912–1914

C LOSE analysis of the suffragette campaigns has had the effect of deflating many, if not all, of the claims made by contemporaries. As we have seen, by 1912–14 the WSPU was in decline and becoming increasingly isolated not just politically but from the rest of the women's movement. Consequently the traditional focus on the militant side of suffragism now seems inappropriate especially if one is trying to explain the eventual success of the cause. Inevitably, as the significance of the Pankhursts has faded, so research has focused increasingly upon the mainstream of suffragism and on the initiatives taken prior to the outbreak of the Great War. One symptom of this change is the shift of interest from Emmeline and Christabel to Sylvia Pankhurst and her activities in London's East End.[1] By seeking a more democratic approach to suffragism, a left-wing alliance, and the mobilization of working-class men and women Sylvia heralded a more realistic strategy. On the other hand, the East End was very much a local effort based on about sixty members and not fully integrated into either the mainstream of suffragism or the Labour Movement. The key development in this period consists in the expansion of the National Union of Women's Suffrage Societies and the shifts in its political tactics in 1912.[2] The renewed emphasis on non-militant suffragism has been promoted by the availability of collections of papers, notably those of Catherine Marshall, a key figure in the National Union's strategy. The picture has also gained depth from some valuable biographies

[1] Patricia Romero, *E. Sylvia Pankhurst* (New Haven: Yale University Press, 1986); Barbara Winslow, *Sylvia Pankhurst* (UCL Press, 1996); Kathryn Dodd, *A Sylvia Pankhurst Reader* (Manchester: Manchester University Press, 1993).

[2] Leslie Parker Hume, *The National Union of Women's Suffrage Societies 1897–1914* (New York: Garland Publishing, 1982); Sandra Stanley Holton, *Feminism and Democracy: Women's Suffrage and Reform Politics in Britain, 1900–1918* (Cambridge: Cambridge University Press, 1986).

of lesser-known non-militant women including Selina Cooper, Ada Nield Chew, Isabella Ford, and Maud Royden.[3]

This material highlights three important trends in the explanation for the eventual outcome of the campaign. First, that while militant suffragism was diminishing before 1914, suffragism as a whole expanded significantly. Second, that this growing movement was moving in the opposite direction, politically, to the WSPU, and was beginning to marshal a range of left-wing organizations of *men* as well as women behind the cause. Third, that in the process suffragism began belatedly to cross the class barrier and to develop into something like a mass movement which was much more difficult for the Asquith government to ignore. Despite this it would be an exaggeration to claim that a complete solution had been found by 1914. The changes during 1912–14 proved to be complicated, and in any case, the war interrupted the process before the new strategy had been fully tested.

The Expansion of the National Union

Much the most conspicuous symptom of the pre-war trend was the development of the NUWSS in terms of a dramatic growth of membership and

TABLE 10.1. The NUWSS, 1897–1914

	Affiliated Societies	Membership
1897	15	
1898	16	
1899	17	
1900	17	
1902	19	
1903	25	
1905	31	
1907	32	
1908	64	8,000 approximately
1909	130	13,161
1910	207	21,571
1911	311	30,408
1912	411	42,438
1913	478	52,336
1914	496	54,592

Sources: The Common Cause; NUWSS, Annual Reports.

[3] Jill Liddington, *The Life and Times of a Respectable Rebel: Selina Cooper* (Virago, 1984); Doris Nield Chew, *Ada Nield Chew* (Virago, 1982); June Hannam, *Isabella Ford* (Oxford: Blackwell, 1989); Sheila Fletcher, *Maud Royden* (Oxford: Blackwell, 1989).

resources. The published figures are not easy to interpret because the National Union's loose structure concealed organization and resources at the local level. In the early years when societies based in large cities presided over satellite branches in the surrounding towns, the national lists of branches probably underrepresent the real strength. During 1903–5 many constituency committees were set up but were not recorded as separate societies until they affiliated later.[4] Conversely, the later increase in affiliated societies probably exaggerates in that it reflects the separation of sub-branches from parent societies, though this obviously reflected the rise in membership.

Despite these qualifications the two growth phases are readily identifiable. The first, which began around 1903, probably reflected initiatives taken by the National Union centrally and the general rise in expectations among Radicals prior to the Liberal victory in 1906. To this extent the expansion pre-dated Edwardian suffragette militancy. But the second and greater phase of growth almost coincided with that of the militant movement. The WSPU grew rapidly from 1907 and the National Union from 1908 when the affiliated societies doubled in number.[5] This expansion appears to have been sustained up to 1914 and is reflected in the membership totals; by 1912 the National Union claimed to be recruiting a thousand members a month.[6] In large part this second phase was a by-product of the suffragette campaigns. The explanation is that many women were greatly stirred and inspired by the risks and sacrifices taken by the militants, but felt loath to undertake militant action personally; joining one of the constitutional societies was a way of reconciling their conflicting emotions. As a result the non-militant movement became much the largest part of suffragism and continued to expand up to 1914 when militancy had passed its peak.[7] One source put the distribution of branches for the three main organizations in 1913 as: NUWSS 460, WSPU 90, WFL 61.[8]

The figures for funds also call for some explanation. The main increase in funds began in 1908, though as in the Victorian period the affiliated societies consistently held more resources than the central organization. Despite the improvement the National Union was eclipsed by the WSPU's fund-raising until the very end of the period when they drew level with around £47,000. By this time the National Union had begun to emulate some aspects of the WSPU's work in raising large sums from single functions, for example, £8,500 from the Pilgrimage in 1913 and over £5,000 from an Albert Hall rally.

[4] *Annual Reports*, NUWSS, 1903–4, 9, 25; 1904–5, 19.
[5] Rosen, *Rise Up Women*, 211–12.   [6] *The Common Cause*, 15 Aug. 1912, 322.
[7] Rosen, *Rise Up Women*, 211–12.
[8] A.J.R. (ed.), *The Suffrage Annual and Woman's Who's Who* (Stanley Paul, 1913).

TABLE 10.2. NUWSS funds, 1904–1913 (in £)

	Central Funds	Local Funds	Election Fighting Fund
1904	1,534		
1905	891		
1906	1,504		
1907	1,470		
1908	3,296	4,000–5,000	
1909	3,385	8,000–10,000	
1910	5,503		
1911	5,734	12,670	
1912	10,486	17,499	4,158
1913	18,886	25,000	4,035

Source: NUWSS, *Annual Reports.*

Yet the growth of the National Union, important though it was, must be seen in a wider context. In addition to its formal membership of 54,000 in 1914, it had recruited around 40,000 'Friends of Women's Suffrage' who paid nothing. It also cooperated with a range of men's suffrage societies, Church groups, the Labour Party, trade unions, trades councils, and Women's Co-operative Guilds by this time. In this way the scattered forces of suffragism became increasingly focused to the point where they resembled a mass movement for the first time. In this wider pattern the organization of support amongst *men* was clearly an important element if only because it helped to mitigate the increasing hostility shown by the WSPU towards the male sex.

Male Suffragism

From the start the relationship between the suffrage movement and men had been complicated; male vested interests formed the target of attack, yet men were also necessary allies in the battle. But the raising of the stakes during the Edwardian period made additional pressure by men appear all the more crucial to the resolution of the controversy. As a result, male pressure groups mushroomed just as they had already done amongst women. First in the field was the Men's League for Women's Suffrage in 1907, followed by the Men's Political Union in 1909, the Men's Society for Women's Rights, the Male Electors' League for Women's Suffrage, the Liberal Men's Association for Women's Suffrage and the Northern Men's Federation for Women's Suffrage, to name only the leading organizations.

It has long been recognized that certain men made major contributions to and sacrifices for the cause. Two journalists, Henry Nevinson and H. N. Brailsford, resigned their jobs at the *Daily News* in 1909 in protest at its criticism of the suffragettes. Even politicians took risks. Both Keir Hardie and George Lansbury jeopardized their standing in the Labour Party by their attempts to make votes for women a higher priority. Among Liberals Henry Harben gave up his candidacy at Barnstaple in 1912, William Barton, the member for Oldham, announced his resignation in 1913, and Sir John Simon risked antagonizing the prime minister by accepting the Vice-Presidency of the Manchester Men's League.[9] Fred Pethick-Lawrence defended suffragettes in court, was forcibly fed in prison, and spent much of his fortune on the WSPU before being bankrupted for the cause and blackballed from his club. Hugh Franklin of the Men's Political Union achieved notoriety for attempting to horsewhip Winston Churchill as Home Secretary and was reputedly forcibly fed a hundred times. William Bell received two months' hard labour for breaking two panes of glass at the Home Office, was forcibly fed for five weeks, denied all contact with his family, and certified insane.[10]

Recently, however, historians have gone beyond these individual cases to analyse the overall phenomenon of male suffragism.[11] About a thousand individuals have been identified in the various male organizations. But an assessment of their significance for the cause has proved elusive. This is partly because the male movement fragmented rapidly as the female one had already done. Also, the attitude adopted by the women towards the men varied a good deal over time. The National Union had always allowed men to join its societies, whereas the WSPU officially excluded them, a policy followed by the WFL despite objections from the rank and file.

Men's motivation for supporting the cause seems fairly clear. Many of those who joined the Men's League were Liberals embarrassed and outraged at the treatment of suffragettes by a Liberal government. Their sympathy overcame the distaste many of them felt for militant methods. Far from being feminists, these men often held rather conventional views about women as the weaker sex towards whom men ought to behave gallantly. In short they were moved by

---

[9] *The Times*, 6 July 1912; Oldham Women's Suffrage Society, 1914: Oldham Local Studies Library, Lees Papers 132; on Harben, see Brian Harrison, *Prudent Revolutionaries* (Oxford: Clarendon Press, 1987).

[10] 'Torture in an English Prison', WSPU, not dated.

[11] Kevin F. White, 'Men Supporting Women: A Study of Men Associated with the Women's Suffrage Movement in Britain and America 1909–20', *The Maryland Historian*, 17 (1987); Leah Leneman, 'Northern Men and Votes for Women', *History Today*, 41 (1991); F. Montgomery, 'Gender and Suffrage: The Manchester Men's League for Women's Suffrage 1908–18', *Bulletin of the John Rylands University Library of Manchester*, 77 (1995); Angela V. John and Claire Eustance (eds.), *The Men's Share: Masculinities, Male Support and Women's Suffrage in Britain 1890–1920* (Routledge, 1997).

a pronounced sense of chivalry.[12] This is evident in Hugh Franklin's comments on Churchill: 'When will cabinet ministers know that their position does not give them the right to insult women?' It was also symbolized by Pethick-Lawrence who, when defending three suffragettes in court in July 1906, saw that the dock was dirty and used his handkerchief to wipe it clean.[13] Similar sentiments drove Keir Hardie and George Lansbury. On one celebrated occasion on 20 June 1912 when the prime minister had been replying to questions about the suffragettes, Lansbury angrily crossed the floor of the Commons to confront Asquith: 'You will go down to history as the man who tortured innocent women.... You ought to be driven from public life.'

Like the middle-class suffragists Lansbury basically regarded women as deserving of protection and respect because of their frailty; they aroused his compassion as did the poor, the helpless, and the oppressed regardless of gender. For some of the younger men chivalry was mixed up with a desire for excitement offered by the campaign, and in some cases by the prospect of romantic fulfilment. Victor Duval married a suffragette, Una Dugdale, while Keir Hardie's fondness for Sylvia Pankhurst is well known.[14] A number of the men seem to have been drawn into the cause by the example set by their female relations or friends. Pethick-Lawrence, for example, admitted he would never have become entangled with the suffragettes but for his wife.[15]

Unfortunately the Pankhursts had no desire to be treated as frail women in need of male protection. Consequently they looked askance at men's contribution to the cause. However, male activities made an impact on the campaign in five main ways. In the first place they had some bearing on the overall public perception of the suffrage issue. Some of the Pankhursts' propaganda created the impression that they sought to wage a sex war, which was tactically unwise since it played into the hands of the Antis. But many women were keen to avoid this. 'I felt that this was not an anti-man movement', wrote Helen Crawfurd, herself a militant.[16] From this perspective the suffragists needed men to counter the Antis' use of women like Violet Markham and Mrs Humphry Ward. The more prominent the Pankhursts became, the more desirable it was to demonstrate that the suffrage cause was not solely female, and thus not a threat to men.

---

[12] 'Christian Chivalry: The Racial Aspect of Women's Enfranchisement', Men's League for Women's Suffrage, not dated.

[13] Harrison, *Prudent Revolutionaries*, 226; June Balshaw, 'The Pethick-Lawrences and Women's Suffrage', 138–45, in John and Eustance (eds.), *The Men's Share*.

[14] See Gillian Hawtin, *Votes for Wimbledon Women* (1993), 55.

[15] F. W. Pethick-Lawrence, *Fate*, 100.

[16] Helen Crawfurd, MS Autobiography, 94, Marx Memorial Library.

On the other hand, the value of the male alliance depended on the credibility of the men involved. They suffered from two problems, the political and the masculine. Politically, they came to be regarded as just another anti-government front, at least by Liberals. More damagingly, aspersions were freely cast upon their masculinity. An underlying part of the Antis' case had always been that as women became more virile, so men grew effeminate and the race deteriorated. Some of the male suffragists invited derision by describing themselves as 'suffragettes in trousers'. In fact several conventional male heroes including the cricketer, Jack Hobbs, supported the cause; and an East End prize fighter, Kosher Hunt, gave Sylvia his protection against all comers. But more typical were the middle-class intellectuals, writers, poets, and journalists such as Israel Zangwill, Lawrence Housman, John Masefield, John Galsworthy, and Gilbert Murray.[17] Prolific and idealistic writers and speechmakers, these figures were nonetheless vulnerable to ridicule in the press, and they lacked influence outside their limited circles.

The second and more tangible contribution of male suffragism lay in the practical and tactical advantages it offered. For example, men were used by the WFL as stewards at meetings. This role proved attractive to workingmen who did not actually join suffrage societies. In Glasgow dockers and navvies cheerfully agreed to help throw out the students who enjoyed breaking up suffrage meetings, while in the East End Sylvia took this a stage further by introducing military drilling.[18] During the early phase of militancy Victor Duval and others had undertaken to interrupt cabinet ministers in meetings from which women had been excluded. At a meeting for Churchill at Manchester's Free Trade Hall in May 1908 'Ladies Tickets' were issued only if signed by a male Liberal Party member who guaranteed their good behaviour; but with men's connivance these elaborate expedients were rendered ineffective, for no sooner had Churchill congratulated the organizers than two women and a male suffragist made their presence known![19]

This example is a reminder of what was potentially the greatest advantage of male suffragism. As voters and as holders of offices within the political parties, the men were surely more likely to be taken seriously. This was indeed the thinking behind the formation of the Men's League in 1907 which included such prominent Liberals as W. H. Dickinson, MP, Leif Jones, MP,

---

[17] See John Masefield, 'My Faith in Woman Suffrage', 1909; Laurence Housman, 'Articles of Faith in the Freedom of Women', 1910.

[18] A. E. Hordern to Mr Beanland, 12 Feb. 1914, John Rylands Library: Manchester Men's League for Women's Suffrage Papers; Helen Crawfurd, MS Autobiography, 108, Marx Memorial Library; Winslow, *Pankhurst*, 56–8.

[19] *Votes for Women*, 4 June 1909, 753; E. Pethick-Lawrence, *My Part*, 233.

Earl Russell, and the Reverend R. J. Campbell.[20] Their position within the party enabled them to voice their objection to the policies of the government at Liberal meetings, but it is far from clear that they achieved anything except a certain amount of embarrassment. A good example was a speech at Aberdeen by Asquith in January 1908 when he was forced to respond to questions about female enfranchisement put by the President of the local Association; when some men in the audience rose to voice their opinions, they were ejected by the stewards, which led to fighting on the platform and to a bitter dispute because tickets had been issued on the understanding that the recipients would keep quiet.[21] However, this kind of pressure failed, as is evident from the decision to form the Liberal Men's Association for Women's Suffrage in 1913. By 1914 this body, along with the Men's League, had begun to focus its efforts on pressurizing local Liberal associations not to adopt Anti-Suffragists as candidates.[22]

Much the most striking attempt to use influence within the party was made by the Northern Men's Federation (NMF) which was formed on the initiative of Maud Arncliffe-Sennett in the aftermath of Emily Wilding Davison's funeral in 1913. After breaking with the Pankhursts she needed a fresh outlet for her energies and her money. The NMF enjoyed the advantage of being based squarely in the towns of Scotland and North-East England; it hoped to demonstrate that suffragism was integral to the heartlands of Liberalism not simply a movement of the drawing-rooms of the Home Counties. Its members were drawn from town councillors, Scots baillies and provosts, JPs, lawyers, clergymen, and chairmen of constituency Liberal Associations. Men in their forties, fifties, and sixties, to judge from their photographs, they were pillars of the community; and as such they had to be taken seriously. But the experience proved disillusioning. By July 1913 the Federation had decided to send a deputation to Asquith. Although the prime minister indicated his reluctance to meet them, they nonetheless travelled to London and duly appeared in Downing Street.[23] But Asquith scuttled away in a taxi leaving his uninvited guests on the doorstep. Although they escaped arrest, unlike female suffragists in the same position, the gentlemen were evidently dismayed by their reception not only from Asquith but from the MPs they saw at Westminster. Even more surprisingly they found themselves held up

[20] *Report*, Men's League for Women's Suffrage, 1907, Museum of London: Suffragette Fellowship Collection 50/82/132.

[21] 'Mr Asquith at Aberdeen', *Votes for Women*, Jan. 1908, 59.

[22] *Manchester Guardian*, 11 Dec. 1913; Men's League for Women's Suffrage, *Newsletter*, No. 52, Feb.–Mar. 1914.

[23] *Edinburgh Evening Dispatch*, 19 July 1913.

to ridicule in the Scottish press: 'The deputation', commented the *Glasgow Herald*, 'has maintained and confirmed the indefeasible right of every private citizen to call upon the prime minister when he is not at home.'[24] As though unable to believe what had happened, the NMF spent the autumn and winter building branches and holding meetings, and in February 1914 it sent a second deputation which Asquith again declined to receive. In a way the Scots had lost sight of the suffrage issue in their concern about the insult to their own dignity. The whole episode deflated the assumption that men could operate more effectively from within the Establishment. Even the women took a disparaging view; Janie Allan declared that she had a low opinion of men who needed a woman to prod them into action, while Mrs Arncliffe-Sennett pronounced them adorable but lacking initiative![25] No doubt their loss of dignity paled by comparison with the physical sufferings of the women at this time.

Ultimately, however, the experience of the NMF is significant in a different context. By 1914 it had joined the other men's groups in a policy of total opposition to the government. The dramatic Liberal defeats at Scottish by-elections at Midlothian and Leith in this period indicate the folly of Asquith's treatment of the men who really were the pillars of his party's dominance in Scotland. By the summer of 1914 they were working in at least six seats held by Anti-Suffragist Scottish Liberals including East Fife which was represented by the prime minister himself.[26] His humiliating defeat at the 1918 election was a belated indication of how out of touch he had become with his own party's supporters.

A fourth and more modest aspect of the male contribution lay in their role as intermediaries. Occasionally they managed to coordinate the suffrage societies despite their divisions over tactics, politics, or personalities, by offering a neutral platform on which the rival leaders could meet. Men such as Brailsford and Lytton also acted as intermediaries between suffragists and politicians, helping to negotiate the truce in 1910–11 while the Conciliation Bill passed through parliament. Brailsford also became a key figure in launching the 1912 electoral pact between the National Union and the Labour Party. As a Radical Liberal Brailsford saw clearly the potential of this strategy and enjoyed sufficient credibility with Labour leaders such as Arthur Henderson and the leading suffragists to carry it out.[27]

Finally, men's participation helped to modify the composition of suffragism by the extensive recruitment of clergymen into the Edwardian campaign.

---

[24] *Glasgow Herald*, 19 July 1913.   [25] Leneman, 'Northern Men', 40.
[26] *Edinburgh Evening News*, 11 May 1914.
[27] F. M. Leventhal, *The Last Dissenter: H. N. Brailsford and His World* (Gollancz, 1985).

For example, 16 per cent of the MLWS membership comprised clergymen. In June 1912 a large meeting at the Queen's Hall in London held to 'consider the religious aspects of the women's movement' enjoyed the support of the Bishops of Lincoln, Durham, Hereford, Hull, Oxford, Southwark, Stepney, and Worcester, the Dean of Peterborough and, among leading Nonconformists, the Reverend R. J. Campbell and the Reverend Dr Scott Lidgett; a supportive letter from the Archbishop of Canterbury was also read.[28] An array of pressure groups catering to all parts of the Christian spectrum duly appeared including the Church League for Women's Suffrage under the presidency of the Bishop of Lincoln, the Free Church League for Women's Suffrage, the Scottish Churches League for Women's Suffrage, and the Catholic Suffrage Society; a Jewish League for Women's Suffrage was also established.

The involvement of churchmen was inevitably controversial because the Antis, many of whom had traditionally based their case on the assumption that women's role in society was God-given, reacted with alarm at the evidence of suffragist sympathies in the Church hierarchy.[29] Clergymen naturally felt vulnerable to the accusation that they were lending respectability to acts of violence; but conversely their prominence on suffragist platforms helped to counter the impression of the cause as largely militant. None of this should be taken as implying that the Church of England as a whole had been converted to suffragism, though it is noteworthy that when the peers debated Lord Lytton's suffrage bill in 1914, the bench of bishops backed him by six to nil. It seems likely that anti-suffrage clergy simply avoided taking a public stance.

The participation of clergymen underlines the point that, by and large, the male contribution to the cause lay on the constitutional side. The Men's League, which was the largest organization, used conventional methods and espoused the constitutional and law-abiding views of the NUWSS, though individual members did cooperate with militant societies. Earl Russell expressed their view when he declared that although it was unwise to break up meetings, it was not for men to dictate how the women's campaign should be conducted.[30] However, divisions inevitably appeared, with the impatient

---

[28] *The Common Cause*, 13 June 1912, 152; *The Standard*, 20 June 1912; *The Times*, 24 June 1912.

[29] See the dispute with Bishop Welldon of Manchester who was accused by the Antis of allowing the Church to be used to support a joint suffrage-Labour demonstration; Secretary to Bishop Welldon, 16 June 1914, Manchester Central Library: Manchester Branch NLOWS, M131/4/12; Leneman, *Guid Cause*, 164.

[30] *Report*, Men's League for Women's Suffrage, 1907, 12, Museum of London: Suffragette Fellowship Collection 50/82/132; MLWS *Newsletter*, No. 54, May 1914.

younger men succumbing to the attractions of militancy.[31] As a result Victor Duval, Henry Nevinson and Charles Gray established the Men's Political Union which adopted the WSPU colours so as to emphasize its adherence to their methods. Among the list of 1,097 suffragette prisoners for 1905–14 are the names of just forty men which suggests that militancy was not typical of male suffragism.[32]

In fact the role of the militant male proved to be an uncomfortable and complicated one. Some men felt aggrieved that the press neglected their activities in favour of those committed by women; Lawrence Housman, for example, recorded that on one occasion he was detained briefly, reprimanded, and then released while women involved with similar offences ended up with three-month sentences![33] More fundamentally, leading suffragettes, notably Christabel Pankhurst, had always entertained reservations about male involvement in spite of their friendship with Keir Hardie and Fred Pethick-Lawrence. She regarded it as essential to keep the WSPU purely female in order to enhance the appeal of the heroism of women. There was, thus, always a danger of men usurping their role, and the Pankhursts invariably reacted with hostility if men took initiatives, even over organizing deputations.[34] They correctly saw that the combination of men's physical strength and their growing frustration would increase the risk of violent encounters with their opponents; Franklin's attack on Churchill is a case in point.

Consequently, towards the end of 1911 relations between male suffragism and the WSPU began to deteriorate. This was partly the indirect effect of the collapse of the Conciliation Bill strategy which discredited men like Brailsford in the eyes of the WSPU. Housman described the Pankhursts as 'exceedingly trying; they want their own way . . . they would take no advice'.[35] Not surprisingly the Men's Political Union had been wound up by 1913. Housman's view is corroborated by the famous split with Pethick-Lawrence in 1912. As long as Christabel had been able to dominate WSPU strategy through the ad hoc committee, it had not mattered that Fred took part without being a member. But by 1912 the Pankhursts decided that he had become a liability, though his ousting was more the result of disagreement over tactics than because of his sex.

[31] *The Common Cause*, 29 Apr. 1909, 34.
[32] 'Roll of Honour: Suffragette Prisoners 1905–14', Manchester Central Library: Mitchell Papers M220/2/2/4.
[33] Housman, *Unexpected Years*, 282–3.
[34] Ibid., 278, gives one such example and wrote that the WSPU 'was persistently belittling our efforts and occasionally resenting our aid'.
[35] Ibid., 275.

These rifts with male suffragists simply accelerated the isolation of the Pankhursts from the broader movement. During the last three years of peace men were increasingly drawn into cooperation with the National Union and the WFL. The more they focused on the new election strategy, the more natural it became for the Men's League to use this as an appropriate outlet for its members.[36]

One is bound to conclude that while the activities of men were helpful in several ways, they by no means offered a breakthrough, and cooperation with the militants proved ultimately a failure. By 1914 the men's suffrage organizations had reached a position of deadlock with the authorities just as the women's had. This, however, is to take a short-term view. The underlying significance of the male role can best be understood in the context of the post-1912 electoral pact between the NUWSS and Labour, in which men, as voters, obviously had a central part to play.

The Origins of the Election Fighting Fund

In negotiating a pact with the Labour Party the constitutional suffragists appeared to be repudiating the strategy they had adopted ever since the 1860s; but it appeared to offer a real prospect of breaking the log-jam in which the cause had become trapped. The immediate origins of the new initiative lay in the events of 1911–12 which had raised hopes for the success of the Conciliation Bill only to dash them again. Officially the National Union had adopted a relaxed view of the government's announcement about its own reform bill. Though it continued to promote the Conciliation Bill, it declared itself content to accept a larger instalment of reform if this became available.[37] However, this stance rapidly became obsolete. In the first place, the National Union was impressed by the debate at the Labour Party conference at Birmingham in January 1912 which resolved for the first time that no franchise reform would be acceptable if it failed to include women. Though less than an unequivocal pledge to vote against a government bill, the resolution, moved by Arthur Henderson and W. C. Anderson and supported by Philip Snowden, showed that at last women's suffrage was becoming less marginal within the party. Ramsay MacDonald underlined this in February when he affirmed Labour's readiness to turn the Liberals out on the issue. These overtures were picked up by Millicent Fawcett who pointedly drew attention to the loyalty of the Labour members in parliamentary divisions; in April she

---

[36] *The Common Cause*, 13 June 1912, 152.   [37] Ibid., 11 Jan. 1912, 686–7.

raised the question whether the time had come for the National Union to modify its policy by supporting Labour candidates.[38]

The second contingency was the shock defeat of the Conciliation Bill by fourteen votes in April 1912. This helped to accelerate the sudden rapprochement between Labour and the National Union. Although the leaders offered a calm analysis for the setback, they had been left severely discredited. After all, forty-two firm suffragist members had voted against the bill and ninety-one had abstained. Many moderates now seemed to recognize how flawed their strategy had been. In a letter symptomatic of the mood Eleanor Acland condemned the entire Conciliation Bill policy as 'dishonest' and concluded: 'I am more and more convinced that our movement has got to be linked to democracy rather than pure feminism. People are *bored* with feminism and the militants have given it a bad name ... we should get much more keenness if one party really liked the Bill.'[39] In fact Acland really wanted a closer link with the Liberals; but Fawcett and her colleagues had become too disenchanted with Asquith to regard this as realistic. To opt for Labour instead had become less risky now that leading Liberal suffragists in the North including Margaret Ashton, Dr Ethel Williams, and Catherine Marshall had reconciled themselves to opposing their old party. At the same time the defeat of the Conciliation Bill had encouraged Philip Snowden to take a fresh look at Labour's strategy. He concluded that the setback should be seen as beneficial for it enhanced Labour's credibility and standing: 'if the Labour Party would, they could force this question. They have only to say ... No Home Rule unless Votes for Women ... and the thing would be done.'[40]

Despite Snowden's optimism, the negotiations over the pact conducted during April 1912 by Henry Brailsford, Arthur Henderson, Kate Courtney, and Millicent Fawcett revealed several problems. Although the Council of the National Union approved the pact in May, Labour's National Executive did not follow suit until July. Essentially the NUWSS was to raise an Election Fighting Fund (EFF) to be used to promote Labour candidates in constituencies chosen with a view to defeating Liberal Anti-Suffragists; it would also send volunteers to help organize the Labour campaign.[41] In this way they hoped both to modify the composition of the House of Commons and to bring effective pressure to bear on the government to introduce legislation.

---

[38] *The Common Cause*, 4 Apr. 1912, 880.
[39] Eleanor Acland to Catherine Marshall, 1 Apr. 1912, Cumbria CRO: Catherine Marshall Papers.
[40] Philip Snowden to Maud Arncliffe-Sennett, 31 Mar. 1912, Arncliffe-Sennett Papers, BL, C 10.245.
[41] Kate Courtney to Arthur Henderson, 23 Apr. 1912, Labour Party Archives, WOM/12/4.

The strength of the EFF policy was that it was symptomatic of a wider sentiment already manifest amongst suffragists. The Men's League had already
begun to focus on assisting Labour candidates.[42] The Women's Liberal
Federation members had increasingly withdrawn from their party. And the
WFL, originally a pro-Labour group of militants, had no reservations about
participating in the new policy.

As the most important initiative during the last three years of the peacetime campaign the EFF requires careful assessment in terms of implementation and results. Did it, for example, make equally good sense for both
parties? The attractions, seen from Labour's point of view, call for explanation if only because 1912 was rather late in the day for a link of this sort. The
party had a chequered history of relations with suffragists, and many Socialists never ceased to regard Mrs Pankhurst as a Tory stooge for her abandonment of the ILP. The party had repudiated her by reaffirming its belief in
adult suffrage on several occasions. Meanwhile Labour had set about building its own organization in the shape of the Women's Labour League which,
though pro-suffrage, was essentially loyalist and non-feminist. Labour
urgently needed to emulate the other parties by recruiting female constituency activists but without in the process introducing a challenge to its
existing priorities. It is significant that since 1906 the Women's Labour
League had been less than a success. By 1914 its membership stood at only
6,000 and it was barely tolerated by many working-class and Socialist candidates. Herein lay the party's dilemma. The movement continued to show its
traditional resistance to female participation; yet with an organization in
barely one constituency in four, Labour urgently needed to expand its local
membership if it was ever to develop into a party on a national scale.

Women's suffrage also raised more fundamental questions about Labour's
programme and its political strategy. A party which claimed to represent the
working-class majority ought logically to have made radical electoral reform
one of its priorities at a time when four out of ten men still lacked a parliamentary vote. But this had not materialized largely because at this stage in its
development the party remained focused on winning the support of the
unionized section of the working class rather than the workers as a whole.
Although Henderson along with Margaret Bondfield and others had promoted the People's Suffrage Federation, they seem to have assumed that
eventually a Liberal government would enact one-man-one-vote. Like the
Liberals, Labour was slow to take up women's suffrage because they did not
regard it as an electoral priority. However, by 1912 there was increasing

---

[42] *The Common Cause*, 30 May 1912, 120; 13 June 1912, 152.

pressure from the activists to extend the movement, and the women in the National Union were becoming less dogmatic about suffrage legislation and more willing to accept a democratic measure.

The cause also had important implications for Labour's relations with the Liberal Party. For several years many local activists had believed the time had come to cease acting as the tame supporters of the government and to strike out with a distinctive radical appeal. But the Liberals had taken so many reforming initiatives since 1908 that there was not much scope. Franchise reform, however, offered an excellent opportunity, for it was a classic liberal cause which had been almost perversely neglected by the Liberal leadership. Women's suffrage could thus be seen as part of MacDonald's wider strategy of outflanking the Liberals by seizing Liberal issues.

Above all, the EFF had practical implications in the shape of more by-election contests against Liberals. In the short term this pleased the activists; but, as Brailsford explained to MacDonald, it would help the party to capture the loyalty of women who first became involved via the EFF policy. 'Tens of thousands who are doing nothing very definite today, or who think they are Liberals, can be won for Socialism almost insensibly,' he claimed. And to Henderson he wrote: 'The Liberal women are in the midst of a split, and all the more active of them are preparing to back our plan ... I believe that in the course of a fighting alliance most of them would end by becoming decided and permanent adherents of the Labour Party.'[43] If slightly optimistic, Brailsford's diagnosis was basically sound, for his claims about the disillusionment amongst Liberal women are readily corroborated. In the long run a larger female membership was to be an essential part of Labour's expansion from the limited bridgeheads won in 1906 and 1910.

Yet despite these compelling arguments, MacDonald and even Henderson evidently took some convincing. MacDonald, in particular, was easily provoked by assertive middle-class women. He continued to denounce the suffragette campaign as 'tomfoolery' and as the creation of 'women who are in a position to throw into collecting plates handed round at the Albert Hall £10,000 at a minute's notice'.[44] As a result he was sensitive towards any signs of feminism within the Women's Labour League at this time.[45] What MacDonald disliked most was the suggestion in the pact that Labour could be bought and used to serve a purpose other than that for which it had been

[43] H. Brailsford to Ramsay MacDonald, 23 Apr. 1912, MacDonald papers PRO 30/69/5; H. Brailsford to Arthur Henderson, 4 May 1912, Labour Party Archives, WOM/12/14.
[44] *Daily Herald*, 29 June 1912.
[45] See discussion in Pugh, 'Labour and Women's Suffrage', in Brown (ed.), *First Labour Party*.

founded.[46] Nor were his fears easily laid to rest, for throughout the inter-war period Labour politicians believed that the Party stood in danger of being hijacked by a handful of feminist infiltrators. Consequently, though Mac-Donald reaffirmed Labour's readiness to vote against a government franchise bill, he tried to prevaricate about making the commitment public, ostensibly on the grounds that it remained uncertain whether all the Labour MPs would fall into line. The National Executive Committee (NEC) would have preferred not to link the EFF to the party, and even to avoid reference to Labour candidates. However, Brailsford reminded them that on such terms the pact would scarcely be worth the National Union's trouble, and so they compromised by agreeing to operate the pact for the benefit of individual Labour candidates rather than the party as such, which actually suited the NUWSS very well. They did not specify in advance precisely which constituencies would be covered by the EFF, which was just as well since this would have shown that the objects of the two partners did not entirely coincide. At least this enabled the EFF to be launched officially in May 1912.

From the National Union's perspective the pact offered a means of putting intense pressure on the Liberals by splitting their vote and eliminating Anti-Suffragists from parliament. Hitherto their by-election policy had lacked impact, but now for the first time they would enjoy the benefits of a clear commitment to one political party. There was less chance of confusion with the WSPU's position since the EFF involved opposition to Anti-Suffragist Liberals not to the party as a whole; indeed, where a Liberal was ranked as a tried supporter the EFF was not to apply at all.

On the other hand, the advantages may have been exaggerated. The Labour MPs *already* voted for women's suffrage bills; and their number had fallen from a maximum of forty-two to only thirty-eight by 1914, hardly enough to have a decisive impact in the Commons. On paper the government could survive a Labour revolt as long as it retained the loyalty of the eighty-two Irish members. However, the National Union evidently believed that Labour could be used to resolve their problem with the Irish.[47] They saw that the biggest factor in the defeat of the Conciliation Bill had been the reversal of the votes of the Irish members who had been frightened into believing that the women's issue might break up Asquith's government and thereby sink the Home Rule Bill too. The National Union concluded that pressure must be brought to bear in the opposite direction. Labour was to interfere with the Home Rule Bill by introducing amendments to enfranchise Irish women.

[46] Interview with MacDonald, 13 May 1912, Fawcett Library: Fawcett Letters 89/2/68.
[47] *The Common Cause*, 8 Nov. 1912; Hume, *The National Union*, 167–9.

However, it is far from clear that this ploy worked. When Snowden put down his amendment it was heavily rejected by 314 to 173; John Redmond was not so easily intimidated while he had the government whips on his side. Although twenty-eight Labour and thirty Liberal members supported Snowden, five Labour members opposed him, and eight abstained. This suggests that if the NUWSS had envisaged the EFF as a means of dealing with the Irish obstacle they had exaggerated both Labour's power and the extent of cooperation by the MPs.

This parliamentary ploy highlighted the underlying flaw in the EFF policy: was Labour yet prepared to risk a break with the Liberals despite the attractions of complete independence? MacDonald and the NEC fully appreciated that to be driven into wholesale electoral conflict with the Liberals would be to destroy the pact which the two parties had operated successfully since 1903 and in the process put most Labour seats at risk. While MacDonald undoubtedly wanted to put pressure on the Liberals by judicious interventions in by-elections, he was far from keen to risk conflict at a general election. For this reason historians are mistaken if they *assume* the success of the EFF strategy. It is certainly possible that over a period of time it might have had the desired effect. Brailsford himself predicted that as cooperation became a habit the pact would become closer, which was to some extent borne out by 1914. By the autumn of 1912 the National Union had gone a little beyond the original agreement by deciding to make support available to sitting Labour MPs, which was a step towards a commitment to the party as opposed to selected candidates.[48] In January 1913 the annual conference pledged the party to vote against any government bill from which women were excluded.

On the other hand, the National Union ran great risks with its own members by going this far. Kate Courtney admitted it was important not to ' prejudice the non-party character of the National Union', and Fawcett insisted that there had been no basic change in that they remained an organization comprising suffragists from all parties who put aside political differences for the sake of the cause.[49] Their support for Labour was thus seen as purely expedient not as indicative of support for its programme let alone for Socialism. This, however, was somewhat disingenuous in the light of the new commitment to sitting Labour members. The best means of reassuring National Union members was to keep the EFF organizationally separate by means of a committee

[48] *The Common Cause*, 17 Oct. 1912, 476; lists of the Labour MPs in Cumbria CRO: Marshall Papers show that fifteen were not to receive help, either because their seats were judged safe or because they disliked rich women in the NUWSS.

[49] Kate Courtney to Arthur Henderson, 23 Apr. 1912, Cumbria CRO; Marshall Papers.

under Catherine Marshall which ran its work. It also compromised by offering support to selected Liberal and even Conservative members.

However, many members refused to be reassured by this. Major societies in Glasgow, Cardiff, and Oldham opposed the new strategy, suggesting it was unlikely to be effective in the short term and would be counter-productive by deterring Liberals from joining suffrage platforms. During 1913 and 1914 substantial losses of members were reported.[50] The leaders had to tread carefully. They wished to encourage their more left-wing activists many of whom genuinely saw the EFF as a step towards the long-term fusion of Labour and the women's movement. They could not, therefore, afford to admit that they were simply using Labour as a weapon against the Liberals, though even Catherine Marshall envisaged withdrawing from the policy before the next general election if sufficient guarantees had been squeezed out of the government.[51] On the other hand, this option had to seem credible to the prominent Liberal and Conservative women in the NUWSS. Fawcett's own views as an anti-Socialist no doubt helped to reassure them. Also the decentralized structure of the National Union proved an advantage here, in that it allowed local societies to abstain from the EFF if they wished. Many of the sceptics simply waited to see what effect the new policy had. In the event the EFF received an unexpected boost from the fiasco over the government's reform bill in January 1913. The National Union had put its weight behind amendments to this bill promoted by Sir Edward Grey and W. H. Dickinson which would have enfranchised married women. This was an important recognition of the necessity to go for a more democratic formula involving around five to six million female voters. Although they were not confident of success owing to the attitude of the Irish members, the suffragists mounted a major campaign during the autumn and winter of 1912 in the hope of pressurizing wavering MPs. These hopes were dashed when the Speaker's ruling killed the bill; but its loss left the constitutional suffragists with no obvious strategy except the Election Fighting Fund.

Suffragism as a Mass Movement?

The most efficacious way of dealing with the misgivings about the EFF was to implement it as quickly as possible. But where? Henderson had mentioned

---

[50] Glasgow and West of Scotland Association for Women's Suffrage, minutes, 11 May 1912: Oldham Local Studies Library, Lees Papers 132; Miss A. M. Dowson to Miss Crookenden, 13 June 1913, and Alice Percy to Miss Crookenden, 23 May 1914, Cumbria CRO: Marshall Papers.

[51] See draft letter to F. D. Acland, 4 Nov. 1913, Cumbria CRO: Marshall Papers.

several constituencies which the National Union was not keen to tackle; conversely the suffragists identified Ipswich, Gateshead, East Bristol, South Shields, Grantham, and Rossendale, all represented by Anti-Suffragist Liberals, which did not suit Labour.[52] However, the mismatch was rapidly resolved by the force of events in the shape of a by-election at Holmfirth in Yorkshire in June 1912. As a vacant Liberal seat Holmfirth left the NUWSS with no option but to put the EFF to the test. Fortunately, as a working-class district with many miners and an active Labour candidate who was a miner himself, it was just the kind of contest Labour's NEC wished to tackle at this time.[53]

Catherine Marshall handled the by-election tactfully. Aware of the need to avoid arousing suspicions that Labour was being taken over by middle-class feminists, she made a point of recruiting organizers who were either working-class or pro-Labour: Margaret Robertson, Selina Cooper, Ada Neild Chew, Annot Robinson, Margaret Ashton, and Isabella Ford. Figures such as Lady Frances Balfour, Lady Selborne, and Millicent Fawcett, whose views were rather right-wing, supported the policy from London but appear to have kept clear of the election itself. The tactics proved successful, and Labour workers from the Chief Agent, Arthur Peters, downwards recorded their appreciation for the efforts of the suffragists. At Holmfirth their technique was to conduct open-air meetings on women's suffrage with a view to attracting audiences away from the other candidates and then to hand over to a Labour speaker.[54] Meanwhile the WSPU also arrived to interrupt Labour meetings, and the National League for Opposing Women's Suffrage subjected all the candidates to questions about female enfranchisement. The Conservative, evidently not intimidated by the volume of female activists, insisted that women must cease their agitation before he would even consider the issue.[55]

As an experiment in collaboration the by-election thus worked well, but the result was difficult to interpret. Labour doubled its general election vote, but remained bottom of the poll; in view of the unpopularity of the government at this time it was slightly disappointing not to have done better in a working-class seat. The Liberals retained Holmfirth; they had lost some votes, but so had the Conservatives, whether because of women's suffrage it is difficult to say.

In June the appointment of Colonel Seeley as Secretary of State for War caused a by-election at Ilkeston in Derbyshire. Since Seeley was a prominent Anti-Suffragist Liberal and the National Union had already undertaken

---

[52] Catherine Marshall to W. C. Andersin (copy), 28 June 1912, Cumbria CRO: Marshall Papers.
[53] *Sheffield Daily Telegraph*, 6 June 1912.　　　[54] *The Common Cause*, 27 June 1912, 184.
[55] *Sheffield Daily Telegraph*, 13 June 1912; 15 June 1912; 17 June 1912.

propaganda in his constituency, the target was tempting for the EFF. But no
Labour candidate stood. A strong rumour that the National Union had
offered £500 to J. T. White to stand for Labour provoked an angry reaction by
the party in London.[56] This was an indication that Labour's interests were
likely to predominate over those of the National Union.

The next vacancy arose at Hanley in the Potteries, a constituency actually
held by Labour under the earlier pact with the Liberals; but all three parties
fought the by-election, and the Liberals triumphantly recovered the seat
while Labour dropped to third place with a humiliating 1,600 votes. Obviously Hanley represented a setback for Labour, but it also cast doubt on the
efficacy of an influx of female workers in places where the party lacked an
existing organization. Despite this the by-election did advance the EFF
policy in the sense that it encouraged Labour to take counter-strikes against
the Liberals. At the same time it alerted the party leadership to the dangers
they now ran, for most of the existing Labour seats would be in jeopardy if the
Liberals decided to contest them.

In spite of these reservations the local campaigning had created some
momentum behind the EFF strategy. By June £3,000 had been donated and
the National Union gladly entered the next by-election at Crewe even
though, once again, the decision reflected the party's interest rather than suffragist pressure. Highly optimistic reports about the enthusiasm generated
by the campaign at Crewe led some suffragists to anticipate securing a victory for Labour.[57] Again, however, they were disappointed as the candidate
came third. On the other hand, this time the Liberal had been defeated. Since
the Liberal majority had been only 1,700 in a straight fight with a Conservative, a new Labour candidate was almost bound to produce this result.
Whether women's suffrage was important in swinging votes is doubtful; the
voting was probably influenced more by the workers' reactions to the
National Insurance Bill and to a recent railway strike in Crewe which had led
the authorities to send troops to the town.[58] On the other hand, as the Conservative won by only 250 votes, the suffragists' role in boosting Labour's poll
might well have been crucial.

At all events the election made the National Union optimistic. 'Our enemies in the Liberal camp have uneasy doubts about how much we are concerned in the revolt of the Labour Party . . . [the government] are at last
beginning to feel there is some risk in putting off the demand for Women's

---

[56] *The Common Cause*, 27 June 1912; *Derby Daily Telegraph*, 11 June 1912; *The Globe*, 19 June 1912;
Hume, *The National Union*, 165.
[57] *The Common Cause*, 11 July 1912, 233; 25 July 1912, 270.
[58] *Crewe Guardian*, 23 July 1913.

Suffrage.'[59] As a result, in the autumn Catherine Marshall proposed to extend the EFF to cover existing Labour constituencies provided the party agreed to contest more Liberal seats.[60] However, it remained uncertain whether Labour was prepared to be hustled into fighting on a much broader front even in by-elections. Henderson refused to get involved in the vacancies arising at NW Manchester, East Carmarthen, and Bolton.[61] The Bolton by-election in November illustrates the dilemma. In this two-member seat Labour and the Liberals shared the representation under the 1903 pact. As this had delivered victories in 1906 and 1910, Labour's wish to respect the agreement was hardly surprising. Frustrated, the National Union simply conducted propaganda and the Liberal retained the seat.[62]

Fortunately the autumn of 1912 provided one dramatic opportunity for Labour-suffragist collaboration in the traditional Liberal seat at Midlothian. Despite high hopes Labour came third, but Midlothian fell narrowly to the Conservatives.[63] As it had been a stronger Liberal seat than Crewe, the loss came as a greater shock; taken together the two losses gave the National Union a satisfying sense that it had drawn blood. In the aftermath of Midlothian the *Manchester Guardian* warned the Liberals that if the suffragists continued in their policy the result would be the return of a Conservative government at the general election.[64] This prospect gained some substance during the winter of 1912–13 as the National Union extended its activities to constituencies presently occupied by prominent Anti-Suffrage Liberals including four who sat in the cabinet: Rotherham (J. A. Pease), Rossendale (Lewis Harcourt), East Bristol (Sir Charles Hobhouse), North Monmouth (Reginald McKenna), Accrington (H. A. Baker), Gateshead (H. L. Elverston), and Bishop Auckland (Sir Henry Havelock Allan).[65] The campaigns in these districts aroused some misgivings in the National Union on the grounds that some of the local workers were becoming too closely involved with the Labour Party. This seems slightly perverse, for the greater the fusion between Labour and suffragism the more likely it was that the party would be

[59]   Report of the EFF, 12 July 1912, Cumbria CRO: Marshall Papers.

[60]   Catherine Marshall to Arthur Henderson (copy), 14 Oct. 1912, Cumbria CRO: Marshall Papers.

[61]   Arthur Henderson to Catherine Marshall, 6 Aug. 1912, Cumbria CRO: Marshall Papers.

[62]   *Bolton Evening News*, 12 Nov. 1912; 18 Nov. 1912.

[63]   *The Common Cause*, 29 Aug. 1912, 362; 19 Sept. 1912, 413–14; *Edinburgh Evening News*, 7 Sept. 1912, 4; *Annual Report*, Edinburgh NSWS, 1913, 7–9.

[64]   *Manchester Guardian*, 22 Sept. 1912.

[65]   *The Common Cause*, 17 Jan. 1913, 70; 23 May 1913, 107; 10 Oct. 1913, 466; 17 Oct. 1913, 485; 24 Oct. 1913, 505.

swept on to attack the Liberals on the broader front that the National Union really required.

Whatever the reactions of Asquith's cabinet, the Pankhursts were certainly provoked by the progress of the EFF, for any rapprochement between Labour and suffragism flew in the face of their own political strategy. Their enthusiasm for Lansbury's Bow and Bromley election in November must be seen in this context, for he was in effect charging Labour with doing far too little to support women's suffrage in parliament. This was obviously an embarrassment for the National Union, and although it supported Lansbury by donating £200 to his campaign, it did so without much enthusiasm to judge from *The Common Cause*. Even this degree of encouragement displeased the Labour Party, especially as the seat was lost.[66] The whole episode was calculated to disrupt the EFF with Lansbury as the unwitting tool of the Pankhursts.

This election was only part of a wider pattern of attacks by Mrs Pankhurst on key figures including Henderson and Snowden whom she denounced in their own constituencies. The National Union interpreted this as an attempt to alienate the party's rank and file from the women's cause.[67] During 1913 the WSPU maintained the pressure by heckling at joint Labour-suffrage meetings addressed by Keir Hardie and Walter Hudson in Newcastle and even shouting down Snowden at York and Gateshead. These interventions culminated in recourse to the police and the stewards (male and female) who bodily removed the interrupters from the hall.[68] Despite the attention they attracted, it is difficult to see what advantage the Pankhursts gained from these efforts. Certainly the EFF continued to operate with undiminished vigour during 1913.

During 1913 and 1914 four more by-elections were tackled with similar results to those of 1912. In February the vacancy at Houghton-le-Spring in County Durham attracted Labour because the party was now keen to assert its claims to mining areas throughout the country. The death of the 88-year-old member who had been unopposed by the Durham Miners' Association since 1890, offered an excellent opportunity to return the Labour candidate, Alderman House who was the current DMA President. However, the local miners, who still ran the Liberal Association, decided almost unanimously to promote another Liberal candidate.[69] Their choice, Tom Wing, was not vulnerable to attack over the suffrage since he had voted for the Conciliation Bill

---

[66] *The Common Cause*, 22 Nov. 1912, 565; 29 Nov. 1912, 587.

[67] Ibid., 24 Oct. 1912, 492; 31 Oct.. 1912, 513.

[68] *Northern Echo*, 11 Feb. 1913, 5; 4 Mar. 1913, 5; 18 Mar. 1913, 5.

[69] Ibid., 15 Feb. 1913, 5; 20 Feb. 1913, 1; 21 Feb. 1913, 1.

when previously an MP.[70] The result was a remarkable Liberal victory in the circumstances, with Labour again in a very respectable third place. It is difficult to assess the impact of women's suffrage, in view of the contrasting evidence. On the one hand, the reports in *The Common Cause* indicated enormous enthusiasm for the women's campaign; on the other, those in the *Northern Echo* threw little light on the issue except to show that Wing was cross-questioned about it. In analysing the result the paper made no reference to the women's issue.[71] However, some of the National Union reports revealed evidence of the underlying hostility towards female suffrage amongst ordinary miners, though this may have reflected reactions to militancy which could be defused amongst those who attended indoor meetings.[72]

There followed a cluster of by-elections at Whitechapel, Leicester, Reading, and West Lothian which Labour left uncontested. At Keighley, which the party had fought previously, it forced a three-cornered contest. However, as the sitting Liberal, Sir Stanley Buckmaster, was ranked as a loyal supporter by the National Union, the EFF was not operated on Labour's behalf. This decision angered some EFF workers like Margaret Robertson whom the National Union leaders regarded as inclined to put Labour interests first and suffragism second.[73] The Liberal women suffragists helped Buckmaster who retained his seat.

The South Lanark by-election in November presented a similar dilemma in that the Liberal was not only pro-suffrage but actually a member of the Edinburgh Women's Suffrage Society. By putting the EFF's resources at the disposal of Labour, the National Union was effectively repudiating one of its own members. Here Labour polled relatively poorly, but in this more marginal seat it was enough to leave the Conservative narrowly in the lead.[74]

January 1914 brought another North-East by-election at North West Durham which Labour also contested. This, too, proved awkward since Aneurin Williams, the Liberal, supported votes for women. The nomination of unmistakably pro-suffrage Liberals at Keighley, S. Lanark, and NW Durham had made some suffragists suspect that the party was trying to frustrate the EFF or create divisions within the National Union. If true, it could be argued that this demonstrated that the strategy was beginning to work by gradually eliminating Antis from the parliamentary party. In the event the

[70] *Northern Echo*, 24 Feb. 1913, 5; 1 Mar. 1913, 1; 4 Mar. 1913, 1.
[71] Ibid., 20 Mar. 1913, 4.
[72] *The Common Cause*, 28 Feb. 1913, 805; 7 Mar. 1913, 821; 14 Mar. 1913, 834–6.
[73] Margaret Robertson and C. M. Gordon to Catherine Marshall, 25 Nov. 1913, Cumbria CRO: Marshall Papers.
[74] *The Common Cause*, 28 Nov. 1913, 623.

National Union insisted that it was already committed to the Labour candidate;[75] indeed, after the resentment caused at Keighley anything less would have put the whole policy at risk. Again the impact of the women's issue is obscure. All three candidates professed to be suffragists, and by sending deputations to Williams the National Union merely helped to publicize his views.[76] Meanwhile the WSPU urged electors to treat the Labour contender as a Liberal, and the Antis advised voters to ignore the women's issue altogether when voting.[77] One may conclude from all the conflicting advice that although enthusiastic meetings were held under EFF auspices, the issue did not greatly influence the outcome. The regional press clearly thought that issues such as land reform were going down well with voters.[78] Though Labour polled strongly in third place, the Liberal does not appear to have been seriously damaged by the EFF for he retained the seat comfortably. One final opportunity for the EFF came at Leith in February where the Labour and EFF campaigns were very effectively integrated. It was usual practice for meetings to commence with suffragist speakers who held the platform until the arrival of the Labour candidate.[79] They also enjoyed the support of the Northern Men's Federation which was anxious to punish Asquith for his ungracious treatment of their deputations. However, the picture was slightly obscured by both the WSPU and the WFL who pronounced the Liberal and Labour candidates to be unsatisfactory.[80] The result was another dramatic Liberal defeat by only sixteen votes, with Labour in third place. However, since the Liberal majority in a straight fight with the Conservatives had been only 1,700, any Labour intervention was bound to put the seat at risk. Local observers attributed the outcome to industrial trouble in the docks which alienated some votes to Labour, and to the Liberal candidate who, as a representative of the older generation of politicians, was seen as too cautious to appeal to the younger workingmen.[81]

Was the National Union's new policy the key to the eventual success of suffragism? Any assessment is complicated by the inconsistent and incomplete nature of the evidence. Considered in the most direct sense the EFF operated in eight by-elections in which the Liberals lost four seats. This, however, demonstrated what was already well-known, that three-cornered

[75] *The Common Cause*, 16 Jan. 1914, 764.
[76] *Northern Echo*, 8 Jan. 1914, 5; 9 Jan. 1914, 1.
[77] Ibid., 20 Jan. 1914, 1.
[78] *Northern Echo*, 29 Jan. 1914, 1; *The Common Cause*, 23 Jan. 1914, 793; 30 Jan. 1914, 812.
[79] *Edinburgh Evening News*, 17 Feb. 1913.
[80] Ibid., 13 Feb. 1914; 14 Feb. 1914; 23 Feb. 1914.
[81] Ibid., 27 Feb. 1914.

tions. Lesley Parker persuaded Labour to undertake these contests.[82] As we have seen, the party had its own reasons for tackling certain seats, and refused to follow the National Union's wishes elsewhere. The most one can say is that in view of the deficiencies in Labour's local organization the EFF's workers and resources encouraged the party to risk new contests. Labour activists sometimes acknowledged that a thousand of their votes were due to the suffragists' efforts. This was positive, but not perhaps enough to encourage the Labour leadership to risk a complete break with the Liberals.[83] After all, the EFF had failed to deliver a single victory, and all four existing Labour seats had been lost in the by-elections of 1912–14.

The key question was what implications the EFF held for the next *general* election which was expected in 1915. From the National Union's side there were two qualifications here. One was simply financial. Although the EFF aimed to raise £10,000, by 1913 it had only £6,900 and during 1914 donations dwindled with the result that resources had to be transferred from the general funds to maintain its expenditure. The second limiting factor was the variation in the local and regional response by NUWSS members. While the Manchester area, the North-East of England, and Edinburgh were enthusiastic, much opposition developed in North and South Wales, in Glasgow and Liverpool. In Holmfirth the suffragist organizations collapsed after the by-election, which suggests that the prospects for extending the fight into a general election were poor. In target seats like N. Monmouth and E. Bristol EFF workers had to be sent in from outside because local suffragists were unhappy about the policy. In the Scottish by-elections, though local members were involved, the campaigns had depended on the arrival of suffragists from England.[84] Though they were effective, this casts some doubt on how far EFF resources would stretch in a general election.

Ultimately the test of the EFF lay in how the politicians themselves reacted to it. They had to consider its likely effect at a general election and the extent to which it created a mass movement by extending suffragism into the working-class organizations. We do have evidence that suffragism and Labour were becoming fused into a common movement in some areas before 1914. One visible symptom of this development was the National Union's

[82] Hume, *The National Union*, 207.

[83] Ibid., 204, incorrectly claims that Labour had decided to contest the seats targeted by the National Union by 1914.

[84] Leneman, *Guid Cause*, 118.

sponsorship of the 'Friends of Women's Suffrage' scheme which was designed to recruit women who were deterred by the cost of membership; they registered their commitment to the cause by signing a form. Even the Oldham suffrage society, which criticized the EFF, recruited 810 'Friends' alongside its 320 members; while Edinburgh claimed 1,517 'Friends'.[85] By August 1914 some 46,000 had joined nationally. The more the working-class women were mobilized the easier it was to refute the long-standing prejudice in Labour circles which equated suffragism with wealthy women. The scheme also had an indirect effect by publicizing the argument that women's enfranchisement would help to raise women's wages. This was the inevitable result of habitual campaigning in industrial areas where the sympathies of the suffragists for the plight of low-paid women was aroused. In Scotland there is evidence that they campaigned as *Socialists* as much as suffragists during this period.[86] In 1913 even *The Common Cause* devoted a report to the success of the Women's Co-operative Guild in raising minimum wages for female CWS employees, citing this as evidence of the use that women could make of their electoral power.[87] Significantly, the Anti-Suffragist organization treated this as a potent argument, and Gladys Pott regularly tried to refute claims that the vote would mean higher wages.[88]

By associating themselves with workingmen and women in the by-election campaigns the suffragists gave themselves more credibility when seeking the formal backing of organizations in the Labour Movement. During 1913 the NUWSS concentrated on securing pro-suffrage resolutions from constituency parties, trades councils, trade union branches, and Women's Co-operative Guilds as well as from local authorities.[89] To mobilize more union support was also a necessary means of maintaining the Labour Party's new position on the issue. The key conference vote in 1912 had been passed by only 919,000 votes to 686,000. Ordinary miners in particular still showed hostility; their union was the heart of anti-suffragism. But after approaches by the National Union prior to the 1913 party conference, the miners agreed to abstain on the women's suffrage resolution which consequently passed more comfortably by 870,000 to 437,000. Finally, at the miners' own conference in October Robert Smillie, the President, promised their support.

These successes in building up popular support enabled the National

[85] *Second Annual Report*, Oldham Society for Women's Suffrage, 1912, Oldham Local Studies Library, Lees Papers 296; *Annual Reports*, Edinburgh NSWS, 1913, 1914.
[86] Leneman, *Guid Cause*, 166.
[87] *The Common Cause*, 3 Jan. 1913, 669–70; 'Vote for Lansbury', WSPU, 1912.
[88] *The Anti-Suffrage Review*, Apr. 1913, 74–5; Dicey, *Letters*, 38–9; Hart, *Woman Suffrage*, 67.
[89] *The Common Cause*, 17 Jan. 1913, 702–3.

Union to sponsor some large-scale displays during 1913–14 just whe.⤳
emasculation of the WSPU by the government's repressive policy h
created a vacuum in the campaign. At a suffrage rally at the Albert Hall in
February 1914 some 342 separate trades unions as well as trades councils and
ILP branches were represented. Such demonstrations were designed to convince the prime minister that a popular demand for the vote now existed
which it would be dangerous for him to ignore. Perhaps the most striking
example of the change in the National Union's style of campaigning was the
Pilgrimage of 1913. This took the form of marches by suffragists along eight
different routes beginning in the far north and west of the country between
the 18th and 26th of July. On the way they gathered supporters to create a
huge but orderly spectacle of bands and banners which culminated in a
demonstration of 70,000 people in Hyde Park. The Pilgrimage proved to
be an unqualified success as judged by the praise it attracted for its law-
abiding character and for what *The Times* called the 'respectful attention'
shown by the crowds.[90] It may be significant that Asquith consented to meet a
deputation of suffragists soon after the Pilgrimage. His response, however,
must be treated with care. On the positive side the prime minister appeared
to accept the National Union's claim that it had fresh evidence of public
support. He gave every sign of being impressed by Margaret Robinson's
claim that in the north of England workingmen had changed their perspective on votes for women; she suggested that their previous hostility had been
to militancy rather than to the vote itself, and that they had begun to see a
common political interest with their wives now that they realized that Anti-
Suffragism was financed by wealthy capitalists.[91]

On the other hand, Asquith made no pretence of having changed his mind
on the issue. But his resistance was now based on a very narrow argument,
namely the absence of a clear demand for the vote. 'We shall bow to the will
of the people,' he declared enigmatically. The most credible interpretation of
this is that Asquith was contemplating how to extricate himself from the
impasse over the women's vote without loss of face. Whether extrication was
now an imminent necessity brings us back to the interpretation of the electoral evidence. Though highly irritating, the loss of by-elections had never
appeared to be a decisive factor; since 1906 the government had passed
through cycles of unpopularity but emerged to retain power in general
elections. Asquith had shown little disposition to be intimidated by the

[90] *The Times*, 28 July 1913; *Morning Post*, 26 July 1913, 7; *Daily Mail*, 28 July 1913, 6; *Daily News*,
26 July 1913, 1; *Daily Chronicle*, 26 July 1913, 1; *Daily Telegraph*, 25 July 1913; *Daily Herald*, 24 July
1913, 6; 26 July 1913, 6.
[91] *The Common Cause*, 15 Aug. 1913, 318–19.

Pankhursts' frequent interventions. However, although the National Union's policy was at one level similar to that of the WSPU, it was both more sophisticated and more comprehensible. They avoided blanket opposition to Liberals and focused on those who opposed the suffrage. Moreover, by linking the women's cause to left-wing politics the suffragists challenged the key achievement of the Edwardian Liberals in putting themselves at the head of progressive opinion. Through the People's Budget, the social welfare reforms, and the attack on the peers' veto they had been remarkably successful in maintaining an alliance of working-class and middle-class radicalism; but by 1912 they were faltering a little. MacDonald, Hardie, and Snowden had perceived that it was possible for Labour to outflank the Liberals on foreign policy, unemployment, and the franchise. This gave the National Union's strategy a logic and a force which extended beyond the immediate results of the pre-war by-elections.

In a way it mattered little how well Labour actually did in the EFF by-elections. If the policy led to three-cornered contests at the general election then it would pose an altogether more serious threat to Asquith. This is why the National Union put so much emphasis on its work in seats held by Anti-Suffragist Liberals where it wanted to create conditions in which a Labour candidature would be unavoidable. Since 1903 the two parties had largely eliminated three-cornered contests at general elections; this is why the Liberals had retained power even in 1910 when the Conservative share of the poll had risen to almost 47 per cent. By 1914 a larger number of candidates were under consideration by the Labour Party, and if they had materialized the prospects of a Conservative victory would have been greatly enhanced.

Yet to recognize that the danger loomed larger as a result of the EFF is not to say that it was about to materialize. By April 1914 Labour's National Executive envisaged fighting thirty-seven existing Labour seats and had sanctioned candidates in a further eighteen. In twenty-two cases the local party had selected a candidate but this had not been approved by the NEC, and a further forty were regarded as 'uncertain'. Since the NEC had drastically reduced the number of possible candidates on previous occasions so as to keep within the pact, it is likely they would have done the same in 1915. From the National Union's point of view the eighteen sanctioned candidates included none except Midlothian which were among its target constituencies. In the twenty-two 'selected' cases, six (Houghton-le-Spring, NW Durham, E. Bristol, Rotherham, N. Monmouth, and Leith) had enjoyed EFF campaigns or were currently targets for its work against Liberals. In the 'uncertain' category seven (Crewe, Gateshead, Accrington, Rossendale, Hanley, Holmfirth, and S. Edinburgh) were seats in which the EFF was active or had been.[92] This gave a total of only thirteen to be attacked, and several of these such as Hanley and Holmfirth were doubtful prospects. Ramsay Mac-Donald had no intention of allowing the National Union to dictate his electoral strategy. He wanted more Labour candidates in some mining districts and in some Tory areas; but at the end of the day he intended to maintain cooperation with the Liberals, for neither his own nor the National Union's resources were yet equal to the hazards of a wholesale conflict with the larger party.

Even if Labour had been willing to extend its challenge, there is some doubt as to whether the National Union could have gone any further without forcing a split in its own organization. Up to 1914 societies in such places as Glasgow and Liverpool continued to try to limit the EFF. Eleanor Rathbone formed a committee to undermine the policy and attacked it at the Council meetings of the NUWSS. A proposal that no EFF work should be done in places where it would result in the election of a Conservative was lost by only five votes.[93] Rathbone accepted that the National Union had committed itself to work for candidates in 26 constituencies, but she aimed to prevent it going beyond these at a general election. She argued cogently that the present policy might prove effective enough to antagonize the government, but not enough to intimidate, and would end up helping more Tories into parliament only to find that women's suffrage was merely referred to a referendum by them. Conversely she insisted that the Liberals remained the best bet for enacting women's suffrage legislation. Helping Labour was unlikely to have a decisive impact.

Fawcett countered that the EFF had already strengthened the cause in the Commons, and Lady Frances Balfour claimed that her meetings with members of the government had convinced her of its effectiveness. Unfortunately there was little outward corroboration of their view up to 1914 except perhaps in Asquith's response to the deputations in 1913 and 1914. However, this dispute within the NUWSS should not be exaggerated. Although Rathbone and others seem to have withdrawn for a time, this did not check the net increase in membership up to the outbreak of war.

The truth was that the National Union leaders were engaged in a game of bluff. They did not really have the resources to challenge the Liberals on a broad front in the general election. But the government could not be sure

---

[92] 'Election Policy', NUWSS Memorandum, Feb. 1913, Fawcett Library: Fawcett Letters 89/2/78.
[93] Glasgow and West of Scotland Association for Women's Suffrage, minutes, 26 Jan. 1914; NUWSS, minutes, 12 Feb. 1914, private and confidential memorandum 5 Mar. 1914 attached, Manchester Central Library M50/1/11.

how much damage they could do. Through her correspondence with Liberal politicians Catherine Marshall realized that they were anxious to know how much assistance would be given to the Labour Party.[94] She contrived to give the impression of a steady expansion of constituency work, and insisted that 'there is nothing to be hoped for from the Liberal Party'.[95] In fact she did not believe there was no alternative to the EFF; she really hoped to push the government into backing down in time to allow the National Union to withdraw from the general election.

There are some grounds for thinking that Marshall was justified in this expectation. In her correspondence with Lloyd George she took some trouble to flatter him into using his influence in the cabinet to force the issue. His papers contain lists of the Liberal MPs *and* prospective candidates with their views on women's suffrage, presumably supplied by the National Union. They wanted Lloyd George to intervene to stop the nomination of Anti-Suffragists or to persuade them to drop their opposition.[96] Though apparently willing to help, he made it clear to Marshall that she would not get votes for women before the election; Irish Home Rule and Welsh Church Disestablishment must be dealt with first. However, this still left the prospect that the government would go into the election with a definite undertaking to legislate for women's suffrage if re-elected. Asquith's surprisingly favourable response to the deputation of East End suffragists under Sylvia Pankhurst on 20 June 1914 seemed to point to this. He endorsed the claims of working women and distinguished them from the suffragettes whom he professed to regard as the real remaining obstacle. Strictly speaking, Asquith's response to the deputation was unnecessary since it represented a small local group. But therein lay its significance. Asquith may have regarded the ELF as part of the broader alliance of left-wing and working-class suffragists which he could not afford to alienate. This was all the more true now that pressure was being applied on the right as well as the left. Catherine Marshall was also endeavouring to raise expectations about a Conservative commitment to female enfranchisement. When Lord Selborne introduced a bill into the House of Lords for the first time in May 1914 it was defeated by only 44 votes which the suffragists interpreted as a very encouraging result. According to Lady Selborne the peers were 'really quite well disposed towards women'.[97] Whether or not she was correct, the point is that by 1914 the suffragists had

---

[94] Notes, 14 Apr. 1913, Cumbria CRO: Marshall Papers.
[95] Catherine Marshall to F. D. Acland (draft), 4 Nov. 1913, Cumbria CRO: Marshall Papers.
[96] House of Lords Record Office: Lloyd George Papers C/17/3/26; C/17/3/27.
[97] Lady Selborne to Catherine Marshall, 15 Oct. 1913, Cumbria CRO: Marshall Papers.

managed to put Asquith in danger of being outflanked by both the Labour and Conservative parties. As a result the likelihood was that all three parties would enter the election with a commitment on votes for women. The Liberals were likely to distinguish their policy from adult suffrage, on the one hand, and from the Conciliation Bill, on the other, by advocating the Dickinson formula designed to incorporate the wives of workingmen. But in view of the dramatic interruption of these manoeuvres by the outbreak of war in August this is as far as one can go.

Epilogue: War and the Vote

WHAT connections were there between the First World War and the pre-war movement for female enfranchisement? So far as the suffragettes were concerned war simply accelerated the existing trends. As we have seen, the campaign was already in decline and suffragettes were gradually accepting the Home Secretary's terms for release. Shortly after the outbreak of war McKenna offered to release the remaining prisoners in return for promises of good behaviour; but he soon retreated from this by offering, in effect, unconditional release. In fact no risk was now involved, for Christabel quickly returned from her exile in Paris to take the opportunity to save the WSPU from what might otherwise have been an ignominious end. On 13 August Emmeline Pankhurst announced the suspension of the suffragette campaign, though in effect it had been abandoned. 'With that patriotism which has nerved women to endure endless torture in prison cells for the national good, we ardently desire that our country shall be victorious,' she wrote.[1] The reinvention of the Pankhursts was already underway.

However, while the suffragette leaders headed enthusiastically for the recruiting platforms and a new career, other suffragist societies were more hesitant. The National Union and the Women's Freedom League contained many Liberal and Labour women who regarded the war as a disaster and as the final proof of the immorality of making government a male monopoly. As Roland Muirhead put it, the war was simply 'male militancy'.[2] A split in the NUWSS was therefore inevitable. Many of its leading figures were drawn into cooperation with feminists in other countries, keen to seek a negotiated settlement and to promote disarmament in the future.[3] However, the National Union remained under the control of Millicent Fawcett whose patriotism was firm if relatively restrained. Yet from the perspective of the women's vote her diagnosis was much the same as the Pankhursts'. 'We know that a War Government cannot busy itself with legislation for franchise

[1] WSPU circular, 13 Aug. 1914.
[2] Roland Muirhead to Jean Lambie (copy), 39 Nov. 1914, Mitchell Library: Muirhead Papers Box 1/37.
[3] J. V. Newberry, 'Anti-War Suffragists', *History*, 62 (1977).

reform.'[4] Unlike the WSPU, however, the NUWSS did not abandon the cause; it maintained its organization and eventually extended it successfully into peacetime. In fact during the first year of hostilities the non-militant societies seem to have retained most of their membership and funds, partly because, like the political parties, they expected a general election to take place fairly soon. The WFL even launched membership drives, perhaps expecting to pick up lapsed WSPU members. In the East End Sylvia also continued the activities of the ELF. But in effect all these organizations focused increasingly on work in support of the war effort rather than on campaigning for the vote.

As for the Election Fighting Fund, it, too, suffered a demise during the war; it was not actually repudiated, it simply lapsed. This was inevitable because the wartime political truce put an end to normal by-elections. In any case, by 1917 the EFF had been overtaken by the expansion of the Labour Party in the constituencies. By 1918 over 380 Labour candidates had been adopted thereby making the EFF irrelevant. But during the 1920s, as thousands of women were recruited into the party's women's organization, the long-term benefits of the 1912 pact began to materialize.

The Pankhursts were by no means the only ones for whom war came as something of a relief. The Anti-Suffragists were just as quick to wind up their work. In theory, the return of leading Antis, such as Curzon and Chamberlain, to office after the formation of a coalition in May 1915 should have enabled them to block all further reform. But they simply joined a minority within the government, and felt reluctant to rock the boat or to risk their own jobs by holding out against female suffrage. For the Antis the crucial stage was to come during the ten months between the cabinet's decision to introduce a reform bill in March 1917 and the debate in the House of Lords in January 1918. But in that period the League failed to launch a campaign or to spend the funds it still had at its disposal.[5] By this time many peers had concluded that it was impossible to resist any longer; they felt that the Antis in the House of Commons were now afraid to oppose the women's vote because they would soon have to face a female electorate.[6] They were right; in the crucial division only twelve Liberals and forty-five Conservatives were prepared to vote against the women's clause. In spite of this Mrs Humphry Ward kept her nerve even though Lord Curzon had clearly lost his. As Leader of the House of Lords Curzon reiterated all the arguments against a female electorate, but

[4] *The Common Cause*, 4 Sept. 1914.

[5] E. Mitchell Innes to Lord Curzon, 6 Apr. 1917; Curzon to Mrs Ward (copy), 26 Dec. 1917, Curzon Papers, BL, F112/37.

[6] Martin Pugh, *Electoral Reform in War and Peace, 1906–1918* (Routledge, 1978), 151–2.

concluded by urging abstention rather than forcing a clash with the Commons. As a result the opposition collapsed ignominiously, and the clause was passed by 134 to 71 votes.

Whether the war influenced the debate about votes for women is rather doubtful. Several suffragists such as Cicely Hamilton and Elizabeth Robins strongly denied that women's wartime work had been in any way responsible for their success.[7] No doubt the war did make the Antis' traditional argument about physical force seem rather redundant, though it had never been particularly credible. In fact the Antis soon realized that they had been outmanoeuvred once the suffragists began to seize the patriotic high ground in the form of voluntary war work of all kinds:

They sew and knit comforts for the soldiers, but with such a perpetual running accompaniment of suffragist self-laudation that they might as well embroider the sacred name of Mrs Pankhurst or Mrs Fawcett on every sock and every muffler, so as to give notice to the soldiers as well as to the country at large that Suffragism alone has the trademark of thoughtful and benevolent patriotism.[8]

Women's voluntary work probably carried more weight with the press than with the politicians. Staunch Antis including J. L. Garvin of *The Observer* and Lord Northcliffe of the *Daily Mail* abandoned their opposition to jump on the bandwagon now that women's enfranchisement seemed inevitable. The role played by young women in munitions factories and other formerly male employment generated excellent copy for the newspapers. But it did not lead men generally to change their ideas about gender roles. The press, the government, the unions, and the employers largely agreed in regarding women's war work as temporary. On the contrary, the war made them see women's traditional roles as wives and mothers as even more important, now that the flower of British manhood was being frittered away in Flanders. But if the war had little impact on the decision to give women the vote, it did almost certainly help to influence the *form* that enfranchisement took in that it strengthened the feeling that the vote should not be a reward for single women so much as a recognition of married women. In this sense the war worked with the grain of politics.

However, the crisis of war went some way to unblocking the log-jam that had built up around women's suffrage, although it did so in indirect ways. Asquith had been greatly relieved when the outbreak of hostilities swept all the domestic controversies off the agenda in August 1914. But his own position was fatally undermined by the decision to form a coalition government

---

[7] Hamilton, *Life Errant*, 67.   [8] *Anti-Suffrage Review*, Mar. 1915.

in May 1915. This destroyed much of his credibility with Liberals, and introduced some keen pro-suffragists into government including Arthur Henderson, Lord Robert Cecil, Lord Selborne, and Lord Lytton. In theory the inclusion of Labour and the Conservatives in the cabinet should have made the idea of a wartime election redundant, but the politicians never ruled it out altogether. As a result, they were forced to maintain the electoral register. Unhappily for the government, the register had been hopelessly disrupted once thousands of men began to move home either to work in munitions or to join the forces. In the process they lost the twelve-month residence required for household voters and ceased to appear on the registers. It was this that forced the cabinet to return to the vexed question of franchise reform in the middle of the war. Consequently by May 1916 even the National Union judged it time to begin writing to the prime minister again. The suffragists agreed not to resume their campaign if the government simply modified the registration system to keep existing voters on the lists, but they would not accept a reform which widened the suffrage.[9] Asquith denied any intention of introducing a reform bill, but in an obscure speech in August 1916 he argued that while he had not changed his views about votes for women, he would find it difficult to exclude them if parliament introduced a new qualification based on service to the state.[10] In the autumn matters were resolved by the appointment of a conference under the Speaker, James Lowther, charged with producing a comprehensive solution to the problems of franchise and registration. It seems fairly certain that Asquith believed that this expedient would get the whole issue off the agenda for the duration of the war if not longer. But in the event the Speaker reported in January 1917 with a full set of proposals. By that time Lloyd George had become prime minister and was keen to show that he could bring in progressive reforms even though his coalition was dominated by the Conservatives.

The conference had proposed a form of female suffrage along the lines urged in 1913 by W. H. Dickinson, who was one of its members. This meant enfranchising women who already had a local government qualification or who were wives of men with a local government vote, subject to an age limit of thirty years.[11] The suffragists were able to exert very little influence on this process, though the WFL put pickets on the Speaker's conference. Attempts by Sylvia Pankhurst and Selina Cooper to arouse public interest with a view to getting full female enfranchisement met with apathy.[12] Even Fawcett

[9] Millicent Fawcett to H. H. Asquith, 4 May 1916, *The Common Cause*, 19 May 1916.
[10] *Hansard, HC Deb.*, 5th Series, LXXXV, 14 Aug. 1916, c. 1451–2.
[11] Pugh, *Electoral Reform*, 84–5.   [12] Pugh, *Women's Movement*, 37.

disliked the proposals in the sense that they excluded daughters living with their parents. Nevertheless, when she led a deputation of suffrage societies to see Lloyd George on 29 March 1917 she adopted a conciliatory attitude: 'we should greatly prefer an imperfect scheme that can pass', she told him.[13]

In some ways the suffragists had got what they wanted: a *government* bill which included women and was therefore almost certain to become law. This was especially true since the conference had got over the long-standing political obstacle by incorporating wives into the electorate; the reservations entertained by Liberal and Labour members no longer applied. After straining over much more limited proposals for decades, the politicians had found it easier to swallow a really democratic measure covering 8.4 million women. But it had not been a capitulation; they had got the vote on their own terms. The thirty-year age limit was illogical and even insulting to women. But it had a certain logic from the politicians' point of view. It kept women in a minority, albeit a large one of 40 per cent. Above all, it excluded the young women about whose ideas and ambitions they had some fears, and it enfranchised the more domesticated women who, they believed, would not destabilize the system. The suffragists had been outflanked. On the other hand, the vote in favour of the women's clause—387 to 57—was so emphatic that there could not be much resistance to a further instalment of reform. Millicent Fawcett retired from the NUWSS feeling justifiably triumphant. But under its new title—the National Union of Societies for Equal Citizenship—her colleagues carried on with a fresh and wider agenda and with the force of a female electorate behind them. By 1928 they had equal franchise in the bag and a female electorate comprising 52 per cent of the entire British electorate.

[13] 'The 1917 Deputation to Lloyd George', Museum of London: Suffragette Fellowship Papers.

SELECT BIBLIOGRAPHY

PRIMARY SOURCES

Papers of Individuals

Janie Allan Papers, National Library of Scotland
Maud Arncliffe-Sennett Papers, British Library
A. J. Balfour Papers, British Library
Lydia Becker Correspondence, Manchester Central Library
Curzon of Kedleston Papers, British Library
T. Billington-Greig Papers, Fawcett Library
Helen Crawfurd MS, Marx Memorial Library
Sir Charles Dilke Papers, British Library
Master of Elibank Papers, National Library of Scotland
Millicent Fawcett Papers, Fawcett Library
Keir Hardie (Emrys Hughes) Papers, National Library of Scotland
S. Lees Papers, Oldham Local Studies Library
David Lloyd George Papers, House of Lords Record Office
Violet Markham Papers, British Library of Political and Economic Science
Catherine Marshall Papers, Cumbria County Record Office
Hannah Mitchell Papers, Manchester Central Library
Roland Muirhead Papers, National Library of Scotland and Mitchell Library

Organizations and Institutions

Glasgow and West of Scotland Association for Women's Suffrage, Mitchell Library
Manchester Society for Women's Suffrage, Manchester Central Library
Manchester Men's League for Women's Suffrage, John Rylands University Library
Manchester League for Opposing Women's Suffrage, Manchester Central Library
National Liberal Federation, *Annual Reports*
National Union of Women's Suffrage Societies, Fawcett Library
Public Record Office (Kew)—HO, PCOM, MEPOL
Scottish Women's Liberal Federation, Edinburgh University Library
Suffragette Fellowship Collection, Museum of London
Women's Liberal Federation, Bristol University Library
Women's Suffrage collections, National Library of Scotland
WSPU Papers, Fawcett Library

Journals

Anti-Suffrage Review
The Common Cause
Conservative and Unionist Women's Franchise Review
Contemporary Review
Fortnightly Review
Macmillan's Magazine
The National Review
The Nineteenth Century
The Suffragette
Votes for Women
Westminster Review
Women's Suffrage Journal

Articles

Barrow, F. H., 'The Political Responsibility of Women', *Westminster Review*, 170 (1908).

Becker, Lydia, 'Female Suffrage', *Contemporary Review*, 4 (Mar. 1867).

—— 'The Women Ratepayers' Right to Vote', *Westminster Review*, 122 (1884).

Bland, J. O. P., 'Woman Suffrage in the United States', *The Nineteenth Century*, 74 (1913).

Cairnes, J. E., 'Woman Suffrage: A Reply', *Macmillan's Magazine*, 30 (1874).

Chapman, Mrs Theo, 'Women's Suffrage', *The Nineteenth Century*, 107 (1886).

—— 'Women's Suffrage Again!', *The Nineteenth Century*, 32 (1897).

Creighton, Louise, 'The Appeal Against Female Suffrage: A Rejoinder', *The Nineteenth Century*, 209 (1889).

Elmy, Mrs Wolstenholme, 'Justice between the Sexes', *Westminster Review*, 169 (1908).

Fawcett, Millicent, 'The Electoral Disabilities of Women', *Fortnightly Review*, 7 (1870).

—— 'The Future of Englishwomen', *The Nineteenth Century*, 4 (1878).

—— 'Women's Suffrage: A Reply', *The Nineteenth Century*, 107 (1886).

—— 'Women's Suffrage: A Reply', *The National Review*, 11 (1888).

—— 'Female Suffrage: A Reply', *The Nineteenth Century*, 209 (July 1889).

—— 'The Women's Suffrage Bill', *Fortnightly Review*, 46 (1889).

Galloway, Countess of, 'Women and Politics', *The Nineteenth Century*, 107 (1886).

Grossman, Enid, 'The Woman Movement in New Zealand', *Westminster Review*, 170 (1908).

Ignota, [no initial given], 'Women's Suffrage', *Westminster Review*, 148 (Oct. 1897).

Jones, Gladys, 'Suffragists Again', *Westminster Review*, 169 (1908).

Mitra, S. M., 'Voice for Women—Without Votes', *The Nineteenth Century*, 74 (1913).

Smith, Goldwin, 'Female Suffrage', *Macmillan's Magazine*, 30 (1874).
—— 'Conservatism and Female Suffrage', *The National Review*, 10 (1888).
Stephen, Caroline E., 'Women and Politics', *The Nineteenth Century*, 61 (1907).
Ward, Mrs Humphry, 'An Appeal Against Women's Suffrage', *The Nineteenth Century*, 209 (June 1889).
Young, Norwood, 'The Truth about Female Suffrage In New Zealand', *Westminster Review*, 142 (1894).

SECONDARY SOURCES

Place of publication is London unless otherwise stated.

ALLEN, MARY, *Lady in Blue* (Stanley Paul, 1936).
ATKINSON, DIANE, *The Purple, White and Green* (Museum of London, 1992).
BALFOUR, Lady FRANCES, *Ne Obliviscaris: Dinna Forget* (Hodder and Stoughton, 1930).
BANKS, OLIVE, *Faces of Feminism* (Oxford: Blackwell, 1981).
—— *Becoming a Feminist* (Brighton: Harvester, 1986).
BILLINGTON, ROSAMUND, 'Women, Politics and Local Liberalism: From Female Suffrage to Votes for Women', *Journal of Regional and Local Studies*, 5 (1985).
BLACKBURN, HELEN (ed.), *Words of a Leader: Being Extracts from the Writings of the Late Miss Lydia Becker* (Bristol: J. W. Arrowsmith, 1897).
—— *Women's Suffrage: A Record of the Women's Suffrage Movement in the British Isles* (Williams and Norgate, 1902).
BLEASE, W. LYON, *The Emancipation of Women* (Constable, 1910).
BLOM, IDA, 'The Struggle for Women's Suffrage in Norway, 1885–1913', *Scandinavian Journal of History*, 5 (1980).
BONDFIELD, MARGARET, *A Life's Work* (Hutchinson, 1948).
BOSTICK, THEODORA, 'The Press and the Launching of the Women's Suffrage Movement, 1866–67', *Victorian Periodicals Review*, 13/4 (1980).
CAINE, BARBARA, 'John Stuart Mill and the English Women's Movement', *Historical Studies*, 18 (1978).
—— 'Beatrice Webb and the Woman Question', *History Workshop Journal*, 14 (1982).
—— *Victorian Feminists* (Oxford: Oxford University Press, 1992).
—— 'Vida Goldstein and the English Militant Campaign', *Women's History Review*, 2/3 (1993).
CARTER, HUNTLY (ed.), *Women's Suffrage and Militancy* (Frank Palmer, 1912).
CHEW, DORIS NIELD, *Ada Nield Chew* (Virago, 1982).
COOK, KAY, and EVANS, NEIL, 'The Petty Antics of the Bell-Ringing, Boisterous Band': The Women's Suffrage Movement in Wales 1890–1898', in Angela V. John (ed.), *Our Mothers' Land: Chapters in Welsh Women's History 1830–1939* (Cardiff: University of Wales Press, 1991).
CREPAZ, ADELE, *The Emancipation of Women* (Swan Sonnenschein, 1893).

CRICHTON, RONALD (ed.), *The Memoirs of Ethel Smythe* (Viking, 1987).

DALZIEL, RAEWYN, 'Presenting the Enfranchisement of New Zealand Women Abroad', in C. Daley and M. Nolan (eds.), *Suffrage and Beyond* (Pluto Press, 1994).

DICEY, A. V., *Letters to a Friend on Votes for Women* (John Murray, 1909).

DODD, KATHRYN, *A Sylvia Pankhurst Reader* (Manchester: Manchester University Press, 1993).

EUSTANCE, CLAIRE, 'Daring to be Free: The Evolution of Women's Political Identities in the Women's Freedom League, 1907–1930', Ph.D. thesis (York University, 1993).

EVANS, RICHARD, *The Feminists* (Croom Helm, 1977).

FLETCHER, SHEILA, *Maud Royden* (Oxford: Blackwell, 1989).

GIFFORD, LEWIS, *Eva Gore-Booth and Esther Roper* (Pandora, 1988).

GOLDMAN, LAWRENCE (ed.), *The Blind Victorian: Henry Fawcett and British Liberalism* (Cambridge: Cambridge University Press, 1989).

GOTTLIEB, JULIE, 'Women and Fascism in Inter-War Britain', Ph.D. thesis (Cambridge University, 1998).

GRIMSHAW, PATRICIA, *Women's Suffrage in New Zealand* (Auckland: Auckland University Press, 1972).

HAMBURGER, JOSEPH, *Intellectual in Politics: J. S. Mill and the Philosophical Radicals* (New Haven: Yale University Press, 1965).

HAMILTON, CICELY, *Life Errant* (J. M. Dent, 1935).

HAMMOND, J. L., and HAMMOND, BARBARA, *James Stansfeld: A Victorian Champion of Sex Equality* (Longman, 1932).

HANNAM, JUNE, *Isabella Ford* (Oxford: Blackwell, 1989).

HARRISON, BRIAN, *Separate Spheres: The Opposition to Women's Suffrage in Britain* (Croom Helm, 1978).

—— 'The Act of Militancy: Violence and the Suffragettes', in *Peaceable Kingdom* (Oxford: Oxford University Press, 1982).

—— 'Women's Suffrage at Westminster, 1866–1928', in M. Bentley and J. Stevenson (eds.), *High and Low Politics in Modern Britain* (Oxford: Clarendon Press, 1983).

—— *Prudent Revolutionaries* (Oxford: Clarendon Press, 1987).

HART, HEBER, *Woman Suffrage: A National Danger* (P. S. King, 1912).

HARVIE, CHRISTOPHER, *The Lights of Liberalism* (Croom Helm, 1976).

HAULTAIN, ARNOLD, *Goldwin Smith: His Life and Opinions* (T. Werner Laurie, 1913).

—— (ed.), *Goldwin Smith's Correspondence* (T. Werner Laurie, 1913).

HERSTEIN, SHEILA, *A Mid-Victorian Feminist: Barbara Leigh Smith Bodichon* (New Haven: Yale University Press, 1985).

HIRSHFIELD, CLAIRE, 'Fractured Faith: Liberal Party Women and the Suffrage Issue in Britain, 1892–1914', *Gender and History*, 2/2 (1990).

HOLLEDGE, JULIE, *Innocent Flowers: Women in the Edwardian Theatre* (Virago, 1981).

HOLLIS, PATRICIA, *Ladies Elect: Women in English Local Government, 1865–1914* (Oxford: Clarendon Press, 1987).

HOLTON, SANDRA STANLEY, *Feminism and Democracy: Women's Suffrage and Reform Politics in Britain, 1900–1918* (Cambridge: Cambridge University Press, 1986).

—— 'The Suffragist and the Average Woman', *Women's History Review*, 1/1 (1992).

—— *Suffrage Days: Stories from the Women's Suffrage Movement* (Routledge, 1996).

HOUSMAN, LAWRENCE, *The Unexpected Years* (Cape, 1937).

HUME, LESLEY P., *The National Union of Women's Suffrage Societies, 1897–1914* (New York: Garland Publishing, 1982).

JALLINNOJA, RIITTA, 'The Women's Liberation Movement in Finland 1880–1910', *Scandinavian Journal of History*, 5 (1980).

JOANNU, M., and PURVIS, J. (eds.), *The Women's Suffrage Movement: New Feminist Perspectives* (I. B. Tauris, 1998).

JOHN, ANGELA V., *Elizabeth Robins: Staging a Life* (Routledge, 1995).

—— and EUSTANCE, CLAIRE (eds.), *The Men's Share: Masculinities, Male Support and Women's Suffrage in Britain 1890–1920* (Routledge, 1997).

JONES, HELEN (ed.), *Duty and Citizenship: The Correspondence and Papers of Violet Markham* (The Historians' Press, 1994).

KENT, SUSAN KINGSLEY, *Sex and Suffrage in Britain, 1860–1914* (Princeton: Princeton University Press, 1987).

KINNAIRD, JOAN K., 'Mary Astell and the Conservative Contribution to English Feminism', *Journal of British Studies*, 19 (1979).

KINZER, B. L., ROBSON, A., and ROBSON, J. M. (eds.), *A Moralist In and Out of Parliament* (Toronto: University of Toronto Press, 1992).

LACEY, CANDIDA, *Barbara Leigh Smith Bodichon and the Ladies of Langham Place* (Routledge, 1987).

LENEMAN, LEAH, *A Guid Cause: The Women's Suffrage Movement in Scotland* (Aberdeen: Aberdeen University Press, 1991).

—— 'Northern Men and Votes for Women', *History Today*, 41 (1991).

LIDDINGTON, JILL, *The Life and Times of a Respectable Rebel: Selina Cooper* (Virago, 1984).

—— and NORRIS, JILL, *One Hand Tied Behind Us: The Rise of the Women's Suffrage Movement* (Virago, 1978).

LINKLATER, ANDRO, *An Unhusbanded Life: Charlotte Despard, Suffragette, Socialist and Sinn Feiner* (Hutchinson, 1980).

MARKHAM, VIOLET, *Return Passage* (Oxford: Clarendon Press, 1953).

MASON, BERTHA, *The Story of the Women's Suffrage Movement* (Sherratt and Hughes, 1912).

MIDDLETON, LUCY (ed.), *Women in the Labour Movement* (Croom Helm, 1977).

MITCHELL, DAVID, *Queen Christabel* (MacDonald and Jane's, 1977).

MITCHELL, GEOFFREY (ed.), *The Hard Way Up: The Autobiography of Hannah Mitchell, Suffragette and Rebel* (Faber and Faber, 1968).

MONTGOMERY, F., 'Gender and Suffrage: The Manchester Men's League for Women's Suffrage, 1908–1918', *Bulletin of the John Rylands University Library of Manchester*, 77 (1995).

MORGAN, DAVID, *Suffragists and Liberals* (Oxford: Oxford University Press, 1975).

MORGAN, K. O., *Keir Hardie: Radical and Socialist* (Methuen, 1975).

MORLEY, ANN, and STANLEY, LIZ, *The Life and Death of Emily Wilding Davison* (The Women's Press, 1989).

NEALE, R. S., 'Working-Class Women and Women's Suffrage', in *Class and Ideology in the Nineteenth Century* (Routledge, 1972).

NEVILLE, DAVID, 'The Women's Suffrage Movement in the North East of England, 1900–1914', M.Phil. thesis (University of Northumbria, 1991).

OLDFIELD, AUDREY, *Woman Suffrage in Australia* (Cambridge: Cambridge University Press, 1992).

OSTROGORSKI, M., *The Rights of Women* (Swan Sonnenschein, 1893).

PANKHURST, CHRISTABEL, *Unshackled: The Story of How We Won the Vote* (Hutchinson, 1959).

PANKHURST, E. SYLVIA, *The Suffragette Movement* (Virago, 1977).

PARKER, JOAN ELIZABETH, 'Lydia Becker: Her Work for Women', Ph.D. thesis (Manchester University, 1990).

PENTLAND, MARJORIE, *A Bonnie Fechter: The Life of Ishbel Marjoribanks, Marchioness of Aberdeen and Temair* (Batsford, 1952).

PETHICK-LAWRENCE, EMMELINE, *My Part in a Changing World* (Gollancz, 1938).

PETHICK-LAWRENCE, F. W., *Fate Has Been Kind* (Hutchinson, 1942).

PUGH, MARTIN, 'Politicians and the Woman's Vote, 1914–1918', *History*, 59 (1974).

—— *Electoral Reform in War and Peace, 1906–1918* (Routledge, 1978).

—— 'Labour and Women's Suffrage', in K. D. Brown (ed.), *The First Labour Party 1906–1914* (Croom Helm, 1985).

—— *The Tories and the People, 1880–1935* (Oxford: Blackwell, 1985).

—— *Women and the Women's Movement in Britain, 1914–1959* (Macmillan, 1992).

PURVIS, JUNE, 'The Prison Experiences of the Suffragettes in Edwardian Britain', *Women's History Review*, 4/1 (1995).

R., A. J. (ed.), *The Suffrage Annual and Women's Who's Who* (Stanley Paul, 1913).

REEVES, WILLIAM PEMBER, *The Long White Cloud* (G. Allen and Unwin, 1898).

—— *State Experiments in Australia and New Zealand* (Grant Richards, 1902).

RENDALL, JANE, *The Origins of Modern Feminism* (Oxford: Blackwell, 1985).

REYNOLDS, K. D., *Aristocratic Women and Political Society in Victorian Britain* (Oxford: Oxford University Press, 1998).

REYNOLDS, STEPHEN, WOOLEY, BOB, and WOOLLEY, TOM, *Seems So! A Working-Class View of Politics* (Macmillan, 1911).

RHONDDA, Viscountess, *This Was My World* (Macmillan, 1933).

RICHARDSON, MARY, *Laugh a Defiance* (Weidenfeld and Nicolson, 1953).

ROBERTS, CHARLES, *The Radical Countess: The History of the Life of Rosalind, Countess of Carlisle* (Carlisle: Steel Bros., 1962).

ROBSON, A. P. W., 'The Founding of the National Society for Women's Suffrage 1866–67', *Canadian Historical Journal*, 8 (Mar. 1973).

ROMERO, PATRICIA, *E. Sylvia Pankhurst* (New Haven: Yale University Press, 1987).

ROSEN, ANDREW, *Rise Up Women! The Militant Campaign of the Women's Social and Political Union 1903–1914* (Routledge, 1978).

ROVER, CONSTANCE, *Women's Suffrage and Party Politics in Britain, 1866–1914* (Routledge, 1967).

RUBINSTEIN, D. W., *Before the Suffragettes* (Brighton: Harvester, 1986).

—— *A Different World for Women: The Life of Millicent Garrett Fawcett* (Brighton: Harvester, 1991).

SMITH, F. B., *Florence Nightingale: Reputation and Power* (Croom Helm, 1982).

STANTON, T. (ed.), *The Woman Question in Europe* (Sampson Low, 1884).

STOCKS, MARY, *My Commonplace Book* (Peter Davies, 1970).

STRACHEY, RAY, *The Cause: A Short History of the Women's Movement in Great Britain* (G. Bell and Sons, 1928).

SUTHERLAND, JOHN, *Mrs Humphry Ward* (Oxford: Oxford University Press, 1990).

SWANWICK, H. M., *I Have Been Young* (Gollancz, 1935).

TICKNER, LIZA, *The Spectacle of Women: Imagery of the Suffragette Campaign, 1907–1914* (Chatto, 1988).

TREVELYAN, JANET, *The Life of Mrs Humphry Ward* (Oxford: Clarendon Press, 1923).

VICINUS, MARTHA, *Independent Women: Work and Community for Single Women 1850–1920* (Virago, 1985).

WHITELAW, LIS, *The Life and Rebellious Times of Cicely Hamilton* (The Women's Press, 1990).

WINSLOW, BARBARA, *Sylvia Pankhurst* (UCL Press, 1996).

WINSTONE, H. V. F., *Gertrude Bell* (Cape, 1978).

INDEX

Lightning Source UK Ltd.
Milton Keynes UK
04 November 2009

145791UK00002B/34/A

9 780199 250226